Democratic Insecurities

Intro,
2, 3, 4, 7

CALIFORNIA SERIES IN PUBLIC ANTHROPOLOGY

The California Series in Public Anthropology emphasizes the anthropologist's role as an engaged intellectual. It continues anthropology's commitment to being an ethnographic witness, to describing, in human terms, how life is lived beyond the borders of many readers' experiences. But it also adds a commitment, through ethnography, to reframing the terms of public debate—transforming received, accepted understandings of social issues with new insights, new framings.

Series Editor: Robert Borofsky (Hawaii Pacific University)

Contributing Editors: Philippe Bourgois (University of Pennsylvania), Paul Farmer (Partners in Health), Alex Hinton (Rutgers University), Carolyn Nordstrom (University of Notre Dame), and Nancy Scheper-Hughes (UC Berkeley)

University of California Press Editor: Naomi Schneider

Democratic Insecurities

Violence, Trauma, and Intervention in Haiti

Erica Caple James

UNIVERSITY OF CALIFORNIA PRESS
Berkeley · Los Angeles · London

University of California Press, one of the most
distinguished university presses in the United States,
enriches lives around the world by advancing
scholarship in the humanities, social sciences, and
natural sciences. Its activities are supported by the UC
Press Foundation and by philanthropic contributions
from individuals and institutions. For more
information, visit www.ucpress.edu.

University of California Press
Berkeley and Los Angeles, California

University of California Press, Ltd.
London, England

Library of Congress Cataloging-in-Publication Data

James, Erica Caple.
    Democratic insecurities : violence, trauma, and
intervention in Haiti / Erica Caple James.
        p.   cm.
    Includes bibliographical references and index.
    ISBN 978-0-520-26053-5 (cloth : alk. paper)
    ISBN 978-0-520-26054-2 (pbk. : alk. paper)
        1. Democratization—Haiti.   2. Political violence—
Haiti.   3. Humanitarian assistance—Haiti.
4. Intervention (International law).   5. Haiti—Politics
and government—1986–   I. Title.

JL1090J36 2010
320.97294—dc22   2009038116

Manufactured in the United States of America

19   18   17   16   15   14   13   12   11   10
10   9   8   7   6   5   4   3   2   1

This book is printed on Cascades Enviro 100, a 100%
post consumer waste, recycled, de-inked fiber. FSC
recycled certified and processed chlorine free. It is acid
free, Ecologo certified, and manufactured by BioGas
energy.

The publisher gratefully acknowledges the generous support of the Anne G. Lipow Endowment Fund for Social Justice and Human Rights of the University of California Press Foundation, which was established by Stephen M. Silberstein.

Contents

Abbreviations

AAAS	American Association for the Advancement of Science
AQOCI	Quebecois Association for International Assistance
ADF	America's Development Foundation
AOJ	USAID Administration of Justice Program
BAI	Bureau des Avocats Internationaux (Office of International Lawyers)
BPS	Bureau Poursuites et Suivi pour les Victimes (Proceedings and Follow-up Office for Victims)
CAPS	Clinician-Administered PTSD Scale
CHR	Conférence Haïtienne des Religieux et des Religieuses (Haitian Conference of the Religious)
CIA	Central Intelligence Agency
CIDA	Canadian International Development Agency
CIFD	Comité Inter-Agences Femmes et Développement Systeme des Nations Unies en Haïti (Inter-Agency Women and Development Committee of the United Nations System in Haiti)
CIMO	Compagnie d'Intervention et de Maintien de l'Ordre

CIVPOL	U.N. Civilian Police
CNVJ	Commission Nationale Verité et Justice (National Truth and Justice Commission)
DPPDH	U.N./OAS Département pour la Promotion et la Protection des Droits de l'homme (Department for the Promotion and Protection of Human Rights)
DRC	Development Research Center
FAD'H	Forces Armées d'Haïti (Armed Forces of Haiti)
FDM	Fon Dwa Moun (Le Fonds des Droits Humains, the Human Rights Fund)
FAVILEK	Fanm Viktim Leve Kanpe (Women Victims Mobilize)
FNCD	Front National pour le Changement et la Démocratie (National Front for Change and Democracy)
FOCAL	Fondation Connaissance et Liberté (Open Society Institute/Haiti)
FRAPH	Front Révolutionnaire pour l'Avancement et le Progrès d'Haïti (Revolutionary Front for the Advancement and Progress of Haiti)
GCAFVCE	Groupe de Concertation des Associations de Femmes Victimes du Coup d'État (Consultative Group of Associations of Women Coup Victims)
GOH	Government of Haiti
HMO	Health Maintenance Organization
HNP	Haitian National Police
HRF	Human Rights Fund
HRW	Human Rights Watch
HRW/A	Human Rights Watch/Americas
HWA	Haitian Women's Association
IACHR	Inter-American Commission on Human Rights
ICITAP	International Criminal Investigative Training Assistance Program
ICM	International Civilian Mission

INSI	Institute for North South Issues
IOM	International Organization for Migration
IPSF	Interim Public Security Force
IRCT	International Rehabilitation Council for Torture Victims
IRI	International Republican Institute
JDG	Justice, Democracy and Governance Program, USAID/ Haiti
JPC	Commission Épiscopale Nationale Justice et Paix (Episcopal Justice and Peace Commission, Justice and Peace Commission)
JRS	Jesuit Refugee Service
LCHR	Lawyers Committee for Human Rights
LFAS	Ligue Féminine d'Action Sociale (Feminine Social Action League)
MAB	Mothers Across Borders
M'AP VIV	Mouvement d'Appui aux Victimes de Violence Organisée (Assistance Movement for Victims of Organized Violence)
MDM	Médecins du Monde (Doctors of the World)
MICIVIH	Mission Civile Internationale en Haïti, OEA/ONU (U.N./OAS International Civilian Mission)
MIPONUH	Mission de Police Civile des Nations Unies en Haïti (United Nations Civilian Police Mission in Haiti)
MNF	Multinational Force
MOVI-30	Mouvman Viktim 30 Sektanm (September 30th Victims' Movement)
MPP	Mouvman Peyizan Papay (Peasant Movement of Papaye)
MSI	Management Systems International
NCHR	National Coalition for Haitian Refugees (National Coalition for Haitian Rights)
NED	National Endowment for Democracy

NGO	nongovernmental organization
NPR	National Partnership for Reinventing Government
NRI	National Republican Institute for International Affairs
OAS	Organization of American States
ONM	Office National pour la Migration (National Office for Migration)
OPC	Office Protecteur du Citoyen (Office for the Protection of Citizens)
OPL	Organisation du Peuple en Lutte (Organization of People in Struggle)
OTI	USAID Office of Transition Initiatives
OVKD	Òganizasyon Viktim Koudeta (Organization of Coup Victims)
PHR	Physicians for Human Rights
PIRÈD	Projet Intégré pour le Renforcement de la Démocratie en Haïti (Integrated Project for the Reinforcement of Democracy in Haiti)
PROMESS	Programme des Médicaments Essentiels en Haïti (Program for Essential Medications in Haiti)
PVO	Private Voluntary Organization
TKL	*ti kominote legliz* (ecclesial base communities)
UNDP	United Nations Development Programme
UNHCR	United Nations High Commissioner for Refugees
UNIFEM	United Nations Development Fund for Women
UNMIH	United Nations Mission in Haiti
USAID	United States Agency for International Development
WHO	World Health Organization
WOH	Washington Office on Haiti
WOLA	Washington Office on Latin America

Illustrations

Acknowledgments

This book is the product of many years of reflection on the long-term consequences of social suffering. It seeks to analyze how individual, organizational, and governmental actors attempted to redress the trauma that resulted from political violence in Haiti. During my research I assessed the efficacy of a variety of efforts to promote individual and collective healing after psychosocial ruptures. I also considered how individuals endured in the face of multiple forms of "insecurity," especially when such rehabilitative measures failed despite their good intentions. A crucial dilemma emerged during the course of this work: how do individual and institutional humanitarian actors grapple successfully with conditions of ongoing insecurity without resorting to the very predatory practices that create such conditions? The conclusions that I reached are solely my own, and I bear full responsibility for what is expressed herein.

* * *

I have been fortunate to receive the support of a number of individuals who helped me to begin considering the moral and ethical dilemmas explored here. I thank Sarah Coakley for her questions regarding whether pain and suffering can be redemptive. For their dedication to Haiti and to challenging the structural roots of poverty worldwide, I express my admiration and appreciation for Paul Farmer and the staff of Partners in Health. Special thanks are owed to Loune Viaud for her early support of my work in Haiti. Ellen Israel, Joel Théodat, and the staff of the UMASS-Boston Haitian Creole Language Institute were integral to facilitating my initial field research.

I would also like to thank my many hosts in Haiti and those individuals and families who graciously allowed me to enter their lives during a very difficult time. Without their trust and generosity, I would not have been able to understand the sense of risk and vulnerability that they experienced, nor would I have witnessed their creativity in the face of despair. Given the frequent shifts in "insecurity" in Haiti, it would be imprudent of me to name them. However, I would like to convey my respect and gratitude to the staff of the three institutions at which I conducted research: "Chanm Fanm," America's Development Foundation (Haiti), and the Mars/Kline Center for Neurology and Psychiatry at the State University Hospital. In addition, I feel fortunate to have been permitted to participate in meetings with the staff members of USAID/ Haiti and their development partners and express thanks for their openness in sharing their personal views on political development assistance.

Several individuals who worked in the domains of human rights, development, public health, and humanitarian aid in Haiti deserve special recognition for their contributions to my research: Ghislaine Adrien, Lise-Marie Dejean, Necker Dessables, Chavannes Douyon, Alexis Gardella, Louis-Jeannie Girard, Mechell Jacob, Mona Jean, Bert Laurent, Ira Lowenthal, Cécile Marotte, Michael Miller, Polycarpe Mvita, Paulette Paul, Terry Rey, and Hugo Triest. I am especially grateful to Hervé Rakoto Razafimbahiny for his support during my research.

The Social Science Research Council/MacArthur Foundation Fellowship on International Peace and Security in a Changing World provided generous financial support for this project. During the course of this fellowship, the methodological suggestions of my SSRC field advisers, Kathryn Sikkink and Charles Hale, were indispensable to the success of this project. I also thank the National Center for PTSD at the Boston Veterans Administration and the Institute for Social Research at the University of Michigan for training me in the use of the CAPS and the CIDI.

This project would not have been possible without the superb instruction and generous financial support that I received from Harvard University, especially from the Department of Anthropology and the Department of Social Medicine at Harvard Medical School. In particular, I thank Michael Herzfeld for his commitment to ethnography and for his ability to see opportunity in the adversities of fieldwork. I also wish to acknowledge the contributions of Begoña Aretxaga, who gave all of her students a grammar with which to think through the seeming illogic of conflict and political violence. The Department of Social Medicine's NIMH Friday Morning Seminar provided a challenging but familial environment for its fellows to engage seriously the politics of global mental health with some of the world's leading scholars and practitioners. I would like to express my heartfelt thanks to Byron Good and Mary-Jo DelVecchio Good for welcoming my participation in the NIMH seminar and for their ongoing support. They have been integral to the critical development of my analysis of mental health and social institutions and have been outstanding role models throughout my career. I can convey only inadequately my appreciation for the mentorship of Arthur Kleinman. From his critical reflections on suffering and morality to his subtle but ever-present support of my work, he has helped me to realize a difficult theoretical and methodological project that I have continued to pursue in subsequent research.

This book has benefited from the careful reading and comments of my colleagues and friends at MIT. They have created a rare atmosphere of academic rigor, congeniality, and fun that has been fortifying as this book took final form. I thank Manduhai Buyandelger, Michael Fischer, Stefan Helmreich, Jim Howe, Jean Jackson, David Jones, Graham Jones, Heather Paxson, Susan Silbey, and Chris Walley. I also express appreciation to former colleagues Joseph Dumit, Hugh Gusterson, and Susan Slyomovics for their comments and advice. I am indebted to graduate students Laurie Denyer and Mia White and to the Ph.D. students in the HASTS ethnography classes for their comments.

Special thanks and appreciation are owed to Peter Agree, Paul Brodwin, Mark Goodale, Antonius Robben, Kate Wahl, and Ken Wissoker for their comments and conversation as the manuscript progressed, as well as to several anonymous reviewers. Thanks also to the production and editing team at UC Press, to Sheila Berg for her dedication to the craft of writing, and to Naomi Schneider for bringing the project to fruition.

My personal debts to friends and family are numerous. Sheri Weiser, Narquis Barak, Kim Burgess, Sonja Plesset, Vanessa Fong, and Nicole Newendorp have been colleagues and friends whose affection and judicious engagement with my ideas have enriched my work and life. I also thank the Dolor and Gabriel families for their support of my personal and professional development.

The bonds of love and family have also nourished me across time and space. My grandmother, Gladys Burns, was a model of strength and grace under fire. My parents, June D. Cargile and Dr. Raymond W. James, enable me to pursue difficult questions away from home with security. Along with my mother, I thank my sister and brother, Lori and Ray, for their love and steadfast encouragement and for their willingness to read chapters in progress. I thank Joseph Lubin for his ongoing friendship and for his support for my research in Haiti. I am grateful to our son, Kieren, for his willingness to brave a new environment in Haiti at a very young age, for his comments on the book, and for his love.

This book would not have reached its final form without the attentive reading and suggestions of my husband, Malick Ghachem. As a legal historian and scholar of Haiti, his questions about the legacies of slavery in contemporary Haiti were essential to the crafting of this book. His thoughtfulness, sacrifices, and love throughout this journey have sustained me through difficult times. Finally, I thank our toddlers, Ayanna and Faisal, for making me laugh, dance, and sing each day.

Preface

On January 12, 2010, as this book entered the final stages of production, Haiti was struck with a catastrophe of unimaginable proportions,
the latest in a long series of catastrophes that have afflicted the nation
and its people. The epicenter of the 7.0 magnitude earthquake was mere
kilometers southwest of the nation's capital, Port-au-Prince, where the
ethnographic research discussed in this book was conducted. Between
1995 and 2000 I worked with survivors of human rights abuses from
the 1991–94 coup years and studied the interveners that attempted to
rehabilitate them as part of my project analyzing the role of humanitarian and development assistance in postconflict reconstruction. Current
estimates are that 80 percent of the capital has been destroyed. As of
this writing I have had little word of the fate of the people with whom
I worked. A few in positions of power, wealth, and security have survived. Others have died. Many are missing. The fate of most of the poor
pro-democracy activists who shared with me their lives of suffering and
resilience remains unknown.

The scale and nature of the recent devastation are unprecedented.
Nonetheless, the physical and psychosocial aftershocks have created
eerie parallels to events analyzed in this book—from accusations that
Haitian culture and religious practices are responsible for this tragedy
and hamper efforts to remedy it to the outpouring of concern for Haitian victims and the influx of aid to the nation. Other parallels that
raise the uncanny specter of déjà vu are the lack of donor coordination,

widespread frustration with the distribution of humanitarian resources, and the escalation of violence among the internally displaced.

Since the ouster of the Duvalier dictatorship in 1986, the Government of Haiti has had only limited capacity to protect its citizens and has struggled to establish security apparatuses that operate transparently and are accountable to Haitian citizens. While the abbreviated tenure of Haiti's first democratically elected president, Jean-Bertrand Aristide, initially raised hopes of peace and security in the nation, his ouster by military coup in 1991 and three subsequent years of repression thwarted those aspirations. Since the political upheaval of 2004 following Aristide's second ouster from the presidency, thousands of UN military peacekeepers, international police, and international and local staffers have worked to arrest crime and promote security, much as was the case in the period following the restoration of democracy in 1994. Many of these individuals were killed during the earthquake, and others are still missing.

Although additional UN and U.S. military forces are currently attempting to restore order and provide humanitarian relief, security remains of paramount concern. The earthquake damaged the national penitentiary. Thousands of former prisoners are currently at large. Some of these escapees undoubtedly orchestrated the destabilization of democracy and security in Haiti in the 1990s and in 2004. Armed gang members who had been imprisoned have reportedly returned to slums they once ruled to reassert their sovereign power.

The struggles of the Government of Haiti to protect its citizens and assert its sovereignty are no better demonstrated than by the actions of an American missionary group recently charged with child trafficking. The group claims it was rescuing children from the chaos of postquake conditions and was taking them to an orphanage in the Dominican Republic where they would be adopted. The group felt a divine call to intervene without authorization by the Haitian state in order to save the children, some of whom still have living parents. As the case has progressed, questions have arisen about the true intentions of this group, the corruption of the Haitian judiciary, and whether justice is for sale or will be meted out according to the rule of law. But the case is also an indicator of the extent to which international actors feel entitled to intervene in order to fulfill their mandates.

There are other parallels to the circumstances documented in this book. As during the 1991–94 period, hundreds of thousands of Haitians have fled to provincial cities, towns, and villages seeking asylum in areas that once depended on their labor in the capital for subsistence. Many Haitians have crossed into the Dominican Republic seeking medical care and new lives. It remains unclear whether the population shift to rural Haiti will result in permanent resettlement and future development of the nation's periphery, as was intended by many of the international development plans that proposed the nation's decentralization in prior years. The United States has also begun to prepare its naval site in Guantánamo Bay, Cuba, to receive a potential influx of refugees should conditions worsen and desperation increase. The detention of Haitian "boat people" in this camp is not new. Long before it was used to house suspected terrorists, Camp Delta held tens of thousands of Haitians for reasons of humanitarian and security concerns during the 1991–94 coup years. The majority of these "inmates" were subsequently returned to Haiti, despite its ongoing political and economic crisis.

Also reminiscent of the conditions described here are reports that have begun to circulate regarding the rape of women and young girls. Haitian women of all classes have traditionally been the pillars of society. They bear greater responsibility for maintaining the household and family than do men, and many do so while also pursuing independent livelihoods to meet their families' needs. Such expectations must be fulfilled regardless of shifts in political, economic, or environmental conditions. Because of these disproportionate obligations, Haitian women have typically been less mobile and more strongly rooted in their communities. For precisely these same reasons, they have also been more susceptible to attacks: it is difficult to flee from persecution when one's livelihood, family, and home are tied to a particular neighborhood, market, or place of work. If current reports are accurate, the makeshift tent cities that currently provide refuge to the internally displaced are sites of further victimization of women rather than sites of asylum, which raises additional questions regarding how security will be established in Haiti. Such conditions also highlight how gender is an integral component of the experience of insecurity and trauma.

Other similarities between the current crisis and the conflict and postconflict period in the 1990s concern the politics of aid. A few recent reports suggest that criminal actors have begun to capitalize on the chaos in order to expand their traffic in persons, drugs, and illicit goods. This book characterizes black market transactions like these as components of occult economies, some of which incorporate hidden exchanges between material and unseen (or immaterial) worlds. Furthermore, scandalous stories have circulated about how humanitarian aid has been diverted from its intended recipients into the black market. Well-intentioned charities have been questioned about the authenticity and legitimacy of their work in Haiti. There have been signs of contention between and among grassroots and international nongovernmental organizations regarding how and to which institutions the hundreds of millions of dollars in charitable gifts that have been donated to aid Haiti will be distributed. These ethical debates involving the just distribution of resources to victims and to the organizations that assist them are described here as components of a political economy of trauma.

As these events continue to unfold, there will come a point at which the numerous agencies and agents now working to provide relief will shift from a framework of emergency to one of reconstruction and rehabilitation. This book analyzes how such transitions occur. It is a cautionary tale documenting how conditions of insecurity have evolved over time. The phenomenon of insecurity incorporates political and criminal violence, economic instability, environmental vulnerability, and long histories of corruption and predation on the part of Haitians *and* foreign interveners. This text also chronicles how the transition from a crisis mode of intervention to one aimed at sustainable development of Haitian institutions—the police, the judiciary, and civil society organizations that promote democracy, human rights, and rehabilitation and reparations for victims—provoked competition and strife *within* the governmental and nongovernmental aid apparatus in the context of insecurity. To some extent the influx of aid had the unintended consequence of exacerbating the conditions that gave rise to military and humanitarian interventions in Haiti in the first place.

Some people have characterized the earthquake tragedy as an opportunity for Haiti's transformation, as long as Haitians remain partners in deciding how plans for their country's redevelopment and reconstruction are to take place. Calls for partnership and greater economic employment opportunities for Haitians are important and necessary. What remains crucial is that Haitians from all social classes and geographic locations participate in such plans. Regardless of the material or infrastructural disparities in power between Haiti and other members of the international community, Haitians must be imbued with equal (if not greater) power than international, national, and local interveners in deciding the course of reconstruction efforts in their country.

As this book demonstrates, it is perilous to consider Haiti and its citizens solely as clients, recipients of welfare or charity, or as victims. This lesson is even more urgent given that there are several populations affected by the earthquake whose status is similar to that of Haiti's victims of human rights abuses following the 1994 restoration of democracy. As was the case then, the Government of Haiti possesses little capacity to provide security, civil services, and medical care for its citizens. Women are increasingly vulnerable to insecurity. The number of orphans has increased exponentially. Thousands of new amputees of all ages require multiple forms of rehabilitation to help them rebuild their lives. If these populations are singled out for greater psychological, physical, economic, and other social supports because they are considered "at risk," but similar opportunities are not made available for all Haitians to flourish as productive citizens, it is possible that these groups may become subject to further stigma and resentment in their communities, as were victims of human rights abuses from the coup and postcoup years.

These issues of population management, the regulation and distribution of resources, identity, and accountability are important considerations for Haitians in Haiti and its diaspora and for those who would aid in rehabilitation and reconstruction efforts. However, such concerns should not overshadow attention to the physical, psychosocial, and spiritual effects of trauma that are the primary focus of this book. Trauma can result from ruptures in the routines of daily life, whether caused by natural, industrial, or human authors. Those who survive such ruptures may experience acute trauma; providers of care to victims may experience secondary trauma during and after a crisis. Trauma and emotional distress are phenomena that are culturally mediated and experienced in bodily ways. Whereas some view the devastation caused by the earthquake as an opportunity to create a blank slate in Haiti, the stories recounted in this book suggest that without effective strategies to address these traumas the power of memory and the embodied legacies of acute victimization will render attempts to mitigate suffering and to promote reconstruction and development ineffective.

Other questions addressed in this book must now be considered anew. How long will the "emergency" funds flow? How are private donations accounted for and to whom? Will the rehabilitation of trauma (whether physical, psychological, infrastructural, or spiritual) be rationed, regulated, and curtailed prematurely, so as to have only limited effect? What identities will emerge for these new "victims" after Haiti's dependence on charity, emergency relief, and other forms of humanitarian and development aid reemerges as a large component of its current economy? If new paths toward sustainable development cannot be created to empower all Haitians and to restore those who wish to rebuild their broken communities, aid interventions risk exacerbating the cycles of insecurity that have ebbed and flowed over the past twenty-five years.

Supported by a rich cultural heritage, the Haitian people retain a capacity for hope, faith, and resilience that remains a tremendous resource for any efforts to rehabilitate the nation and its people. Even when a powerful minority—whether Haitian or foreign—has posed obstacles to democracy, human rights, justice, and economic possibilities for all, the majority has endured. They must participate as equal partners in the reconstruction of their nation.

Cambridge, Massachusetts
March 2010

Introduction

Democracy, Insecurity, and the
Commodification of Suffering

What has dehumanized me has become a commodity, which I
offer for sale.

> Jean Améry, *At the Mind's Limits*

In this book I trace the links between military and humanitarian interventions in contemporary Haiti and the nation's ongoing struggles to
consolidate democracy and combat insecurity. I first chronicle the historic roots and practices of terror apparatuses and then describe how the
coup regime targeted Haitian pro-democracy activists with cruel forms
of domination during the 1991–94 period of de facto rule. I recount
how members of the coup apparatus used sexual and gender violence
as tools of repression to terrorize the poor pro-democracy sector. I also
describe the disordered subjectivities that such traumatic experiences
produced in women and men whom I encountered during my work.
However, this book does not focus exclusively on the assemblage of
sex, gender, violence, and trauma—a negative nexus of power that has
plagued sociopolitical realities in Haiti from the colonial era to the present (James 1989 [1963]; James 2003; Renda 2001; Rey 1999). Rather,
it describes the processes by which individuals and families targeted for
repression formulated new political subjectivities as apparatuses of terror *and* compassion intervened in their lives.

On December 16, 1990, the citizens of Haiti elected the former
priest Jean-Bertrand Aristide president of the republic. The democratic
election was historic after nearly thirty years of the brutal hereditary
Duvalier dictatorship (François "Papa Doc" Duvalier, 1957–71, and
Jean-Claude "Baby Doc" Duvalier, 1971–86) and five years of "Duvalierism without Duvalier," a period in which Duvalierist armed forces

sought to maintain political control by means of violent repression of pro-democratic sectors in civil society (Barthélemy 1992; Fatton 2002: 64–70). Aristide, a charismatic activist, espoused the ethics of liberation theology and promised to exercise a "preferential option for the poor."[1] The Lavalas coalition,[2] a network of grassroots, pro-democracy advocacy groups, endorsed Aristide as a candidate, and he won 67 percent of the popular vote. The historic inauguration of President Aristide on February 7, 1991, gave many Haitians hope that democracy, the rule of law, justice, human rights, governmental accountability, and socioeconomic equality might become enduring conditions in the nation.[3] But the meaning of these concepts has been at the heart of conflict in and over the Haitian nation throughout its history. To the consternation of those who supported the popular movement for democracy, the power to define and measure such conditions has remained in the hands of the international, national, and local actors whose interests in Haiti are often in opposition to those of the poor majority. These powerful actors routinely intervene to alter the course of Haiti's affairs.

Dreams of sociopolitical transformation in Haiti were short-lived. On September 30, 1991, Aristide was ousted by a military coup d'état. In the three years that followed, tens of thousands of paramilitary gunmen known as *atache* (attachés) aligned with the military to repress the population.[4] The terror apparatus murdered, raped, and "disappeared" fellow citizens in the poor pro-democracy sector, using methods of torture with historical roots in the brutal discipline of the slave plantations. Three hundred thousand Haitians were internally displaced, and tens of thousands of Haitian "boat people" fled to other Caribbean nations, South America, and the United States. Most Haitian refugees who reached U.S. shores were imprisoned in detention centers or repatriated. They were characterized as "economic migrants" fleeing poverty rather than granted the status of political asylum seekers.

On October 15, 1994, the U.S.-led Multinational Force (MNF), a twenty-eight-nation coalition of military forces sanctioned by U.N. Security Council Resolution 940, restored Aristide to power. International, national, and local humanitarian and development aid organizations worked alongside the peacekeeping and humanitarian military mission to rehabilitate the embattled nation and its traumatized citizens, much as they had begun to do during the period of unconstitutional military rule. Since the 1994 restoration of constitutional order, Haiti has recommenced the process of transforming systemic and systematic predatory state practices into practices of governmental accountability

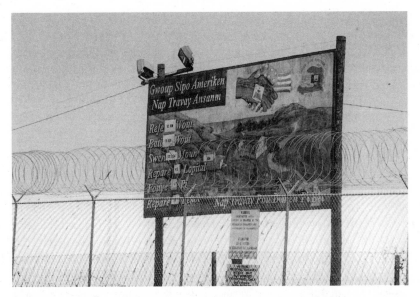

Figure 1. U.S. military "Support Group" mural, Camp Fairwinds, Port-au-Prince. The Haitian Creole text from the upper left corner to the bottom of the sign reads as follows: Gwoup Sipo Ameriken: American Support Group; Nap Travay Ansanm: We're Working Together; Refe Wout: Rebuild Roads; Bati Wout: Construct Roads; Swen Moun: Treat People; Repare Lopital: Repair Hospitals; Fouye Pi: Dig Wells; Repare Lekol: Repair Schools; Nap Travay Pou Demen Pi Bèl: We're Working for a Better Tomorrow. Photo credit: Erica Caple James.

and transparency. Nevertheless, it continues to struggle with ongoing political and economic insecurity.

In 1995 I arrived in Haiti to study Haitian Creole and to conduct research on religion and healing practices in anticipation of future Ph.D. work in medical anthropology. This first visit to Haiti occurred nine months after the MNF military intervention and during the United Nations Mission in Haiti (UNMIH) peacekeeping occupation, a mission that included soldiers from the United States, Bangladesh, Pakistan, India, the Netherlands, and Canada, among other nations. In addition to the peacekeepers, U.S. military forces engaged in "humanitarian civic assistance" to rebuild Haiti's infrastructure and provide medical care to Haitians in need. Many Haitians perceived the peacekeepers as a new kind of security force, one able to suspend the horror of the events that had transpired between 1991 and 1994. Throughout Port-au-Prince, the capital of Haiti, armored tanks and other military trucks commanded the roads. The soldiers who operated these imposing vehicles seemed to receive welcoming gestures from pedestrians passing through the streets.

The experience of living under such conditions drastically reshaped my future ethnographic research. Dr. Marie George and her family hosted me at their home in the upper Delmas section of Port-au-Prince during this first visit.[5] The neighborhood was residential, and to my untrained eye, it seemed calm and peaceful. The house was modest but comfortable, and I settled in to continue learning Haitian Creole with the George family, despite the challenges facing urban residents in daily life. That summer was one of the hottest I had ever experienced, and my hosts confirmed it seemed unusually warm. There was very little potable water, and we had electricity for only an hour or two each evening. We often cooked by candlelight while listening to hymns sung at a home-based Pentecostal church a few doors away. I was unsettled by the presence of high, gated walls around many of the homes. Broken glass or iron spikes were secured in mortar on top of these walls to prevent unwanted outsiders from entering. I began to sense the fear that still plagued Haiti despite the recent "restoration of democracy." It was as if the population had not yet awoken from a nightmare, one that left palpable traces on individuals, families, and communities.

During my first few days in Haiti, my Creole instructor took me to visit his family and to tour Port-au-Prince. In addition to the foreign military forces patrolling the city, I saw private uniformed security guards whom business and home owners with financial means routinely hired for protection, a practice that is common in many parts of Latin America[6] and increasingly characterizes many North American communities (Low 2003). The security firms that employed these men had names like Citadelle and Panther. These names evoked the power of the Haitians who triumphed over the country's enemies when it won its independence from France in 1804 and during struggles against foreign intervention in the postcolonial period. Private security companies first came on the scene after the 1986 ouster of Jean-Claude Duvalier. Some of the guards were former members of the coup apparatus (Stotzky 1997: 203–4); others were civilians who were unable to find work in their chosen profession. As a whole, these security firms managed an armed force that could be deployed for private and political ends should the need arise. While at first I was shocked to see the guards, armed with rifles or automatic weapons, posted in front of grocery stores and banks, by the end of the summer I no longer saw them. They had become invisible.

At home, Dr. George was extremely concerned about our personal safety as there had been a number of recent robberies in the neighborhood. Earlier that spring an elderly couple living a few doors down was murdered during a burglary. Dr. George said that most people assumed that the *gason lakou* (yard boy, caretaker) had allowed the thieves to enter the home. No one was sure what had actually happened. In the shadow of these extreme events, our day-to-day life was strangely predictable, despite the persistent anxiety about what might happen if we were not vigilant about our security. Dr. George made almost daily trips downtown to the clinic where she worked near the National Palace. When I accompanied her on these occasions, we were always careful to return home well before nightfall and not to make any unnecessary stops.

While en route we sometimes discussed how difficult life had been during the coup years, but these occasions were rare. Dr. George was reluctant to talk about those times, and it was not clear that they were truly in the past. After the coup the international community imposed a porous economic embargo intended to pressure the de facto regime to relinquish power. The military obstinately maintained its unconstitutional rule despite these so-called sanctions and profited from the black market that the sanctions encouraged.[7] Food was scarce and extremely expensive during the embargo. During especially uncertain times, Dr. George often remained at home to avoid the risk of going downtown to work at the clinic. She explained that these years reminded her of the social upheaval that directly affected her family after the fall of Duvalier.

Dr. George's brother, a businessman and manager of private schools that were owned by her extended family, was a target of *dechoukaj* (uprooting),[8] the retributive violence following the ouster of Duvalier directed against alleged Duvalierists. His house in the posh Laboule section in the mountains above Pétionville was razed to the ground by a mob of poor Haitians. Dr. George said that the group accused her brother of being a *tonton makout*—one of the agents and beneficiaries of the Duvalier terror apparatus. The lingering effects of this attack on her middle-class family were manifested in Dr. George's apprehensions about the inhabitants of her home, including me. Like many other Haitian homes, the George residence could be locked from the outside to prevent the door from being opened even by those who remained within. All keys to the home, rooms, and cabinets remained in her hands; thus she controlled when we entered and exited the domestic sphere. To exit the home, I needed to be with her. The attempt to secure our domestic space behind the clawed walls and locked doors of the gate and home only emphasized the specter of disorder in the social space outside.

Encounters with three other individuals would have a direct influence on my subsequent ethnographic research in Haiti on postconflict or posttrauma rehabilitation for individuals, groups, and even nations, especially in contexts of widespread social, political, and economic instability. In the mini-*bidonvil* (slum, shantytown) near the Georges' house, a woman could often be seen walking the streets at midday, crying out as if she were a bird or some other animal. I asked Dr. George about this woman and was told that she practiced Vodou. Sometimes the woman became possessed and walked the streets. "She's just crazy," I was told, "just ignore it." Nevertheless, I wondered if her possession was actually taking place in the context of ritual, or if there might have been some other factor that precipitated her dissociative state—especially considering the recent murder on the same street and the overwhelming climate of tension in the city as a whole.

Dr. George's dismissal of this woman's condition raised several questions regarding whether the local disruptions in social space and the broader context of political and economic instability disordered some individuals' subjectivity—their sense of self, identity, and bodily experience—more than others. Were there culturally patterned ways in which emotional distress manifested in Haiti, and did these vary according to gender, class, or social status? In what contexts did individuals dissociate, and when was it socially appropriate? From my previous study of religion and healing, I was aware that in ritual contexts of Haitian Vodou dissociation is considered a desirable spiritual state that precedes the embodiment of the spirits. How did those Haitians whose understanding of the body, emotion, and illness rested on the epistemology of Vodou express and interpret psychological distress? Were instances such as these markers of some sort of posttraumatic stress disorder (PTSD) as it is understood in biomedical contexts? If so, what methods of healing existed in Haitian culture to restore the integrity of the person? Were they effective for the victims of violence, torture, and rape who continued to struggle in the insecure environment?

A visit by a member of Dr. George's family gave me more questions to ponder about the relationship between political, social, and economic instability and the processes of establishing democracy and security in Haiti. Nathalie St. Pierre, a cousin of Dr. George, occasionally stayed with us while she worked as a translator at the nearby civilian police academy. We often spoke about her work with the U.S. Department of

Justice International Criminal Investigative Training Assistance Program (ICITAP), which provided instruction to civilian police forces globally. The new Haitian National Police force had been established recently, and American, Canadian, and French police gave technical assistance to the new classes of Haitian officers. Nathalie described the officer candidates as very young and inexperienced and said that translating across cultural and linguistic boundaries was often difficult. I wondered how this young police force would be able to provide security in such an unstable social and economic environment.

The third individual who encouraged me to think about the challenges of promoting democracy, the rule of law, and justice in Haiti was a Belgian priest of the Scheut Mission, Fr. Hugo Triest (1932–2003), a human rights activist, journalist, and former director of the Catholic Radio Soleil. Father Hugo had promoted human rights in Haiti since the Duvalier period. He visited me at Dr. George's home that summer and invited me to accompany him to the Carrefour neighborhood where he frequently celebrated Mass for disabled young adults at a residential center. Carrefour was one of the areas hardest hit by violence during the period of de facto military rule. In our conversations I learned about the overwhelming difficulties his Haitian colleagues and he had faced during decades of promoting human rights in the nation. Their efforts were hampered by repression and violence, the population's overarching illiteracy, and the difficulties of everyday social engagements.

Father Hugo told me, furthermore, that it was often impossible for the network of Haitian human rights organizations to achieve consensus on courses of action. He lamented the competition, suspicion, and indecision that some of these organizations exhibited. But he also challenged me to consider that it was not just the violations of what are viewed as civil and political rights that were affronts to humanity; violations of economic, social, and cultural rights can be equally if not more devastating. I will never forget his words that summer: "In Haiti misery is a violence."[9] They remained with me as I learned how Haitian governmental and nongovernmental actors, as well as international interveners, approached the work of postconflict transition in Haiti between 1996 and 2000.

This book examines the paradox that many of the efforts to rehabilitate the nation and its citizens, and to promote democracy and economic stability, inadvertently reinforced the practices of predation, corruption, and repression that they were intended to repair. In response to the proliferation of human rights abuses during the coup years, the humanitarian and development aid apparatuses—international, national, and local governmental and nongovernmental institutions assisting Haiti through improvised as well as "planned" interventions (Ferguson 1994: 20)—offered crisis assistance to victims and documented human rights violations as they were occurring. In the postconflict period the aid apparatus generated numerous and sometimes competing initiatives to rehabilitate these victims as a component of interventions to strengthen democracy in Haiti.

Integral to the processes by which aid apparatuses indirectly fomented social unrest was the pernicious presence of *ensekirite* (Haitian Creole for "insecurity"): the seemingly random political and criminal violence that ebbed and flowed in waves amid ongoing economic, social, and environmental decline. Through the course of my work in Haiti, I observed how ensekirite was experienced as vulnerability, anxiety, and a heightened sense of risk at a sensory level, especially by those who were most vulnerable. The sense of risk and vulnerability crossed racial, class, and gender boundaries and even threatened members of expatriate communities and agencies—whether governmental or nongovernmental—although to varying degrees.

I understand ensekirite as the embodied uncertainty generated by political, criminal, economic, and also spiritual ruptures that many individuals and groups continue to experience in Haiti (James 2008). The lived experience of ensekirite incorporates not only the threats residing in material space but also the perception of unseen malevolent forces that covertly intervene in Haitian society—whether such forces are natural or supernatural, individual or collective, organized or arbitrary, or domestic or foreign. Thus another goal of this work is to capture how individual, institutional, and government actors perceive and make sense of the hidden or occult powers that are integral to the generation of ensekirite.

HISTORIC ROOTS OF ENSEKIRITE

Haiti (formerly Saint-Domingue) is one of many nations attempting the transition from authoritarian regimes, civil war, colonial rule, and political violence to a state of social and economic stability. Haiti is also generally known as the "poorest country in the Western Hemisphere." This oft-cited negative description renders opaque the way in which international and national political and economic powers have contributed to its dire state. Many have questioned why the world's first black republic still struggles to consolidate democracy after gaining independence in

1804. To some degree the answer is straightforward: the majority of Haitian citizens lack security. Without security it is difficult to build lasting social and political institutions that support democratic processes and economic growth. Embedded in this seemingly simple answer are complex historical practices of international exploitation and disenfranchisement, domestic terror and economic predation, and long-standing societal ills and injustices.

The dilemmas of representation are a necessary starting point for this book. A long tradition of misrepresenting the Haitian nation and its culture, especially on the part of Westerners, complicates many recent as well as older depictions of the country's plight (Dash 1997; Farmer 1992, 1994; Lawless 1992; Renda 2001). Haiti remains infamous for the widespread practice of Vodou, the historically maligned religion that enabled former slaves to survive and to create other forms of spiritual governance in Haiti's postcolonial era. It is a religion that has been considered both a positive and a negative force for "development" at various periods in the nation's history (Desmangles 1992: 6; Mars 1977 [1946]; Price-Mars 1983). Undoubtedly, the ambivalence about its practice colors the way the nation and its people have been treated internationally (Farmer 1992; Sabatier 1988).

Questions about Haiti's capacity to achieve democratic governance and representations that depict violence and the Vodou religion as the hallmarks of Haiti's so-called national character also have deep political and historical roots. These representations mark their authors as occupying positions of privilege and power that the majority of Haitians have never approached. Frequently, observers of Haiti also deny any connection between their privileged position and the nation's ongoing struggles with democracy. Furthermore, representations of Haiti and its people, history, and culture directly influence foreign policies applied to and interventions in the nation.

The roots of Haiti's challenges in consolidating democracy are long and deep. They can be traced to eighteenth-century colonial plantation regimes in which overseers extracted material resources through slave labor in order to enrich European metropolitan centers. But Haiti is also the only nation to successfully liberate itself from the extreme brutality of the plantation regime, largely through rebellion and revolution by the slave majority. Between 1791 and 1803 there were approximately 450,000 African slaves, 40,000 ruling whites, and 30,000 mixed-race persons, as well as a small population of free blacks (Lundahl 1983: 68; Nicholls 1985: 23; Nicholls 1996: 20–21).[10] In the course of the rebellion and revolution, the Saint-Domingue slaves overcame Spanish, British, and French forces (Davis 2006: 159, 166–67). These intrepid slaves ultimately defeated Napoleon Bonaparte's efforts to reestablish French colonial domination between 1802 and 1803 and declared independence from France on January 1, 1804. The country's unique history is related to its current troubled state.

In its quest for sovereignty, equality, and liberation from tyranny—values promoted in the preceding American and French revolutions—Haiti entered its postcolonial era as both an outcast from colonizing and slaveholding nations and a symbol of freedom for the enslaved and colonized. In 1825 Haiti was compelled to pay a hefty indemnity to France of 150 million francs to compensate former plantation owners for losses sustained during the revolutionary period. The indemnity agreement, a condition of political recognition of Haiti's independence, put an end to France's attempts to reacquire its former colony but severely hampered the fledgling nation economically (Farmer 1994: 76). After adding the interest on loans required to pay the indemnity, the figure equaled more than U.S.$21 billion in today's dollars (Charles 2003). As a further indignity, it was more than half a century before Haiti received formal recognition as a sovereign nation from the Vatican (in 1860) and the United States (in 1862, after the South seceded from the Union at the commencement of the Civil War) (Logan 1941: 303; Trouillot 1990: 51, 53).

The achievement of independence did not lead to the eradication of exploitative domestic practices. In the early nineteenth century Haiti's postcolonial leaders reproduced the colonial system of political and economic repression in parts of the nation, including the brutal discipline of workers (Trouillot 1990: 48–50). As the nineteenth century progressed the racial and class conflict between a "mulatto, city-based, commercial elite, and a black, rural, and military elite . . . was frequently such that each would prefer to invite foreign intervention in the affairs of Haiti than to allow its rivals to gain power" (Nicholls 1996: 8). The poor black peasant majority that cultivated the land was largely excluded from political decisions but mobilized to resist foreign intervention when Haiti's sovereignty was challenged by the collusion of foreign and domestic actors. By the end of the nineteenth century the former French colony that was once the most economically productive in the world received two-thirds of its imports from trade with the United States (Trouillot 1990: 54). In the early twentieth century U.S. control of Haiti's import market would also be accompanied by military occupation.

In the twentieth century decades of U.S. occupation, political instability, and economic development strategies favoring foreign investors
reinforced the late-nineteenth-century position of the Haitian state and
its agents as predators (Fatton 2002; McCoy 1997; Rotberg 1971;
Smith 2001). The occupation also increased the nation's dependency
on imports. Between 1957 and 1986 the Duvalier dictators deployed
what Achille Mbembe (2003) has termed "necropolitics"—the power of
death to subjugate life—in order to control the population. This repression occurred with the tacit approval of the international community
because it produced a docile labor force that was available for industrial
export production. The profit from the commodities that Haitians produced—items such as baseballs, microelectronics, textiles, apparel, and
toys (Farmer 1988b; Grunwald, Delatour, and Voltaire 1984, 1985)—
remained in the hands of the Haitian elite and foreign business owners.
These international and national practices of political and economic
extraction are major contributors to Haiti's current status as what is
widely regarded as a failed state.

Predatory practices did not occur without resistance. Between 1986
and 1990 poor, pro-democratic forces struggled with former Duvalierists, at times violently, to determine the course of Haiti's future. Despite
the reciprocal violence occurring in the period before its democratic
elections, national and international observers considered President
Aristide's election legitimate. But hopes for changing the endemic
oppression and corruption were dashed by the September 30, 1991,
military coup d'état, President Aristide's subsequent protracted exile,
and the brutal suppression of the pro-democracy sector.

In light of the brief history recounted thus far, it is important to discuss another set of representations that depicted Haiti's political economy during the time of my research between 1995 and 2000. The *World
Development Report 2000/2001* listed Haiti as a "low income" country
(170th out of 206 economies), with a gross national product (GNP) of
only U.S.$460 per capita (World Bank 2001). The U.N. Development
Programme's (UNDP's) *Human Development Report 2000* stated that
63 percent of the population lacked access to safe water, 55 percent
lacked access to health services, and 75 percent lacked access to basic
sanitation. Adult illiteracy rates were at least 55 percent, and possibly
higher. At least 28 percent of children under age five were below normal
weight. Infant mortality rates were nearly 64 per 1,000 live births.

Such dire conditions have not changed much in recent years. The CIA
World Factbook of 2008 estimated life expectancy at slightly more than

fifty-eight years for women and fifty-five years for men. The same report cited an HIV/AIDS prevalence rate of nearly 6 percent for the entire population of Haiti.[11] Overall, at least 80 percent of the population lives in poverty and 56 percent in abject poverty. Haiti's current external debt is U.S.$1.3 billion, and unemployment is currently estimated at nearly 70 percent (CIA 2008). Given statistics such as these, one might ask, What has happened in Haiti? Or, rather, What hasn't happened?

When President Aristide was restored to power in 1994, the international community, through its multilateral and bilateral aid institutions, proposed the "development" of Haiti by instituting neoliberal economic interventions: export-led agricultural production, continued privatization of national industries, expansion of the industrial assembly sector, and additional stabilization and structural adjustment efforts, among others. These plans were contested, as they required that the nation and its economy be open to nearly unrestricted foreign extraction of resources and exploitation of "cheap" labor. Foreign assistance came primarily in the form of loans. Such measures meant that for the most part profits would accumulate in the hands of the elite or circulate outside Haiti rather than "trickle down" to build state infrastructure and improve the status of the poor majority. While some of these efforts were implemented, ongoing political disputes in Haiti and in the international community disrupted aid flows.

Aristide's truncated term concluded in 1995 after peaceful elections. The transition that followed brought to power René Préval, who was once known as Aristide's protégé and who served as prime minister during Aristide's first term. In 2000, as President Préval completed his five-year term, Aristide was reelected to a second term as president, raising hopes that the unrealized promises of his first interrupted term could finally be accomplished. But despite these indicators of the development of democratic processes, the international community suspended direct foreign assistance to Haiti because of allegations that the election was fraudulent.[12] Multilateral and bilateral aid agencies filtered emergency funds through international nongovernmental humanitarian and development aid agencies rather than disburse them directly to Haitian institutions. After the 1994 restoration of democracy, close to half a billion dollars in direct international aid was withheld.

This suspension of aid was continued after yet another escalation in Haiti's sociopolitical instability. On February 29, 2004, Aristide was forced into exile for the second time. Armed forces in the north of Haiti composed of members of the terror apparatus from the 1991–94 coup period and other anti-Aristide actors joined together in a campaign to take control of Port-au-Prince. In this instance the international community did not intervene. Rather, President Aristide was presented with the "choice" to resign and immediately leave the country or to face more civilian killings and his government's destruction. The unwillingness of the United States, Canada, France, and other nations to intervene in the crisis permitted a virtual coup d'état that Aristide sympathizers have termed a "kidnapping" (Aristide 2004; Chomsky, Farmer, and Goodman 2004; Hallward 2007; Robinson 2007). These events plunged the nation into another cycle of violence, and since that time another round of military and humanitarian intervention has attempted to restore order and democratic rule. Ensekirite continues to proliferate despite (or as a consequence of) these processes.

Haiti's cycles of economic decline and political and criminal insecurity are inextricably linked with this history of the masses' suffering and resistance. Of course, these cycles are also influenced by foreign military, political, and economic interventions that are inextricably connected to the circulation of commodities in the global capitalist economy. Thus criticisms of Haiti's apparent failure to achieve democracy and postconflict security must be assessed in the context of the country's unique geopolitical and economic position.

SOVEREIGNTY, SECURITY, AND INTERVENTION

Theorists of international relations have traditionally deployed the concepts of sovereignty and security to describe a given state's political independence: its freedom from external interference, right to self-government, and right to protect its national interests from the threat of other sovereign polities. Likewise, international relations theorists have conventionally considered the ethics and politics of intervention in the context of war. In the aftermath of World War II and the Holocaust, however, the parameters of scholarship on sovereignty and related security discourses have shifted.

The evolution of the prevailing "culture of national security" (Katzenstein 1996) accompanied the formal development of the international human rights regime by the Allied powers at the end of World War II. After the war European nations were faced with the challenge of resurrecting societies and transforming national war economies into economies that alleviated suffering and promoted social, economic, and political recovery. On June 5, 1947, U.S. Secretary of State George

Marshall extended U.S. assistance to "rehabilitate" the ruined countries and economies of Europe as a humanitarian concern—one that had a direct influence on global peace and security, as well as on U.S. national security.[13] Underlying the concern to alleviate suffering, however, were nascent cold war fears that Europeans, out of desperation, social chaos, and poverty, would turn to Communism rather than to democracy.[14]

The postwar period was also significant for the establishment of international institutions dedicated to promoting global peace, security, democracy, and human rights, alongside economic development. Governmental and nonstate actors alike began to affirm that the security of individuals and groups residing *within* a sovereign nation was a matter of international interest rather than a matter solely of domestic policy, a concept currently understood as "human security" (Rothschild 1995). On October 24, 1945, the U.N. Charter was ratified. It created an international institution committed to global peace and security; to justice, human rights, and equitable social and economic development; and to protect citizens from the repressive acts of their own governments. At the state level, membership in the U.N. required, among other things, that a government promote and protect human rights. As a consequence, states must also agree to external surveillance of their domestic affairs. Such monitoring could result in interventions in the affairs of sovereign nations that were violating such rights.

The international human rights regime codified ideals for regulating interpersonal, institutional, and intergovernmental interaction through the December 10, 1948, ratification of the Universal Declaration of Human Rights (UDHR) and the subsequent ratification of covenants, charters, statutes, and other legal instruments. Through such efforts human rights stakeholders have, in effect, defined what it means to be "human" in universal terms, even as these definitions remain hotly contested. As has been noted by numerous scholars of the human rights regime, vigorous debates continue to unfold around issues of culture, gender, and individual versus collective rights; a tendency to privilege the surveillance and enforcement of "civil and political" rights over the "economic, cultural, and social rights"; a Western or "Eurocentric" orientation to foundational human rights documents; and historical debates over the lesser influence of later entrants into the U.N. system after World War II (the newly independent postcolonial and postsocialist states, among others).

In the decades since the inauguration of the formal human rights regime, the dynamic nature of conflict and the plurality of settings in which it occurs have impelled revisions and refinement of these conceptions of human rights and notions of security. Historically, the sphere of individual civil and political rights and the specter of violent threats in interstate wars have received greatest emphasis. As a result, classifying types of violence as "state-sponsored" or "organized" has been an essential step in the human rights regime's procedures for intervening in the affairs of a predatory sovereign state. Given consensus that such criteria have been met, governmental and nongovernmental actors have implemented military and humanitarian interventions across the borders of sovereign states in order to reduce suffering and promote human security during and after periods of political strife. These interveners characteristically demand that transitional nations promote democracy, human rights, the rule of law, and justice—as well as embrace free market economies—as they undergo postconflict development. They also advocate that transitions take place in circumstances of governmental accountability and transparency. These activities constitute what has come to be called nation building.

Even given consensus that a population is suffering from human rights violations and an absence of security, the Haitian case demonstrates that refugees escaping instability and ensekirite can also be perceived as threats to the security of the nations to which they flee. These perceptions of threat, in turn, evoke conventional understandings of and debates about national security that prevail over concerns for human security. Thus the state—whether sovereign and legitimate, illegitimate, accountable, or failed—remains at the heart of these theoretical discourses, despite notions of a "new world order" in the post–cold war world.

Both conventional and human security discourses are largely framed in the shadow of paradigms that view the state and its organized agents as malevolent perpetrators or negligent patriarchs in opposition to vulnerable, "feminized," or subjugated populations. In response, transnational interventions to craft democracies from "transitional" societies frequently adopt modern, universal discourses of law, human rights, and development to remedy the disparities in power between states and their civilian populations. In many transitional states, "cultures of insecurity" (Weldes et al. 1999) hamper efforts to consolidate democratic processes and economic growth. What must not be forgotten, however, is that these "new" conflicts have deep historical roots. Foreign and domestic powers may have instigated, manipulated, or suppressed violent disputes in order to maintain the previous dominant position of state, ruling class, or colonial power. In some respects interventions aimed at social rehabilitation of transitional states are reminiscent of the missions of colonial expansion, the joint military and humanitarian interventions of the imperial past that sought to civilize their objects of intercession.

I use the terms *neomodern* and *neomodernism* in this book to refer to the resurgence of Enlightenment theories and practices of intervention that arise in relationship to the crisis of the state in the post–cold war era (Alexander 1995).[15] In addition to characterizing new modes of warfare, neomodernism refers to the interventionist practices of nation building. Crucial to the neomodernist mission is the deployment of "governmentalities" (Foucault 1991: 103)—government rationalities or technologies of governance—to targets of intervention.

Neomodern doctrines of evolution and salvation are expressed through discourses of modernization and development (Escobar 1995: 194). A key tenet is the belief that the harmonious linkages of law-abiding nations that promote human rights and democracy and maintain open markets will inevitably achieve global peace and security. These secular creeds provide new flames to keep that motivate the zeal characterizing many well-intentioned interveners (Hopgood 2006).[16] Neomodern principles of social engineering are also secular "theodicies"—theories explaining the origin of "evil" or suffering in the face of justice (or the goodness of God)—that seek to account for and remedy misfortune encountered across and within sovereign borders (Herzfeld 1992: 9–10). Nonetheless, intervention practices arising from such ideals frequently ignore political and economic disparities across and within nations that may ultimately underlie the eruption of "emergencies" (Agamben 1998 [1995]; Boltanski 1999 [1993]; Hopgood 2006). Despite possessing lofty ideals, the actual practices of promoting human rights, democracy, and economic growth abroad can be prejudiced, unequal, and unjust: some nations that desire to join the global community of nations are denied, whereas others are forced to follow the neomodernist path of development.

Another goal of this book is to show that these paradigms and the interventions engendered by neomodern discourses are inadequate to remedy chronic climates of ensekirite such as those that persist in Haïti. The limitations of conceptions of violence and vulnerability—as well as those of human rights, human security, and human development—likewise challenge the effectiveness of efforts to prevent, adjust, heal, or restore the cleavages wrought by ensekirite. I argue, furthermore, that the contradictions between neomodernist ideals and practices of governance produce ethical and moral dilemmas for the agencies and agents working to facilitate Haiti's postconflict rehabilitation. These contradictions also create "double binds" (Fortun 2001) and untenable dilemmas of representation and identity for individuals who are both victims of human rights abuses and targets of aid intervention. Participating in and observing such processes as they unfolded also produced ethical challenges for the anthropologist.

ETHICS OF RESEARCH AND REPRESENTATION

In the introduction to *Anthropology and the Colonial Encounter*, Talal Asad exhorts anthropologists to examine the ways in which the discipline's history, suppositions, and practices are rooted in asymmetries of power. As producers of knowledge, anthropologists' expertise may "have contributed to the cultural heritage of the societies they study. . . . But they have also contributed, sometimes indirectly, towards maintaining the structures of power represented by the colonial system" (1973: 17). These remarks are still relevant for the type of ethnographic practice that many anthropologists conduct today, known as activist or "critically engaged" anthropology.

In recent years the role of anthropologists as champions of their subjects has received considerable attention. The 1995 debate between Nancy Scheper-Hughes and Roy D'Andrade in *Current Anthropology* and the accompanying commentary on their perspectives raised questions about what moral obligations anthropologists have to relieve suffering rather than simply describe and analyze it. Are we, as Scheper-Hughes (1995: 417–18) admonishes, to act as "barefoot anthropologists" who are committed to siding with those who are downtrodden? Does such an activist position compromise the anthropologist's ability to record a politically neutral account? Is neutrality truly possible in the face of misery, or does such a position lean toward indifference?

Despite such tensions, anthropologists are actively advocating for human rights while simultaneously opening the theoretical space to challenge the universalism of its tenets (Goodale 2006; Merry 2006; Slyomovics 2005; Speed 2006). While the critically engaged anthropologist faces questions of how best to use ethnographic practices to represent their subjects' interests, she also faces the double bind of what truths to tell, especially when portraying complexity "on the ground" may undermine a particular political struggle (Fortun 2001: 52–54).

There are also current ethical debates about the role of anthropologists as cultural "experts" or translators in service of neocolonial, imperial, or military interventions.[17] Such anthropologists are *embedded in* the systems and structures of power against which many activist anthropologists are advocating. For example, Arturo Escobar (1995: 15), affirming Stacey Leigh Pigg's (1992) reflections on anthropologists working in the field of development, has said, "Anthropologists have been for the most part either inside development, as applied anthropologists, or outside development, as the champions of the authentically indigenous and the 'native's point of view.'" But "embedded anthropologists" are also ideally positioned to study the powerful effects of institutions, policies, and practices on their objects of intervention (Nader 1999; Pandolfi 2003, 2008).

Many of the actors designing and implementing the social engineering strategies in Haiti are both theoretical and applied anthropologists. They may be individuals with cross-cultural expertise from formal study of social theory or from humanitarian work. The anthropologists and social theorists with whom I studied and worked in Haiti are multiply positioned as activists, investigators, and experts. All of us were deeply implicated in the ethical dilemmas and failures of intervention depicted in this book. I critically assess the outcomes of these interventions with ambivalence, as I recognize that many of the sociocultural experts whose work is critiqued in this ethnography were the same ones who permitted me to participate in and observe the work in practice.

In writing this book, I have been forced to ask how the anthropologist describes Haiti's difficulties traveling along a chosen democratic path without reinforcing negative stereotypes about the nation and its people or demonizing the political spectrum of international interveners that sought to craft such processes. How does one discuss the problems of interpersonal strife, political violence, and pathological social cleavages without reinforcing the perception that Haiti is a pathological state? Is political neutrality possible when describing the processes that are transforming the social identities of both givers and receivers of aid in a climate of manifest insecurity? How does the methodology used to construct knowledge about the historical production of ensekirite—as well as the intersubjective, institutional, and governmental responses ensekirite provokes—generate additional dilemmas of representation?

In answer to these questions, I have chosen an interdisciplinary mode of analysis. I build on the insights of theology, medical and psychiatric anthropology, law and political science, human rights and humanitarian studies, and studies of race, gender, and religion; however, I am unable to delve deeply into the conceptual genealogies of each field without sacrificing the narrative that I want to recount. As a discursive strategy, much of the analysis is presented as it was lived: the interpretation of events is sparsely interwoven in or immediately following the vignettes depicted. My intent is to give the *sense* of ensekirite that was experienced by Haitian activists targeted for repression and by those who sought to assist them.

The interdisciplinary character of this book also reflects the challenges that arose from the methodology used to gather data for the analysis. I conducted long-term, multisited ethnographic research tracing the international, national, and local responses to violence, trauma, and injustice in Haiti. I was in a unique position to evaluate interventions to assist Haitians who were targeted for political repression and to witness the unintended consequences of those interventions. I was also able to gauge the effects of ensekirite on both givers and receivers of aid. As George Marcus (1998: 98–99) has suggested regarding the challenges of multisited ethnography, the multiplicity of my participant-observation work necessarily shifted into "circumstantial activism." I was often cast in the role of translator or advocate when the epistemologies and practices of agents and agencies involved in such gift exchanges conflicted with the needs and desires of aid recipients.

Negotiating the politics, discourses, expectations, and constraints of all these spaces over the course of several years was extremely difficult. The complexity of this project raised serious ethical problems concerning how to maintain a position of integrity when sometimes violently confronted by the competing frames of knowledge and practice to which I was exposed. In this regard, however, it is useful to recall Donna Haraway's (1991: 192) statement: "A commitment to mobile positioning and to passionate detachment is dependent on the impossibility of innocent 'identity' politics and epistemologies as strategies for seeing from the standpoints of the subjugated in order to see well." We must always recognize that the situatedness of knowledge produced in the locations we study, and our own shifting position in these locations over time, can constrain our power to see and act. Changes in my position and the responses to them among those with whom I worked became ethnographic tools for me to understand some of the more elusive features of contemporary life in Haiti. As I discuss later in this book, they were also the basis for threats to my own security.

Between 1995 and 2000 I spent more than twenty-seven months in Haiti studying transnational efforts to craft democracy and civil society in Haiti's "post-trauma polity" (Fischer 1991). I accompanied victims of human rights abuses from the 1991–94 de facto period as they sought justice, healing, and reparations from the aid apparatus. These individuals called themselves _viktim_ (victims, pronounced "veek-teem"),[18] not only to signify their status as a class of political martyrs for Haitian democracy, but also to draw attention to their particular needs for psychosocial rehabilitation and reparations. Most viktim were nonliterate, unemployed, and struggling with chronic emotional and physical illnesses resulting from their victimization.

My goal was to understand better the long-term medical, psychological, material, and spiritual consequences of having been targeted by the terror apparatus amid the ongoing climate of ensekirite. Early in my research many viktim claimed the identity of _militan_ (activist). By the end of my work most emphasized the identity of viktim to the exclusion of other identities. The transformation of militan into viktim is one of the many troubling processes that I describe here. It is for this reason that I use the Haitian Creole form of the term to denote a political class of individuals from a particular period in Haiti and to denaturalize the concept of victimization as it is understood in a Western, liberal context.

I worked with viktim as a therapeutic practitioner and ethnographic researcher in multiple sites. From 1996 to 2000 I volunteered at a privately funded women's clinic in Martissant that I call Chanm Fanm (Women's Room). In my capacity as a practitioner of the Trager® Approach,[19] a form of physical therapy, I treated women who were victims of politically motivated rape. Most of these women were first-generation migrants from rural areas who came to the capital in the 1970s and 1980s to work in assembly factories. Exploitative conditions compelled many of them to seek employment as small-scale merchants. In times of scarcity they may also have engaged in sex work to support their families. Financial insecurity corraled most of these women within sprawling slums, where they and their families became targets of torture and terror because of their struggles for economic justice and democracy. As my research progressed, I followed these women, their families, and a broad network of victims' associations as they learned to negotiate the humanitarian and development aid apparatus that was based primarily in Port-au-Prince.

In spring 1997 I was a paid consultant for America's Development Foundation (ADF), a private voluntary organization with headquarters near Washington, D.C., that received funding from the United States Agency for International Development (USAID). Many have called the USAID/Haiti Mission a "state within a state," speaking to the tremendous power and resources that it wielded in the country and to its virtual sovereignty. In 1994 USAID/Haiti and ADF inaugurated Fon Dwa Moun (Le Fond des Droits Humains, the Human Rights Fund) in Port-au-Prince. In May 1997 the Fund, as it was called in English, began housing the Victim Assistance and Rehabilitation Program (hereafter the Rehabilitation or Rehab Program) for Haitian victims of organized violence. To support this initiative, I designed and participated in a training program for Haitian mental health practitioners who, as members of the Human Rights Fund's medical network, treated torture survivors. The training took place in June 1997 in Boston, Massachusetts. I also studied conventional conceptions of PTSD and trained to use the Clinician-Administered PTSD Scale (CAPS) in order to learn more about the psychosocial distress that survivors of traumatic events might experience. The authors of this diagnostic instrument at the Boston Veterans Administration National Center for PTSD provided additional instruction in recognizing the classic signs of posttraumatic stress.[20]

In fall 1997 and from summer 1998 to spring 2000, I conducted archival research and participant observation at the ADF Human Rights Fund in Port-au-Prince. I studied case files representing more than 2,500 viktim to track patterns of violence from the coup years. Until the suspension of its services in May 1999, I also participated in the Rehabilitation Program therapy groups for victims of human rights violations as a volunteer co-facilitator and ethnographic researcher. Through my affiliation with current and former ADF staff, I was able to attend the USAID/Haiti Justice, Democracy and Governance (JDG) Program planning meetings to understand how the agency implemented political development assistance. I interviewed USAID/Haiti staff members and conducted additional archival research to learn more about the history of U.S. military, humanitarian, and development interventions in the nation.

Finally, from fall 1998 to spring 1999, I also studied with Haitian mental health practitioners in outpatient therapy sessions at the State University Hospital Mars/Kline Center for Neurology and Psychiatry in Port-au-Prince. This internship permitted me to learn many of the cultural idioms Haitians use to articulate emotional and psychological distress. I interviewed individuals working in these and other institutions that intervened to serve viktim. Wherever possible, interviews were tape-recorded.

Throughout these years in Haiti, I continued to treat and accompany viktim outside these institutional spaces as they sought reparations, rehabilitation, and justice. This allowed me to observe how a discourse of trauma became an organizing trope producing new forms of bureaucratic practices throughout Haiti, much as it has in sites of disaster across the globe (Bracken and Petty 1998). Postconflict psychosocial rehabilitation projects reflect the growing prevalence of the concept of trauma in Western culture and the desire to define or classify the "unthinkable" horrors of social ruptures (Trouillot 1995), whether produced by human agency or other causes. The traumas resulting from conflict, from industrial, technological, and medical disasters, and from environmental causes, were "comorbid"—that is, they occurred at the same time but not always related to or arising from the same source.

As I discuss below, additional aspects of ensekirite exacerbated the social prevalence of traumatic comorbidity in Haiti. More generally, conditions of trauma resulting from disasters of human or "natural" authorship are global phenomena indicative of state insecurity. These complex circumstances have been identified in Indonesia (Good and Good 2008; Good et al. 2006; Good et al. 2007), India (Cohen 1999; Das 1995; Fortun 2001), Ukraine (Petryna 2002), and many other fragile or failed states.

Despite the prevalence of traumatic comorbidity, the etiology of suffering is a factor in the type of interventions undertaken. "Acts of God" cannot be controlled and are (usually) perceived as having morally neutral origins. Survivors of a natural disaster may become the objects of state bureaucratic management and rehabilitation and often receive care from charitable organizations and other benevolent associations simultaneously. These natural calamities and the interventions that flow as a result may reveal the fractures and disparities of power among their victims, as has been revealed following the Hurricane Katrina disaster in the United States.[21]

Similarly, survivors of industrial or manufactured disasters such as the residents of Chernobyl (Petryna 2002) and Bhopal (Das 1995; Fortun 2001) are targets of humanitarian intervention. In some ways these catastrophes can be characterized as unintended rather than malicious, despite their human authorship. Such "accidents" resulting from the negligence of transnational corporations or governments also generated movements for reparations and justice for victims.

In contrast, victims of conventionally recognized human rights abuses grapple with the question of "evil." They confront the issue of whether their experiences of victimization were intentional. Individuals designed and carried out malefic action against them as part of individual and institutional efforts to extract power from and otherwise control or punish them. Thus the moral, ethical, and political concerns evoked by the victims of state-authored conflict make assistance to them a thorny matter in the international political arena. All these societal ruptures can precipitate new identities for victims based solely on suffering or injury, especially when occurring in insecure states.

Along with analyzing how and by whom the discourse of trauma was employed in Haiti, I evaluated the rhetorics of rights, rehabilitation, and reparations that shaped institutional practices. Prompted by the work of the philosopher Michel Foucault on madness (1988 [1965]), biopolitics (1990 [1978]), discipline (1979), and governmentality (1991), I suggest that the discourse of trauma and rights reflects concerns for security for individuals, organizations, and governments that result from a crisis of the sovereign state, especially those deemed fragile or failed. The Government of Haiti's (GOH) response to the plight of traumatized viktim was hampered not only by insufficient material resources but also by a legacy of corruption, nepotism, and graft from previous administrations. Thus international, national, and local aid agencies and agents intervened between viktim and international political actors, the Haitian state, and their own communities but always within limits-defined by the prevailing climate of ensekirite. Regardless of such restrictions, many Haitians perceived these institutions as invaders over which they had no control (Étienne 1997).

Categorizing intervening actors according to the conventional designations "local," "national," and "international," as well as "governmental" and "nongovernmental," was difficult. Many aid institutions in Haiti were satellites of international agencies and had both Haitian and expatriate staff members. If an expatriate was hired in Haiti, he or she was considered "local." Over time, many humanitarian relief and development projects had overlapping or intersecting mandates and memberships, or acted beyond the confines of their mandates in the midst of a "crisis." Furthermore, while international and national nongovernmental organizations (NGOs) and associations largely filled the gap between what the state could provide for its citizenry and what it could not, these were not disinterested actors: demonstrating success in providing aid to "victims" was also a means to secure additional institutional funds.

At the international level, viktim worked with the U.N. system and bilateral institutions such as USAID and the Canadian International Development Agency. The joint U.N. and Organization of American States (OAS) International Civilian Mission of Human Rights Observers (MICIVIH)[22] and international medical and human rights missions such as Médecins du Monde (Doctors of the World) provided medical relief services to Haitian victims of human rights abuses while documenting the violations. Viktim also gave testimonies of suffering to Physicians for Human Rights, Amnesty International, Human Rights Watch, and the National Coalition for Haitian Refugees (now called the National Coalition for Haitian Rights), missionary groups, and other organizations.

At the national level, viktim sought assistance from Haiti's Ministry for Women, the Ministry of Justice, National Commission for Truth and Justice, numerous Haitian human rights and development organizations, and the Haitian public health system. In their local communities they formed victims' advocacy organizations and joined with church groups, neighborhood associations, artisans' groups, and other community-based organizations in an effort to find security.

I evaluated the successes and failures of this diverse aid apparatus in providing to Haitian viktim what they termed *ankadreman*, or support (lit., "framing"), amid chronic ensekirite. The trope of ankadreman referred to the way that multiple forms of assistance—social, material, institutional, infrastructural, and informational—engendered a sense of security, protection, and social connection that enabled individuals and families to reconstruct lives disrupted by violence.

Central to this study, therefore, is an analysis of the individual and intersubjective experience of viktim. As I demonstrate, aspects of identity such as gender and sexuality shaped the way Haitians were targeted for repression. These factors also influenced how viktim experienced trauma. Gender and sexuality, among other markers, also influenced how viktim were represented by the bureaucratic languages and practices of the humanitarian and development assistance assemblage. Thus access to care was itself tinged with international, national, and local conceptions of gender and sexuality and social processes with roots in earlier periods of Haitian history and international relations that I explore later in this book.

I observed how the role of Haiti's viktim as militan—political activists—was to some degree eclipsed by a focus on their victimization during the coup years and on their subsequent traumatic suffering. The actors providing postconflict assistance tended to view victims of human rights abuses through lenses that objectified or medicalized suffering. They were viewed categorically as "women," the "poorest of the poor," "patients," or "vulnerable populations" rather than in terms of their contributions to democratic processes. Viktim were largely excluded from the international policy debates about Haiti's political and economic future, despite the fact that they themselves initiated the fight for liberty, *[handwritten annotations: "viictims engage in international discourse to gain legitimacy ↳ victim identity → empowerment (aid)" "political economy of trauma" "vicious cycle 25"]*

freedom, and democracy. They were often objectified, vilified, or ignored by the larger society in which they lived. Such processes evoke the theoretical attention in recent anthropology to refugees and asylum seekers in so-called secure states (Fassin 2005; James 2009; Malkki 1995, 1996; Ticktin 2006) and to survivors of disasters in "insecure" states (Fortun 2001; Petryna 2002) who gain recognition or citizenship on the basis of injury, displacement, or biological condition (Brown 1995; Das 1995; James 2004). As Ratna Kapur (2005) discusses in her work on law and feminism in postcolonial contexts, the Western liberal gaze tends to view post/colonial, racial, and gendered subjects in iconic or stereotypical ways through the lenses of victimization, powerlessness, or suffering. However, these subjugated actors may use the very categories by which their identities become essentialized as tools of resistance or means of garnering power, even in the most dire circumstances.

Thus viktim were not without agency. During my research I traced how they learned to engage the international discourses relating to human rights, women's rights, public health, and democracy to gain medical, legal, material, and other assistance from the aid apparatus. I also observed how they resisted, adopted, or transformed the discourses and practices of the institutions and organizations that worked with them. In many examples, viktim appropriated their own suffering and the victim identity as means toward recognition or political subjectivity (Aretxaga 1997), as well as strategies for survival and resistance. At times their tactics were also effective measures to empower themselves vis-à-vis the Haitian state and the international community. I also show, however, that some of the social practices they used to resist terror, economic inequality, and political ostracism reproduced an overarching pattern of predation that has existed historically in sectors of Haitian society and political culture. These heartbreaking practices reveal some of the ways in which the engagement with the aid apparatus worsened the subjective experience of trauma, grief, and suffering and generated what I call a "political economy of trauma" (James 2004).

THE POLITICAL ECONOMY OF TRAUMA

The term *economy* generally evokes the production, distribution, and consumption of goods and services or "the social life of things" (Appadurai 1986). It refers to financial systems and the circulation of wealth, whether in a global market or a household. Economies can be informal and unregulated. They encompass trade, barter, or gift exchanges. They

political economy of trauma
terror economies   *compassion economies*

can also be unlawful and evoke the black market, or illicit traffic, in desired commodities. I use *economy* because it best describes what I learned in Haiti: the suffering of another person, when extracted, transformed, and commodified through maleficent or beneficent interventions, can become a source of profit for the intervener. Through acts of intimidation, destruction of property, theft, torture, and murder, agents of torture and repression generated what I call *terror economies*. Through documenting horror, treating victims, and providing asylum, psychotherapy, legal aid, and material assistance, the aid apparatus generated *compassion economies.* Both economies intersected or overlapped in the political economy of trauma.

In this political economy the activists' pain and suffering became commodity "fetishes" (Marx 1867; Pietz 1985, 1987, 1988, 1993), powerful products of material and symbolic value created through the transformation of raw materials that circulated in both terror and compassion economies (James 2004; see also Nussbaum 2003). In both economies individual and collective pain and suffering was extracted and remade into something "productive" but with opposite goals. In terror economies the extraction of pain and suffering was a tool to augment the illegitimate power of the de facto regime. In the compassion economy products of transformed suffering circulated in humanitarian markets alongside the aid dispensed to Haiti to assist with its transition. Such processes arose from a complex assemblage of forces comprising the major themes of this book: torture, trauma, and truth. Each theme portrays conflicts about suffering, its documentation, and its veracity that are also aspects of the political economy of trauma. As I elaborate in subsequent chapters, the following case serves as a paradigm for how these processes evolved over time and how humanitarian and development interventions can contribute to the commodification of suffering despite their benevolent intent. Recounting this narrative also presents dilemmas of representation that are explored further in this book.

FROM MILITAN TO VIKTIM

Liliane Saint-Jean, a small-scale merchant, was fifty-eight years old in July 1996 when I interviewed and provided physical therapy to her in Martissant, a poor, densely populated area just outside the capital. I was volunteering at Chanm Fanm, a women's clinic that had been established that year through the partnership of a U.S. and a Haitian women's rights organization with funding from the Episcopal Church.

Liliane explained that she had pain in her bones, problems with her head, and a hard mass that had congealed underneath a stab wound in her back that hurt continually. I asked, "Who stabbed you?" She then began sharing fragments of the haunting story of her suffering:

> The stuff during the coup d'état . . . I suffered a lot. I had to sleep in the woods, I had a lot of problems . . . my child . . . my child had a child out in the brush. During the period of the coup d'état we received a lot of shocks. I was in hiding. Here is why I was a target. There was a brigade [a neighborhood watch group] in a quarter of the zone—I had to cook food, provide drinks, coffee, rum.

I interrupted and asked for clarification. "I would like to know when the violence began. Why were you in hiding? What was the date?" Liliane sighed and shifted to a narrative style that I recognized as having been shaped by legal depositions that require testimonies to have a rational, linear, teleological plot (Mattingly 1998):   "trauma narrative"

> On the fourth of February 1994, they came and entered my house. They beat me and they beat my husband. They raped me and they raped my daughter. They put a gun against my son's ear and told him to lay face-down on the ground. They beat my husband and beat him until they saw that he peed blood. He couldn't move or do anything. . . . [T]hey raped me, they took my niece who helped me in life, who helped me. When I escaped [after the rape] they came after me. In the morning I was so ashamed. When others in the neighborhood ridiculed me [because of having been raped], I went into hiding. I went to the provinces for three months. When I came back this organization was documenting what had happened. They came and got me. If it wasn't for that I could have died already. An older person like me. Then I was fifty-six. legitimacy through style of internationally recognized testimony

My request for Liliane's story during our initial interview and therapeutic work was not the first, nor would it be the last. I had hoped to understand better what had happened to her and to provide relief with as much empathy and compassion as possible. In asking her to reframe her narrative, I was participating in the professional transformation of Liliane's suffering (Kleinman and Kleinman 1991) through clinical and bureaucratic procedures. After this therapeutic encounter with Liliane, I learned that in addition to my requests for her "trauma narrative" (James 2004), she had previously given testimony to an international investigative team advocating that rape be recognized as a human rights abuse that warranted political asylum under international law. Her case was also included in the final report of Haiti's National Commission for Truth and Justice.[23]

The reshaping or translating of Liliane's suffering using the discourses and practices of clinical, legal, or other forms of intervention were intended to promote her civil or human rights, healing, and security. Such acts represented the benevolent side of what I characterize as "bureaucraft." In the compassion economy professional bureaucratic discourses and practices that arise from expert or "secret" knowledge are employed to reframe and transform the experience of suffering, thereby generating social, political, legal, economic, symbolic, and even spiritual power and capital for the recipient of aid. As I discuss in this book, bureaucraft is not employed solely to extract from negative conditions something that is generative or productive for the recipient of aid; it is also employed to generate multiple forms of power and capital for the provider of aid.

As Haitian viktim observed the flows of information, material resources, and other benefits that accrued in the hands of those who intervened in their lives, they began to employ bureaucraft themselves to participate in these processes as active agents, although with varying degrees of success. In November 1997, while attending the International Tribunal against Violence toward Women, an ad hoc tribunal organized by a coalition of Haitian women's organizations with the support of international development organizations (see chapter 3), I unexpectedly encountered Liliane and other women viktim I knew from my work at Chanm Fanm. At the event's conclusion we arranged to meet at the clinic so that I could learn how their lives had been since our last meeting the previous year. I also hoped that I could facilitate their access to the Human Rights Fund's rehabilitation services. I came to the clinic a few days later and was met by a large group of women. We decided to move the meeting to Liliane's home.

Liliane lived in an area called the zone *siyon* (Zion), referring to an open-walled Pentecostal church located high in the hills that was one of a few in the city to which hundreds of residents went to fast (*fè jèn*) and pray each week. The siyon was in the middle of a sprawling squatter settlement and had provided internally displaced Haitians with asylum during the de facto period.[24] After exchanging pleasantries, the meeting quickly became a formal one for which I was unprepared. The women began "testifying" about their victimization and asked me to document their trauma narratives.

Liliane's story was most troubling. She revealed that she had been the victim of *another* act of violence in the period following our therapeutic work together in 1996. She stated before everyone that earlier in the year she had borrowed money from a lending house in *lavil*, downtown Port-au-Prince, to restart her business. When she left the moneylender— essentially a loan shark—there were men waiting who knew she had just received some money. Liliane asserted:

> They followed me toward the Bicentennial road where there is a hideout where they kidnap the poor who've just bought things. Five men came on motorcycles and took me down by the sea where there are all kinds of foul things. They took me and beat me when they saw I didn't want to give my sack. They cut me . . . cut out my teeth. My head swelled completely, and I was there for three days. No one knew where I was. Finally, someone saw me and helped me.

As a witness and listener I was shocked and saddened by the ongoing dangers that these poor women and their families faced while simply trying to survive and support their families. I responded with pledges to assist the group with their efforts to find stability and security, and subsequently they were able to become beneficiaries of the Human Rights Fund's Rehabilitation Program. Two years after hearing Liliane's story of attack, theft, and extortion, I learned from participants at the gathering that the story was false: in the shadow of the International Tribunal against Violence toward Women the story had been performed for me with the tacit support of the other women at the meeting. The effectiveness of trauma narratives in motivating intervention is an indicator of the global saturation of cultural forms of testimony and lamentation as means of recognition and redress for sufferers. Thus the performance of trauma narratives has become a necessary transaction in order for sufferers to participate in local, national, and international compassion economies. In humanitarian contexts, stories of misery are frequently solicited from "victims" in the course of providing social or judicial services to them.

As such, the creation, performance, and circulation of false stories were means by which resource-poor viktim sought security, capital, and power, especially when their ongoing struggles were no longer considered acute. Liliane's second story of tragedy echoed the style of testimonies presented during the Tribunal and other quasi-legal or therapeutic settings. It was a form of testimony that had previously given her local and national recognition and was convincing to me as an ontological lament. The purpose of Liliane's second narrative, although never acknowledged, was to elicit sympathy and to provoke empathy and action using the "power of horror" (Kristeva 1982) to shock or compel intervention from the consumer of the story (Boltanski 1999 [1993]).

performance - "power of horror" - shock - evoke compassion

To my knowledge Liliane never repeated this second story, not even in a therapy group for victims of organized violence in which we were both participants in fall 1998 in the Rehabilitation Program—in our respective capacities as beneficiary and co-facilitator and ethnographer.

Whether authentic or false, trauma narratives are efficacious because of their ability to evoke horror and compassion. The combination of these two sentiments instills a desire to distance oneself from the unthinkable shock of violation at the same time that it inspires empathy and the feeling of identification with the victim. The contradiction in the two sentiments may be that which propels action or intervention regardless of the truth, *if* one recognizes the humanity or worth of the victim. Furthermore, by dramatizing a fictional "critical situation"—"a set of circumstances which—for whatever reason—radically disrupts accustomed routines of daily life" (Giddens 1979: 124), the gaze of humanitarian actors like me who were no longer explicitly focused on the plight of Liliane and others like her in Haiti was returned to local conditions of unrelenting misery.

Regardless of its truth, Liliane's second story of traumatic vulnerability represented an archetype of the experiences of danger, economic vulnerability, and gendered insecurity in Haiti. It was also emblematic of the micropolitics of truth in the local realm. Accusations that viktim were not authentic or had fabricated trauma narratives circulated in Martissant—especially when access to aid was threatened or its supply decreased. Rumors, gossip, and allegations about the veracity of viktim status also circulated in the institutions that served them.

The politics of truth and its connection to global material and symbolic resources produced a similar process that I witnessed in the bilateral and international realms of humanitarian and development aid. Staff members of institutions that competed for donor funds or for victim clients also made accusations against other agents and agencies when the supply of aid dwindled after the crisis during the period of "democratic consolidation." Interveners accused each other of falsehood, misrepresentation, or fraud in the context of financial scarcity. Rumors flowed about their histories, their motives for action, and their hidden connections to occult institutions operating within and outside Haiti.

At stake were questions of speculation, accumulation, and consumption of resources in what can be regarded as "occult economies" (Comaroff and Comaroff 1999, 2003; James 2004). Jean Comaroff and John Comaroff describe occult economies as the real or imagined transactions of magic or sorcery for material or political gain in African polities *goals: modernity, transparency, truth, development, accountability, power, justice*

that are embracing market economies. The concept also refers to the "effort to eradicate people held to enrich themselves by [occult] means; through the illegitimate appropriation, that is, not just of the bodies and things of others, but also of the forces of production and reproduction themselves" (Comaroff and Comaroff 1999: 284). Occult economies range from the illicit or unregulated traffic in commodities or other tangible and intangible items of value to the nefarious transactions between individuals and hidden forces, both spiritual and material, to attain power. In Haiti occult economies are not solely the product of traditional beliefs in Vodou or black markets controlled by criminal regimes: they are also generated by the secrecy and opacity of modern bureaucratic technologies and practices. *lack of transparency*

Like the witchcraft accusations that are stereotypical of traditional societies in times of political and economic insecurity (Ashforth 2005; Dolan 2002; Evans-Pritchard 1976; Farmer 1992; Favret-Saada 1980 [1977]; Geschiere 1997; Stewart and Strathern 2004), the competition for knowledge, resources, and institutional territory within the aid apparatus produced what I observed as the malevolent side of bureaucraft. Occult bureaucratic strategies employed to garner political and social capital generated conflict, contests for power, and accusations of illicit capital accumulation in the compassion economy. In international debates about national transitions, transparency, accountability, law, and justice are powerful discourses meant to oppose and transform practices of secrecy, corruption, impunity, and injustice—at interpersonal, institutional, and governmental levels. Supposed "premodern" practices of duplicity or corruption are viewed as needing reform because they are perceived to be obstacles to "modernity." For the intervening agencies and agents in Haiti, truth and transparency were central indicators of progress toward rehabilitation to be documented at the level of individual experience, in organizations, and in governmental practices. Nonetheless, stated concerns for transparency and accountability were frequently belied by the actual practices humanitarian and development interveners employed to promote development, democracy, justice, and social restoration.

Thus the bureaucraft concept addresses the spectrum of benevolent and malevolent practices that contributed to the political economy of trauma. As discussed above, well-intended professional practices to transform suffering into something productive contributed to the objectification and circulation of trauma narratives during the course of aid interventions. One aspect of the malevolent sense of the term arose

good intentions → exacerbation

from discourses and practices linking witchcraft, suffering, misfortune, and insecurity to the opaque and sometimes corrupt bureaucratic practices of individuals and institutions operating in the aid apparatus. As I observed them, the very rules and procedures that these complex aid apparatuses inculcated in Haiti created new spaces in which hidden, occult, or corrupt practices could flourish, especially in an overall insecure political and economic climate. Ultimately, competing perceptions of the right or just acquisition of power were at stake. This is yet another aspect of the political economy of trauma that highlights the link between intervention, Haiti's chronic ensekirite, and truth.

The extraction of truth was integral to the broad spectrum of intervention practices that are described in this ethnography. At one extreme in the spectrum of regimes of truth (Foucault 1980) were actors in the terror apparatus who used what I call "technologies of torture" to extract confessions and to control, damage, or destroy a particular target of intervention (see chapter 1). Their purpose was not solely to determine the truth of a victim's political activity or connection to pro-democracy forces; rather, it was to establish their own personal and institutional security in the face of external illegitimacy (Crelinsten 1995; Scarry 1985). The use of technologies of torture created the conditions for action at the opposite spectrum of cultures of truth.

The aid apparatus employed "technologies of trauma"—rational, bureaucratic, scientific practices intended to diagnose and authenticate the suffering of victims—such as forensic anthropology, physical examinations, photography, psychiatric tests, and affidavits for legal and therapeutic purposes, among other practices. Viktim were often recognized (Fraser 1995; Taylor 1994) solely through the technical languages of medicine, psychiatry, law, feminism, and others that speak the discourse of trauma and psychosocial rehabilitation. The intervener witnessed, authenticated, and transformed the suffering of the target of technologies of torture. Such practices of translation could also be used to authenticate the suffering of nearly any "client category" (Escobar 1995). Through the use of technologies of trauma, interventions to assist Haitian viktim produced symbolic and material emblems of extracted power.

Viktim were sometimes called upon as "tokens" to support many international and national organizations' quests for legitimacy and additional funding—a conversion and appropriation of their suffering that was in many ways a denial of their experience (Das 1995; Kleinman and Kleinman 1991; Petryna 2002; Povinelli 2002). In some instances

Haitian victims' performances of suffering enabled interveners to acquire international cultural capital through their links with the global social movement for justice and reparations. This positioned some victims and victims' advocacy organizations as desired political allies. The category "victim of human rights violations" lay at the intersection of ideological conflicts about the nation-state, security, and moral accountability and was often sacrificed by the ambiguity and indecisiveness of those conflicts.

commodity

victim identity

The opaque and sometimes secret crafts of activists, bureaucrats, and other humanitarian and development experts aiding Haiti made suffering productive. Their labor converted the suffering that embodies individuals after malevolent, inhumane interventions into what I call "trauma portfolios" (James 2004), the aggregate of paraphernalia compiled to document and authenticate the experience of individual, family, or collective sufferers. The work of conversion created the identity of "victims" or "survivors" for individuals who were once militan. It was a professional transformation of suffering that fed a growing humanitarian market.   ✓ *authenticate victim*

Trauma portfolios were circulated and exchanged in the local, national, and global humanitarian markets as commodities or currencies. At the individual level they resembled a portfolio of economic investment and were symbolic indices of material holdings or social capital. They were also material and symbolic signs of viktim status or identity. Interveners with the power to do so provided documents, photographs, medical records, psychological evaluations, letters of reference, and affidavits that authenticated victimization. These paraphernalia added to the value of the portfolio relative to those of other sufferers when circulated in the humanitarian market.

At the community or collective level viktim joined forces and created advocacy groups—often with the support or at the instigation of international and national interveners who provided them with bureaucratized forms of care. Viktim pooled their trauma portfolios to improve the chances that they would receive rehabilitation, restitution, and justice—if not from the Government of Haiti, then from the domestic and international aid apparatus. Such aid frequently engendered occult economies and developed independent "social lives" (Appadurai 1986, 2006) both within and outside the formal realms of exchange between donors and beneficiaries.

Trauma brokers facilitate these transactions. In local communities the humanitarian market generated gatekeepers who managed the "initial

give aid to promote security
trauma portfolios to gain funding / support
(legit)

public offerings" of tales of woe to the interveners. Brokers might be individual speculators in the local realm with access to actors or institutions in the humanitarian assemblage, or they might be institutions such as the Human Rights Fund or other victim assistance projects that used their collection of trauma portfolios to solicit funding from bilateral or multilateral donors.

Actors and institutions in the aid apparatus collected trauma portfolios in order to advocate for viktim and "do good" (Fisher 1997). Through the use of bureaucraft we collected them in order to support benevolent interventions in the nations, institutions, minds, and bodies of others but also to support our own efforts to acquire funding and political capital—in other words, to promote our security. In analyzing the practices of interveners deploying technologies of trauma, one can say that at times the purpose was not to determine truth but rather to establish personal and institutional security in the face of external illegitimacy.

Trauma portfolios represent the legitimacy and accountability of the interveners and their institutions to their *own* donors and stakeholders. In this manner technologies of trauma are mechanisms of "audit cultures" (Strathern 2000), in which diversified trauma portfolios are the indicators of an agent's or agency's authenticity and accountability in the overall political economy. Nevertheless, while the trauma portfolio is a commodity representing the transformed suffering of an individual, a family, or a group that can function as currency, it can also be devalued when there is no longer demand in the humanitarian market.

Thus false trauma narratives like Liliane's reveal the political economy of trauma in states of insecurity—one subject to the ebbs and flows of supply and demand in the global humanitarian market. False narratives are close enough to the commodities and currency of authentic trauma that they are circulated in this market without confirming evidence unless interested parties challenge their provenance. These sham currencies recall Bill Maurer's (2005: 59) discussion of the "counterfeit": "[A] counterfeit is only known when its circulation, its flow, is halted. If it circulates, even if it is 'false,' it is nonetheless 'true' in the now of the transaction: it is efficacious."

Counterfeit stories of injury demonstrate the power that has coalesced in postconflict cultures of truth and in institutional endeavors at history making, assessment of the past, justice, and reparations. But they also represent the challenges of engaging with humanitarian and development assemblages that are characterized by impermanence, flexible accountability, and transnationality. In such cases one must also

*trauma portfolio —
both rehumanization translation of suffering
AND
commoditization / dehumanization*

ask what processes or conditions convert compassionate intentions into bureaucratic indifference (Herzfeld 1992) or produce bureaucraft. One must also assess the long-term consequences of such interventions on the political subjectivity of their targets.

In previous work I have named the status attained by viktim "traumatic citizenship" (James 2004). I recognized in Haiti a parallel social process from which has emerged the concepts of biological citizenship (Petryna 2002; Rose and Novas 2005), therapeutic citizenship (Nguyen 2005), and other tropes of identity formation based on injury (Fassin 2005; Ticktin 2006). These identities of victimization may engender limited types of sociopolitical inclusion and material entitlements (Brown 1995). However, I no longer view the status attained by viktim as a type of citizenship; their client status depends on assemblages and apparatuses that are fleeting and myopic in their gaze.

Humanitarian and development actors are in some senses "mobile sovereigns" (Appadurai 1996) or "migrant sovereignties" (Pandolfi 2003). They rarely maintain a lasting presence in their terrains of intervention and are seldom accountable to the states in which they work. Furthermore, recognition of the needs of clients—women, rape survivors, victims of human rights abuses, trafficked persons, and child slaves, of which Haiti has many—depends on the will and mandates of institutions that may only retain these specific interests for a limited period. Thus forms of inclusion and "citizenship" based on such interests are unstable and impermanent, as is the focus of the humanitarian market generated by these practices.

I describe in this ethnography what I call the "social life of aid," the path that products of intervention—such as trauma narratives and the material assistance that these narratives generate—may follow once circulated. Arjun Appadurai (1986, 2006) theorizes the way objects like works of art can circulate and have social lives. During the course of their social trajectory, things—whether objects or persons—can "make the journey from commodity to singularity and back. Slaves, once sold as chattel, can become gradually humanized, personified, and reenchanted by the investiture of humanity. But they can also be recommoditized, turned once again into mere bodies or tools, put back in the marketplace, available for a price, dumped into the world of mere things" (Appadurai 2006: 15).

As an object, the trauma portfolio facilitates a kind of rehumanization of the viktim through the translation of suffering. But when aggregated for political and economic purposes, trauma portfolios are commoditized and subject to the humanitarian market, effectively rendering viktim mere bodies or even tools for others' personal, institutional, or governmental security.

Thus humanitarian and development interventions lie at the nexus of economies of terror and compassion and in the space between gift economies and commodity economies (Appadurai 2006: 19). They operate as one spectrum of a process in which suffering is abstracted to give power to an intervener. The suffering of viktim makes the journey from singularity (unmediated distress or misery) to commodity (the trauma portfolio) and back to singularity when it is no longer a focus of the humanitarian market. Such processes constitute the political economy of trauma.

* * *

Here this ethnography encounters another dilemma of representation. I want to be clear that it is not my intention to equate torturers and humanitarian interveners.—Far from it. Rather, I want to draw attention to the ethical quandaries that can arise from the uses and misuses of power from the vilest to the most benevolent realms of human engagement. I am also ambivalent about pronouncing judgment on the truths of suffering during the 1991–94 coup period. If the truths of Haitian suffering are debated, discounted, or denied, especially by the very governmental interveners that may have contributed to their suffering—and that may withhold humanitarian and development aid or release it indirectly or sparingly—might revealing the existence of fictitious trauma narratives and trauma portfolios endanger or suspend these unequal exchanges completely?

On the other hand, might discussing the extent to which advocacy institutions appropriate the suffering of others in order to secure their own interests jeopardize the benevolent work of grassroots, privately funded associations? Despite these very real concerns, it is nonetheless important to analyze the flow of practices, technologies, exchanges, and discourses that circumscribe and define individual, collective, institutional, and governmental identities in an environment of ensekirite. My hope is that this story of trauma in Haiti can provoke further dialogue about the effectiveness of postconflict reconstruction and political development interventions in fragile and failed states across the globe.

Chapter 1 is a genealogy of sovereign forms of violence in Haiti that subjugate life to the power of death. The chapter begins with a narrative that depicts ethical dilemmas generated by discourses of torture, trauma, and truth, then traces key periods in Haitian history when violence, sexuality, and gender intersected in the context of economies of extraction.

Chapter 2 maps the diverse spectrum of agents and agencies that intervened to rehabilitate Haiti's victims. I discuss how their competing and sometimes conflicting bureaucratic mandates, technologies, and identities produced ethical and moral dilemmas not only for the interveners but also for their clients, contributing to bureaucraft.

Chapter 3 analyzes the lived experience of gendered insecurity among *viktim.* I demonstrate how the aid apparatus employed bureaucratic categories to diagnose the causes of trauma that failed to encompass the complexity of suffering, vulnerability, activism, and resistance. The limitations of professional languages created tensions for *viktim* in representing the truths of torture and trauma. These epistemological and technological limitations produced additional moral and ethical dilemmas for victim clients.

Chapter 4 depicts how institutions such as the Human Rights Fund faced the challenges of mediating or brokering aid between donors and recipients operating in what can be characterized as a *grant economy,* one governed by an audit culture. I outline how routines of rupture impeded humanitarian and development actors from achieving their goal to transform suffering through technologies of trauma. Accusations of witchcraft and bureaucraft emerged as means to assign blame for suffering. I demonstrate how occult economies of trauma flourished in the gap between Government of Haiti accountability and the intervention of humanitarian actors.

Chapter 5 continues the analysis of witchcraft, bureaucraft, and the double binds generated by the circulation of aid by tracking contests about victim identity from the Human Rights Fund to Martissant.

Chapter 6 chronicles the closure of the Rehabilitation Program in the context of multiple attacks on America's Development Foundation, the Human Rights Fund, and the Rehabilitation Program staff members. These attacks took place at the crest of another wave of ensekirite and culminated in scapegoating and violence.

The conclusion argues that while aid agents and agencies may inculcate new political subjectivities based on secular theodicies of human rights, democracy, women's rights, law, and psychiatry, the overarching insecurities in their terrains of operation may also generate accusations of witchcraft, sorcery, and bureaucraft in the social life of aid. The unintended consequences of aid created conditions that reproduced the cycles of economic decline and political and criminal instability in zones of intervention.

* * *

The story told in the following pages is one without heroes. No one, including me, is blameless or free from error. It is a story of violence, suffering, and loss and how word of these conditions circulates. It is an account of hope for change, of change, and of more of the same misery. It is a description of interventions in the lives of the Haitian people, both for good and for ill, and of the results of those interventions. It is a story of how suffering has become a commodity in Haiti. As the story is refracted through different lenses, truth and the foundations for its discernment collapse.

CHAPTER I

The Terror Apparatus

One of the most troubling images of Haitian history and culture is that of endemic violence, in particular, sexual violence.[1] It is impossible to understand the development of the political economy of trauma in Haiti without relating it to this long-standing image and its historical evolution. During the 1991–94 coup years, the de facto regime employed sexual and gendered violence to repress the pro-democracy movement.[2] Rape, including gang rape, and even forced incest were among the forms of torture used strategically to damage and control not only individuals but also families and larger communities.

Analyzing the many forms of violence perpetrated in societies that have undergone political conflict is a complex task. In places such as Haiti where the state apparatus attacks its own citizens, it can be difficult to distinguish between political and criminal motives for abuses. State-sponsored violence that is directed at a nation's own civilians also challenges theories that have assumed separation between the political and domestic spheres and between public and private actions since John Locke's *Second Treatise* on civil government (Pateman 1988). Such assumptions also underlie the perceived divide between human rights and criminal violations.

Contemporary discourses about rape must be analyzed in the context of discussions about gender and race and culture, history, and power. Rape has been an especially "thorny" problem in Western political discourses because of debates over whether the act is about sex, power, or violence (or some combination of the three) (Bell 1991). Additional questions concern whether rape is an interpersonal crime or should be considered the product of historical, global structural inequalities between the sexes.[3] In the 1970s women anthropologists evaluated why "women are treated, culturally and socially, as inferior, in virtually all societies in the world" (Rosaldo and Lamphere 1974: v) and whether disparities in status between men and women were the product of biological "nature" or cultural "nurture."[4] To refute interpretations of the phenomenon of sexual violence as inevitable, universal, or of biological origin, some anthropologists have posited the controversial view that societies are either "rape-prone" or relatively "rape-free" (e.g., Sanday 1981), thereby suggesting that acts of sexual violence are products of "nurture," or learned behavior. Such approaches still tended to neglect the political, economic, and historical roots of different forms of violence and were based on questionable data. Feminist social theorists have also depicted the sexual violence that men perpetrate against women as a global, historical strategy by which women have been subjugated as an entire class by means of fear of violation (e.g., Brownmiller 1975). According to these views, sexual and gender violence is a means by which the power of the state and its institutions reinforce male domination (MacKinnon 1989). Other theorists of rape have written about the way that sexual coercion of women was racialized and institutionalized in colonial slavery (Davis 1981; Hartman 1997), embedded in military cultures (Enloe 1993), endemic in contemporary civil ethnic and nationalist conflict (Das 1995; Stiglmayer 1994), and an omnipresent component of international wars (Brownmiller 1975).

Discourses about politically motivated sexual violence are challenging not only because of these debates about public versus private; nature versus culture; sexuality, gender, and race; and power and violence. This type of sexual violence also blurs the distinctions between state and individual sovereignty. These classifications have been crucial to pursuits of justice as each evokes domains of law that have traditionally been separate: international human rights law and domestic civil and criminal law (Copelon 1994; Seifert 1994). But in nations such as Haiti where it has been difficult to prosecute rape because of a so-called culture of impunity and the social stigma attached to rape, its systematic use as a weapon of terror has become the subject of heated international political debate.

During the period of unconstitutional rule, narratives proliferated both within and outside Haiti that challenged the truth of reports of human rights abuses, especially reports of politically motivated rape. Combined with the prevailing negative stereotypes about Haitian history and culture and the general resistance of sexual and gender violence to unambiguous categorization, these contested accounts were circulated by governmental and nongovernmental actors to justify or rationalize their political choices. On the one hand, denying abuses of Haitian human rights argued against military and humanitarian intervention to uphold Haiti's democracy; on the other, recognition of human rights abuses in Haiti justified intervention. As I discuss below, these positioned rhetorics reflected conflicts over the meaning of sovereignty for the embodied individual, for the state, and for the populations whose sovereignty the state is theoretically obligated to protect and preserve.

Arguments about whether to recognize sexual and gender violence as human rights abuses are examples of the historical "biopolitics" of intervention (Foucault 1990 [1978]). In *The History of Sexuality*, Foucault suggested that a shift had occurred between the seventeenth and nineteenth centuries regarding conceptions of the body and the practices such conceptions produced. Foucault describes a change from a politics of alliance[5]—the regulation of persons based on notions of blood, kinship, and reproduction in units like the family—to a focus on "sexuality." Sexuality is a construct that incorporates the regulation and production of knowledge about the social and lived body in relation to the economy (Foucault 1990 [1978]: 106–7). In societies of sexuality, power manifests through the categorization, surveillance, and control of bodies to engender productive, disciplined populations—what Foucault (145–46; 1979: 207–8) calls biopolitics. Both modes of regulation, the biopolitics of alliance and of sexuality, concern the law (what is held to be permissible or forbidden). Each mode reflects concerns about political and economic production and reproduction at different levels of society and is relevant to this ongoing analysis.

Foucault's schema has been criticized for its lack of attention to subjective experience, individual agency, and gender, as well as its historical emphasis on the European context (Hartsock 1990; Stoler 1995). Nonetheless, his broad formulation of the relationships between power, body, and subjectivity, as well as economies and governance, are useful for thinking through the discourses surrounding politically motivated rape. In analyzing the "politics of sex," Foucault argues:

> To return to sex and the discourses of truth that have taken charge of
> it, the question that we must address, then, is not: Given a specific state

structure, how and why is it that power needs to establish a knowledge of
sex? . . . It is rather: In a specific type of discourse on sex, in a specific form
of extortion of truth, appearing historically and in specific places[,] . . .
what were the most immediate, the most local power relations at work?
(1990 [1978]: 97)

Both of Foucault's questions are necessary to contextualize practices
of torture and the presumed extraction of truth from the bodies and
minds of sexed and gendered victims. Foucault's questions about truth,
power, and the knowledge of sex are also relevant to framing discourses
about and representations of sexual and gender violence in Haiti. The
participation of several "regimes of truth" (Foucault 1980) in debates
concerning the truth of violence in Haiti during the period of de facto
rule contributed to the growth of the political economy of trauma, as
the terror economies and the compassion economies collided.

This chapter examines the historical roots of sexual and gender violence in Haiti and presents details of its deployment during certain periods that contributed to the evolution of ensekirite. My goal is to place
in context the terror apparatus as it emerged and operated in the twentieth century. I begin with a resume of the events of the 1991–94 coup
period and highlight the controversy surrounding a 1994 U.S. diplomatic cablegram that demonstrates the continued influence of negative
historical representations of violence in Haiti and ongoing contests over
the truths of sexual and gender violence. The analysis of the scandal
that the cablegram provoked provides a framework for examining some
of the ethical challenges that are inherent in representations of violence.

I next trace the relationship between political violence and political
economies in Haiti by presenting paradigmatic episodes in Haitian history that have contributed to the production of ensekirite. These are key
periods in which violence, sexuality, and gender intersected with economies of extraction. I survey the 1915–34 American occupation of Haiti
out of which arose the Duvalier dictatorships, then briefly examine the
expulsion of Jean-Claude Duvalier and the resurgence of Duvalierist
antidemocratic violence perpetrated against civil society in the postdictatorship period. Despite attempts to thwart the democratic process, this
period culminated in the presidential election of Jean-Bertrand Aristide.

I conclude with a detailed examination of the technologies of torture
perpetrated during the 1991–94 coup period. I use the term *technologies*
to indicate evidence of the patterned manner in which such violence was
deployed (and documented).[6] During this period of de facto rule, the
intensity, frequency, and timing of attacks on the pro-democracy sector

suggest that violence was perpetrated systematically: the deployment of torture and terror had the character of an orchestrated campaign. Furthermore, sexed and gendered technologies of torture were also linked to their historical roots in the brutal forms of discipline used against the slaves of Saint-Domingue. I argue that in its use of necropolitical violence (Mbembe 2003), the terror apparatus irreparably harmed the foundations for its victims' security, thereby establishing ensekirite as a pervasive existential experience in Haiti.

BIOPOLITICS, NECROPOLITICS, AND INTERVENTION

In the post–cold war era, international disputes over the truth of violence and human rights abuses in conflict and postconflict settings indicated the presence of underlying political struggles over power, knowledge, and state sovereignty, aspects of what I term elsewhere the "condition of neo-modernity" (James 2009). In the 1990s discourses of sex, sexual violence, trauma, and political victimization became entangled in global debates about the need for military and humanitarian interventions in conflict settings such as Haiti. The governmental and nongovernmental actors engaged in such discussions tended to recognize or designate women as vulnerable "victims," as a class or population in need of intervention or regulation, especially in states undergoing crises or emergencies. Furthermore, the neomodern focus on sexual violence perpetrated against women was "à la mode" in the aid apparatus in Haiti (Bell 2001: 96). In part, the national and international emphasis on sexual and gender violence as human rights violations deserving of international recognition and intervention accompanied the perception of a real shift in the nature of political conflict to forms that explicitly targeted civilian or vulnerable populations. Such modes of political violence are a type of biopolitics; they are also examples of necropolitics.

Necropolitics describes forms of conflict or warfare that deploy torture against populations to inculcate terror and to subjugate life itself to the power of death. In proposing this term, Mbembe (2003) sought to remedy the inadequacies of Foucault's theories of biopower and biopolitics. Foucault's theories rely on European or Western models of sovereignty and lack a detailed consideration of how imperial or colonial violence and practices of torture buttressed and were embedded in the evolution of liberal capitalism and the modern state. In addition to this, Foucault (1979: 194) depicted the individual as a product of disciplinary technologies of power, devoting little attention to individual agency or motive for participating in or resisting such disciplinary structures.

Mbembe (2003: 11) questions conventional ideas of sovereignty that locate power within the confines of the "nation-state, within institutions empowered by the state, or within supranational institutions and networks." Drawing on Giorgio Agamben's (1998 [1995], 2005) elaboration of Schmitt's theory of the "state of exception," as well as Georges Bataille's (1985, 1988) ideas of sovereignty and death, Mbembe describes state (sovereign) violence as that arising from the aggregate of individual self-interested acts, even as such individuals are components of larger apparatuses of power. He further asks whether the concept of biopower is "sufficient to account for the contemporary ways in which the political, under the guise of war, of resistance, or of the fight against terror, makes the murder of the enemy its primary and absolute objective" (Mbembe 2003: 12).

The actors involved in current warfare and their tools of repression extend beyond those of national armies with the presumed legitimate monopoly over the use of force, as has been conventionally described of modern warfare (Weber 1946: 77–78). Much like the imperial and colonial campaigns of past centuries, the agents of neomodern violence include private security forces, urban gangs, warlords, rebel groups, and mobs. These actors have often been armed, supplied, and directed by the overt and covert material and financial resources of private, national, and international powers (Mbembe 2003; Nordstrom 2004; Tambiah 1996). Agents of neomodern violence are often unallied "mobile sovereigns" whose loyalty may be purchased;[7] they may hold the power of life and death over their targets of intervention long after the intervention itself has been completed. These private agents work within networks that are flexible, transnational, or "transboundary." Their ability to act across and within borders challenges dualistic categories of the global and the local (Callaghy, Kassimir, and Latham 2001: ix–x).

Necropolitics produces social, political, and economic disorder through forms of violence that inculcate terror and attack the moral foundations of family and society. What is at stake is "not the struggle for autonomy but *the generalized instrumentalization of human existence and the material destruction of human bodies and populations*" (Mbembe 2003: 14; emphasis in original). Sovereignty is expressed by a willingness to transgress cultural boundaries or taboos, even within the realms of "sexuality, filth, excrement," and especially death (16). Such actions are undertaken, in part, as a way of attaining security for the sovereign, the person or assemblage of actors seeking to maintain or expand their power. The sovereign "continuously refers and appeals to exception, emergency, and a fictionalized notion of the enemy" as justifications for destructive interventions (16). The dissemination of negative representations of the "enemy" creates a perception of threat on the basis of attributes such as race, sex, and gender; ethnicity, political affiliation, and religion; and economic status.

Because necropolitics operates to destroy human bodies and populations through the violation of taboos such as rape and forced incest, it is not surprising that the deployment of sexual and gendered violence is typical of these "new" forms of warfare (Brownmiller 1975). What makes neomodern necropolitics distinct in the Haitian context is the way mobile sovereigns have been deployed to perpetrate forms of violence designed to destroy even culture itself. But where necropolitics intersects with Foucault's conceptions of biopower and biopolitics is in the way that the truths of such horrific forms of violence were authenticated and denied by conflicting regimes of power and knowledge.

THE COUP AND THE CABLEGRAM

Between September 30, 1991, and October 15, 1994, the coup apparatus in Haiti inflicted increasing extremes of torture on pro-democracy militan and their families. The military regime terrorized poor neighborhoods known to support the democracy movement. Thousands of Haitians fled across the border to the Dominican Republic. Tens of thousands journeyed in rickety, overcrowded boats to reach sanctuary in South America, the United States, and other Caribbean nations. In sharp contrast to the experience of refugees from many other countries, however, Haitians who sought asylum in the United States were usually detained in centers that could be equated with prisons.[8] The United States characterized them as "economic migrants" rather than as legitimate seekers of asylum, abiding by an interdiction policy established under the Reagan administration in the early 1980s (Little and al-Sahli 2004; Miller 1984). Some Haitians were ultimately granted asylum; however, most were apprehended at sea and turned back from U.S. shores without the hearings that are considered a human right according to the conventions of international law.[9] Although the plight of Haitian boat people received some media attention during the coup years, the suffering of the estimated three hundred thousand individuals who were displaced within Haiti was less visible (HRW/A, JRS/USA, and NCHR 1994).

The desperation of Haitians targeted by the military regime eventually gained attention through the reports of a variety of independent actors. The humanitarian and development aid apparatus disseminated press releases describing the horror that was unfolding in Haiti to the international media and throughout their advocacy networks. The exiled Aristide government issued similar statements to alert the international community about the condition of Haitian citizens. In Haiti itself many courageous physicians and health professionals, human rights groups, religious organizations, and women's rights groups and their international counterparts documented the violence perpetrated by the military junta while caring for its victims. As a result, in 1992 the OAS, a regional bureau within the U.N. system, sent the Inter-American Commission on Human Rights, composed of autonomous human rights observers, to assess the crisis in Haiti. In February 1993 the U.N. and the OAS formed the International Civilian Mission to monitor the ongoing crisis in Haiti and to aid internally displaced Haitians. In June 1993 Haitian women's rights activists, who had also been helping displaced Haitians, presented the general situation of human rights abuses and the specific targeting of women through sexual and gender violence at the U.N. World Conference on Human Rights in Vienna. Friends of Haiti and members of the Congressional Black Caucus in the United States sent delegations to Haiti and lobbied on behalf of Haitians in Washington, D.C., in order to pressure the U.S. government to recognize the human rights of Haitian victims of violence and to address the growing humanitarian emergency in Haiti. These actors also pressured the United States to honor its regional and international legal obligation to uphold Haiti's legitimate government through intervention.

Contemporary with the Haitian crisis, a tremendous amount of global attention was focused on reports of ethnic cleansing in the former Yugoslavia. Shocking stories surfaced about the forcible impregnation of Bosnian Muslim women by Serbian men, that is, the use of rape as a method of genocide (Stiglmayer 1994).[10] Although the humanitarian assemblage had publicized similar reports of the systematic use of sexual and gender violence in Haiti, the Haitian case did not initially draw the same global outrage. Rather, U.S. government officials and domestic and international opponents of the Aristide administration contested many of these reports, as demonstrated by a U.S. Department of State memo.

On April 12, 1994, at the height of the most repressive period of violence perpetrated by the coup regime, a confidential cablegram was

sent from the U.S. Embassy in Port-au-Prince to Secretary of State Warren Christopher in Washington, D.C. The cablegram was apparently
written by Political Officer Ellen Cosgrove and approved by Ambassador William Lacy Swing. Cosgrove's staffers reputedly leaked the
document to pro-democracy activists in Haiti, Friends of Haiti abroad,
and the media (U.S. Embassy/Haiti 1994).[11] The text denied the reports
of human rights abuses that were circulating among international and
national human rights NGOs at the time. In my copy of the document,
which I received from a Washington, D.C.-based pro-Aristide organization, point 4 states:

> The Haitian left manipulates and fabricates human rights abuses as a
> propaganda tool, wittingly or unwittingly assisted in this effort by human
> rights NGOs and by the ICM [U.N./OAS International Civilian Mission].
> Immigration is primarily caused by economic conditions, but is aggravated
> by violent institutions which ordinarily guarantee human rights, like an
> independent judiciary and professional law enforcement entities, do not
> exist in Haiti [sic]. (U.S. Embassy/Haiti 1994)

These comments imply that American diplomats did not believe that
the flight of Haitian refugees was motivated by a "well-founded fear
of being persecuted," which under international human rights law was
a basis for granting refugee status and political asylum. Denying the
plausibility of such fears was a way for the embassy to avoid granting
asylum to tens of thousands of Haitians, even as there is some acknowledgment in the cablegram that the flight of Haitians was aggravated by
the Haitian state's use of "illegitimate" violence. The cablegram asserts
that rather than use its presumed monopoly over legitimate forms of
violence to inculcate the rule of law in the nation, the state has often
used its power to violate the rights of Haitian citizens in egregious ways.
   Another issue to which this excerpt refers is a seeming ideological
contradiction in discourses of American sovereignty and discourses of
rights and security. On the one hand, the Cosgrove memo articulates
concerns about security: the United States must protect itself against the
increasing influx of (black) Haitian refugees. On the other hand, what is
at stake is the image of the United States as a nation that has been committed to democracy, human rights, and the protection of asylum seekers.
Haitians, consistently defined as economic versus political refugees and
stigmatized as disease carriers (Farmer 1992), force the United States and
its policy makers to ask the following question: Will the United States
maintain an image as a generous, open-armed "motherland of liberty"
or as a "disciplinary global father" that must secure its borders against

those historically deemed threats to national security? That this issue of national identity and U.S. sovereignty was a challenge is revealed in the critique of the ICM as having been manipulated and deceived.

The cablegram accuses Haitian pro-democracy activists of fabricating the truth in another sense. Point 13 of this document alleges that President Aristide himself and his supporters in Washington, D.C., "consistently manipulate or even fabricate human rights abuses as a propaganda tool. Their justification for doing this is that they are an unarmed force arrayed against an armed and brutal military. Under these circumstances they see the truth as a flexible means to obtain a worthy political end." The suggestion that Haitian political actors, and even the president, may have ensnared human rights NGOs and the International Civilian Mission in a magical web of lies or some kind of deceptive spell is one with many antecedents in Haiti history. This statement echoes accusations made against Haitian political leaders since the colonial period regarding their use of sorcery, fetishism, and the malefic charisma of Vodou. Such accusations have long pervaded relations between Haiti and the international community (James 2003).

Accusations about human rights practices and their documentation, and the politics of truth itself, are integral to the political economy of trauma. The American diplomats, the International Civilian Mission observers, and human rights activists in Haiti and abroad can be considered political factions in the aid apparatus. Possessing unequal power, they nonetheless all focused on representing and authenticating the truths of sexuality, human rights, and democracy. As further context for these debates, there was already ongoing criticism of the United States for having refused to ratify numerous conventions that would obligate it to provide additional assistance to asylum seekers (but could also leave U.S. military personnel vulnerable to prosecution for their own abusive behaviors abroad). As these arguments unfolded, the United States was also chastised for its arrears to the U.N., for which it would temporarily lose its seat on the U.N. Human Rights Commission in 2001. Thus MICIVIH and the Haitian human rights NGOs challenged the U.S. Mission's expert knowledge and, concomitantly, its power by asserting competing claims regarding the human rights abuses perpetrated during the de facto period. At stake was the image of the United States as a promoter of human rights and democracy and the corresponding ethical obligation to intervene in situations of crisis.

The accusations about truth flowing between competing groups engaged in producing knowledge about torture and trauma are also nascent examples of bureaucraft.[12] While advocates in the aid apparatus document and circulate reports of suffering in order to generate multiple forms of intervention, these professional practices are still subject to scrutiny and suspicion by other interveners in Haiti. Thus another point from the infamous cablegram is relevant to place in context the politics underlying these conflicts. Under the subheading "The NGO's and the ICM: Truth, Lies, and Politics," the memo discredits the testimony of a nun (who was also a registered nurse) who had lived among Haiti's poor for five years. She had sheltered a family who claimed to have been tortured by the "anti-gang" unit of the municipal police force, which was known for its brutal attacks against Lavalas party militan. When one of the family members alleged that he had been beaten with "wet towels," the supposedly benign manner of torture was questioned. On this case the memo states:

> We have to assume that she [the nun] knows more about old and recent scars, about child psychology, and even—having lived among Haiti's poor for five years—about beatings at anti-gang than we do. Certainly she believed the account of their troubles, as did the ICM. The problem is that we do not believe it, chiefly because we know all too much about the way the police and the army really handle suspected Aristide supporters—and it is not with wet towels.

The statements made about how the Haitian armed forces punish their victims and the authenticity of torture practices in Haiti also raise the question of the relationship between Haitian and U.S. armed forces and security apparatuses, as discussed below. But once again, this excerpt suggests that the Samaritan acts of the nun to provide asylum to the Haitian family was a product of deception or confabulation, whether on the part of the nun, the NGOs, or the family.

It is the embassy memo's accusation of the fabrication of *particular kinds* of human rights abuses, however, that is important here. The subheading "The Rape Epidemic—Equating Haiti and Bosnia," under point 14, demonstrates that Haiti has not received international recognition of its political and economic difficulties and that notions of sex, violence, and truth are crystallized in the struggles for sovereignty between the Haitian and U.S. governments and in the international realm (Foucault 1990 [1978]: 97):

> A case in point is the sudden epidemic of rapes reported by pro-Aristide human rights activists and by the ICM. *For a range of cultural reasons (not pleasant to contemplate),* rape has never been considered or reported as a serious crime here. Hardline, ideological Aristide supporters here regularly

compare the human rights situation in Haiti to the carnage in Bosnia. Some
have called recent violence in Port-au-Prince slums "political cleansing,"
equating this with "ethnic cleansing" against Muslims by Bosnian Serbs. . . .
We are, frankly, suspicious of the sudden, high number of reported rapes,
particularly in this culture, occurring at the same time that Aristide activists
seek to draw a comparison between Haiti and Bosnia. (My emphasis)

The phrases highlighting the otherness of Haitian cultural practices suggest that if systematic rape has occurred, it is systemic or natural in
Haitian culture and not something that inflicts suffering. This assertion echoes eighteenth- and nineteenth-century discourses that denied
Haitians' moral capacity to love others and to feel pain (James 2003).
Statements like this also efface Haitian history: sexual violation was
integral to the French colonial enterprise, Haiti's war of independence,
and the U.S. occupation of Haiti (James 1989 [1963]; Renda 2001; Rey
1999). The cablegram implies that because rape has never been considered a crime in Haiti, an escalation in the number of rapes should not
be viewed as a mass violation of human rights, or as a form of genocide
or political cleansing. If rape has never been reported as a serious crime,
then an escalation in reports of rape is by definition suspect.

The cablegram also challenges the way human rights activists compared the reputed systematic use of sexual violence in Haiti with the
plight of Europeans in the former Yugoslavia, whose victimization and
subsequent suffering is unquestioned. There is an implicit disbelief in the
commensurability between the suffering of poor black men and women
in Haiti and that of the embattled ethnic groups in the Balkans. By extension, Haitians, for whom sexual violence is reputedly natural or cultural,
could not possibly suffer from trauma and need psychosocial assistance
in a culture in which political, criminal, and sexual violence are stereo-
typed as the norm. The cablegram can also be viewed as a denial and
devaluation of Haitian suffering and humanity—additional aspects of the
political economy of trauma that I examine later. The explicit statements
of moral relativism and the unspoken assertion of a radical difference in
humanity between the women and men of Bosnia and those of Haiti are
disheartening. More troubling but less transparent implications of this
claim have firm historical roots in international rhetorics about Haiti.
They arise from a tension that has been embedded in U.S. foreign policy
since the early twentieth century: between the protection of domestic
security interests and the promotion of democracy and security abroad.

What does it mean to state that rape is part of Haitian culture? If
rape has a historical presence in Haiti, does this preclude considering its

targets as victims of crime or human rights abuses? In what way is its use cultural, historical, political, interpersonal, or all of the above? How is sexual and gender violence related to the use of force and interventions to control a geographic, political, economic, or social terrain? A state's use of egregious forms of subjugation to violate the sovereignty of its civilian population raises an inescapable question: what motivates individuals to participate in and carry out such acts? The remainder of this chapter proposes to address these questions by examining the historical relationships between social, political, and economic inequalities and between identity and subjectivity for both perpetrators of violence and their victims in Haiti. In other words, the analysis considers the relationship between structures of power and individual or collective agency, without reducing the causes of (politically motivated) violence to either structure or agency.

RETHINKING "STRUCTURAL VIOLENCE"

Many scholars use the concept of structural violence (Galtung 1969, 1990) to refer to the linkages between social inequalities, suffering, and individual power or agency (see, e.g., Bourgois 1995, 2004; Farmer 1996, 2003, 2004; Farmer, Connors, and Simmons 1996; Merry 2007; Scheper-Hughes and Bourgois 2004). Johan Galtung (1969: 170–71) described structural violence as "violence where there is no actor," or as violence "built into the structure [that] shows up as unequal power and consequently as unequal life chances". Conditions of suffering that are "objectively avoidable," such as starvation and poverty, are forms of structural violence; therefore, *social injustice* is considered an equivalent term (171). The concept has been important to signify the way that seemingly agentless or "invisible" conditions of social inequality—and the unequal distribution of resources—can have powerfully negative effects that are experienced much like direct or physical violence. It also has some limitations.

Contemporary anthropologists have used the analytic framework of structural violence not only to indicate forms of systemic injustice but also to place in context individuals' use of direct or physical violence as a reflection of their structural location in society. While not identical, such usages are similar to the idea of the "culture of poverty" (Lewis 1959). I suggest that violence cannot be regarded solely as a product of social structures of inequality or brutal cultures of poverty. I do not view malicious social acts as products of structural violence—as has become common in anthropological, human rights, peace, and public health literatures—even as such acts may be placed in sociopolitical, economic, and historical contexts. I also do not hold the view that (sexual) violence is a matter of instinctive or natural drives embedded in biology. Furthermore, I deemphasize the notion of a gendered subject who acts according to a predetermined psychoanalytic script of cultural possibilities for action because of his or her unconscious drives or particular social location. The use of the term *structural violence* to highlight the suffering that structural inequalities may inflict on persons tends to reify the artificial divide between and the priority placed on the civil and political rights over the economic, social, and cultural rights in human rights discourse. All these stances minimize the extent to which in many cases of political conflict few members of a population may resort to physical or direct violence to violate the embodied sovereignty of others.

In addition to considering structural conditions that may engender some individuals to use violence against others, theorists of violence must consider concepts of identity, fantasy, desire, and reputation as factors affecting both perpetrators and victims as they negotiate their respective statuses in the context of contested power relations. In examining violence, torture, and subsequent iterations of ensekirite, I postulate that members of the terror apparatus perpetrated malevolent acts in partial response to threats to gender identity. I propose that changes in Haiti's political and economic arenas affected gender ideals and power relations between the sexes. Such shifts influenced the style of violence used by the coup regime in Haiti, including its choice of targets. And this style of violence emerged at the nexus of conflicting international, national, and local power relations (Moore 1994: 142). The specific modes of violence committed during the coup years can be linked to historical forms of sexual and gender repression based in the histories and practices of exploitation generated by the transnational political economy of extraction.

THE U.S. OCCUPATION OF HAITI: 1915–1934

The conjunction of military intervention and violence targeting civilians goes back at least to the American occupation of Haiti, beginning in 1915. From 1870 to 1915 Haiti was the site of political and economic contests between England, France, Germany, and the United States, as each power attempted to dominate the Caribbean and Latin America (Dupuy 1989: 129; Farmer 1992: 173–76; Nicholls 1985). World War

I was the geopolitical backdrop against which the United States occupied Haiti. The stated rationale for intervention was "maintaining stability" in Haiti's chaotic domestic arena; the implicit or covert motive was to ensure U.S. financial interests abroad (Trouillot 1990: 100). U.S. Marines were deployed to massacre northern *caco* (resistance) forces and to seize control of Haitian financial institutions, customshouses, and administrative bodies to centralize and stabilize the economy (Nicholls 1996; Plummer 1992; Schmidt 1995).

The United States granted concessions that favored prospective foreign investors, "such as rights to use water ways, the monopoly on the production and sale of crops abroad, and equally as important, a cheap and abundant labor force whose wages were only 25 to 30 cents for a twelve-hour day" (Dupuy 1989: 135). The Haitian masses were viewed as a source of exploitable labor in the service of foreign capitalism, just as they had been during the colonial period, that would also enrich the Haitian elite. In many respects, the U.S. occupation reinforced a political economy of extraction.

These political and economic interventions altered traditional kinship and gender relations. Land that was previously unavailable to foreign owners because of legal restrictions was leased or sold to U.S. companies for agricultural production. The Haitian peasants who had worked these lands had to move elsewhere. This forced removal of Haitian peasants from their traditional sources of livelihood compelled many Haitians to seek work abroad in order to survive. Thousands of Haitian men found work in fruit plantations owned by several U.S. multinationals, such as the Atlantic Fruit Company and the United Fruit Company (Martinez 1995: 136–37).[13] Often these migrant workers had left behind families whose major support would be the single mother—a pattern that continues today (Martinez 1995: 136–37; see also Laguerre 1976, 1987b).

In addition to alterations in agricultural production, economic interventions increased Haiti's dependence on the United States by expanding the export of coffee, which made up 74 percent of all exports (Trouillot 1990: 103). Furthermore, by the end of the occupation in 1934,

U.S. companies controlled the production and export of sugar, sisal, and bananas, and tourism emerged as a subsidiary industry linked to the use of Port-au-Prince as a liberty port for the U.S. Navy. Haitian banking and finance were now controlled by U.S. banks, and the Haitian currency was pegged to the dollar rather than the French franc. The United States became the single most important market for Haitian exports and imports. (Dupuy 1989: 141)

With U.S. control of customs, import duties increased on staples from 23 percent to 46 percent by the end of the occupation, which, of course, drastically increased their price. While this measure benefited the United States, it placed a terrible financial burden on the Haitian poor (Trouillot 1990: 103). But the welfare of Haitian citizens was of little concern to the U.S. military forces, who saw the former essentially as forced laborers.

In some respects the U.S. occupation revived the practices of the plantation slavery period: brutality and sexual coercion and violence. In 1915 U.S. forces created a new "Haitian" institution, the Gendarmerie, which reinforced this modern economy of extraction through coercive practices. The Gendarmerie policed the peasantry and ensured Haiti's continued economic productivity by means of forced labor (Renda 2001: 31–32). Toward the end of the occupation the Gendarmerie was transformed into the Garde d'Haïti, an institution that received ongoing training from the U.S. Marine Corps and that was the basis for Haiti's modern army and policing force (Weinstein and Segal 1992: 32–33). The Marines became known for their sexual exploitation of Haitian women, which reinforced gender and sexual violence as tools of repression. According to Rey (1999: 83), "Stories of rape committed by U.S. Marines during the first American occupation of Haiti (1915–1934) are still widely told. The satirical Haitian jest that USMC should stand for *Use Sans Moindre Contrôle* (use without the least control) was mainly generated as a critique of the marines' infamous lewdness and drunkenness, a state in which many of their alleged conquest rapes of Haitian women were probably committed." Mary A. Renda (2001: 163) argues further, "In fact, Americans' repeated deprecation of Haitian women did much to create and maintain an atmosphere in which rape would go unrecognized, unnamed, and, of course, unpunished."

U.S. forces also committed atrocities that have the character of necropolitical violence. The Women's International League for Peace and Freedom described how U.S. forces tortured Haitians with fire and even burned men and women alive. They executed children and destroyed crops, distilleries, mills, and houses (Bellegarde-Smith 2004: 111, citing Balch 1927: 126–27). It is important to note that the deployment of sexual and gender violence and the brutal repression of Haitian citizens were undertaken by a military force that trained the modern Haitian armed forces.

In addition to the reputed threats to U.S. political and economic interests in Haiti and the region, military and economic intervention was justified by cultural discourses about Haitian racial, intellectual, and biological inferiority. U.S. foreign policy on Haiti was based on implicit theories of race, kinship, and gender. These representations of Haitians that circulated in political discourses at the time would have lasting effects on Haitian domestic politics, and their legacy manifests as implicit stereotypical references in the 1994 embassy cablegram. Such discourses also justified other contemporaneous U.S. interventions in Latin America and the Caribbean (Tickner 1992: 49).

Central to the ideology of early-twentieth-century U.S. foreign policy was the notion that peoples of African descent were incapable of self-governance or sovereignty. In 1921 a U.S. State Department official made an overt racialist statement that prefigures the tone of the embassy's 1994 cablegram:

> It is well to distinguish at once between the Dominicans and the Haitians. The former, while in many ways not advanced far enough for the highest type of self-government, yet have a preponderance of white blood and culture. The Haitians on the other hand are negro for the most part, and, barring a very few highly educated politicians, are almost in a state of savagery and complete ignorance. The two situations thus demand different treatment. In Haiti it is necessary to have as complete a rule within a rule by Americans as possible. This sort of control will be required for a long period of time, until the general average of education and enlightenment is raised. In the Dominican Republic, on the other hand, I believe we should endeavor rather to counsel than control.[14]

In alignment with such racialist views, the United States employed Levantine Arab merchants who had begun migrating to the Haiti in the 1890s to implement its covert "rule within a rule" and to further its efforts to dominate Haiti's economy and resources (Shannon 1996). On entering Haiti, "the arabs [sic] moved quite quickly into the import-export trade, challenging the position of foreign and local elites" (Nicholls 1985: 140–41). Similarly, the "German/French encroachment led the US State Department to assist American business in using Syrians as agents to regain some of the Haitian import market through more liberal credit terms on mass-consumption merchandise" (Shannon 1996: 5). Over time these Levantines married into the mulatto elite who had controlled Haiti economically and politically since the nation's independence in 1804. The U.S. political and economic preference for a "rule within a rule" had long-term consequences in Haiti.

A brief story from my time in Haiti demonstrates the links between biopolitical alliances and economies of extraction in contemporary

Haiti. In summer 1996 a Haitian friend introduced me to a member of a prominent Haitian family of Levantine origin—whom I will call Joseph Cassis—to help me understand how early-twentieth-century politics continues to be enmeshed with issues of race and kinship. Early one evening, as we drove along the Pan American Road leading from Port-au-Prince to the lush foothills of Pétionville to Cassis's affluent estate, my friend explained that Cassis's extended family and associates were in control of Cité Soleil. Cité Soleil is a shantytown in the capital known for its cyclical violence, rapid population increase due to rural-to-urban migration and high fertility rates, and expanding drug trade (Maternowska 2006).

As we drove up the long driveway, the Cassis children were engaged in twilight target practice on the front lawn. Cassis's wife welcomed us inside the house but did not join in the conversation. Joseph (as I was asked to call him) appeared quite inebriated, which may have accounted for the conversation's content. He had been educated at a prominent American Ivy League university, and we spoke in English. He explained to me that his family was Christian. They had fled from religious persecution in Palestine to Haiti at the beginning of the twentieth century. The extended family entered small-scale commerce and expanded their business during the American occupation. In the course of the conversation, I was surprised by his open affirmation that his father had given financial support to the dictator François Duvalier in his ascent to the presidency. Perhaps bravado or alcohol was a component of this revelation to my Haitian friend and me; however, I am inclined to accept these statements as true.

After leaving the Cassis residence, my Haitian friend and I discussed the conversation with Joseph. My friend told me that during the coup years, Cassis had brought General Raoul Cédras to his home in the middle of the night so that his wife might translate a document for him. Cassis's close association with Cédras gives credence to the assertions that some members of Haiti's elite were covert, if not overt, supporters of the coup.

I had read many accounts of the involvement of the mulatto elite in bringing about President Aristide's first ouster, but this was the first time I had firsthand confirmation of these stories. The United States favored those Haitians who would facilitate as complete a rule within a rule as possible. The mulatto elite and perhaps other covert foreign actors intervened in Haiti's national security and political economy throughout the twentieth century by supporting Haitian political leaders who used repressive practices to control the population. Of those, François Duvalier is perhaps the most notorious for his strategic use of neomodern necropolitics.

THE POLITICAL ECONOMY OF DUVALIERIST VIOLENCE

One can argue that the Duvalier dictatorships brought the manipulation and violation of cultural norms to new levels. Duvalierist repression, while rooted in a Haitian cultural and historical context, was not unlike the dirty wars that unfolded in other parts of the globe, such as Argentina (Arditti 1999). However, François Duvalier inculcated a "new kind of state violence" (Trouillot 1990: 166) that has subsequently been used to characterize state repression in postcolonial African regimes—what Mbembe (2001: 83) calls the "lapse into 'tonton-macoutism.'" Duvalier's terror apparatus employed forms of necropolitical violence that violated corporeal and physical boundaries. It transgressed cultural taboos to exploit, control, and destroy individual and collective bodies. It manipulated Haitian Vodou beliefs, kinship practices, and the sex and gender system in the forms of violence it deployed. The violation of sex, gender, and kinship norms was intrinsic to the Duvalierist apparatus. In this respect, Duvalierist necropolitical violence targeted not just the material body but also the cultural and psychological foundations of identity.

François Duvalier, a physician and ethnologist who had studied the folklore of the poor majority, entered politics in an era when many Haitian intellectuals were protesting the influence and interventions of foreign polities, especially the United States. A political platform of nationalist, anticolonial, and pro-African rhetoric carried him to the presidency by "democratic" election on September 22, 1957.[15] Patrick Bellegarde-Smith (2004: 123–26) suggests, furthermore, that Duvalier received the covert support of the United States (and also of members of the Haitian business class). In order to strengthen his domestic and international position, Duvalier used brutal forms of repression to eliminate his enemies and to inculcate a pervasive climate of terror, creating an atmosphere in Haiti known as *lapè simityè*, fear or peace of the cemetery.[16]

On entering office, Duvalier restructured the Haitian army to ensure that individuals loyal to him were in positions of power (Laguerre 1993: 110–14). He also created a paramilitary network that was diffused throughout the nation, a prime example of the use of mobile sovereigns in necropolitics. Called the *cagoulards,* these individuals hid their faces behind ski masks and operated primarily at night as a secret police force. However, by "1958–59, members of that secret police had replaced their masks with dark glasses and operated increasingly in public view, even though the regime denied their existence. They came to be referred to by the people as *tonton-makout* and became the living symbols of Duvalierist coercion" (Trouillot 1990: 189). In this respect Papa Doc's training in ethnology was useful for instilling fear.

Duvalier's makout also evoked traditional Vodou symbolism in their dress. The symbolic figure Tonton Makout (Uncle Strawsack) is a bogeyman from Haitian folklore that is said to "disappear" disobedient children into his *makout* (sack) at night (Wilentz 1989: 34). The style of clothing Duvalier's tonton makout adopted served to create a sense of ambiguity. The identities of religious practitioner and makout—as well as visible markers of state, paramilitary, or civilian actors—overlapped and, perhaps, were indistinguishable:

> In town, Papa Doc's Macoutes wore blue jeans, denim hats and sometimes sunglasses and red bandanas. More rarely, they wore suits, fedoras and sunglasses, and *often they wore no uniform at all*. In the provinces, the Macoutes sometimes topped the denim outfit with broad peasant hats. At voodoo pilgrimages in the countryside it was hard to tell the difference between the voodoo priests, who wore the blue denims, red scarves and broad peasant hat that represent the voodoo agricultural god Cousin Zaka, and the Tontons Macoute, similarly garbed. Often the only difference was that the voodoo priest had a machete, and the Macoute had an old Enfield rifle. Often, the priest and the Macoute were one and the same. (Wilentz 1989: 34; my emphasis)

The elision of Duvalier's secret police with the Vodou religious clergy was intended to manipulate Haitian peasants' loyalties to their land, extended families, and ancestors. Duvalier himself dressed in a manner that recalled Baron Samedi (Bawon Samdi), chief of the spirits of the dead, by wearing a black suit and sunglasses in his public appearances (Brown 1991: 185 n.). Through these symbolic associations, Duvalier invoked his sovereign power over life and death.

Duvalier also enlisted networks of Vodou temples and servants of the Haitian *lwa* (spirits) in his efforts to survey or "discipline" a particular area (Laguerre 1989: 116). The reasons for Vodou clerics' participation in Duvalier's terror apparatus were complicated. Priests wanted freedom of religion, power over a particular territory, security for their congregants, political recognition, and a salary, and they wanted to survive (116–17). Vodou priests used their charisma, as well as repressive practices, to police the peasant population. In this manner, Duvalierist violence, while visible in very material and symbolic ways, literally became an occult, or hidden, source of fear.

The Duvalierist apparatus blurred the boundaries between the state and civil society by co-opting local agents. Generally, the makout were drawn from a large group of economically disenfranchised individuals in both rural and urban areas. Allegiance to the makout apparatus was initially a lucrative endeavor, yielding political patronage and monetary compensation (Trouillot 1990: 154). Duvalier ensured that makout remained loyal through the use of these financial incentives but also through kinship ties and the ever-present threat of death. Duvalier placed loyal makout in key positions in the army and encouraged them to marry only into other Duvalierist families. However, lower-ranked army officers were encouraged to survey and inform on the actions of their superiors (Laguerre 1993: 112–13). The financial incentive for political support helped to create a geographically extended social base comprising both men and women that was willing to betray and use violence against their associates to ensure their own political and economic gain. The parasitic system of patronage trickled down through the apparatus from the army officers and makout into civil society. Michel Laguerre (1993: 148–60) notes that this instituted "military corruption as a *sui generis* system." The nation's continuing economic decline ensured that there were many individuals willing to join the makout apparatus, thereby establishing a terror economy.

The specific techniques of violence perpetrated by the Duvalierist apparatus are of special significance to this discussion and recall Mbembe's (2003: 16) description of how a "fictionalized notion of the enemy" justifies necropolitical violence. Michel-Rolph Trouillot (1990: 166) observes further: "Duvalierism distinguished itself by [introducing] a *new kind* of state violence, one that systematically violated the codes governing the use of force by the state" (emphasis in original). Categories of people formerly considered "innocents," including children and the elderly but especially women, were attacked (166–67). Leaders of civil society—religious clerics, doctors, intellectuals, and so on—were no longer considered immune from victimization and may have been forced to participate in the violence (166). From 1960 to 1986, when Jean-Claude Duvalier was forced to flee Haiti, the Duvalier regime attacked any civilian institutions or ideological apparatuses that were seen to threaten the regime, regardless of any overt political stance. Churches, schools, trade unions, women's organizations, universities, the media, professional associations, and sports clubs—all were targets of random attacks (159–60, 167–68). The tools of social control included curfews, martial law, extortion, imprisonment, torture, and murder. But Duvalier did not solely target civic associations.

Racial, kinship, and gender ideals also determined the targets of necropolitical violence. Just before his assumption of power in 1957, François Duvalier's affiliates attacked mulatto political opponents and their supporters. In summer 1964 in Jérémie, after a group of youths protested against Duvalier, whole mulatto families vanished. In the attack on the town, "infants were raped and killed for offenses against the state committed by cousins twice removed, or even by former neighbors" (Trouillot 1990: 168).[17] The constant threat of repression created a climate of terror in which traditional alliances and solidarities in civil society and the family were shattered. Fear and suspicion of one's own family members was a reality:

> Duvalierist violence recognized as legitimate targets *all* individuals who had a relationship with a political subject, regardless of the nature of that relationship. It thus succeeded in casting a pall over most relationships.Fathers repudiated sons, sometimes publicly. Neighbors denounced neighbors. Cabinet Minister Luckner Cambronne summarized the Duvalierist desire to submit all traditional solidarities to the principles of the state: "A good Duvalierist must be ready to sacrifice his own mother." (168–69; emphasis in original)

It has been estimated that more than sixty thousand people were murdered over the course of the Duvaliers' rule (Farmer 1994: 128). In this manner the Duvalier regime was a quintessential embodiment of necropolitics. Social trust was undermined at all levels of society. The random, limitless nature of the violence perpetrated by mobile sovereigns generated state hegemony: "The victims were so many sacrificial offerings, confirming the permanence of power, a reminder to the people of their smallness in regard to the state, a reminder to the executioners of the omnipotence of their chief" (Trouillot 1990: 169). The appropriation of power through brutal repression of the population and through manipulation of religious leaders is a form of "state fetishism" in the extreme (Taussig 1992; see also Mbembe 2001).

By the time of François Duvalier's death and Jean-Claude's ascendance to power, civil society was oppressed and repressed to the point that resistance was practically nonexistent. Patrick Lemoine, who was tortured in the infamous Fort-Dimanche prison, describes the climate of fear at this time of transition:

In 1971, it appeared that no political opposition existed. The only voice of dissent was that of the exiled community. It was hard to accept the calm that surfaced after the death of the tyrant, *Papa Doc*, on April 21, 1971. Not a single weapon was discharged; not a firecracker was heard. Not a single cry for justice was uttered despite the known abuses, the atrocities, and the assortment of crimes that the *tonton macoutes* had committed. Yet, almost every level of society had been affected by the repressive actions of the government. (1997: 12–13; italics in original)

Some argue that in spite of the overarching climate of fear, the Duvaliers established alternative paths to citizenship for members of its terror apparatus (e.g., Charles 1995). Indeed, Mbembe (2001: 83–84) defines citizens in a parasitic system of "tonton-macoutism" as "those who can have access to the networks of the parallel economy, and to the means of livelihood for survival that economy makes possible." While some members of the makout may have chosen to participate in the Duvalierist apparatus to protect themselves and their families, involvement in Duvalier's broader civilian militia system was a means for economic improvement, regardless of one's actual allegiance to the state. For the rural and urban poor, membership in the terror apparatus may have been one of few paths to upward mobility (Trouillot 1990: 191). To a certain degree Duvalierism destabilized paths to economic solvency and political power that were traditionally under the control of the mulatto elite. Duvalierist necropolitics also established the terror economy as a parallel means of financial mobility. Participation in military and paramilitary forces gave formerly disenfranchised individuals means to control existing economies or to establish literal occult economies by means of violence, extortion, and crime, as long as such activities did not undermine state power.

Carolle Charles (1995) argues, further, that Duvalierist practices created new forms of citizenship for women. In rural and urban Haiti conjugal unions take several forms, ranging from *maryaj* (legal marriages), the most prestigious but least prevalent, to *plasaj* (common law marriage), the most common relationship. Couples who are *plase* assume the responsibilities of a legal marriage without a formal ceremony (Lowenthal 1984, 1987; Vieux 1989: 9). Haitian men are expected to provide financially for their families. It is often presumed, however, that they will engage in polygamous relationships and maintain a *fanm deyò*, a "wife" or partner living outside the primary household. They are also obligated to support any children born from these unions.

Women are the recognized *potomitan* (pillars) of the community.[18] They are responsible for the household and are expected to remain monogamous (CIFD 1992: 57–59; Maternowska 2006: 44–74). The gender division of labor is such that *konbit,* large-scale, cooperative agricultural production outside the home, is generally viewed as a male activity—despite women's and children's participation in the sowing and harvesting of crops—while the sale of the produce is *travay fanm,* women's work (Herskovits 1975 [1937]: 85; Lowenthal 1984: 18). Women also control the sale and distribution of produce in local markets; however, they must also ensure that the household requirements are met from the cash generated from that sale (Lowenthal 1984: 18–19). Even with this integral role in the management of the domestic economy, it is unclear to what extent the woman in the conjugal household retains control over the remainder of the proceeds (Nicholls 1985: 126). To supplement her income she may participate in the informal economy as a *madanm sara* (small-scale market woman), the profits from which are hers to control (Brown 1987: 125).

Sexual partnerships between men and women have also been made for mutual economic aid when faced with a lack of other alternatives (Lowenthal 1984, 1987; Maternowska 2006). In his ethnographic research in rural Haiti, Ira P. Lowenthal (1984: 22) found that sexual exchange is another form of alienated labor that can produce wealth.[19] In this regard, the aphorism "Chak fanm fèt ak yon kawo tè—nan mitan janm-ni" (Each woman is born with a *kawo* of land—between her legs) reveals some measure of the resources women are viewed to possess innately.

Less has been written about the status of women and men in elite sectors of Haitian society. Historically, kinship and gender relations have been much more circumscribed among wealthy families, many of which are mulatto. These families attempted to gain economic and political power by means of strategic intermarriages and the control of women. Efforts to limit the boundaries of this social "caste" were assisted directly by the Catholic orders of priests and nuns that arrived after the Concordat of 1860. Under their influence, from the mid-nineteenth to the early twentieth century there were greater possibilities for the education of elite women but also for their discipline and control (Bouchereau 1957: 76–78). Nonetheless, the general expectation that women are responsible for the domestic sphere cuts across classes.

According to Charles (1995: 139), the gender ideology of the Duvalier nationalist state transformed women "into political agents of social change" over and against a "prevailing conception of women as passive political actors, devoted mothers, and political innocents." Women participated in the Duvalierist terrorist apparatus, and a woman even directed the makout apparatus (Trouillot 1990: 191). Women's participation in the apparatus afforded them greater power, but it may also have provided protection for self and family. Charles's (1995: 139) argument suggests this interpretation: "In contrast to other dictatorial regimes of Latin America that appeal to the image of the suffering, self-sacrificing, patriotic mother who has no place in the political arena, the Duvalierist state focused on the 'patriotic woman' whose allegiance was first to Duvalier's nation and state. Any woman or man who did not adhere to these policies became an enemy subject to political repression."

Given the potential insecurity produced by nonparticipation in the terror apparatus, Charles's next assertions are open to dispute. She states that in targeting women for detention, rape, torture, forced exile, or execution, "state violence created, for the first time, gender equality" (140), especially in an environment in which the cultural ideal of women's weakness was strong. She continues, "Because of the systematic use of state violence by the Duvalierist regime, Haitian women became increasingly aware of their role and were able to situate themselves within the political framework of the struggle for democracy" (141).

It is true that sexual violence was deployed against women activists, as well as the female kin of Duvalier's political opponents, in attacks that were both political and personal: "Under the Duvaliers, women were sometimes treated the same as men, often worse. Many women were attacked because a husband or male relative was out of reach—in exile or in a foreign embassy. The Duvalierist preference for the sexual 'conquest' of females associated with the political opposition, from torture-rape to acquaintance-rape to marriage, infused the politicization of gender with violence" (Trouillot 1990: 167). One could also argue that Duvalierist practices infused the politicization of violence with gender. But are these forms of violence means by which women and other targets are recognized as equal, or acquire citizenship, as Charles suggests? The following examples complicate this interpretation. On August 7, 1957, just before the presidential elections, the Women's Political Bureau of the mulatto senator Louis Déjoie was attacked (Trouillot 1990: 153). In 1958 Yvonne Hakime-Rimpel, a journalist and Déjoie supporter, was brutally raped by the tonton makout as "a blunt warning to the opposition" (Diederich and Burt 1986: 105).[20] I suggest that women who were targeted for violence were already viewed as political subjects and threats to the Duvalierist regime for their activism and position in the racial hierarchy, even as they were targeted as surrogates for absent males. They were also viewed as threats to conventional gender ideals. It can be argued that politically active elite women, who were traditionally relegated to the domestic sphere, were far more threatening to the ideal sex-gender system than working-class rural and urban women.

The perpetration of violence against women in Haiti was undoubtedly a means to renegotiate shifts in traditional sex and gender roles. In considering the deployment of violence against women in the Duvalier era, I adopt the anthropologist Henrietta L. Moore's (1994: 154) perspective that we should view violence not "as a breakdown in the social order—something gone wrong—[but] . . . as the sign of a struggle for the maintenance of certain fantasies of identity and power." Haitian women had been increasingly politically active since the U.S. occupation. They solicited funds to send a delegation of Haitians to the United States to protest the occupation, and in 1930 elite Haitian women coordinated a processional march with Catholic priests to chant odes that demanded the liberation of Haiti (Bouchereau 1957: 81). In 1934 Madeleine Sylvain Bouchereau and other elite women formed the Ligue Féminine d'Action Sociale (Feminine Social Action League, LFAS) to set up literacy classes for women and to advocate for women's suffrage (Charles 1995: 146–47; Nicholls 1985: 128). Unfortunately, these pro-suffrage efforts were viewed as disloyal to nation, race, family, and men (LFAS 1946: 29–30), despite the fact that Haiti ratified the U.N. Charter in 1945 and the Universal Declaration of Human Rights in 1948, documents that promote equal rights for all. Haitian women were granted the right to vote only in 1950. Nevertheless, until an October 8, 1982, decree revised the Haitian Civil Code, married women were considered "minors" under the protection of their spouse, as had been the case in the Napoleonic Code on which the Civil Code had been based in 1825 (Collectif de femmes Haïtiennes 1980: 23; Trouillot 1983). Thus it is possible to interpret (political) violence against women as a reflection of male anxieties about a perceived breakdown in the social order, one that destabilized the traditional balance of power between women and men.

Changes in women's status over time were also linked to Haiti's position in the political economy of extraction. In the 1970s and early 1980s the specter of widespread Duvalierist violence and the decline in traditional modes of agricultural production were factors in the massive displacement of individuals to urban centers. Although officially condemned by the international community, the routinization of violence under the Duvaliers contributed to the flight of "disciplined" Haitians from rural to urban areas (Laguerre 1987b: 120–21). These migrants could be brought into the industrial sector as cheap labor for international assembly factories without fear that they would form unions or agitate for higher wages (Garrity 1981: 27). As during the U.S. occupation, gender was a factor in these population shifts. Women were considered ideal employees in the assembly sectors because of their reputed docility and dexterity (Grunwald, Delatour, and Voltaire 1984, 1985). Because of their market skills, and the preference for women in assemblage factories, "women [became] breadwinners and their relationships with men, many of whom have significantly less earning power, have become more unstable as a result" (Brown 1987: 125).

The challenges to Haiti's traditional sex and gender system increased in the 1980s. The international community insisted that the Duvalier dynasty respect human rights as a condition of development assistance. Such conditional aid pressured Jean-Claude Duvalier to liberate civil society, thereby opening the space for Haitians to agitate for civil, women's, and human rights.

DEMOCRACY AND DUVALIERISM WITHOUT DUVALIER

The international pressure placed on Jean-Claude Duvalier meant that popular resistance to the regime increased in the early 1980s. The food riots of 1984 were the first massive display of dissent in more than twenty years. In 1985 Fr. Jean-Bertrand Aristide returned to Haiti after study abroad. He joined a growing public movement that opposed the poverty and repression in Haiti by broadcasting antistate sermons on the radio. While peasants organized in protest in the countryside, Aristide helped church youths to form Solidarite Ant Jen (Solidarity among Youth). These groups, in turn, joined with the *ti kominote legliz* (ecclesial base communities, TKL). The TKL had adopted the politics of liberation theology to form collective resistance against state repression.[21] Women were actively involved in all stages of the democracy movement (Racine 1995: 10–11). The domestic and international pressures culminated in the forced exile of Duvalier in February 1986 (Bellegarde-Smith 2004; Farmer 1994: 120–25).

The dechoukaj, or uprooting, period—the massive, violent backlash against the tonton makout and Vodou practitioners assumed to be members of the Duvalier apparatus—commenced after Duvalier left the country. The Haitian masses burned and murdered reputed Duvalierist affiliates and looted their property (Danner 1987; Wilentz 1989: 53). Popular revenge was quickly curbed, however, as the provisional

government, led by former Duvalier military officers, responded by escalating the repressive Duvalier techniques of social control in what has
been called "Duvalierism without Duvalier."[22] To some extent this government was supported by foreign aid from the United States (Dupuy
1997: 50–54; Farmer 1994: 132).

Nonetheless, the increased freedom of association permitted women
to organize protests against the structures of domination and exploitation that continued to exist in both the public and private spheres.
Women activists returned from overseas political exile to join the movement for participatory democracy. They formed both urban and rural
organizations concerned with health care, literacy, political inclusion,
and economic equality (Charles 1995; Racine 1995). When domestic
and international pressures forced the provisional government to schedule elections, women's organizations, rural peasant workers groups, the
TKL, and other groups joined the Lavalas movement to support Father
Aristide as a candidate for president.[23] Aristide began his campaign in
the Salomon market to honor merchant women's participation in the
political coalition. He explicitly incorporated women's concerns into
his platform and won the presidency on December 16, 1990. President
Aristide appointed women as directors of four ministries, including
Finance and Foreign Affairs (Racine 1995: 11).

COUP D'ÉTAT

On September 30, 1991, after less than eight months in power, the seven-
thousand-member Haitian military (Forces Armées d'Haïti, FAD'H)—led
by General Cédras and backed by Haiti's traditional bourgeoisie—drove
the democratically elected President Aristide from power. The international community imposed a porous economic embargo intended to
pressure the coup regime, but despite "sanctions" the military held firm.
From the coup d'état until Artistide's restoration by Operation Uphold
Democracy on October 15, 1994, the de facto state perpetrated violence
against the masses of Aristide supporters that is said to have far sur-
passed the worst violence and terror of the Duvaliers (Fuller and Wilentz
1991: 2).

The coup regime enlisted remnants of Duvalier's tonton makout to
mobilize against Aristide's supporters. Chèf seksyon (section chiefs),
rural members of the makout organization, were given the task of policing rural Haiti (Fuller and Wilentz 1991: 11–13). The army took control
of all forms of communication and shut down all radio stations—the

only source of information for most of the predominantly illiterate population. Popular organizations were terrorized and silenced. Most leaders of civic associations were arrested or forced *an mawonaj,* into hiding within Haiti.[24] Neighborhoods and slums supportive of Aristide were targets of burnings and massive gunfire. Disappearances, beatings, assassinations, torture, and detention were once again modes of social control (HRW/A and NCHR 1994: 32–33). Simply having a picture of Aristide in the home put one at risk (Fuller and Wilentz: 1–2). Mutilated and dismembered bodies—some of them peppered with gunshot wounds—turned up in "killing fields" (Williams 1994: 21). Bodies littered the Titanyen mass grave,[25] the sides of roads, and the slums of Cité Soleil and washed up on beaches (HRW and NCHR 1994: 5). These brutal acts revived lapè simityè and were visible reminders of what could happen to anyone, at any time.[26] The result of this random violence and ensekirite (HRW 1993: 105) was the internal displacement of more than 300,000 Haitians (HRW/A, JRS/USA and NCHR 1994: 2–3).

The coup apparatus's state of terror was implemented by a diffuse network of actors. After the September 30, 1991, coup, FAD'H armed tens of thousands of paramilitary atache to control the population. In September 1993 the controversial Revolutionary Front for the Advancement and Progress of Haiti (Front Révolutionnaire pour l'Avancement et le Progrès d'Haïti, FRAPH) began to function.[27] The reporter Allan Nairn asserts that FRAPH was established with the financial support of the U.S. government through the CIA—which has had FRAPH's leaders on its payroll—and the assistance of U.S. Special Forces (Arnove 1995). Further, the United States used FRAPH to undermine the democratic movement and to force Aristide to accede to its vision of restored democracy—one that would be favorable financially to American business interests.

Many of FRAPH's members were former tonton makout who openly displayed their loyalty to "neo-Duvalierism" in symbolic ways that were clearly meant to intimidate and evoke the history of necropolitical terror. On September 22, 1993, the anniversary of François Duvalier's 1957 election, FRAPH emerged publicly by carrying the Duvalier black-and-red flag to a museum exhibition of Papa Doc's personal items (HRW/A and NCHR 1994: 12). Others joined FRAPH in order to secure their livelihoods in the face of the economic crisis that resulted from the embargo or to protect their families by affiliating with the coup apparatus.

The final group of perpetrators of violence during and after the coup period, the *zenglendo,* were "criminals . . . recruited from groups ranging from the marginal social strata found in working-class districts to police officers themselves usually acting at night, in civilian clothes and with official weapons" (HRW and NCHR 1994: 2). This group of mobile sovereigns, like the tonton makout, blurs the boundaries between the state and civil society, making it difficult to categorize their acts as state-sponsored human rights violations or as interpersonal crime.

TECHNOLOGIES OF TORTURE

As Das and Nandy (1985) have observed in their discussion of sacrificial and political violence in South Asia, there were differences in the style of violence employed to maintain the climate of terror in Haiti during the 1991–94 coup years. The terror apparatus employed techniques of repression that violated cultural ideals of sexuality, gender, and kinship. They also targeted their victims' capacities for production and reproduction. These strategies reveal how social alliances remain integral to local power relations, despite Duvalierist attempts to undermine traditional solidarities in society.

Supporters of Aristide were deemed "enemies" of the coup apparatus by virtue of their poverty and presumed support for a pro-democracy platform. During the attacks, the majority of the poor who were targeted were rebuked as "Lavalasyen," partisans of the pro-democracy party. There were differences, however, in how attacks were deployed against the sexes. Men were attacked directly for their involvement as organizers or supporters of the popular democracy movement. When apprehended, they usually were arrested or kidnapped, interrogated in a detention facility, beaten, whipped, and humiliated. Attacks on the body included torture of the genitalia, not only to inflict pain but also to damage the sexual organs permanently, thereby destroying men's reproductive capacity. In general, the attacks on men's bodies and minds accompanied theft and destruction of property, livestock, or other possessions.

Such violence emasculated or "feminized" these men socially. One man I knew from my participation in the Human Rights Fund therapy groups came from the Artibonite region. He had been a farmer and activist affiliated with the Mouvman Peyizan Papay (MPP)—an organization that advocated on behalf of peasant rights in rural areas. He was arrested for his political activities and detained in the local prison. His captors stripped him naked, restrained him, and beat him severely during his interrogation. Throughout the rituallike extraction of "truth," his torturers stressed that he was nothing more than a slave or an animal. To emphasize the point they found a long rope encrusted with excrement that had been used to tether pigs and tied him up with it. After his release and eventual recuperation at a northern hospital, he fled to the Dominican Republic and worked on a *batèy* (sugarcane plantation) until "democracy" was restored. When he returned to Haiti, however, he learned that not only his wife but his livestock and property as well had been "appropriated" by one of his torturers. When I met him in the therapy group in fall 1998, he expressed feelings of indignation and humiliation about his experience. Especially painful was his captors' treatment of him as a beast. This example of a man's loss of livelihood and productive capacity is echoed in other forms of torture and intimidation.

The terror apparatus inflicted forms of torture intended to damage the body permanently, if the victims of abuse survived their attack. To ensure that male "enemies" never again performed manual labor or other work, their hands may have been chopped off or irreparably mutilated. Another man I knew from the Human Rights Fund therapy groups played the trumpet in a Rara band during the Lenten season.[28] His mouth had suffered such extensive damage during his torture that he could no longer play his instrument.

Women were targeted for their political activism and their economic autonomy in ways intended to harm their productive and reproductive capacity. Members of civil associations, such as churches or women's rights groups, were raped. Sexual violence and assault were also used to punish women who were not organizers but were still politically active. Some women were merely accused of pro-Aristide political activism. In addition, the madanm sara, many of whom were politically active, were attacked because of their financial independence. In general, market women were often unable to go into hiding because of their domestic responsibilities for their children and the household and because commercial activities bound them to local markets.

The following case demonstrates how both political and economic motives characterize the human rights abuses perpetrated against women during the de facto period.

> My name is ____. I am 42 years old. I live in ____. I heard they were out looking for young men and killing them. I have two sons and a daughter. I sent my sons to the countryside. I was at home. Three of them came in the house. I had a little restaurant, and I was cooking food. They took every last thing in the house. After they took everything in the house, they said, "Where's the money[?] Give me the money." I said, "I don't have any money." That's when they raped me. Then they made me lift the bed to

give them $300. When I gave them the $300, they ate all the food from the
pan. As they left they said, "We'll be back. We'll be back." After that I had
to go into hiding. I didn't stay in my house at all. I was in hiding. I asked
friends for a place to sleep. . . . While they were raping me they said I was
a Lavalasienne. They repeated that I was a Lavalasienne and they said they
were going to kill all the Lavalasienne. One of them said, "If it's a member
of Aristide's . . . I'll kill them all."[29]

The attackers depersonalized, objectified, and "translated" this woman
into a political enemy. She was not only a "Lavalasienne"; she was also
a gendered subject standing for Haitian women as a whole. The atrocity was intended to destroy self, body, and future agency: by raping her,
they were threatening both her productive and reproductive capacity.
Given the political and economic climate, it was difficult for the poor to
regain their livelihoods, so the theft of such a large sum was devastating.
By raping this woman, the perpetrators stole another form of wealth—
the way female sexuality can be economically productive in the informal economy as *travay* (sex work). The style of violence was predicated
on reified notions of sexuality and gender and the fact that this woman
was an autonomous, productive, and reproductive agent.

Sexual violence also occurred among illegally imprisoned women
who were forced to have sex in exchange for their release. Torturers
abused other women in detention to damage their reproductive capacity.
Such acts were intended to produce miscarriage and potential infertil-
ity. For example, the Platform of Haitian Human Rights Organizations
reported, "A pregnant woman, abducted during a demonstration, heard
the soldier who was taking her to prison say while mistreating her, I'll
keep on beating you until you have to give birth by the nostrils." Other
examples of the deployment of sex and gender violence reported by this
organization include burning of the breasts and stabbings in the vaginal area.[30] Battery of women, therefore, was designed to injure sexual
organs in an effort to strip women of their "femaleness."

Women were also victimized as surrogates for absent husbands,
fathers, brothers, or male associates. They became what René Girard
(1977) has called "sacrificial substitutes." As during the Duvalier dictatorships, rape often occurred when local section chiefs, attachés, and
uniformed soldiers would come to homes searching for the husband or
partner (HRW and NCHR 1994: 5–6). By attacking the absent male's
kin, perpetrators sought to keep the men from returning and to prevent
the women from engaging in any sort of resistance.

The use of sex and gender violence was inextricably linked to the political economy of the household, blurring a conventional distinction between politically motivated and interpersonal violence. The anthropologist M. Catherine Maternowska (2006) observed in her research in the Cité Soleil slum during the coup years that already dire economic conditions were worsened by the embargo. Men had difficulty surviving according to traditional modes of production. The deteriorating economy rendered them unable to perform their ideal role as patriarchs within the conjugal union, as well as in public settings where it was necessary to perform their masculinity. Men were more inclined to use punitive violence against their conjugal partners out of frustration and anger. The gap between ideal gender norms and the material reality of scarcity produced practices that were often detrimental for women. Maternowska (2006: 70) writes, "In the face of these grim prospects, men appear to be clinging even more doggedly to their only power—that over women. . . . [T]hrough acts of violence and rape, men are responding to the structural systems—both political and economic—that control them. Violence in its many forms is a way of reasserting the eroding male identity." If a woman failed to perform her expected domestic role of keeping her partner's needs fulfilled, whether materially or sexually, she was "vulnerable to verbal and physical assault" (61). If she was unable to provide food, for example, she may also have been subject to violence that she was resigned to accept. Given the worsening political and economic insecurity, remaining in an abusive domestic relationship may have been preferable to the risks of maintaining the household alone. During this period, many women in female-headed households were compelled to engage in periodic sex work to survive. Such work was considered a humiliation and made them vulnerable to sexually transmitted diseases (67–68).

Political and economic pressures constrained poor men and women's agency during the coup years. However, as discussed above, I resist an analysis that contextualizes men's use of violence against women solely as products of "structural violence." It is true that individuals whose social position has been threatened may resort to force to regain or consolidate power. I suggest, however, that the use of sex and gender violence also reflects issues of identity, reputation, and social performance. Moore's concept "thwarting" is relevant to this interpretation.

> Thwarting can be understood as the inability to sustain or properly take up a gendered subject position, resulting in a crisis, real or imagined, of

self-representation and/or social evaluation. . . . Thwarting can also be the result of contradictions arising from the taking-up of multiple subject positions, and the pressure of multiple expectations about self-identity or social presentation. It may also come about as the result of other persons refusing to take up or sustain their subject positions *vis-à-vis* oneself and thereby calling one's self-identity into question. . . . In all such situations, what is crucial is the way in which the behaviour of others threatens the self-representations and social evaluations of oneself. Thus, it is the perpetrator of violence who is threatened and experiences thwarting. (1994: 151)

As some Haitian men were unable to uphold the "ideal" of masculinity according to traditional concepts of sex and gender—and as women were unable or chose not to maintain their respective subordinate position according to the traditional gender ideology—an identity crisis resulted for some men that was externalized and enacted on women's bodies.

By extension, I argue that a similar process occurred at the collective or national level. As the coup years wore on, the terror apparatus expanded its reach throughout Haiti by adding civilian affiliates. Human rights abuses escalated in frequency and severity, especially politically motivated rape. Although incidences of politically motivated rape occurred immediately after the coup (Amnesty International 1992: 36), by late 1993 not only rape but also gang rape and even forced incest were beginning to appear.

These forms of necropolitical violence were used systematically as methods of repression to terrorize families and communities more generally but women specifically. For example: "A woman who was a member of a merchant's cooperative and a democratic group was tied up and forced to watch armed FRAPH members gang-rape her twelve year old daughter. They then burned her house down."[31] Here the woman's femaleness and motherhood were attacked, even though her daughter was the one who was directly violated. Being made to watch the violation of a loved one was intended to instill a sense of powerlessness and failure to uphold an ideal of motherhood. In addition to violating her daughter's body, the perpetrators shamed the family socially because of the stigma of rape.

Another woman's narrative, presented below, similarly emphasizes the link between sex and gender violence and necropolitical power, in that such violence transgresses moral norms of kinship using abject forms of violation (Kristeva 1982). Perpetrators sought not only to destroy women, their families, their livelihoods, and their prospects for the future but also the moral fabric of Haitian culture. These forms of violence are the penultimate expression of necropolitics. As the coup regime realized that a transition of power was inevitable, its members targeted the nation by means of forced incest.

> A woman was in her home with her son and daughter when soldiers burst in. One of the soldiers threatened to kill the son unless he raped his mother and sister. The boy tried to refuse but his mother told him that he must do it "because I didn't want to lose him and I knew he would be killed." The son did as he was told. Afterwards, the woman and daughter were raped by the soldiers while the boy was forced to watch. The family's trauma was compounded by the son and daughter's having run away after the episode, too ashamed to face their mother. "If they return it is only at night because they cannot look me in the eye."[32]

Forced incest, forced witnessing of rape, and gang rape were intended to dehumanize this family. Not only are all three victims made to have sex in violation of incest taboos, but the familial bonds of love or caring are also manipulated. The shame and guilt that resulted from these violations of cultural and moral taboos fragmented this family. One wonders if it will recover from such degradation. Such egregious acts also proved devastating for the prospects of long-term social rehabilitation in Haiti.

The proliferation of egregious forms of sexual violence that violated traditional norms of permissible contact correlated with phases of negotiations between Aristide, the de facto regime, and the U.N. (and implicitly the United States) to establish the terms for Aristide's return to power. Human Rights Watch reports that killings and other forms of violence intensified in the period between the July 3, 1993, signing of the Governors Island Accord—an agreement stipulating the de facto leadership's relinquishing of power with blanket amnesty—and October 30, 1993, the date when the transfer of power was to take place (HRW/A and NCHR 1994: 6–30). My clients at Chanm Fanm told me that during the Governors Island Accord negotiations, the military rode through the local market and announced over loudspeakers that they intended to punish the community in the place of Aristide. They threatened, "You'd better hope that he returns, or we're going to bomb you!" This initial date of transfer failed for reasons that are discussed in the next chapter. The failure to restore constitutional rule in October 1993 had devastating consequences for those deemed enemies of the coup apparatus.

In the intervening year, 1993–94, incidences of violence continued to escalate. Even more individuals were driven into hiding, the majority of whom were men, leaving the less mobile women and children

vulnerable to further attacks. The escalation in abuses at this historical moment recalls Elaine Scarry's (1985) description of the culture of
torture. In these cultures the "material factuality" of the human body is
appropriated to lend realness or certainty to an ideology or construct
whose validity is doubted or challenged (1985: 13–14). Trouillot (1990:
169) states similarly that the "sacrifice" of Haitians through Duvalierist forms of violence was a ritualistic endeavor to confirm the power
of the state. This macropolitical analysis parallels Moore's micropolitical theories of thwarting—where an individual commits violence when
there is a threat to his or her own identity or power in relation to others.
These theories of violence echo Scarry's "analogical verification" and
"analogical substantiation."

> At particular moments when there is within a society a crisis of belief—that
> is when some central idea or ideology or cultural construct has ceased
> to elicit a population's belief either because it is manifestly fictitious or
> because it has for some reasons been divested of ordinary forms of substan-
> tiation—the sheer material factualness of the human body will be borrowed
> to lend that cultural construct the aura of "realness" and "certainty." . . .
> [T]he felt-characteristics of pain—one of which is its compelling vibrancy
> or its incontestable reality or simply its "certainty"—can be appropriated
> away from the body and presented as the attributes of something else
> (something which by itself lacks those attributes, something which does not
> in itself appear vibrant, real, or certain). (1985: 13–14)

The technologies of torture perpetrated by the coup regime were exercises in analogical substantiation that occurred on both the level of
the individual and the level of the state. By this I mean that on one
level individual perpetrators inflicted pain on the bodies and minds of
women and men as a means to augment their personal sense of power
and masculinity. Through these sovereign interventions, individuals
exercised power to extract certainty or legitimacy from the victim. But
at the same time, many of these individuals were agents of the de facto
military apparatus. The extraction of legitimacy through sexual and
gender violence and the accompanying destruction and appropriation
of the victim's material property were attempts to crystallize the power
of the de facto regime, especially when its authority was denounced as
illegitimate by both the pro-democratic masses within Haiti and the
international forces outside Haiti.

Another likely reason for the escalation of violence between 1993
and 1994 was the increase in the number of paramilitary affiliates of the
coup apparatus (the atache and zenglendo) as these individuals sought

protection and economic security for themselves and their families—factors that had motivated individuals to join the Duvalier apparatus in earlier periods. I speculate that the increase also correlated with men's need to compensate for feelings of emasculation and disempowerment in the climate of ensekirite. The historic permissiveness of the military and makout apparatus and the impunity with which the terror apparatus controlled the population conferred greater political, economic, and interpersonal power on its members. Affiliation with the apparatus may also have conferred power on those in its members' kinship and social networks. In general, collaborators with the de facto regime potentially attained the masculine "ideal" through violence and extortion but also through violent, sexualized crimes against women *and* men.

Such violence conferred factuality or "certainty" on the de facto state when its authority was questioned by both the pro-democratic Haitian masses and international forces. On the international level, the U.S./UN initiation of negotiations between President Aristide and General Cédras to restore democracy in Haiti stripped the coup regime of power, thereby "feminizing" it. It also denied them desired or fantasized power on the national and personal levels. The reaction to this thwarting gave rise to increased violence against the people of Haiti and to an intensification in the use of sexual violence.

Cases of thwarted rape display the way sexual violence emphasized or reified cultural norms that may have been in flux. Human Rights Watch reports an attack that occurred on August 14, 1993, in which a policeman, two soldiers, and two atache, all of whom were armed, forcibly entered the house of M.B. in search of her father-in-law. In his absence they robbed the family, murdered her twenty-three-month-old daughter, molested M.B.'s cousin, and attempted to rape M.B. herself. However, M.B. was menstruating at the time, which prevented her from being raped. The family was forced into hiding after this event (HRW and NCHR 1994: 8–9).

Despite the horror of this story, it is striking that the very femaleness or "negative" power of menstrual blood saved M.B. from further violation. Considered an impure or profane fluid meant to cleanse and balance a woman's body, menstrual blood nevertheless represents a baneful source of power. In traditional Haitian concepts of embodiment, contact with menstrual blood endangers men. Girard asserts:

> To understand the impurity of menstrual blood we must trace its relationship to blood spilt by violence, as well as to sexuality. The fact that the

sexual organs of women periodically emit a flow of blood has always made
a great impression on men; it seems to confirm an affinity between sexuality and those diverse forms of violence that invariably lead to bloodshed.
(1977: 34–35)

It is possible that the presence of blood, prior to the rapist's act of violence, strips the act of its ability to confer sacrificial power on both the
individual male and, by extension, the de facto state. It is interesting,
therefore, that in the realm of necropolitics some cultural boundaries
remain intact.

OCCULT ECONOMIES

Occult economies range from black market transactions—illicit, unregulated traffic in commodities or other items of value—to the nefarious
exchanges to attain spiritual and material power that occur between
individuals and hidden forces. As discussed earlier, the Duvalier apparatus manipulated the symbols and practices of the baneful Vodou tradition to gain power. I suggest now that a dimension of the technologies
of torture perpetrated during the coup period was a means by which
pain and suffering were transformed into occult forms of capital or
spiritual power. As the following narrative suggests, these forms of terror were sometimes literally sacrificial or fetishistic.

Sylvain Charles was a young man I knew from the Delmas 31 section
of Port-au-Prince who resided near a police station known as a site of
egregious torture during the coup years. His friends had nicknamed him
"Preacher" because after converting to an Evangelical Protestant sect he
often gave extemporaneous sermons. I asked Sylvain about the different
styles of violence perpetrated by the terror apparatus when a group of
us were talking about events that had transpired in the neighborhood
during the coup years. Sylvain stated that while some members of the
coup apparatus had joined to protect their own families, others had
joined to gain economic and spiritual power. As our group continued
the discussion, everyone confirmed Sylvain's interpretation that the violence possessed a sacrificial, occult nature.

Sylvain stated that the killings had a particular character that marked
them as ritualistic in the baneful Vodou tradition: "When someone was
going to be killed, they would sometimes dig a hole and put them in it,
cover them with honey, and let the ants eat them. This was a sacrifice in
order to gain power." Two Haitian nurses with whom I worked at the
Human Rights Fund (one of whom was the daughter of a Vodou priest)

also discussed how such murders were ritual sacrifices intended to win the perpetrator *pwen* (power points): a force or immaterial energy that can be harnessed for good or malevolent purposes. As I elaborate in subsequent chapters, the *zonbi* (disembodied souls) of those who have died unnatural deaths can be extracted or appropriated, transformed, and cultivated for self-protection or to harm others (Brown 1991: 189; Davis 1988: 52, 59, 253; Larose 1977: 93; McAlister 2002). Zonbi can also be made to labor for their captors to acquire power or material resources.

Sacrificial forms of torture are not new in Haiti. The sinister form of murder by burial described above and other equally cruel forms of torture were deployed during the period of plantation slavery to discipline and terrorize slaves (De Vaissière 1909; James 1989 [1963]). Slaves were buried alive in tombs that they themselves were forced to dig (Pluchon 1984: 166). These burials took place in front of other slaves in an *atelier* (work group). Some slaves were buried up to the neck; then sugar was poured over their heads to increase the appetite of the flies that devoured them. Other slaves were stripped naked, rubbed with sugar, and tied near an anthill. To expedite the torture, the ants were poured over their bodies (De Vaissière 1909: 193–94). As in colonial Saint-Domingue, Haitian victims between 1991 and 1994 were forced to watch their loved ones being violated sexually, mutilated, or murdered. Like their slave forebears, men were "hamstrung" in order to prevent them from fleeing and to cripple them for life. During colonial times the slaves' anus or vagina was packed with gunpowder that would be ignited. The bodies exploded like a cannon, in what was known as the *bombarde*. By comparison, during the coup period many women were shot in the vagina.

The Episcopal Justice and Peace Commission was one organization that documented human rights abuses between 1991 and 1994 that confirmed the historical roots of neomodern torture in Haiti in the brutality of the plantation regime. Gilles Danroc and Daniel Roussière (1995: 44), who documented the forms of repression used daily in the Gonaïves diocese, made the following observation: "the use of methods [of torture], that in the end differ very little from colonial tortures (beatings, *djak:* ankles and wrists lashed together), attests to the integration of the historic heritage in contemporary Haiti."[33] These authors argued further that the violent remnants of this heritage in practices of torture prevent Haiti from becoming a free nation. While this claim may be true, what must be emphasized is that the use of historical forms of torture in contemporary Haiti suggests that the international political economy of extraction remains tethered to and buttressed by forms of necropolitical brutality. In addition to arising from the acts of individuals seeking to promote and protect their own interests, such forms of repression have always been linked to foreign and domestic political and economic interventions, whether of organizations or of sovereign states.

LEGACIES OF NECROPOLITICAL VIOLENCE

It is clear from the examples above that necropolitical violence has several purposes that are not always explicit. Over the course of the Duvalier dictatorships and in the postdictatorship period, traditional ideals of sex and gender—and the social inequalities that they encode— were shifting, in part in response to changes in the political economy of extraction. The blurring of boundaries between gender stereotypes occurred in a domestic context of economic and political exploitation and repression. The terror economy reproduced the system of predation by channeling some individuals toward a double bind: the choice to use violence to dominate others or risk becoming a victim. Those who participated in the terror apparatuses inextricably intertwined their identities with power at the state level. By resorting to domestic violence at the micropolitical level, however, these individuals attempted to redress the crisis of personal authority and legitimacy.

The de facto period revived Duvalierist methods, which reached new heights of horror. At the macropolitical level the de facto regime used technologies of torture against women, children, and the nation as a whole to extract power and authority when its legitimacy was questioned domestically and internationally. Nonetheless, interpreting the use of systematic rape during the coup years is difficult because of the complexity of the subjectivity of both the perpetrator and the victim. These subjects simultaneously occupied kinship, social, and political positions as members of families, communities, and the state. If an unarmed man in civilian clothes, thereby lacking visible insignia of power, entered a home to rape a woman during the coup period, it was difficult to determine whether he was affiliated with the state. Is this a case of politically motivated rape? Or is it a case of an individual taking advantage of the chaos to gain power and fulfill repressed desire? It is also nearly impossible to determine if the systematic raping was an unconscious (or conscious) strategy to maintain state power, reinstate traditional gender hierarchies, express frustration through aggression, fulfill desire, or some combination of all of these micro- and macrolevel possibilities.

As elsewhere, rape in Haiti carries a stigma that "taints" the reputation of the victim and her family (HRW and NCHR 1994: 20–21). There are many instances when a spouse, partner, or family has abandoned a rape survivor because of the imputed shame accompanying rape. It is precisely because of the massive silence that follows such shame that it is difficult to determine how many were victimized. Occurrences of rape during this period are estimated to range from five thousand to ten thousand.[34] Admittedly, it is difficult to determine the exact number of rape survivors, even after years of research. This is not solely because of the politics of truth described in the introduction and earlier in this chapter but also because of the shame and fear of speaking publicly about sexual victimization. For every person who did come forward, I suspect there were many times that number who did not. But as previously discussed, there are other challenges to documenting and accounting human rights violations.

Analyses of the sequelae or long-term psychosocial legacies of torture and terror cannot solely focus on the individual "body in pain" (Scarry 1985). As conceptions of selfhood, personhood, and subjectivity are complex across cultures, this depiction negates how torture targets the social body (Lock and Scheper-Hughes 1996). Scarry (1985: 35) has suggested that the senselessness of torture reduces the victim to a nonentity; that through interrogation and infliction of intense pain on the *individual* material body, the torturer has the ability to destroy language and the world. While this characterization is in some part true, it obscures how many technologies of torture are also attacks on kinship or lineage, family, and community, in addition to targeting the embodied individual. As necropolitical violence is deployed against the sexes, one aim is to reinforce idealized differences and power between men and women and to ensure both the long-term devastation of the economic productivity and the reproductive capacity of the individual victim. But another intent of such necropolitical acts is the destruction of social bonds between the direct target of violence and his or her family and community.

The ultimate aim of these punitive acts, beyond the initial attempt to extract legitimacy and power from victims, is to inculcate a state of social death and "natal alienation" (Patterson 1982). In this case, social death and natal alienation are the isolation of the victim from communities of responsibility—social, kinship, political, and economic

networks linking individuals in relationships of obligation and reciprocity. Many men, women, and children who were targets of torture and
terror now endure physical and psychological trauma alone. Numerous
women who survived rape acquired AIDS or other sexually transmitted
diseases. Some women have to care for additional children who are the
products of rape and whose presence is a daily reminder of their violation. Others continue to wait for their disappeared family members to
return from hiding—knowing they might never return.

One of the most devastating consequences of necropolitical violence
is its impact over the course of generations. As I discuss in subsequent
chapters, Haitian traditional culture conceives the person in material
and symbolic relationship to the extended family, including ancestors,
and the lwa. Thus acts of torture can be viewed as relational attacks
intended to silence and disempower not only the individual victim but
also the social community in which he or she is temporally and spatially
embedded. The physical assault and accompanying material losses that
coup victims suffered hampered their ability to maintain gendered obligations to partners, family, and the deceased. It is in the moral domain,
however, that the sequelae of torture and repression—psychophysical
debilitation and disease, the humiliation and shame accompanying
victimization, loss of social status, the stigma of rape, the inability to
maintain a livelihood, and in some cases the breakdown of the family
(among others)—are revealed. In this respect, the intention of torture in
Haiti was the destruction of society across space and time.

CHAPTER 2

The Aid Apparatus and the Politics of Victimization

MOBILIZING INTERVENTION

Human rights, humanitarian, development, and other advocacy organizations and institutions use similar strategies to generate the political will and material support for interventions across and within national borders. Both nongovernmental human rights advocates and humanitarian relief organizations identify and publish accounts of calamities across the globe to generate a sense of urgency in consumers of these materials. By raising awareness of emergencies, these interveners desire to provoke individual, institutional, and governmental responses to curtail abuses, mitigate disaster, and restore or build security. When successful, reports of crises across and within borders pressure nongovernmental and governmental actors in the international community to confront several dilemmas:[1] how to maintain a politically neutral stance of compassionate humanitarianism but also advocate for the rights of foreign and domestic others while simultaneously protecting their own international, regional, and domestic interests.

In the Haitian case, actors "on the ground" joined together to circulate the truths of the human rights crisis to audiences at a distance using exposés, documents, or spectacles of traumatic suffering (Boltanski 1999 [1993]: 3, 5, 12). The narratives were iconic representations of victimization that evoked pity and alarm intended to engender intervention to alleviate suffering. Stories of horrific violation in Haiti garnered the attention of many democracy advocates, human rights activists, development practitioners, and Friends of Haiti abroad. The moral response that these portrayals generated turned the gaze of principled issue actors outside the nation toward conditions of crisis in Haiti. However, these actors frequently differed in their approaches to the duration of an intervention: some intervened to witness and document suffering in the short term, and others attempted to reengineer societal structures and reshape individual and collective action in the long term. In the midst of a crisis, however, such distinctions may dissolve.

The process of mobilizing foreign and domestic actors to intercede in Haiti's affairs was protracted and controversial. There was tremendous debate about the meaning of democracy in Haiti and whether or not incidences of violence targeting certain groups should be recognized as legitimate human rights abuses. The representations of Haitian viktim were contested for their authenticity and devalued as mere rumor, fabrications, or outright lies, in part because these individuals were not members of political groups that the U.S. government had traditionally supported (or funded). Disputes about the accuracy of depictions of Haitian suffering generated accusations and counteraccusations about the competence of pro-Haiti advocates to document human rights abuses while resisting the occult charisma of Haitians who reputedly duped them with their stories. These struggles over truth occurred through the vehicle of several public incidents that recall the circuits of rumor, accusation, and "scandal publicity" that Lawrence Cohen (1999) has described in the organ transplant market in India.[2] In the Haitian case, rumors, accusations, and scandal concerning the truth of human rights abuses arose from struggles over power, knowledge, and policies that would be applied to those deemed legitimate "victims."

There are several examples of scandal publicity to mobilize political will and material support for intervention in Haiti. One instance of an attempt to foment outrage against U.S. foreign policy vis-à-vis Haiti was the public disclosure of the April 1994 diplomatic cablegram from the U.S. Embassy there, which questioned the use of politically motivated rape and the competence of the human rights assemblage to document human rights abuses in language that could be interpreted as racist. In addition to this, a series of stories appeared in the media that alleged U.S. government involvement in the training and even financing of leaders of the 1991 coup ("Nightmare in Haiti" 1994). In response, members of the Congressional Black Caucus led public protests against the disparate treatment Haitian refugees were receiving.

Randall Robinson, a prominent African American lobbyist, activist, and founder of the TransAfrica Forum, began what would become a twenty-seven-day hunger strike to press for the equitable treatment of Haitian refugees and for U.S. military intervention in Haiti. The hunger strike was much discussed in White House press conferences (Myers 1994a, 1994b). Ultimately, on the evening of September 15, 1994, President Bill Clinton addressed the nation on television to announce that the United States would be leading "an international effort to restore democracy in Haiti" by military force (Clinton 1994).

The impetus for the intervention was compassionate; however, the rationale for intervention was much more complex than a mission to save Haitian victims and concerned U.S. national security. Military intervention was portrayed as essential to prevent the unconstitutional regime from continuing its reign of terror in the emerging democracy.

> General Raoul Cédras led a military coup that overthrew President Aristide, the man who had appointed Cédras to lead the army. Resistors were beaten and murdered. The dictators launched a horrible intimidation campaign of rape, torture, and mutilation. . . . International observers uncovered a terrifying pattern of soldiers and policemen raping the wives and daughters of suspected political dissidents, young girls, 13, 16 years old, people slain and mutilated with body parts left as warnings to terrify others, children forced to watch as their mothers' faces are slashed with machetes. (Clinton 1994)

In terms of the politics of truth, it is significant that the statement acknowledged and validated the knowledge claims of the international observers. But the decision to intervene was also geopolitical. President Clinton cited President George H.W. Bush's assessment of the status of Haiti as one that is "an unusual and extraordinary threat to the national security, foreign policy, and economy of the United States." As an additional justification for intervention, he stated that in addition to the thousands of Haitian refugees receiving humanitarian support in Guantánamo, at the cost to the U.S. of hundreds of millions of dollars, "three hundred thousand more Haitians, 5 percent of their entire population, are in hiding in their own country. If we don't act they could be the next wave of refugees at our door. We will continue to face the threat of a mass exodus of refugees and its constant threat to stability in our region and control of our borders." The risk was financial but also clearly related to questions of domestic security, much as it had been before the 1915–34 U.S. occupation of Haiti. Embattled Haitian citizens were cast as potential threats to U.S. national security. Thus the logic of the 1994 military and humanitarian intervention in Haiti stemmed as much from concerns over America's image as a protector and promoter of human rights and democracy as from concerns for domestic and regional political and economic security.

Operation Uphold Democracy commenced on September 19, 1994, when the U.S.-led Multinational Force disembarked in Haiti to restore peace and constitutional order. Unfortunately, one intervention during this operation had negative consequences for Haiti's ability to establish accountability and to promote truth and justice during its postconflict transition: When the MNF entered Haiti, the United States seized thousands of administrative documents and "trophy" photos from FAD'H and FRAPH headquarters said to depict the torture of Haitian militan (the so-called FRAPH documents). These materials are thought to provide evidence of the terror apparatus's bureaucratic accounting procedures and may reveal the details of how the coup was implemented and sustained by terror. The documents might also confirm the systematic deployment of sexual and gender violence against the population during these years, as well as much more direct involvement on the part of the United States to foment instability in Haiti.[3]

Although the truths of rape in Haiti remain contested, the crisis and its representation during the de facto period engendered new programs, organizations, and governmental interventions in Haiti aimed at rehabilitating "victims of organized violence." International NGOs and Haitian women's rights organizations collaborated to create the Chanm Fanm women's clinic in Martissant. The fallout from the U.S. Embassy cablegram and the concerns about the public image of the United States as a defender of democracy and human rights resulted in the establishment of the Human Rights Fund in the America's Development Foundation in Port-au-Prince. By circulating between these two institutions as I traced the paths of viktim, I learned much about the political economy of trauma and the politics of victimization.

This chapter has two objectives. First, I present a cross section of the aid apparatus in Haiti that provided formal and informal support to victims in the so-called postconflict period.[4] The broad field of local, national, and international agencies and agents that channeled gifts and grants of aid to viktim occupied diverse political positions along a spectrum. Each possessed distinct ideologies regarding how to provide aid to others in need, as well as regarding how to promote rights, democracy, and postconflict rehabilitation. Each organization or agency operated in administrative bureaucracies of varying degrees of complexity and faced demands to document and authenticate the suffering of their clients, as well as to demonstrate the effectiveness of their interventions. As I elaborate in later chapters, these practices of authentication and justification were necessary, especially for institutions dependent on public and private funds. Recipients of publicly funded foreign aid, however, faced tremendous additional pressures to document, rationalize, and bureaucratize their interventions. While some of these actors collaborated, there was frequently tension, suspicion, and even antagonism between, among, and within these agencies and agents.

Thus the second objective of this chapter is to show that the aid apparatus is structured by dilemmas and double binds that are produced in part by competing and sometimes conflicting mandates and practices but also by a need to generate and justify the uses of funding. The aid that these assemblages provided was crucial to individuals who were attacked during the coup years but also contributed to the growth of Haiti's political economy of trauma. By mapping the linkages between and among the institutional actors over time, I demonstrate how terror and compassion apparatuses intersected within the political economy of trauma and generated new cultures and institutions.

Aid apparatuses are networks of international, national, and local governmental and nongovernmental agencies and agents that have a common "principled issue" (Keck and Sikkink 1998; Sikkink 1993) motivating their work or defining their identity. Aid apparatuses are also "semantic networks" (Good 1977), social webs of meaning making, and "assemblages" (Deleuze 1988; Deleuze and Guattari 1987; Latour 2005; Ong and Collier 2005), temporary groupings of actors that emerge, transform, and dissolve in response to the ebbs and flows of global crises such as natural and industrial disasters or political conflict. Like the terror apparatuses described in chapter 1, aid apparatuses also work within and establish economies.

In the Haitian case, such networks comprised the benevolent spectrum of the political economy of trauma, or the compassion economy. I define *compassion economies* as the finite flows of beneficent material resources, knowledge and expertise, technologies, therapies, and other forms of exchange circulating between the aid apparatus and its clients and between the aid apparatus and its donors. Terror and aid apparatuses, and the economies that they generate, intersect in the way each apparatus elicits truth or knowledge from its targets. Both categorize or represent their objects of intervention in ways that tend to reduce the complexity of identity and experience. Both can transform pain and suffering into something that is productive, but such practices are by no means equivalent. The transformation of suffering occurs through technologies of torture in terror economies and technologies of trauma in compassion economies. While I describe in this chapter the emergence of compassion apparatuses and economies in Haiti, such developments represent phenomena that can be witnessed globally.

The aid apparatus in Haiti comprised the plethora of governmental, nongovernmental, multilateral, bilateral, and private organizations acting to rehabilitate or transform the nation, including domestic agencies and agents. The primary goal linking the diverse group of actors and institutions was, in theory, the promotion of democracy, human and civil rights, and justice; however, each agency (and agent) possessed varying degrees of power and resources to implement this goal. Many interlocutors in the aid apparatus claimed that foreign and domestic powers that espoused support of Haitian democracy had actually fomented violence against the poor, pro-democracy sector. How and by whom such principled issues were conceived was a matter of life and death that pitted participants in both terror and aid apparatuses against each other through overt and covert means.

The aid apparatus provided humanitarian and development assistance to viktim in response to the necropolitical repression perpetrated during and after the Duvalier dictatorships and after the 1991 ouster of Aristide. This apparatus grew exponentially after the 1994 "restoration of democracy," leading many Haitians to describe its presence as an "invasion" (Étienne 1997). Thus, in addition to ameliorating the direct effects of political victimization, aid was distributed to viktim in recognition of the deleterious effects of chronic ensekirite. As waves of ensekirite crested, humanitarian and development interventions intersected, overlapped, and merged. Because Haiti's chronic ensekirite has meant that its states of "exception" or "emergency" are actually the rule (Agamben 1998 [1995], 2005), the call for immediate emergency action to mitigate acute suffering "prevail[ed] over considerations of justice" for viktim in the long term (Boltanski 1999 [1993]: 5).

I begin with a brief overview of the privately funded, grassroots actors and organizations that contributed to the creation of Chanm Fanm. I next provide a preliminary review of the politics embedded in the international collaborations between the ICM and human rights and humanitarian organizations aiding viktim. I end with an extended analysis of the publicly funded U.S. agencies and agents responsible for the establishment of the Human Rights Fund and other similar U.S.-sponsored "victim" rehabilitation programs. This section highlights the politics of democracy promotion and postconflict transition assistance abroad but also illustrates how terror and compassion economies can intersect. I discuss the ideologies and technologies of trauma employed by each institution as aspects of their broader mandates. Their ideologies, technologies, and practices to rehabilitate viktim generated benevolent aspects of bureaucraft. As aid resources diminished over time despite the persistence of Haiti's ongoing ensekirite, I observed that malevolent dimensions of bureaucraft began to emerge. As aid actors were perceived to employ covert bureaucratic strategies to generate personal and organizational power, discourses about such activities fomented accusations of illicit capital accumulation and even violent conflict.

BUREAUCRAFT

In the anthropological literature, witchcraft, sorcery, and magic have been foundational concepts to describe not only the benevolent and baneful practices of occult practitioners but also patterns of accusation regarding suspected occult activities. These practices and patterns are frequently depicted as emerging from tensions between members of kin or other closely related social groups in traditional or developing societies, especially in conflicts over land, commodities, and other material resources (Evans-Pritchard 1976). The social dynamics are not limited to societies of the past. In contemporary social groups across cultures, such processes have unfolded in response to general concerns about uncertainty, scarcity, and risk.[5] I argue that such patterns are not only seen in subjugated, traditional, or developing groups; they are also characteristic of modern, bureaucratic echelons of power.

In contemporary literature on modern witchcraft, concerns regarding justice and the equitable accumulation of resources frequently underlie witchcraft discourses and practices. Peter Geschiere (1997) describes the way in which conceptions of witchcraft in Cameroon encompass ideas of how the powerful accumulate resources and wealth, as well as ideas of how the weak "level" or eradicate disparities in power through occult means. As Pamela J. Stewart and Andrew Strathern (2004) have similarly noted, rumors, gossip, and the public revelation of scandal may catalyze accusations of witchcraft, sorcery, and magic, as well as episodes of social and political scapegoating and violence. Catherine S. Dolan (2002) has observed the unintended consequences of agricultural development efforts in Kenya in the 1980s and 1990s. When these interventions exacerbated existing gender inequalities through the unequal distribution of aid in the household, women threatened to use witch-craft or poison against their husbands as means to level these disparities in income. Under such circumstances of perceived injustice, witchcraft is a "signifier for the contradictions and tensions emanating from con-temporary processes of missionization, urbanization, state domination and globalization" (Dolan 2002: 663).

Similarly, the interactions between bureaucracy, humanitarian and development aid, and political economy in Haiti contributed to specula-tion about professional expertise, knowledge, and practices, as well as the distribution of resources in the compassion economy. Max Weber (1968 [1956]: 922) observed of bureaucracies that "administration always tends to exclude the public, to hide its knowledge and action from criticism as well as it can." He claims, furthermore:

> This tendency toward secrecy is in certain administrative fields a conse-quence of their objective nature: namely, wherever power interests of the given structure of domination *toward the outside* are at stake, whether this be the case of economic competitors of a private enterprise or that of potentially hostile foreign polities in the public field. . . . However, the pure power interests of bureaucracy exert their effects far beyond these areas of functionally motivated secrecy. (992; emphasis in original)

Just as professional practices can be used to aid clients, administra-tive experts cultivate the opacity and insularity of bureaucratic proce-dures to maintain power and to galvanize resources within a competitive field. In this regard, Michael Herzfeld (1992: 62) likens the work of state bureaucrats to the rituals of occult practitioners: "Bureaucrats work on the categories of social existence in much the same way as sorcerers are supposed to work on the hair or nail clippings of their intended victims. Their religion is nationalism, and their actions, like those of most ritual practitioners, pragmatically aim to draw the powers of the reified cos-mos into the pursuit of immediate goals." Bureaucrats, like ritual experts, employ ideologies and practices to achieve concrete goals, whether those of their clients or their own. As Foucault suggests, the processes by which power is deployed are not inherently negative or malevolent but can be productive. Thus the bureaucraft concept refers to a spectrum of inter-ventions that are perceived as benevolent or malevolent depending on the political position of the actor.

The shared goal of promoting postconflict rehabilitation, human rights, democracy, and justice in Haiti positioned the diverse actors in the humanitarian and development aid apparatus as members of a closely related social group, albeit with different degrees of power. Each actor functioned for the most part in administrative bureaucracies of varying size and complexity that permitted the pursuit of their clients' goals to limited degrees. Each institution employed technologies and practices that at times implemented "national" ideologies, even though they did not always act on behalf of state bureaucracies. Furthermore, actors in Haiti's aid apparatus preached the secular creeds of human rights, democracy, sustainable development, women's rights, law, and even psychiatry to their clients through a variety of bureaucratic and therapeutic practices, including technologies of trauma. Each actor also inculcated neomodernist doctrines of civility, governance, rights, and rationality that attempted to transcend the bounds of the nation-state by means of globalizing bureaucratic practices of transparency and accountability. Such practices are increasingly hegemonic in the domain of development assistance and are concrete representations of rationalities that have the character of secular theodicies.

Herzfeld (1992) rightly highlights how bureaucratic practices and the logics that they encode are more similar to the craft of ritual practitioners than they are different, containing aspects of divination, magic, and ritual. The aid apparatus employed diagnostic practices and logics that were means of "explaining away one's own misfortunes or the successes of one's competitors" (9). Secular explanations of suffering were employed in several ways. Administrative experts in the aid apparatus used professional discourses and practices to document, analyze, treat, and transform the pain and suffering of victims into something productive (Kleinman and Kleinman 1991), what I have termed the "trauma portfolios" (James 2004). They also used these same technologies and portfolios to solicit additional funding within finite compassion economies of varying formality. Such professional strategies also provided means to rationalize individual and institutional losses or gains.

For both aid donors and aid recipients, these bureaucratic diagnostic procedures were productive in that they frequently reinforced both individual and institutional security. Over time, however, especially in a field of competing aid institutions possessing limited resources, the malevolent side of bureaucraft was manifested in the aid apparatus as a partial product of numerous ethical dilemmas. The activist anthropologist Kim Fortun (2001) describes the challenges of representing the suffering of victims of the 1984 Bhopal industrial disaster in India for multiple, conflicting audiences as a "double bind." Advocates such as Fortun knowingly elided the particularity of the disaster and its effects in order to achieve global recognition of collective suffering and justice (Fortun

2001: 53–54). Double binds also resulted when actors were "confronted with dual or multiple obligations that are related and equally valued, but incongruent": "Double-bind situations create a persistent mismatch between explanations and everyday life, forcing ethical agents to 'dream up' new ways of understanding and engaging the world. They provided a lens for observing experiences produced by established rules and systems, yet not adequately described in standard explanations of how these systems function and change" (13). In part, what Fortun alludes to here are the challenges of working with(in) bureaucracies. These requirements produced double binds for these actors (and their clients) and contributed to the commodification of suffering.

Theorists of human rights and humanitarianism have depicted these ethical challenges as arising from processes of selective recognition. During a crisis or emergency the humanitarian gaze tends to focus on certain forms of victimization or victim identities deemed emblematic of acute suffering (Fassin 2007; Malkki 1995; Pandolfi 2003, 2008; Redfield 2005; Ticktin 2006). Selective recognition practices frequently generate "triage" interventions that remedy immediate or acute suffering rather than transform the structural political, economic, and social conditions that contribute to chronic forms of insecurity (Hopgood 2006; Redfield 2008). In so doing, interventions directed to categories such as victims of human rights abuses, rape survivors, refugees, trafficked women, or sufferers of other forms of abuses target their objects at the level of "bare life" (Agamben 1998 [1995])—at the biological or "prepolitical" body. This is in part because such interventions are frequently conducted under organizational and contextual constraints that permit enactments only of what Peter Redfield (2005: 344) calls a "minimalist biopolitics," a "temporary administration of survival." Thus, however well intended they may be, when triage interventions depoliticize the roots of chronic conditions of sociopolitical instability (like Haiti's ensekirite) in favor of immediate palliative responses, they can reinforce or exacerbate preexisting power inequalities between actors across and within borders (Agamben 1998 [1995]: 126–35; Terry 2002): "In the final analysis . . . humanitarian organizations . . . can only grasp human life in the figure of bare or sacred life, and therefore, despite themselves, maintain a secret solidarity with the very powers that they ought to fight" (Agamben 1998 [1995]: 133).

The temporal framework "emergency" is crucial to how selective recognition and depoliticization processes unfold in humanitarian exchanges, but these dynamics are by no means exclusive to contexts of crisis or states of exception. These processes also occur during interventions intended to have long-term effects, such as exchanges between donors and recipients of development aid (Ferguson 1994). Arturo Escobar (1995) describes how the "development gaze" objectifies general client categories such as women, peasants, the poor, or the environment as targets of intervention. The development apparatus "packages" or represents the intended recipients of aid through specific discourses and practices that transform them into highly visible "spectacles of modernity" (Escobar 1995: 155). During the period of unconstitutional rule in Haiti, the similarities in practice, intent, and expert knowledge that such aid actors possessed encouraged collaboration. In the so-called postconflict period, ideological and methodological similarities between aid interveners also contributed to conflicts over viktim as a specific category of political actors and to competition for finite sources of funding for their public and private endeavors.

Humanitarian actors in Haiti were obligated to use the transformed products of suffering, the trauma portfolios, as means to generate further material and political capital for their work. In the years after the restoration of democracy, aid for victims of organized violence diminished. Thus agencies and agents in the viktim assistance apparatus began demonstrating what Agger and Jensen (1996: 208) have observed in their work with mental health initiatives assisting survivors of torture in Chile: "The reduction of international economic aid has increased the internal competition between the different centres for the scarce funding which is available, although there is enough work for many more centres. The competition is also expressed on the intellectual/academic level with a limited amount of collaboration between the different centres and teams." At the same time, nongovernmental actors surveying the human rights crisis in Haiti also investigated the postconflict victim assistance programs created in response to this emergency. The results were disseminated using the print and visual media, the Internet, and other vehicles that could generate both "ethical" and "scandal publicity" (Cohen 1999: 147). Their goals were either to rationalize aid interventions or to question the occult motivations of other interveners. These acts produced a series of events that unfolded tragically over time.

The conflicts over truth, secret knowledge, and covert action ensnared both aid patrons and their victim clients in contests over the meaning of democracy, rights, and the best practices to facilitate Haiti's postconflict transition. In short, such conflicts were about ethics. In the context of these ethical and political struggles, Haitian clients began making their transition from militan to viktim. Over time these viktim adopted subject positions in this contested terrain of political meaning, although with unequal power. Their participation stemmed in part from desires to exercise individual, collective, and national sovereignty in order to determine Haiti's future but also to mitigate the ongoing struggles of living with ensekirite. In the context of ensekirite, even viktim learned to appropriate their own suffering through bureaucraft to generate multiple forms of capital.

Despite efforts to promote and demonstrate transparency, the opaque quality of bureaucratic administrative practices in the aid apparatus rendered the institutions and actors employed within them subject to rumor, speculation, gossip, scandal, and accusations of malevolent witchcraft. When these tensions went unresolved, the debates about bureaucratic knowledge and practices led to leveling, scapegoating, and even forms of violence between and among aid institutions and their clients, especially as scarce institutional resources declined. I observed a similar pattern outside these institutions in which the scarcity of resources and social instability produced predation in networks of victims' advocacy groups in local communities. These controversial dynamics in economies of compassion are also aspects of the political economy of trauma. Underlying these processes are struggles over power, knowledge, policy, expertise, and experience. In the remainder of this chapter I describe how these processes began to unfold.

DRAMATIS PERSONAE

In the early 1980s international political pressure on the Duvalier regime enabled networks of national and expatriate individuals and groups to promote democracy and human rights openly in Haiti. The 1986 ouster of Jean-Claude Duvalier gave grassroots NGOs the opportunity to reconstruct the social space they were compelled to abdicate during the dictatorship of father and son. Exiled activists working abroad returned to Haiti and established satellites of their foreign-based advocacy organizations. Expatriate Haitian intellectuals and others still living in Haiti also created new, independent organizations in the postdictatorship period. Their work revived the social movement for democracy and civil rights that had begun in the 1930s and 1940s (Nicholls 1985, 1996). The task that faced the democracy and rights movements was to reclaim social and geographic space as well as engender new forms of political discourse.

During the 1991–94 crisis years, these institutions and their partisans once again came under attack. As the international community responded to the crisis, domestic civil society associations linked in new ways and joined with international military and nongovernmental interveners to document the crisis and provide humanitarian assistance to Haitian victims. Some of these international groups maintained permanent institutional satellites in Haiti; others disembarked in Haiti with the U.S.-led MNF and left soon after the restoration of democracy. Several Haitian and foreign-based NGOs attempted to assess and redress the damage inflicted on the population through various networks of health care, information sharing, and support.[6]

The Development Research Center

The Development Research Center (DRC) was established in 1987, just after the ouster of Jean-Claude Duvalier. The institution worked to meet the needs of women at all levels of society, in particular, those living in the countryside and in *bidonvil* (slums), called the *sektè popilè* (popular sector) by residents of these areas. The DRC offered humanitarian and development aid through microfinancial assistance, advocacy training—educational workshops to help women organize in their local communities—and other programs. After the 1991 coup d'état, the DRC partnered with the Haitian Women's Association to uncover the extent of human rights violations that had been perpetrated in Cité Soleil, Martissant, and in rural areas. As many *viktim* were market women who had been stripped of their wares, the DRC provided them with small loans to rebuild their businesses. Such aid was important to rehabilitate their lives. It also was an example of how instances of extreme suffering gained victims political recognition and material compensation or reparations, an aspect of the emerging political economy of trauma.

The Haitian Women's Association

A similar analysis can be applied to the emergence and work of the Haitian Women's Association (HWA), which was established in 1986 to continue the long tradition of women's activism in Haiti. The HWA focused on social problems and gender-related issues for professional women, peasant women, and poor urban market women residing in the sektè popilè. At the time of the coup, there were general attacks on Aristide supporters and activists in the pro-democracy movement. Some HWA members were targeted not only in their capacity as political activists but also as women who had viable financial resources or employment at the time of the embargo. The DRC employed a few HWA members, so the two organizations began to explore together how to provide immediate crisis assistance and long-term rehabilitation services to victims of violence. Jointly, they were able to offer emergency medical care to victims of violence in Martissant and Cité Soleil and began to document the abuses perpetrated in these and other zones.

As their work progressed from 1994 to 1995, these Haitian activists recognized the need to establish permanent facilities that could provide ongoing health services, educational classes, and support in local neighborhoods. By summer 1996 the DRC mobile clinic was functioning in Cité Soleil and provided minimal emergency care to its residents. Many of its staff members documented human rights violations that had been perpetrated during the coup years while treating patients. The HWA established a small depot in Martissant that provided basic supplies, food, and other necessities to its members residing in the community. Through a partnership with Mothers Across Borders, the HWA also established a women's clinic in Martissant that was designed to meet the health needs of victims from the coup years.

Mothers Across Borders

Established in the early 1980s, Mothers Across Borders (MAB) is a U.S.-based women's human rights organization that initiated several humanitarian assistance projects throughout the developing world and in postconflict areas. MAB's founding members traveled to Central and Latin America to witness the plight of women who they felt were direct victims of U.S. covert military interventions in the region and pledged to document and share these women's stories of suffering. Since its founding the organization has worked with women worldwide through education programs, health and human rights projects, and other programs aimed at eradicating the political and social conditions that give rise to women's human rights abuses.

MAB's mandate is to hold governments accountable for their actions. The organization presents itself as a watchdog that informs its partisans and the world at large about the devastating impact of U.S. foreign policies. Toward this end, MAB employs both ethical and scandal publicity to evoke in its supporters a sense of urgently needed action, as well as concern and compassion for the plight of distant women. However, the use of these forms of publicity to turn the gaze of viewers toward conditions of distant suffering is also a means to generate charitable donations for MAB's human rights and postconflict assistance.

In 1993 the HWA sent a delegation to the U.N. Conference on Human Rights in Vienna to report the increased use of rape as a weapon of terror in Haiti. While at the conference they met MAB's executive director and staff members. Over time the two organizations discussed a political and material alliance to promote health, human rights, and justice for Haitian women viktim. Following this meeting, MAB sponsored delegations to Haiti composed of international lawyers, representatives of other U.S.-based women's advocacy NGOs, and academics to document the human rights violations from the coup years. To build support for this joint effort, prominent Haitian women activists toured the United States with MAB publicizing the horrors and the challenges facing Haitian women, while the HWA's local bases in Martissant and other urban and rural areas mobilized action in Haiti.

The DRC, HWA, and MAB also sponsored several groups of rape survivors that formed during and after the coup years. These survivors' groups operated simultaneously as human rights, women's rights, and victims' advocacy organizations. All these actors strove to establish a permanent clinic to aid women who had never had access to medical or legal assistance of any kind—especially those living in areas hardest hit by organized violence. The work of documenting cases of politically motivated rape was critical to the goal of having Haitian women's suffering recognized as human rights violations. Women's rape cases were presented before the OAS Inter-American Court of Human Rights delegation in October 1994 (IACHR 1995). The recording of traumatic testimony and its public presentation and circulation were also means by which these organizations solicited funding. After receiving private funding from independent donors and several U.S.-based church organizations, the coalition was ultimately successful in creating Chanm Fanm, the women's clinic in Martissant.

The Haitian Medical Network

During the coup years the Haitian medical community had been engaged at great personal risk in protecting and treating victims of human rights abuses at the State University General Hospital (l'Hôpital Général). Members of the terror apparatus frequently searched in this hospital for victims they had previously attacked, bringing the war against democracy into what many argue should have been a politically neutral space. At the height of the violent repression, physicians, nurses, psychologists, and other health care personnel also treated viktim in private clinics, churches, and other settings. Foreign physicians cared for viktim at health centers affiliated with international medical missions; however, most of these clinicians were based in urban centers that were inaccessible to the nation's rural majority. With the limited capacity of the Haitian state, physicians working in the public sector were unable to establish an independent, sustainable institution that could provide rehabilitation services to victims of violence without foreign assistance.

The MICIVIH Medical Unit

In February 1993, another international assemblage was instituted at President Jean-Bertrand Aristide's request, the UN/OAS International Civilian Mission in Haiti. MICIVIH operated at a level of much greater complexity and formality in the aid apparatus but still maintained close links with the "local" grassroots organizations and the privately and publicly funded medical professionals who were aiding viktim. MICIVIH was highly contested in the international aid apparatus, as were its attempts to craft a sustainable Haitian institution for victims of organized violence. The mission operated successfully until the security situation forced its observers to evacuate to the Dominican Republic in mid-October 1993 (UN/OAS International Civilian Mission 1995: 1).[7] Its observers resumed activities in Haiti from the end of January 1994 to mid-July 1994, when they were once again evacuated after the de facto authorities declared their presence undesirable (1). On October 26, 1994, on returning from its second evacuation, MICIVIH resumed its monitoring and documenting of human rights abuses. Other mandated activities were promoting civic education, addressing the problems of arbitrary and illegal detentions, assisting with the repatriation and resettlement of the internally and externally displaced, and facilitating medical care for victims of human rights abuses (2).

The Medical Unit, a small medical department within the MICIVIH administrative apparatus, worked with the network of Haitian health care providers and foreign physicians based in Haiti to treat victims of repression. The Medical Unit aided 587 Haitians, the majority of whom were targeted in 1994. When it resumed its crisis treatment of viktim after the October 15, 1994, restoration of democracy, there were more than 100 new cases: human rights abuses had continued unabated while MICIVIH was in the Dominican Republic. Less than two months later MICIVIH amended the Medical Unit mandate from the provision of direct care to victims to the documentation and certification of human rights abuse cases without medical treatment. The rationale for this change was that the records could be used to promote justice in the nation, should there be future attempts to prosecute perpetrators of violence (UN/OAS International Civilian Mission 1995: 5). The modification of the mandate also marked the departure from a bureaucratic rationale of "emergency" to one of "consolidation." By advocating a legalistic, human rights approach to reconciliation, MICIVIH attempted to support Haiti's legislative development. Nonetheless, this shift may have been untimely given victims' immediate need for therapeutic care and subsistence support.

Former MICIVIH members told me that the revision of the Medical Unit's mandate was complex and contested. In addition to the reputed rationale of judicial reform, another issue that influenced the decision was funding. MICIVIH could not pay for victims' orthopedic treatment and reconstructive surgeries indefinitely, despite the additional U.S.$60,000 the Canadian embassy donated for these services. In December 1994 MICIVIH signed an agreement with Médecins du Monde (MDM). It transferred to MDM the work of caring for victims and the task of creating a local permanent victim assistance institution. In 1995 MICIVIH announced plans for the establishment of the Haitian Community Clinic for Victims of Trauma in partnership with MDM. MICIVIH foresaw that this center would continue the work conducted by its Medical Unit between 1993 and 1995, as the latter would be terminated in February 1996 (UN/OAS International Civilian Mission 1995: 5).

In my early interviews with former members of the Medical Unit, I was told that the decision to close the medical department concerned issues of power, knowledge, and questionable humanitarian ethics. It was also personal. There were ongoing disputes in the general body of human rights observers between health care providers and nonmedical staff that reflected the tensions of a number of double binds. These disputes related to the extent to which observers could intervene to assist Haitian victims under the MICIVIH mandate. One of the primary concerns for the MICIVIH command structure was protecting the security of its observers and maintaining neutrality for the Medical Unit. Observers were exhorted to document cases of human rights abuses while deferring to the chain of command before initiating action to assist viktim. This position conflicted with the Medical Unit's health care providers' desire to intervene actively to obtain long-term biomedical and psychological care for their patients. Some members of the unit felt that an independent Haitian institution, rather than one created by MICIVIH or its affiliates, should assume the responsibility for future material, medical, psychological, and legal victim assistance. In effect, the obligation to follow MICIVIH regulations conflicted with humanitarian medical ethics. However, other disputes between the Medical Unit and the general body of MICIVIH observers influenced the decision to terminate the unit.

I was also told that there were contests for authority and legitimacy between the "human rights clique"—MICIVIH observers affiliated with the London-based Amnesty International and other international rights groups—and the physicians affiliated with international medical missions. One factor concerned expertise in using technologies of trauma to document and verify human rights abuses in Haiti. The MICIVIH human rights observers did not possess equal skills in assessing human rights abuse cases. Civilian observers were trained to use a violation checklist to record and classify testimonies of alleged abuses. This diagnostic assessment tool categorized human rights infringements under the following subheadings: violations of the right to life; the right to integrity, security, and liberty of the person; the right to freedom of expression and association; and the right to justice. The use of the checklist to document and verify human rights abuses was somewhat limited in terms of its reliability. Observers depended on the oral testimony of complainants and witnesses or the reports of local NGOs that were considered reputable and competent to authenticate such allegations.[8] Many MICIVIH observers had limited to no fluency in Haitian Creole, which is the language of the majority of Haitians and especially of the poor pro-democracy activists.[9] These limitations contributed to the reliance on local Haitian aid actors to verify reports of abuse. The need for local Haitian information brokers to supply and authenticate stories of traumatic suffering was a factor causing U.S. political officers to dispute the accuracy of their work. At least two of the Medical Unit's members were fluent in Haitian Creole, which gave them an advantage in communicating directly with Haitian victims.

The use of therapeutic skills provided another means by which health practitioners could document and verify human rights abuse cases. In a statement made a few months after the April 1994 U.S. Embassy cablegram questioned the veracity of reports of systematic rape, the U.N. Mission stated that the use of medical technologies and practices to document human rights abuses cases engendered more credible trauma portfolios:

> Many relevant medical tasks, ranging from physical examination of individuals to forensic exhumation of mass graves[,] can produce evidence of abuse which is usually more credible and less vulnerable to challenge than traditional methods of case reporting. Such medical documentation is far more difficult to refute than oral or written testimonies of abuse, no matter how well corroborated by witnesses. (UN/OAS International Civilian Mission 1995: 4)

In addition to completing the questionnaires and checklists to document a human rights case, Medical Unit physicians were able to provide hands-on assessments of physical evidence as they evaluated Haitian victims. Their scientific and forensic training lent greater authority to the Medical Unit members' human rights appraisals; however, these observers did not possess bureaucratic power in the Mission.

I learned through my interviews with other MICIVIH staff members that there was competition between what were essentially political factions within the general Mission. Observers affiliated with Amnesty International were viewed as having acquired positions of power and influence, despite their lesser experience and expertise. Some of the African observers claimed that, despite their superior qualifications, individuals who did not have college degrees sometimes supervised them. These human rights observers had personal relationships with others higher up in the chain of command, which supported the view that nepotism and patronage were keys to acquiring lucrative positions in the U.N.[10]

Furthermore, the overall quality of the dossiers assembled by the general body of human rights observers can be questioned. Between 1997 and 1999 I asked MICIVIH Executive Director Colin Granderson in person and in writing for access to the victims' case files for my research. I assured him I would protect the identity of those whose cases had been documented. Each time I was told that the files were not in good shape or that key personnel who managed the archives were unavailable to assist me. I also asked the deputy director of the Human Rights Unit, the Argentine lawyer Rodolfo Mattarollo, for the same academic privilege. Finally, I was told in an interview with Mattarollo that fewer than eighty-five written human rights cases were of sufficient quality and credibility to have been forwarded to the National

Commission for Truth and Justice (CNVJ) and that it would be impossible for me to have access to the archive.

It is troubling that so few case files of traumatic suffering had been deemed of sufficient quality to warrant their inclusion in the work of the Haitian truth commission. MICIVIH states, "At its peak in October 1993 MICIVIH's staff had reached 230 people of 45 nationalities, and its observers operated from 13 offices spread throughout all Haiti's nine geographic departments. As of August, 1995, the Mission had 193 human rights staff (89 OAS, 104 UN in post) operating from its headquarters at the Montagne Noire above Pétionville and 11 regional offices" (UN/OAS International Civilian Mission 1995: 1). MICIVIH reports that it transmitted 142 cases to the CNVJ. Of these, the CNVJ chose 73 cases as "priorities" emblematic of the repression employed by the de facto regime. How is it possible that so few cases were deemed legitimate or representative, given the number of observers, their length of time in the field, their expertise, and the amount of resources deployed to support them?[11] Had MICIVIH and the CNVJ chosen to present the most robust trauma portfolios rather than the aggregate of alleged violations in order to have greater impact? Is such a selective representation an accurate portrayal of truth? Or were there in fact questions of veracity in the information accumulated by the ICM, as was maintained in the U.S. Embassy cablegram? I suspect that the Medical Unit compiled the case files that were forwarded to the CNVJ, especially given MICIVIH's stated judgment that the medical department dossiers were those with the most credible evidence. In light of this, the rationale to close the unit at the time becomes more perplexing.

The February 1996 closing of the Medical Unit caused another conflict within MICIVIH regarding the ownership of human rights case files, the trauma portfolios. Medical Unit staff stated that for bureaucratic reasons the Mission refused to release a victim's dossier to the individual about whom it had been compiled, despite the fact that the documents might be beneficial for that individual's long-term pursuit of justice. Instead, all the medical case files were transferred to MDM and soon appeared under their own institutional letterhead, as if the data were movable goods or valuable territory to be sold, traded, or usurped. Although a proposal to create a sustainable Haitian victim assistance institution emerged from the controversial partnership between MICIVIH and MDM, no attention was given to the possibility of future problems related to treating trauma portfolios as intellectual property.

M'AP VIV

In February and June 1995 MICIVIH held two "Days of Reflection" on repression and psychological trauma in preparation for the task of inaugurating a permanent rehabilitation center in Haiti for victims of organized violence. Like the joint work of the DRC, the HWA, and MAB, MICIVIH formed a committee after the first Day of Reflection to explore how to establish a sustainable institution that could address the long-term psychosocial needs of victims of violence. Among those who participated in these early meetings were members of the Medical Unit, members of the Haitian mental health community with whom I would later train in Boston and in Haiti, Haitian rights activists, and foreign health professionals. Like the collaboration between the DRC, HWA, and MAB, these participants organized viktim into an advocacy association—in this case, M'AP VIV, the Assistance Movement for Victims of Organized Violence (Le Mouvement d'Appui aux Victimes de Violence Organisée).[12] It was anticipated that M'AP VIV would eventually evolve into a sustainable organization that would carry on the initiative to create a permanent rehabilitation center for victims of human rights abuses in Haiti.

That M'AP VIV was being positioned as a long-term actor with the technical capacity to serve the needs of victims of human rights abuses is indicated by the bureaucratic rationalization of its tasks. In its organizational literature M'AP VIV presented itself as an association that would "be a hope for those who had been humiliated, tortured and raped to be able to live tomorrow without fear, shame and guilt." It would be a "wager [pari] for the future and against forgetting" the violence of the past. Its principal objective was the rehabilitation of victims of organized violence. As described in its institutional literature, M'AP VIV's "scope of work" was the following:

- to train individuals capable of intervening at the community level with the victim population;
- to support the establishment of projects aimed at the physical and mental recuperation of the victim population as well as their social and economic rehabilitation;
- to analyze social realities that result in organized violence;
- to educate the public in general and local institutions regarding these questions;
- to find legal assistance for victims; and

- to establish a network of popular organizations and notably the organizations of victims around the project M'AP VIV.

As a further indication of the professional development of this organization, in September 1995 M'AP VIV began to train small groups of victims as *"intervenants"* (local investigators or interveners) who worked at the community level to identify victims needing assistance. In addition to making contact with local human rights organizations and victims' associations, M'AP VIV established links with international human rights groups.[13]

The expansion and specialization of victim assistance organizations was inevitably political and politicized, even as such organizations aided in the transformation of militan into viktim. For example, as the MDM/M'AP VIV partnership began to function, some members of the Medical Unit felt that a "coup d'état" had taken place that forced them out of the UN/OAS Mission. Such complaints about how bureaucratic decisions were made through covert political machinations were aspects of bureaucraft.

In fall 1997 Dr. Christine Thomas, a former member of the Medical Unit who later directed the Human Rights Fund Rehabilitation Program, spoke about the politics of victim assistance in Haiti in my interview with her. Dr. Thomas had training in psychology, philosophy, and ethnopsychiatry, a method of cross-cultural psychotherapy developed by the "Hungarian-born, French and U.S.-trained anthropologist-psychoanalyst George Devereux" and the Haitian psychiatrist Louis Mars (Gaines 1992: 4). In the 1970s and early 1980s Thomas had studied with Devereux and his protégé, Tobie Nathan, in France. She later completed research in clinical psychology and clinical ethnopsychiatry with Haitian refugees in the Caribbean and Canada.[14] Thomas was also a survivor of organized violence. On more than one occasion her family was threatened when her former husband, a prominent Haitian intellectual, had been targeted after the ouster of Jean-Claude Duvalier. These attacks on her household took place during the postdictatorship period when the reciprocal violence between pro- and antidemocratic sectors accelerated. Eventually she and her family had to flee. It was during her exile from Haiti that Thomas conducted research and therapeutic work with Haitian refugees. Her expertise in the needs of Haitians and her experience with the volatile political shifts in Haiti made her an attractive candidate for the U.N.'s rehabilitation work in Haiti.

During the 1994 evacuation to the Dominican Republic, MICIVIH recognized that its Medical Unit lacked a psychotherapeutic component—not only to assist Haitians but also to provide emotional support for its own civilian human rights observers. Such additional support to MICIVIH staff was essential if they were to resume work in Haiti after the restoration of democracy. Some observers already suffered from the stresses of the work, so Dr. Thomas was invited to take charge of this new service. She joined the U.N. early in 1995; however, she had been with MICIVIH for less than a year when institutional politics unfurled in a manner that ended her position. With a lingering sense of exasperation and anger, Thomas described having been sent by MICIVIH in January 1996 to participate in a ten-day training session with the Copenhagen-based International Rehabilitation Council for Torture Victims (IRCT).[15] On her return to Haiti she discovered that both her position and that of Raphael Manata, an African emergency physician working with the Medical Unit, had been suspended when the Medical Unit was terminated.

Dr. Thomas and Dr. Manata both expressed chagrin at the abrupt curtailment of the Medical Unit and their employment. They maintained that much of their previous work to articulate a strategy for the long-term rehabilitation of Haitian viktim had been usurped during institutional politicking and covert deals between other human rights organizations. Both alleged that when MICIVIH's Department for the Promotion and Protection of Human Rights (Département pour la Promotion et la Protection des Droits de l'homme, DPPDH) came under the direction of a member of another international human rights organization, the National Coalition for Haitian Rights (NCHR),[16] they were forced out of MICIVIH.

There is some evidence corroborating these accusations of hidden politicking and competition in the aid apparatus. When one compares early MICIVIH reports describing the activities of the Medical Unit with the institutional history presented in the DPPDH's June 1997 volume, *Haiti: Droits de l'Homme et Réhabilitation des Victimes* (Human Rights and the Rehabilitation of Victims), there are factual discrepancies. Major differences concern the timing and authorship of the idea to create an independent Haitian victim assistance center. The 1997 document states that MDM itself initiated this effort:

> In 1995, the Medical Unit [UM] pursued the work of assistance while collaborating, in view toward relief [from the activity of direct assistance], with the establishment of the Médecins du Monde Mission and the development of the local organization MAP VIV.
>
> In April 1995, at the request of MICIVIH's Director of Human Rights, the organization "Amnesty International" commissioned an expert

physician to evaluate, on the one hand, the needs of the population of victims, and on the other hand, the possibility to put in place an assistance network organized for the rehabilitation of victims.

In accord with the work undertaken by the UM, the expert recommended notably: to continue the initiative of training and education alongside health professionals and social scientists; to support the development of a community network for medical and psychological assistance.

In this sense, in February of 1996, again with relief *[relève]*[17] assured by Médecins du Monde, the UM stopped its activities, and the Department for the Promotion and Protection of Human Rights put in place a program destined to encourage local initiatives in favor of rehabilitation of victims. (UN/OAS International Civilian Mission 1997: 19)

The partnership between MICIVIH, MDM, and M'AP VIV was just one controversial linkage in the assemblage of institutions acting locally to assist Haitian victims. It emerged within a contested field in which aid actors vied for power to control the trauma portfolios and to represent and rehabilitate the population of Haitian viktim.

MICIVIH, MDM, and M'AP VIV professionalized, routinized, and propagated victim assistance efforts in Haiti. The intervenants branched out throughout the nation to form additional victim assistance and advocacy organizations in what would eventually become a small-scale humanitarian industry. That M'AP VIV had received international political support and financial backing from a variety of institutions ensured that it possessed the social and cultural capital to endure in a volatile humanitarian market.

The controversial status of the Medical Unit and its members and the debates about what professional techniques most accurately recorded credible human rights violations were aspects of the political economy of trauma. The accusations leveled by former MICIVIH members, from the general body of observers to the specialized Medical Unit members, indicated a high degree of political tension within the overall Mission. Speculations about the motives for bureaucratic decisions—as well as the technologies that supported them—were nascent aspects of negative bureaucraft within the political economy of trauma that escalated in frequency and severity over time.

Fondasyon 30 Sektanm

The final Haitian victims' advocacy organization introduced here would find itself at the heart of contests between viktim, the Government of

Figure 2. Place des Martyrs, Port-au-Prince. Photo credit: Erica Caple James

Haiti, and actors in the international aid apparatus over the just dis-
tribution of aid to victims of human rights abuses. In 1996 Françoise
Boucard, former president of the National Commission for Truth and
Justice, and Pierre-Antoine Lovinsky,[18] a founding member of M'AP
VIV and representative of the National Office for Migration (Office
National pour la Migration, ONM), formed the Fondasyon 30 Sektanm
(the September 30 Foundation). Its goal was to represent survivors of
the September 30, 1991, coup d'état.

In 1997 Fondasyon activities kept the quest for rehabilitation, justice, and reparations for victims from the coup period in the public eye
through meetings with staff in the Ministry of Justice, September 30
commemorative events, and other activities. Early in 1998 the organization began to hold weekly sit-ins and marches at the Place des Martyrs—a monument for coup victims located near the Champs de Mars
and the National Palace in Port-au-Prince. These marches recalled the
peaceful protests of the Mothers and Grandmothers of Plaza de Mayo
in Argentina (Arditti 1999).

By fall 1998 the organization had grown in influence and gained
greater political visibility. In a proposal for funding submitted to the
Ministry of Justice, the Fondasyon promoted itself as an umbrella

organization for victims' associations, with representatives in seven of nine departments. During the time of my research the organization remained closely linked with MICIVIH's M'AP VIV.

Bureau Poursuites et Suivi pour les Victimes

The Government of Haiti had limited capacity to assist viktim through specific programs and funding but remained an influential broker between local, national, and international aid organizations and through partnerships with institutions such as the Human Rights Fund. The state's practices and initiatives to remedy the suffering of Haitian-viktim would also render the state subject to charges of corruption, nepotism, and processes that can be recognized as bureaucraft. In fall 1997 the Ministry of Justice began to consult with international and national human rights organizations about its intent to establish the Bureau Poursuites et Suivi pour les Victimes (Proceedings and Follow-up Office for Victims, BPS) through which to begin implementing some of the recommendations of Haiti's CNVJ. Organizations that partici-pated in these consultations included the Justice and Peace Commission, the Human Rights Fund, MDM, M'AP VIV, Fondasyon 30 Sektanm, the Bureau des Avocats Internationaux (Office of International Law-yers, BAI),[19] the Aristide Foundation for Democracy, victims' organiza-tions from all parts of the country, and various organizations within Haitian civil society.

The ministry formally announced the establishment of the BPS in a press release on February 13, 1998. The release listed particular violent episodes and patterns of systematic terror to which Haitians had been subjected in recent years. After cataloging categories of victims of politi-cally motivated brutality, the ministry stated:

> The Haitian population is thirsty for justice. The history of our judicial institutions, marked by the negation of law and by arbitrariness, exacer-bated the frustrations of those to whom it is accountable. . . . Impunity is sustained as much by infrastructural failures [carences] as by the absence of political will or by corruption and the carelessness [incurie] of the judicial apparatus. . . . To overthrow the state of general denial of justice, to move beyond [enterrer] crime, injustice and to establish a true democracy, it is necessary to work against the culture of impunity.

The BPS was designated as the state institution that would implement these goals, as well as distribute reparations to victims. The minis-try provided the BPS with 60 million *gourdes,* approximately U.S.$4 million at the time. The funds were allocated for legal, medical, and economic assistance and a public media campaign to help victims gain justice. Other aims of the BPS were the following: to build sustainable social peace through the reestablishment of judicial authority founded on the rule of law and the legitimate use of force, to prevent the reemergence of summary justice, to guarantee the rights of the person to life and physical integrity, to promote the spread of fundamental human rights, and to restore public confidence in the powers vested in the state.

From 1997 to 1999 the BPS provided medical assistance primarily by brokering referrals to other programs that offered medical care to victims of human rights abuses, in particular, the Human Rights Fund. Viktim received direct care through the HRF medical referral network discussed below. Because of its limited capacity, the Haitian state did not distribute direct economic grants or reparations to individual viktim. Assistance was, therefore, *collective* and infrastructural. The BPS distributed the CNVJ report, met with victims' organizations throughout the nation, helped victims with the preparation of legal dossiers, and funded some of the development efforts of victims' organizations. Prominent among the organizations receiving support was the Fondasyon 30 Sektanm, founded by Françoise Boucard.

In addition to working with national and international partners, the BPS funded projects to build schools and distribute school materials. It also financed projects to rebuild homes that had been destroyed during the coup years in the Northern, Artibonite, Western, and Southern Departments. Furthermore, the BPS established memorial sites and "supported the struggle for the demands for restitution [*revendications*]" of the society's majority (Ministère de la Justice et de la Sécurité Publique 1999: 6–7). Over the course of its activity from 1998 to 1999, when the BPS closed in the heat of controversy, these funds sparked competition and contention among victim advocacy groups. Disputes over these funds would also contribute to the untimely demise of the Human Rights Fund Rehabilitation Program.

U.S.-FUNDED POLITICAL DEVELOPMENT PROGRAMS

Many of the victims' assistance and advocacy groups described above were considered Haitian "civil society" organizations, even as their membership, founding partners, and supporters were local, national, and international. There were also parallel "Haitian" victim assistance institutions more closely tied to U.S. governmental efforts to promote democracy and human rights in Haiti. The presence of U.S.-sponsored programs providing aid to others who were considered "victims" further politicized and polarized the aid apparatus. Among these efforts, the ADF Human Rights Fund was a controversial, ambiguous, and malleable institution with which many of the aforementioned individuals and organizations would eventually collaborate. Rumor, gossip, accusations, and scandal about this institution, its personnel, and its programs in Haiti would emerge within flows of speculation about U.S. political development assistance abroad.

The Human Rights Fund I

Just days after the leaking and dissemination of the April 12, 1994, U.S. Embassy memo, the CBS 60 Minutes news program aired "Nightmare in Haiti," an exposé that further damaged the reputation of the United States as a supporter of human rights. The piece began with an interview of the coup's leader, General Raoul Cédras, who appeared disaffected and unapologetic when confronted with Haitian and international human rights groups' reports of killings, rapes, and disappearances of Haitian activists. The exposé also highlighted how the U.S.-backed economic embargo had far more of a negative impact on the poor than it had on the military regime.[20]

The program presented an interview with Emmanuel "Toto" Constant that was especially damaging. Constant is the son of one of Duvalier's former generals and an intimate associate of the repressive police chief during the coup years, Colonel Michel François. He is known as the founder of the FRAPH paramilitary organization, despite allegations that the United States was involved in forming what it called a "political party."[21] On October 11, 1993, Constant and members of FRAPH successfully faced down the USS Harlan County. They prevented U.S. forces from docking and disembarking as had been agreed in the plan to restore Aristide to power, the July 1993 Governors Island Accord. In his interview with Constant, Ed Bradley asked about this victory over the most powerful armed force in the world.

> EB: Did you think on that day you were standing up to President Clinton?
>
> EC: Yes, because he's the one that gave the order directly to the Harlan County to move and come to Haiti. So in fact, there was something between Clinton and me.

EB (voiceover): And on that day, if it was between Constant and the president, then the Haitian won. To everyone's surprise, a day later, the White House aborted the mission. Washington was fearful that American soldiers might be attacked and killed if the *Harlan County* tried to dock.

Sen. Tom Harkin (D-Iowa): Just think about it. Here we are, the— the most powerful military nation on earth. No one can even remotely challenge us. And a rag-tag bunch of thugs, less than a hundred of them, turns back a United States ship. And if they say they rolled President Clinton, well, I guess they did.

After the embarrassing failure of the United States to restore democracy as planned, human rights abuses reigned unchecked. In the face of such a loss to the "rag-tag bunch of thugs," the honor, strength, masculinity, and competence of President Clinton and the United States were at stake. Where did the Human Rights Fund fit into the picture?

The U.S. Mission in Haiti began plans to provide direct assistance to *viktim* in Haiti in the aftermath of these public scandals. The allegations of U.S. involvement in the coup d'état against Aristide and the failure to restore democracy in Haiti contributed to the creation of the Human Rights Fund:

> Haitian credibility placed on U.S. concern for human rights is low. The project is designed to demonstrate the commitment of the United States for the protection of human rights in Haiti, and to help alleviate pain and suffering of the victims whose rights have been abused. To regain and build USG credibility as a human rights leader, an immediate and significant change in the size and scope of assistance is called for through the Human Rights Fund (the "Fund"). (USAID/Haiti 1994)

Assisting Haitians at this juncture was crucial to the image of the United States. Aiding individuals and families who might otherwise have lost their lives trying to reach asylum in the United States was in theory a step toward building U.S. authority or standing with Haitian civil society. As discussed above, there were implicit (or covert) dimensions to this humanitarian concern. One rationale for aid was the need to secure the United States against a potentially threatening population of Haitian refugees. Furthermore, supporting these individuals was presented as a potential strain on state and federal resources. Thus the original Human Rights Fund (HRFI) was created in July 1994 and housed in the ADF.

Figure 3. America's Development Foundation Headquarters, Port-au-Prince.
Photo credit: Erica Caple James.

The creation of the Fund fueled accusations of occult motives for U.S. military and humanitarian intervention in Haiti on the part of Haitian and international human rights advocates that became more concentrated as time progressed. Since the early 1990s the ADF's Integrated Project for the Reinforcement of Democracy in Haiti (Projet Intégré pour le Renforcement de la Démocratie en Haïti, ADF PIRÈD)[22]—had been promoting democracy. During the coup period PIRÈD staff provided informal emergency relief to Haitians who were targets of political repression. Staff members sheltered internally displaced persons at their homes and on the grounds of the ADF physical plant in Port-au-Prince. ADF PIRÈD staff members also helped persecuted grassroots activists gain asylum in the United States through an in-country processing program that had been initiated in February 1992.

Rumors about the activities of ADF, PIRÈD, and eventually the Fund indicated the flourishing of a negative speculative economy in which the truth was an object of contested power and knowledge. In discussions with staff members who worked at ADF during this period, I was told that the involvement of PIRÈD personnel in facilitating asylum applications for Haitian activists and intellectuals was politicized. Grassroots pro-Haiti activists spread rumors that the asylum program was covertly gathering intelligence on Haitian activists. Secondarily, these activists alleged that the goal of the program was intended to "decapitate" the democratic movement by sending its active members into exile. Even years after its inauguration, accusations about the PIRÈD program and the institution through which it was implemented circulated in the print media and in discourse among grassroots NGOs and the Friends of Haiti.

In part, the opacity of bureaucratic procedures and concerns about the actors who implemented U.S. foreign policy and development strategies in Haiti may have contributed to suspicions about ADF and the Fund. The U.S. government funded HRFI with congressional approval as an extension of ADF's "Cooperative Agreement" with USAID/Haiti.[23] Its staff compiled a database of human rights abuse cases that were perpetrated during the coup years. In addition to this, HRFI provided emergency support to victims of persecution in Haiti from July 1994 until February 1995. The bulk of the assistance was distributed between July and November 1994. Aid consisted of "critically needed services, including urgent medical care and trauma counseling, temporary housing, safe haven and subsistence allowances, and legal aid, asylum advice and prison monitoring to nearly 2,500 families, including over 700 direct victims of violence" (USAID/Haiti 1995: 1). The standard weekly stipend for an eligible family of four was 250 gourdes—approximately U.S.$15 at the time. Some additional payments were given so that families could find shelter (USAID/Haiti 1995: 6). The Fund paid for surgeries for acute trauma victims through its affiliation with CITYMED, an organization with USAID support that had emergency and primary care clinics in the capital and rural areas. Counseling services were provided to victims through the Centre Médico-Psycho-Pédagogique, an institution under the direction of a Canadian psychologist. HRFI also provided financial assistance for the burial of victims: at the request of its beneficiaries, the Fund underwrote in whole or in part the cost of twenty-eight funerals. As the crisis period shifted to one of consolidation, reports of human rights abuses decreased; presumably, there was less need for emergency assistance. In mid-February 1995, therefore, HRFI shifted its emphasis to civic education training. By June 1995, when HRFI was terminated, USAID claimed that it had trained more than 740 Haitian civil society organizations in the use of its materials (USAID/Haiti 1995: 8).

The HRFI initiative was rejected by the majority of Haitian rights groups from its inception. Late in April 1994 the U.S. Mission in Haiti sent a series of letters inviting these groups to participate in "roundtable" discussions on the Fund's design. They were invited to participate as members of an advisory board that would act as "the conscience of the Fund." In response to these invitations, the Platform of Haitian Human Rights Organizations (La Plate-Forme des Organizations Haïtiennes des Droits de l'Homme) wrote U.S. Ambassador William Lacy Swing to inform him that as a human rights consortium it could not align itself with a foreign diplomatic mission. No collaboration was possible, especially given that the April 12 embassy cablegram had not been "clearly and categorically disavowed" (Platform 1994). At stake were questions of power and knowledge: not only was the Platform's reputation as experts on the human rights abuse crisis still discredited by U.S. actors, but the Platform rejected the ethical challenges of collaborating with an institution that was funded by the very government purported to have covertly orchestrated the terror between 1991 and 1994.

A July 21, 1994, letter that once again invited the participation of the Haitian human rights community in the Fund was similarly rejected. On August 1, 1994, the national executive secretary of the Episcopal Justice and Peace Commission (Commission Episcopale Nationale Justice et Paix, JPC) responded to USAID Mission Director Larry Crandall:

> While thanking those who wanted to give me this honor, I must make a point of saying that [participating] is not at all possible. And this I say as an individual as well as in my capacity as an emeritus leader of the human rights community in Haiti.

The additional July 31, 1994, response to Crandall by Father Hugo Triest on behalf of the Platform contained pointed critiques that will frame part of the analysis in the remainder of this book:

> While appreciating your effort I find myself, however, in a position that does not permit me to accept your invitation. . . . Here is why it is impossible for me to accept:
> * Saying that the Fund is "the fruit of dialogue between the Haitian Human Rights Community and the American Mission who had been invited to sit around a Fund that is already pre-established and functioning"
> * Not wanting to negate the need to come to the aid of victims of the repression, it is, however, much more important and necessary to work to cease the massive violations. Neither direct assistance nor programs of education will replace the need to take measures to put an end to this situation. . . . I fear that the Fund, in focusing itself on the victims, will drown in the efforts to heal the symptoms instead of the illness. What are USAID and the American Mission doing to combat the causes of abuses? Embargo. Sanctions. Refugee Policies? All those who are in

power today in Haiti are precisely those who destroyed the emergence of democracy in December 1990. How is it that they are still in power after three years? Yes, it is necessary to bury the bodies, but by not putting an end to the forces of destruction it is to compromise with . . . delaying tactics that keep this situation [in] crisis.

This statement was written before the "restoration of democracy" by the U.S.-led MNF. Nevertheless, it emphasized the need to address political and structural inequalities in Haiti rather than the symptoms of social unrest and ensekirite. Father Triest's response recalls both Agamben's and Boltanski's respective critiques of humanitarian acts described above that selectively recognize "victims" in their capacity as sufferers in moments of crisis or emergency. Combating the causes of abuses that contributed to multiple forms of victimization, however, was not easily undertaken or resolved with this foreign peacekeeping mission. The process of postconflict consolidation in Haiti is one that reveals the many conflicts between international and national governmental and nongovernmental actors over truth, sovereignty, and the meaning of democracy, as well as definitions of human rights and issues of political recognition.

America's Development Foundation

In addition to criticizing the process by which the Fund was established, Haitian human rights groups and their international partners questioned the covert motives for the effort while criticizing both USAID and ADF/PIRÈD as institutions. As I discuss later, this pattern of accusation and questioning of truth and hidden motives was something that also occurred *within* the U.S.-funded development realm between actors in federally funded institutions. What was problematic about ADF? According to its institutional literature ADF was established in 1980 as a tax-exempt, private voluntary organization (PVO) "dedicated to assisting the international development of democracy" through funding from "USAID, the National Endowment for Democracy (NED), international organizations, private foundations, corporations, and individuals."[24] In a proposal to seek additional funding for one of its Haiti projects ADF states that its "expertise is in assisting civil society organizations (CSOs) to build democratic societies and the rule of law" (ADF 1999: 1).

According to NGOs that are highly critical of U.S. foreign policy, ADF was not always focused on overseas political development assistance. GroupWatch reports that "prior to 1988, ADF focused on projects that helped people in the third world nations feed themselves, through improved nutrition and increased agricultural production . . . with U.S. PL 480 and Section 416 food assistance programs of the U.S. Agency for International Development (AID)."[25] By the late 1980s ADF was increasingly focused on political development assistance abroad.

Other civil society advocacy organizations that monitor the funding that the U.S. government grants as part of its foreign assistance have remarked that ADF's position as the institutional host for the Fund was problematic:

> This Fund is to be administered by a group whose parent organization was intimately involved with AID's (and the National Endowment for Democracy's) now-disavowed activities in Central America throughout the 1980's. America's Development Foundation (ADF) created PIRED (Projet Integré [sic] de la Renforcement de la Democratie [sic]) as the umbrella management unit of AID's "Democracy Enhancement Project" which began in 1991. As demonstrated in Central America, "democracy enhancement" is more properly termed democracy *intervention*, whether funded by AID or the controversial National Endowment for Democracy (NED). Neither AID nor NED has any credible track record in human rights. (WOH 1994: 18; emphasis in original)

ADF was controversial in Central America for receiving grants directly from the National Republican Institute for International Affairs (NRI)[26]—the Republican Party's channel for NED funding—in order to assist U.S.-backed Nicaraguan opposition groups.[27]

ADF began working in Haiti in 1985 shortly before Jean-Claude Duvalier was ousted as "President for Life." Its institutional literature states that between 1985 and 1991, its NED-funded civic education work in Haiti consisted of examining

> issues of democratic, economic and social development with members of the government, the nonprofit sector and private citizens. ADF, with its partner Haitian CSOs [civil society organizations], helped citizens learn about the importance of being able to voice one's opinions. The second phase of this activity led up to and followed the adoption of a democratic Constitution for Haiti in 1987. Technical and financial assistance was provided to Haitian NGOs with widespread and nationwide networks of grassroots organizations to undertake civic education to instruct Haitians in basic democratic principles and the content of the new Constitution. This led to ADF support for Haiti's electoral process through voter registration activities, get-out-the-vote programs and civic education programs with core information needed to participate in Haiti's first democratic elections in 1991.[28]

While ADF's "self-presentation" might seem benign and positive, Haitian pro-democracy activists and their grassroots foreign supporters criticized the controversial organizations with which it worked. The Washington Office on Haiti (WOH) also expressed concerns about ADF's programs in Haiti:

> ADF has two major NGO's in Haiti, IHRED and PIRED. . . . IHRED (Institut International d'Haiti de la Recherche et du Développment [sic]) is presented as a Haitian NGO dedicated to research and civic education pursuits. In fact, it was founded in 1986 with a $100,247 grant from NED to the Institute for North South Issues (INSI), a "non-profit" NED-funded organization founded in the early 1980's and dissolved when the Iran-Contra hearings clarified its role as a channel for illegal funds. . . . IHRED was vigorously involved in promoting U.S.-favored candidate [Marc] Bazin both before the 1990 elections and after the coup. (WOH 1994: 19)

I have not been able to determine the exact relationship between INSI and the IHRED project, or whether INSI was a subcontractor of or separate institution from ADF. Nevertheless, in its critique WOH goes on to make an interesting point:

> The kind of "democracy" sought in democracy enhancement is not one which reflects self-determination, real grassroots participation, or the interests of the poor majorities in Third World countries. . . . Democracy enhancement, more properly termed democracy *intervention,* evolved over the past decade as a primary nonmilitary mechanism of low intensity conflict. (WOH 1994: 20; emphasis in original)

According to this watchdog group, "assistance" and "intervention" are linked and sometimes identical in twentieth-century U.S. policies and practices in the Western Hemisphere. Strategies to achieve political and economic security for the United States often conflict with and contradict notions of security articulated in local realms such as Haiti.

Thus another important point to consider is how democracy and security are conceived and by whom. A speech given by former Secretary of State Madeleine Albright during the Clinton administration provides initial answers. In October 1997 Albright gave the keynote address at the conference "Promoting Democracy, Human Rights and Reintegration in Post-Conflict Societies." The following excerpt outlines the rationale for American participation in "peacekeeping, humanitarian relief and development"—activities that are sometimes arbitrarily separated both conceptually and in practice.

We do, after all, have a security interest in preventing conflicts from re-
igniting, spreading across international borders, drawing in regional powers
and creating a risk that our armed forces will have to respond to. We have
an economic interest in opening new opportunities for American commerce, and in preventing new demands on the resources we have available
for emergency relief and refugees. We have a budgetary and social interest
in helping the people of other countries to build a future for themselves
at home, instead of being forced—out of fear or desperation—to flee to
our shores. We have a political interest in helping post-conflict societies
to embrace democracy and to become part of a solution to global threats
such as proliferation, pollution, illegal narcotics and trans-national crime.
Finally, we have a humanitarian interest in helping those who have survived
the cauldron of war or—in a case such as Haiti, the cruelty of repression—
to revitalize their societies. (Albright 1997)

Albright states that U.S. domestic security, economic *and* political, is the
key issue in overseas interventions. Peacekeeping, humanitarian relief,
and economic development are expressly interdependent: these interventions target refugees or internally displaced persons for assistance,
relief, and management, in order to promote economic productivity not
only within the nations receiving assistance but also as potential new
markets for American commerce. Furthermore, Albright presents a neomodernist vision of America's manifest destiny. It is America's mandate
to promote and protect democracy, not only in the Western Hemisphere,
but also throughout the world. In this secular theology, democracy and
capitalism bring salvation and are the logical endpoints of all national
development.

In May 1999, in conversations with USAID/Haiti personnel in its
Economic Growth program, we discussed how the United States conceived the relationship between democratic development and economic
growth. One of the directors of this office offered a perspective that
countered the official political rhetoric of the United States and affirmed
that while the promotion of democracy buttresses economic development, it is not essential, given that many nations have become economically successful without democracy. This individual also affirmed that
conflicts often arose about foreign policy toward Haiti between USAID's
development strategies and the U.S. Department of State's intention that
economic growth occur through export-led development. Conflicts in
the rationale for economic intervention tended to disproportionately
benefit the business interests of foreign investors in Haiti and only indirectly strengthened the Haitian state's infrastructure and the economic
and political welfare of Haitian civil society.

In March 1999 I interviewed David Hunter, an anthropologist and controversial former employee of ADF,[29] who at the time was working with another political development assistance project funded by USAID, in order to gain additional perspectives on the relationship between democratic development and economic growth. Hunter was a charismatic expert on political development who typified the bureaucratic "sorcerer" or the ethnographic "spin doctor" (Geschiere 2003)—especially in his ability to shape-shift between the realities of rural Haiti and the halls of USAID/Haiti. The interview provided context for how NGOs became involved in exporting democracy but also the hidden or covert ways that policy is created and implemented. In the interview I asked about ADF's politics, rationales, and practices of political development assistance. Hunter discussed some of the mistakes that USAID had made in entering the democracy assistance sector in Haiti in the late 1980s:

EJ: So you just mentioned that AID has had more than one democracy initiative. . . . At what point did AID include democracy or sustaining it, strengthening it at all as part of its mission?

DH: Well, AID started way back in 1985 with a minimalist democracy program. . . . Their first support—project support—went to an institution called IHRED, the Haitian Institute for Research and Development[,] . . . headed by someone . . . who came out of the development sector, where he had once worked for the Haitian Development Foundation in a rural credit program. [He] was an up and coming young, bright guy who formed his own institute with the notion, I believe at the time relatively sincerely, of promoting open debate on Haiti's political situation and conducting a variety of research projects. It was his own little . . . "business," you know in quotes, in the context of development. He's still a player. He subsequently went on to a position which was somewhat compromising during the coup period, and he's now . . . relatively associated with the far right. . . .
In retrospect it seems, and no one could have known this, that AID made a big fatal error, not a fatal error, but a poor choice in terms of its initial assistance vehicle in democracy because the guy's later actions tended to be picked up by critics of U.S. policy. And accusations of continuing support to IHRED during the coup period, for example, and even following the coup period, dogged the AID democracy program over the years. Even at the time that we were establishing the Human Rights Fund it came

back to haunt us in terms of misperceptions within the human rights community that we were still working very closely with IHRED, when in fact we had not been. And ADF was involved as an institution for a long time and maybe way back when under the IHRED program, in fact, in the democracy sector. And ADF is also sort of a small business . . . and it's operated like a small business. . . . But Michael's [ADF President Michael D. Miller] background actually is in naval intelligence.

EJ: He admits it.

DH: No, exactly, it's not a secret. That also may have been a poor tactical choice from the point of view of USAID if they had known what was going to happen. It's very easy to criticize in retrospect. But at the time that they started in 1985 it was clear that Duvalier was on his way out. AID was looking—as was the U.S. government I think—to a sort of rapid transition to the technocrats who had recently returned to Haiti with Marc Bazin at their head. But Marc Bazin, I remember, brought back Leslie Delatour . . . and the Americans' plan—to the extent that it was a coherent plan at all—but their expectation was that with the fall of Duvalier, a more rational portion of the elite spectrum would take over. Marc Bazin came out of the World Bank and was very highly respected, Delatour came out of [the] Chicago Economics program, and they didn't foresee anything like what's going on here now. They can't really be faulted in retrospect for not having prepared themselves or positioned themselves properly for what was coming. I don't think anyone really expected this quite that early, back in '85.

Hunter's statements emphasized the ambiguity of U.S. intentions, whether to assist or to intervene, as well as the unpredictability of the political, social, and economic environment in which the United States operated. As discussed in chapter 1, the goal of promoting democracy was not one that had been present historically in U.S. foreign policy toward Haiti. Thus one might evaluate USAID's political development assistance as a form of recognition of Haitian capacity and rationality, and the choice of personnel and procurement structures with hidden political backgrounds as a matter of poor judgment.

When ADF's president, Michael Miller, came to Haiti to meet with the staff of ADF/Haiti, staff members and I had dinner with him on a number of occasions that shed light on the ideology of the relationship between democracy promotion and economic growth. He was open to a certain extent about the path that led him to democracy assistance work, noting that as a young man he had served in U.S. Naval Intelligence. Subsequently he worked with Vice President Nelson Rockefeller's initiatives to expand trade relations between the United States and Latin America. Prepared by his experience in business, he established ADF during the Reagan administration. When President Reagan announced that the promotion of democracy abroad would be a significant focus during his tenure in office, ADF began to pursue funding for democracy and civil society work abroad.

In June 1982 President Reagan announced an initiative called "Project Democracy" before the British Parliament as a "war of ideas" meant to minimize the threat of worldwide Marxism-Leninism (Carothers 1991: 200). By February 1983 the project was presented to Congress for approval but received tremendous criticism for its overtly propagandistic rhetoric. Two months later an independent, bipartisan initiative called for the creation of the National Endowment for Democracy, "an umbrella organization that would disburse most of its funds to four subcomponent organizations operated by U.S. labor, business, and the Democratic and Republican parties" (Carothers 1991: 204). Eventually more acceptable to Congress than was the Project Democracy, this initiative began operation in 1984.

After the cold war the emergence of newly independent states (NIS) engendered the reformulation of the rationale for USAID's assistance abroad. The new strategy was based on the idea that political (democratic) development *must* accompany economic development. Thus political development assistance—electoral assistance, judicial reform efforts, legal aid, human rights work, local governance strengthening, and other forms of "capacity building"—is still relatively new in the USAID development arsenal.

USAID increasingly outsourced its projects to for-profit and not-for-profit NGOs that were willing to compete for contracts in its development portfolio. These contractors are often U.S.-based management consulting firms or NGOs such as ADF that have experience in infrastructural development, especially agricultural reform. Initiatives like ADF/PIRÈD were among the first organizations federally funded as part of this accelerating governmental trend to assist "transitional societies." Like the Democracy Enhancement Program or USAID's subsequent multimillion-dollar Administration of Justice Program (AOJ), these U.S government–funded projects are lucrative, even when the parent institution is a nonprofit charity or PVO like ADF. The institutional procurement structure for these projects receives substantial indirect funding for overseas management.

The history of Hunter's development work sheds light on how USAID made the transition to promoting political development assistance, as well as whether it involved overt or covert military and humanitarian intervention. In addition, his statement raises questions about how the United States viewed the prospects for democracy in Haiti. On another level, however, Hunter's political development work raises ethical questions about the uses of ethnographic knowledge and the role of anthropologists as activists, advocates, interlopers, spies, or even mobile sovereigns of a different kind.[30]

> *EJ:* So in '85, do you remember what name the democracy effort was given? I've seen names like the "Democracy Enhancement Program." I've seen "Democracy Initiative" . . .
>
> *DH:* The Democracy Enhancement Program didn't start until 1989. That, I can give you the whole history on that. . . . Anyway, IHRED got the first grant.
>
> *EJ:* Around then wasn't ADF involved in . . .
>
> *DH:* ADF was the intermediary, but that was after the fall [of Jean-Claude Duvalier]. Then . . . toward the end of 1985 obviously things heated up here. I had the opportunity at that time to be in an informal working group that was comprised entirely of anthropologists—actually and this is just nasty stuff. It's great that you're going to ruin my reputation. Ummm, we were called together. We happened to all be in the country on various other activities. I was managing the agricultural project then for AID, _____ was managing the PADF [Pan American Development Foundation] portion of that program for AID, and actually you should be discrete about naming the people I am naming in your work . . .
>
> *EJ:* I'd ask for permission.
>
> *DH:* You can name me, but you'd need to talk to them or not. . . . Anyway, we had a little kitchen cabinet for the ambassador at the time. [Ambassador Clayton E.] McManaway was a career diplomat who was intelligent enough to try to find something out about the country as it was coming apart. And called upon

us—obviously amongst a bunch of other people—to talk through
basically on a weekly basis what the administration—where they
were headed. . . . And at the time the Reagan State Department
rigorously opposed the removal of Jean-Claude Duvalier. They
were quite comfortable with Duvalier's regime, they had as we
learned subsequently made considerable investments in intelligence assets in the Haitian Army and in the Duvalier government; and—Anyhow we were meeting with McManaway, and
McManaway was getting a lot of resistance on direction from
the State Department concerning keeping Duvalier in place. And
the fear at the time—as old-fashioned as it seems in retrospect
from the point of view of the State Department, in addition to
trying to preserve its assets and investments here—was that Haiti
would be prone to a Communist takeover in the wake of the fall
of the dictatorship.

Our job as we defined it amongst ourselves, the anthropologists, [was] to disabuse the ambassador of this notion and to
explain in very clear social scientific terms that . . . that was not
a possibility for Haiti, given the structure of the land tenure
system, given the social organization, given the country's history,
that wasn't even a dim prospect. We may have even oversold that
case, but we were all quite firmly committed to moving beyond
Duvalier—we didn't quite know where. . . . So McManaway
learned from us and began parading us in front of State Department officials who came down during that time at dinners and all
sorts of other things to make his case once he was convinced that
we needed to go forward. . . . And so it was that I was somewhat
involved in the advent of the dechoukaj and then essentially went
through it like everyone else who was here at the time. Quite
happily. It was a very interesting time.

Hunter was controversial within the pro-democracy sector for this previous work with ADF and USAID. He was also, however, a key actor in
the creation of HRFI and subsequent iterations of the program. A brief
history of our first meeting is relevant to this discussion of how bureaucraft evolved over time in the aid apparatus in Haiti.

In early 1996, before I began working at Chanm Fanm, I had been
criticized by a few American pro-Aristide activists for citing Hunter's
work in a 1996 manuscript, "'Political Cleansing' in Haiti: 1991–1994."
These activists claimed that Hunter worked for the CIA—rumors that

he openly discussed but never confirmed or denied. His notoriety centered in part on having been involved in political development as an anthropologist, reviving criticisms of anthropology as a discipline with historical links to colonial and imperial projects (Asad 1973). These accusations also stemmed from the critiques of development as a discipline.[31] I had also heard praise of Hunter because of his humanitarian work with victims of human rights abuses during the coup years. He was instrumental in aiding grassroots activists who were persecuted between 1991 and 1994. Hunter and his wife, Patricia Roberts, another anthropologist working with a project funded by USAID, had hosted internally displaced Haitians in their home in Haiti during the coup years. Hunter was also integral to the formalization of the PIRÈD crisis work as the HRFI program, which was in some respects a formal mechanism for the United States to provide limited reparations and institutional support to Haitian viktim.

I first discussed victim assistance work with Hunter in fall 1996 when we met at the Haitian Studies Association meeting in Haiti. By chance I happened to sit at his dinner table on the first night of the conference. Seeing his name tag, I realized that I had cited him in my manuscript. We spoke about my therapeutic and ethnographic work at Chanm Fanm, and he offered to introduce me to an organization of rape victims who had survived during the coup years by hiding in caves in the mountain range that ringed the capital. I also told Hunter about a victim assistance proposal based on Dr. Thomas and Dr. Manata's work with the MICIVIH Medical Unit that was going to be presented at the conference the next day.[32]

Dr. Thomas and Dr. Manata were critical of the supply and distribution of postcoup reconstruction assistance. International financial institutions and bilateral agencies such as USAID directed tens of millions of dollars toward "rehabilitating" and crafting new Haitian state institutions and personnel—for example, the former military and new civilian police forces. Millions of dollars were funneled through USAID's AOJ Program and other neoliberal programs to modernize Haiti's infrastructure. Few funds or technical support were earmarked to assist the poor population that the coup regime and its agents had terrorized. Thus their proposal was intended to redistribute postconflict aid to "true" victims.

Hunter and another colleague at ADF, Marcus Belmonte, attended the presentation. After its conclusion they approached Dr. Thomas and Dr. Manata and the four agreed to work together to find funding for what would become known as the Victim Assistance Rehabilitation

Program. The ADF Human Rights Fund became the structure through which USAID funded the rehabilitation proposal in April 1997. The Rehabilitation Program was proposed as a temporary project that would build the foundation of a permanent independent institution. It was intended that Haitian health professionals in collaboration with health professionals in developed countries would administer this new structure and that national and international funds from both private and public sources would endow it. Despite these intentions, the Rehabilitation Program was hampered not only by its institutional location within ADF but also by the unintended consequences of other U.S.-supported "victim" rehabilitation programs in Haiti.

HAITI'S OTHER "VICTIMS"

When President Aristide returned to office, the Haitian army was dismantled. A major issue facing postconflict transition efforts was how to reconcile the repressive force that had terrorized the Haitian masses during the coup years with the viktim they had targeted. In 1994 USAID created the Office of Transition Initiatives (OTI) under its Bureau of Humanitarian Response. In September 1994, just prior to the entrance of the U.S./U.N. peacekeeping mission, the OTI designed a program to demobilize and reintegrate FAD'H members into Haitian civilian society.

The program operated between November 1994 and November 1996. It provided stipends and six months of vocational training to former military personnel on the condition that they disarm, with the hope that they would find gainful employment as civilians. The U.S.$8.7 million effort was reportedly "paid by the Haitian government from foreign donor government balance of payments relief" (Dworken, Moore, and Siegel 1997: 1). The International Organization for Migration (IOM) implemented the program. Of the estimated 7,000 soldiers in the army, 6,250 were "demobilized" and 88 percent (5,482) of those registered with the IOM; however, "only one FAd'H officer participated in the program, and most of the soldiers did not enter training until after the U.S. military transferred the operation to the United Nations" (2–3). Of those who participated, 4,867 graduated, but only 304 found employment through the Opportunity and Referral Service.

> The low employment rate among the former FAd'H is due to poor economic conditions in Haiti, lower-than-expected economic growth, and the stigma of being a former soldier. The essential determinant of reintegration and security, though, is Haiti's economy. Without a stronger economy, the

former FAd'H will remain unemployed, alienated from society, and a possibly disruptive source of insecurity—though not one capable of toppling
the government. (3)

USAID felt that its program was instrumental in creating "breathing
space": the democratic process could be consolidated and protected
from the threat of violence that former FAD'H members represented (3).
Nonetheless, USAID acknowledges that the program had limited success because of its uneven coordination, its failure to link with other aid
programs, and the limited participation of high-level Haitian officials.

Understandably, representatives of the legitimate Government of
Haiti and other assistance projects that were supporting the "transition
to democracy" would hesitate to be associated with such a program.
However, another factor in its limited success was that former soldiers
viewed themselves as "victims" of the democratic process.

> Despite several efforts, IOM was unable to introduce civic education
> into the program (the FAd'H continued to view themselves as "entitled"
> victims of an unjust dismissal). There were also no *systematic* attempts by
> IOM to promote the efforts of some schools to foster local reconciliation
> through local projects, although IOM tried to support such programming.
> (Dworken, Moore, and Siegel 1997: 2; emphasis in original)

Supporting the view that the Haitian armed forces had been victimized,
former president and commander in chief of the Haitian army, General
Prosper Avril, described the entrance of the U.S.-led peacekeeping mission on September 19, 1994. He called it a day that was "even more
ignominious and shameful than the day of July 29, 1915 [the inception
of the 1915–34 U.S. occupation], because at this time the occupation
of the country occurred by the will of a Haitian who, in order to attain
his own goals, abused the legitimate authority given to him by a mandate of the Haitian people" (Avril 1999: xxiii). Avril accused President
Aristide of betraying the nation. Furthermore, he castigated the work of
other Haitian scholars who had written on the army as "accusations, as
a search for scapegoats or indeed as designed to only discredit the military institution, which they tend to accuse of being responsible for the
confused and chaotic situation of Haiti" (xxviii). Correspondingly, Avril
called the Haitian army the "mute victim" of the democratic process
(321): "My thesis is different. I am convinced that even though many
members of the Haitian army committed errors, a great many errors, or
had a reprehensible conduct, the military institution itself is necessarily
a victim" (xxviii).

Avril's assertions represent the perspective that the army had been humiliated, emasculated (or perhaps even "raped"), and was without a voice to protest. Nevertheless, the army received extensive assistance and preferential treatment in the immediate postcoup period in the context of a virtual amnesty for the military and its affiliates.[33] These personnel also received positions in the new government.

Policing and Public Security

In addition to the program to rehabilitate the former FAD'H, the United States supported a program for "victims" from both political spectrums—an interim policing force that would have devastating consequences for Haiti's ongoing ensekirite. This example also demonstrates the use of scandal publicity to diagnose causality or assign blame for the continuing insecurity in Haiti. In the uncertain political and economic climate, allegations of bureaucratic incompetence and occult motives for action, as well as blame for the failures of aid, flowed freely in print and public discourse between the United States, the U.N., the Government of Haiti, and human rights NGOs.

In October 1994 the U.S. assisted the Government of Haiti in forming the Interim Public Security Force (IPSF), comprising mostly former members of FAD'H (U.S. Congress 1996: 10). The United States attempted a vetting process to screen out perpetrators of human rights abuses during the coup years, but perpetrators were rarely identified. Former soldiers were thrown together with another group from the opposite end of the political spectrum: interdicted Haitian boat people from the Guantánamo detention camp. Both factions received minimal training in public security to support the MNF (U.S. Congress 1996: 9). These individuals, representing anti- and pro-democracy actors, perpetrators and victims, were funneled into the U.S. Department of Justice's International Criminal Investigative Training Assistance Program. ICITAP was one of the primary institutions recruiting and training the new civilian Haitian National Police (HNP) (HRW/A, NCHR, and WOLA 1997: 3–4).

On March 31, 1995, the MNF withdrew most of the 20,000 American soldiers who had disembarked in Haiti. The U.N. Mission in Haiti (UNMIH) took over as the primary peacekeeping force. By October 12, 1995, in a total U.N. peacekeeping contingent of 6,000, only a smaller force of 2,500 U.S. soldiers remained (HRW/A, NCHR, and WOLA 1997: 4; U.S. Congress 1995: 17). The transfer of the mission from the MNF to the U.N. had profound consequences. The U.N.'s civilian police contingent (CIVPOL) was among the institutions responsible for the new Haitian National Police. Human rights organizations raised questions about the competence of this body: "We are . . . concerned that CivPol field monitoring of the HNP does not appear to have been effective in preventing or stemming police abuse and the CivPol officers repeatedly defer their responsibility for human rights monitoring to the human rights observers of the U.N./OAS International Civilian Mission" (HRW/A, NCHR, and WOLA 1997: 4). Furthermore, an insufficient number of officers had been adequately trained to provide security when the external peacekeeping missions ended. The U.N. recommended that the GOH permit former FAD'H to train as new police. This decision was made against the advice of the United States.

The United States eventually cast blame for the failures of the Haitian National Police on the U.N. and the Haitian government. On January 4, 1996, the House Committee on International Relations held the hearing, "Haiti: Human Rights and Police Issues." Robert S. Gelbard, then assistant secretary of state for International Narcotics and Legal Affairs, stated:

> While we understand that the United Nations based its recommendations on feedback from its corps of 600 police monitors serving in the field, we nevertheless differed in our assessment and in our advice to the GOH. . . . [W]e hold our deepest concern over the inclusion of individuals in the HNP's ranks who may have committed criminal acts. We will not support a force which harbors criminals in its ranks. (U.S. Congress 1996: 12)

Violent conflicts erupted between factions within the HNP, especially in Martissant and other contested areas. These battles contributed to a pervasive sense of insecurity, and they were an indirect consequence of the lack of coordination and consensus among international interveners. An unintended consequence of this aid intervention was fighting between the HNP and gangs for control over crime. This is also an example of how occult economies can develop from political economies of trauma.

In addition to the U.N. forces and ICITAP, however, there were other national security forces involved in crafting the HNP. American, French, Canadian, and Haitian government representatives recruited men and women throughout Haiti to meet the initial goal of five thousand candidates (U.S. Congress 1996: 10). At the Haitian National Police Academy, U.S. police officers, members of the Royal Canadian Mounted Police, and French police instructors conducted the training. I was told by one of the officials managing the ICITAP program that the differing national and cultural approaches to policing proved problematic. Under the "merit-based recruitment" strategy, psychological and medical tests were administered to identify appropriate candidates and to exclude former perpetrators of criminal activity and human rights abuses. These diagnostic procedures, like the technologies of trauma employed by MICIVIH and other human rights groups, can be questioned for their validity. All candidates were reportedly vetted for past criminal acts (U.S. Congress 1996: 10), but despite such precautions, the international conflicts over the direction and tutelage of the police in particular and Haiti's democratic process generally created the conditions for a future struggle for power that would embattle Haiti's civilian communities.

As can be expected, in the months after the first class of civilian police had graduated and began acting as agents of the state, additional reports of human rights abuses surfaced. Conflicts between HNP factions played out throughout the country and contributed to the escalation of ensekirite in Port-au-Prince. Such abuses also were the impetus for the revival of the Human Rights Fund in 1996 as a victim assistance program for persons abused by the HNP.

The Human Rights Fund II

In July 1996, in response to reports of abuses perpetrated by members of the new "U.S.-trained" Haitian National Police force, the Fund was reactivated under ADF's Democracy Enhancement Cooperative Agreement. Under HRFII, victims of human rights abuses who had been targeted after January 1, 1995—the date when HRFI ceased assisting victims of abuses perpetrated during the coup years—were eligible for direct medical, legal, and psychosocial aid.[34] U.S. efforts to build or craft "local capacity" by encouraging nonviolence and the rule of law are striking examples of neomodern development discourses. They are also additional examples of how suffering can be appropriated (Das 1995; Kleinman 1995; Kleinman and Kleinman 1991) and transformed to create an image of accountability or legitimacy for the donor at the same time that there was authentic desire to do good by helping Haitian victims of organized violence.

The recognition of the trauma and suffering of Haitian victims of human rights abuses perpetrated by the HNP occurred in the aftermath of another public scandal. New accusations appeared in the U.S. media criticizing the U.S. government's failure to train a responsible Haitian civilian police force that respected human rights. The media leveled charges that the Human Rights Fund was a screen for covert activity. The reporter Tammerlin Drummond went to Haiti to investigate the HNP crisis in response to a report issued by Human Rights Watch/Americas, the National Coalition for Haitian Rights, and the Washington Office on Latin America titled "Haiti: The Human Rights Record of the Haitian National Police" (HRW/A, NCHR, and WOLA 1997). Drummond's article, "A Constabulary of Thugs," which appeared in *Time* magazine on February 19, 1997, was a devastating critique. It charged the United States with complete responsibility for the failures of the democratic reconstruction process in Haiti. Drummond had interviewed HRFII's director, an American sociologist who vacated the position in June 1997. The article pointed out the irony that the U.S. government spent $65 million of taxpayer money to train the new police force. Now taxpayers supported another U.S.-authored program to protect people from these same police.

Drummond did not provide a detailed history of the HNP, nor did she discuss the involvement of the multiple international and domestic actors involved in the institution. Rather, she described the case of a Haitian man who had been shot by the police without cause. After his family complained, they became the targets of threats and needed protection from police brutality.

> Fearing for their lives, Charles' cousin and brother finally did what many Haitians are doing these days when they find themselves abused, tortured or terrorized by the police. They paid a visit to the offices of an organization called the Human Rights Fund. The group offers a number of services, including a special protection program for people who have been savaged by police officers whom the U.S. recruited, trained and turned loose on the streets of Haiti in July of 1995. This, needless to say, does not come cheap. But fortunately there is a ready source of cash. That's because, like the officers who commit these crimes, the program to shelter their victims is funded by American tax dollars.
>
> Up until now this program remained a closely held secret within the community of American and U.N. officials who administer Haiti's billion-dollar reconstruction effort. . . . It was in the spring of 1996, say U.S. officials, that "we began receiving a lot of reports of killings and torture." At this point they started casting about for a way to protect the people who had witnessed these crimes. The solution was the Human Rights Fund. With the help of a $500,000 appropriation, the group has paid for the funerals of 11 people killed by the police in the past seven months and for the medical care of another 60 who were beaten or wounded. The fund also has enabled witnesses to disappear quietly by providing them with safe houses, legal aid and a stipend for living.

Sometimes, however, this protection is not enough. Shortly after one of Jean Bernard Charles' relatives moved into a safe house that the Human Rights Fund had rented for him, four men forced him into a white Nissan pickup truck (the same type of vehicle driven by the Haitian National Police). They took him to habitation Leclerc—a remote field where the former military used to torture people. There the men broke both his knees and razored his back. When officials of the Human Rights Fund arrived at work on Monday morning, the man was slumped on the front stops. One ear was hanging from the side of his face. He is in hiding again. (Drummond 1997: 62–63)

USAID and the American embassy were incensed by the depiction of the Human Rights Fund project. They questioned the Fund director about his portrayal of the institution and its history in his interview with Drummond. In a 1997 memo titled "Account of HRF's Contact with Time Magazine," ADF states:

In response to more general questions posed by Ms. Drummond during the interview, the Fund director traced the history of the Fund as well as describing for her the nature of HRF's collaboration with the MICIVIH, NCHR and other prominent institutions with explicit human rights concerns in Haiti, both governmental and non-governmental, and the HNP Inspector General's Office and Special Investigative Unit (Brigade Criminel). . . . In this context was also highlighted HRF's contact with the Haitian Senatorial Justice and Human Rights Commissions. There was *never* a question of the Fund's activities being secretive as reported in Ms. Drummond's article, except to the extent that HRF's casework is treated with considerable discretion in order to protect victim's privacy and safety.[35] [Emphasis in original]

In the early months of 1997, therefore, the Human Rights Fund still lacked "credibility" with both the Haitian and international human rights communities, making it an example of U.S. "failures" and "incompetence." On some level the Fund's visibility made it an easier target than the Haitian state, the failures of which were considered so pervasive that it remained invisible or shielded from the criticism. It is in the context of this politically charged and highly scrutinized environment that negotiations took place to house the new Rehabilitation Program at the Fund. The addition of former members of the U.N.'s defunct Medical Unit, and advocacy by the various actors and external circumstances described above, enabled the Fund to be extended from March 1997 to June 30, 1997, then again from July 1, 1997, to June 30, 1998. ADF received an additional $500,000 for the Fund—not including the funding for indirect costs that it received to manage the project—which brought the total moneys received in direct costs to $1 million.

* * *

The process of implementing victim assistance during the crisis and postconflict period was thoroughly politicized, from the "international" realms of politics in the U.S. Congress and the United Nations to the "local" or grassroots realm in Haiti. Each aid institution or program operated within an administrative structure that required the demonstration of accountability and competence to promote postconflict development as well as to promote the institution's security, whether political or financial. Each institution or organization had a mandate, whether explicit or implicit, that generated technologies of trauma. Such technologies were employed to recognize, categorize, and authenticate the experience of "victims" according to a number of criteria. Once victim status was recognized, this client identity yielded social and material forms of compensation, whether for "perpetrators" or their "victims." Such processes were politicized and contested.

Throughout this aid apparatus, accusation, counteraccusation, rumor, and gossip flowed concerning the competence and motives of institutions, their policies, and the persons charged with executing these policies. Political auditors—human rights organizations and other watchdog agencies—employed both ethical and scandal publicity to mobilize response and have garnered considerable power to challenge government practices in the domestic and international arena. Ironically, although some Haitian rights groups and their international partners emphasized the failures of U.S. and Haitian governmental initiatives in their reports, they quietly collaborated with them, both as institutions and as individuals, even to the point of accepting federal funds.

The processes depicted in this chapter characterize nascent aspects of bureaucraft in the domain of victim assistance. It is a politics of truth, knowledge, and ethics as debated by direct and indirect means throughout the victim assistance apparatus. Absent so far from this analysis of bureaucratized forms of aid within the governmental and nongovernmental realm is a depiction of the lived experience of encountering these institutions as a client, patient, or viktim. In what way did the insidious presence of ensekirite affect the assemblages of humanitarian and development organizations and victims' advocacy groups? How does trauma manifest itself, and in what way does interaction with the diverse technologies of trauma shape or craft suffering? What is the process of shifting from militan to viktim? What are the long-term consequences of these interventions and their failures versus nonintervention?

As each institutional node in the governmental and nongovernmental victim assistance network faced the challenge of limited resources to address the chronic and acute needs of victims of all kinds, the institutional pressures mounted, as did the frustration of the beneficiaries of these institutions. Consequently, viktim scrambled to meet their needs as best they could, given the ebb and flow of aid. I consider these questions in the following chapters as I moved among Chanm Fanm, the Human Rights Fund, and the Martissant community.

CHAPTER 3

Routines of Rupture and Spaces of (In)Security

The ghost is not simply a dead or missing person, but a social figure, and investigating it can lead to that dense site where history and subjectivity make social life. . . . Being haunted draws us affectively, sometimes against our will and always a bit magically, into the structure of feeling of a reality we come to experience, not as cold knowledge, but as transformative recognition.

Avery F. Gordon, Ghostly Matters

Viktim experience psychosocial trauma while grappling with the heightened state of social risk that ensekirite creates. Living with Haiti's ensekirite worsens traumatic suffering, especially for viktim who do not have social and institutional forms of support. For many viktim, continuous traumatic stressors, what I call routines of rupture (James 2008), exacerbate psychosocial suffering. These are multiple ongoing disruptions to daily life rather than single traumatic events after which there is a "post-," as suggested by the conventional notion of posttraumatic stress disorder. The experience of ensekirite has political, economic, legal, social, and spiritual dimensions. Ensekirite reflects the degree of fragility individuals and social groups feel in everyday life. Through discussions, physical therapy, and participation in therapeutic groups with traumatized women and men, I learned to see that the experience of ensekirite is gendered. Although I did not provide physical therapy to Haitian men who were targets of human rights abuses, my interviews and participation in therapeutic settings with these viktim suggest that development efforts with a gender focus must direct their interventions to both sexes, as well as to family systems, in order to achieve human security.

The sociologist Anthony Giddens (1984: 375) defines "ontological security" as "confidence or trust that the natural and social worlds are as they appear to be, including the basic existential parameters of self and social identity." An individual experiences security when there is autonomy of bodily control, bodily integrity, and a "sense of trust in the continuity of the object-world and in the fabric of social activity" (60). The routinization of daily life creates the *sense* of security. That sense is the fundamental ground of embodiment, agency, and, ultimately, the reproduction of social structures such as the family. The notions of routinization and predictability of daily life are integral to analyses of subjective experience in secure *and* insecure environments.

The reality of ensekirite is that constancy, safety, or trust cannot be assumed for either the individual or the group, especially not for the poor living in the slums of the capital. In the context of chronic political and economic ruptures one cannot take for granted that social institutions are permanent. On the contrary, ontological insecurity forms the ground of subjectivity when ruptures of routine social institutions and practices are the rule (Giddens 1984: 62). When ruptures are routine and arise within an overall climate of political and economic instability, we must ask how the broader societal "nervousness" (Taussig 1992) influences the experience of subjectivity and embodiment on both the individual and collective levels.

I introduce here the concept of *spaces of security* to describe therapeutic interventions that created spatial and temporal intervals or breaks in the otherwise unremitting ensekirite of Port-au-Prince. In these temporary spaces of exception viktim gave traumatic testimony before witnesses and found healing, reparation, and political recognition. This chapter begins with a narrative of my introduction to the women of Martissant by the grassroots development and human rights organizations that were assisting them. I present the ontological ground of ensekirite in a brief history of Port-au-Prince and Martissant. I then map the terrain of embodied ensekirite by outlining concepts of emotion, illness, and embodiment that I learned in therapeutic contexts with Haitians. The "sensory biographies" (Desjarlais 2003) of women to whom I provided physical therapy at Chanm Fanm reveal the complex lived experience of Haiti's ensekirite for its poorest citizens. I then present traumatic testimonies of men with whom I participated in therapy groups at the HRF Rehabilitation Program. I conclude with an analysis of another space of (in)security, the November 1997 International Tribunal against Violence toward Women. The event was one that revealed the political economy of trauma, as well as the occult economies that emerge within them.

WOMEN'S RIGHTS UNDER HAITIAN LAW

The birth of the Chanm Fanm clinic was the culmination of transnational and international advocacy work by the Haitian Women's Association and Mothers Across Borders. In fall 1995 I learned of the joint initiative to create the women's health center from Judy Williams, a friend with whom I had been studying Haitian Creole in Boston. She had worked in Haiti and Central America for many years as a nurse-midwife and women's reproductive health activist. She provided her expertise to help establish the women's clinic and kept me apprised of its progress. Among its routine clinical services, there would be training programs for *fanm saj* (lay midwives) to professionalize their skills and introduce international best practice standards. Clinic staff were being recruited from the state school of nursing and among health practitioners.

Judy knew that I practiced the Trager Approach and that I planned to conduct research in Haiti. I immediately agreed when she asked if I would consider volunteering to work with rape survivors at the Martissant clinic in Port-au-Prince. In the months preceding my arrival, she introduced me to the MAB executive director and staff and a Boston-based human rights lawyer who were jointly compiling legal human rights dossiers on Haitian women and girls who had been raped between 1991 and 1994. At that meeting we discussed the physical therapy work that I would provide once the clinic began offering care to women, as well as my interest in researching gender violence in Haiti. The clinic opened on March 8, 1996, International Women's Day. In July 1996 I returned to Haiti to work with rape survivors at Chanm Fanm.

When I arrived in Port-au-Prince, the DRC was sponsoring a series of residential seminars on the topic "Women's Rights under Haitian Law" for women's organizations from rural and urban areas and for three groups of rape survivors from the poorest areas of Port-au-Prince. Staff members of MAB, the DRC, and the HWA decided that it would be best for me to meet the women with whom I would work at Chanm Fanm by participating in these seminars. The morning of the first day of the training, DRC staff picked me up at the home of my hosts, a Haitian family living just outside downtown Port-au-Prince. I will never forget the look of shock that the women wore on their faces when they arrived

and saw me. Although I was a *blan,* a foreigner, as they had anticipated, I was not *blan*—white. I also spoke passable Haitian Creole at
this stage. After a few laughs about their foiled expectations we were on
our way to the seminar that was being held at the DRC offices—a large
home in a residential section of upper Delmas. After introducing me to
many of the staff members, they led me to the main room where the
training would take place. Already seated were some of the participants
with whom I would develop close relationships over the next four years.

Marie sat against one wall. I introduced myself as an American student interested in gender issues. I explained that I would be providing a
form of physical therapy during the workshop and at Chanm Fanm for
the rest of the summer. She immediately spoke up and asked me quite
sharply, "What can you do for me? I have an infection in my vagina
that won't go away. Can you do anything for that?" Taken aback by her
challenging tone, I said no, the work that I did was more for stress and
other physical pain but that I'd see what I could do to help.

Another woman approached me, one with whom I developed a
research collaboration that was later to end badly. Sylvie Saint-Fleur
was a tiny woman whose willingness to speak up, at times quite critically, more than compensated for her size. She attended the training
with her fourteen-year-old daughter, Natasha, who was called *bèbè*
because she was deaf and mute. A group of young men in the Martissant neighborhood had gang-raped Natasha earlier that year because
her disability prevented her from speaking. Sylvie and her family had
also been victimized during the coup period, but I didn't learn more
about their stories until a few weeks later when we met in the privacy
of the clinic. Sylvie approached me with an offer of calculated friendship. She wrote me notes on her daughter's behalf and boldly told me
that Natasha wanted my friendship. She needed help to go to a school
that specialized in training people with disabilities. I told Sylvie that we
could talk about it at Chanm Fanm after the seminar had concluded.

By this time the room had begun to fill with many women who
belonged to one of the support groups for rape survivors. Our facilitator was a young Haitian human rights activist and lawyer from the Faculty of Law, Mèt (*maître,* attorney) Stephanie Joseph. She had helped
the Boston lawyers prepare the women's human rights dossiers in order
to present their cases to the Inter-American Court of Human Rights.
At this training session, however, the focus was on imparting everyday
knowledge of the Haitian legal system that would aid the participants in

their daily battles against personal injustice. The facilitators introduced me to the group as a foreign student interested in questions of gender relations in Haiti, someone who would also be giving "massage" at the Martissant clinic to aid their physical and emotional recovery. I later demonstrated the Trager work during the training and gave abbreviated physical therapy sessions to participants.

The seminar opened with a discussion of parental responsibility. Some of the participants had been in long-term, stable relationships, but the majority spoke about the difficulties of raising their children without sufficient support from their partners. As previously discussed, women are known as the potomitan—pillars—of the Haitian family.[1] Sex and gender ideals place expectations on Haitian women to maintain the conjugal household, care for children, and manage the household economy. Women also supplement the economic activities of their male partners in small-scale trade, domestic work and, more recently, in employment in the assembly sectors of urban Haiti.

Partners often abandoned women who were raped, as well as children who might have been conceived from rape, because of the associated shame—especially in the aftermath of the 1991–94 coup period. During the group discussion a woman asked if there was recourse under the law to force a man to take care of his children, even when there was no birth certificate verifying paternity. Her child's father disavowed his status. The woman lamented in exasperation, "I can say for myself that I don't understand what's in the law, but I know that if I have a child with a man he should take care of that child. If he doesn't take care of the child we know that we don't have priority with him." There were also cases in which a partner denied his own children by saying that they were the rapist's, even when there was no ambiguity in the timing of conception.

Sylvie added with much bitterness:

> In reality, even when men acknowledge their paternity [bay yon pitit batistè-a] they do not take care of the child, because I've seen near my neighborhood a friend of mine who is married. Her spouse left her with six children and four others who aren't hers. Because . . . when you see that you've had children with a man, whether you're married or not, if . . . you go to an officer of the public records bureau [ofisye leta sivil] to lodge a complaint in order to force him to help you with the child, you know what the judge will say? "Woman, men never will give you what he hasn't already. Why would you have children with him? You know that [justice] here is not like overseas, so you just have to accept it [ou oblije reziyen-w']."

Sylvie's neighbor Denise added:

> Many times when you're married to a man and he acknowledges the
> children, all of the responsibility falls on the woman. At one moment things
> can be fine between you, but sometimes a partner can become jealous and
> then leave you and find another woman. I have eight children and I've
> never found a man who'll take care of me.

The discussion then shifted to an aggrieved chorus of protests about
how their partners had failed or betrayed them. This patterned narrative
style, what I call a discourse of lament, is characterized by frustrated testimonies of betrayal, rejection, vulnerability, and loss. It was a common
mode of expression that I would encounter in one-on-one, group, and
public discussions in daily life. Discourses of lament recall Fiona Ross's
(2003) discussion of women's testimonies in the South African Truth
and Reconciliation Commission. She describes their narrative style as
"lamentations, forms of sorrowing and grieving" that was a product of
the gendered division of mourning practices (51, 180).

Discourses of lament also resemble Atwood Gaines and Paul E.
Farmer's (1986) concept of rhetorics of complaint. Gaines and Farmer
surveyed cross-cultural idioms of distress. They describe a form of communication in Mediterranean cultures through which individuals nar-
rate lives of routine suffering and victimization, what Goffman (1959)
would refer to as a "presentation of self." Such laments are meant to
validate the self and to establish self-worth publicly while forestalling
rumor, gossip, or accusations about the state of an individual's fortune.

> In the Mediterranean, one seeks to minimize the perceived risk of fall-
> ing prey to supernatural and natural forces, the latter including the envy
> and jealousy of others, by presenting oneself as unfortunate, battered by
> the winds of fate and scarcely able to continue the struggle for life. The
> micropolitics of social life in the Mediterranean governed by gossip . . .
> demand that individuals conceal good fortune and demonstrate their wor-
> thiness by a rhetoric indicative of a lack of success or good fortune. One
> verbalizes a social life of problems or mundane developments which try
> one's patience. (Gaines and Farmer 1986: 305)

Atwood and Gaines note a general style of complaining meant to ward
off supernatural, natural, or human-authored adversity. Haitian wom-
en's laments of everyday suffering have some of this character. They also
follow a pattern that Farmer observed in the mid-1980s in his clinical
work with AIDS patients in rural Haiti. The downfall of Jean-Claude
Duvalier opened space for general complaints in political discourse that

influenced the way people talked about the appearance of AIDS (Farmer 1990: 11). Similarly, women viktim linked human rights abuses they suffered during the coup years to more general dynamics of sex and gender in Haitian society.

Byron Good (1994: 147) similarly presents the notion of rhetorics of complaint in his analysis of Turkish epilepsy narratives. Stories of tragedy and illness were "plotted"—temporally structured—and "emplotted"—recounted or performed for readers or witnesses in order to determine cause, course, meaning, and modes of redress, as well as the connection between incidents of suffering and individual and collective life events (144, 148).[2] As I began to study Haitian women's narratives of embodied misfortune and life histories of suffering, I observed a similar pattern. Many narratives had a temporal sequence or plot in which routine stressors culminated first in a crisis and then some form of resolution through the intercession of interveners.

Good (1994: 143), drawing on Victor Turner's (1957) theories of performance and social dramas, observes, "Narrative accounts, along with ritual, efforts at legal redress, and other social dramas, are organized in relation to the contradictions structured into societies . . . that [become] evident at moments of breach and crisis." Some of the contradictions embedded in Haitian society are the gaps between the ideals of the sex and gender system and the real limitations the majority of Haitians find in meeting the expectations of their communities of responsibility. Individuals who have lost or who lack agency to perform these expected social roles feel tremendous pressure and stress. Such thwarting (Moore 1994) can influence the negative actions a person may perpetrate or suffer. Thwarting also influences the experience of trauma in gendered ways.

In this analysis, however, I distinguish discourses of lament from rhetorics of complaint. Laments are not simply positioned rhetorics meant to deflect envy or to establish public worth, saintliness, or martyrdom in the face of misery. Similar to Douglas Wood Holland and Jane C. Wellenkamp's (1994: 221–22) findings in their ethnographic work with Toraja villagers in Indonesia, the prevalence of misfortune in Haiti makes discourses of lament relatively straightforward accounts of life's challenges. That having been said, these accounts sometimes had a performative or persuasive dimension (Robben 1995), even as they were also tales of authentic crisis. Multiple bureaucratic discourses and professional practices crafted or transformed general laments of suffering to make them efficacious as "trauma narratives"

(James 2004). Through the work of interveners, stories of suffering were molded, tested, and transformed to validate victims' suffering as authentic according to preestablished criteria. The work of transformation also demonstrated the competence and accountability of the intervener. The trauma portfolios of which such structured narratives become part could also permit the victim and the brokers of suffering to gain social and material capital.

When discourses of lament were articulated in the workshop on women's rights, I did not yet recognize the narrative structure as significant or patterned. Despite the prevalence of such forms of communication, other participants who witnessed these performances sometimes challenged them. Mèt Joseph interjected two crucial statements to disrupt the growing negativism in the discussion. The goal of the seminar, she said, was not simply to *voye wòch sou gason* (criticize men). Rather, it was for us to critique the situation that exists in society: "It is a fact that because men doubt women they may not take care of the children. We're not saying here that men are not good, but we're going to denounce what isn't good within society. There are men that aren't good as well as women, because we're human." I recalled her words when I began to interview these women, provide them with physical therapy, and visit them at their homes near the Martissant clinic. It was then that the reality of their daily struggles with ensekirite became apparent. I realized that by freeing participants from their everyday worries, this seminar had provided a space of rest, unguarded speech, social support, and temporary security for its participants. The space of security that workshops like this one offered was integral to building civil society, especially given the decades of repression that Haiti had suffered under lapè simityè, the deathly silence of the Duvalier regime, and amid the continuing ensekirite in Martissant.

MARTISSANT

The population of Port-au-Prince, currently estimated at two million, is expanding rapidly without an organized plan for urban management. Sabine Manigat compares Port-au-Prince to a "drifting ship":

> It is a city full of activities in search of a unifying project and new institutions capable of channeling the aspirations and political participation of its citizens. In spite of the social movements that have emerged in the city . . . the absence of urban management in Port-au-Prince has been a constant failure during the past thirty years. (1997: 112–13)

The population increase in the capital is the result of a long process of shifts in governance from the colonial to the postcolonial period. Port-au-Prince became the administrative capital of Haiti in 1750, four decades before the war of independence began in 1791. The U.S. occupation of Haiti between 1915 and 1934 reinforced the centralization of administrative, economic, and military power in the capital (Dupuy 1989; Renda 2001; Trouillot 1990). Thus Port-au-Prince became the hub through which commerce, communication, and production flowed domestically and internationally. During the Duvalier administrations the decline in agricultural production, combined with widespread political repression, forced the migration of peasants from rural to urban areas (Laguerre 1987b). According to Huldrych Locher (1978: 50), the population of Port-au-Prince grew from 143,534 to 493,692 between 1950 and 1971. Of that increase, more than 334,000 people were recent migrants from rural areas (Locher 1978: 52). By the late 1970s and early 1980s the growth of the assembly industry for export—and its preference for cheap, docile, dexterous female laborers—encouraged the migration of women to the city (Grunwald, Delatour, and Voltaire 1984: 238). Many of the women I worked with in the slums of Martissant were the first members of large extended families to arrive in Port-au-Prince, followed later by other close relatives.

Martissant is just west of Port-au-Prince along the Carrefour road that extends to the southern peninsula. In the nineteenth century British Consul-General Spenser St. John described "Marquissant" as a zone of debauchery and depravity. St. John depicted it as the place where President Salnave reputedly consulted with a Vodou priest, bathed in the blood of goats, and agreed to ritual human sacrifice to gain spiritual power to stem the tides of civil war that threatened his administration (St. John 1884: 184). In the decades following the U.S. occupation, many bourgeois families built estates in the verdant foothills of Martissant and the nearby Carrefour area. In the 1980s, however, the greater Carrefour area that adjoined Martissant became notorious as a zone for prostitutes and Vodou practitioners, even as its concentrated poverty encouraged the development of pro-democracy groups (Wilentz 1989).

In 1995 I toured Martissant and Carrefour with Father Triest. As we drove, we passed garbage heaped alongside the road awaiting the infrequent pickups by the state-owned disposal service. Vendors lined some of the high walls that separated the road from neighborhoods and commercial buildings along the route. The traffic along the road, both vehicular and pedestrian, was often jammed (as it still was when I began working at the Chanm Fanm clinic the next year).

Figure 4. Market, Martissant. Photo credit: Erica Caple James

Even so, sectors of Martissant retained their beauty. The middle class in this poor, highly populated area lived in the subdivision between the Carrefour road and the mountain's base. Here the homes were more permanent, and the residents had lived in Martissant for longer periods than those of the bidonvil near the sea or the ravines of the mountain above them. The majority of my clients at Chanm Fanm and their families resided in a geographic "block" of thousands of ramshackle homes bordered in the east by Fifth Avenue in the Bolosse section of town and in the west by the Martissant 17 road. To the north was the vast slum that has arisen on the landfill bordering the sea; in the south, squatter settlements in the high ravines of the southern mountain range.

The population of this area was difficult to determine, but six to twelve or more individuals inhabited nearly every household that I visited, from the sea to the mountains. These homes were cramped, one-room, corrugated tin-roofed houses whose haphazard arrangement gave the zone a labyrinthine appearance. The houses of the better-off were constructed of cinder blocks or wood siding. Those of the poorest were made of scrap metal sheeting or at worst, cardboard. The lack of proper drainage and waste management in some of these areas, combined with the extreme population density,[3] meant that water contamination, the

Figure 5. Legacy of Hurricane Gordon, Martissant.
Photo credit: Erica Caple James.

proliferation of malarial mosquitoes, and bacterial infections were additional sources of risk and insecurity for residents.

The state had done little to improve these areas apart from expansion of the Carrefour road to reduce the traffic jams at an intersection
leading into the city. In fact, during the years of my research, much of
Martissant had been forgotten by the state. The 1994 "liberation" of
Haiti only temporarily decreased the violent immiseration of Martissant residents. To make matters worse, in November 1994, just a few
weeks after the restoration of democracy, Hurricane Gordon killed more
than fifty residents of the mountainside bidonvil, as avalanches of mud
from its eroded hillsides suffocated entire families. During the storm the
road that once connected this neighborhood to a more frequently traveled thoroughfare was washed out, making this part of the zone even

more inaccessible to the civilian police force.[4] In 1998 two additional hurricanes (Georges and Mitch) worsened erosion and destroyed more property and households.

In addition to the environmental threats, there were issues of security. Many of my informants told me to leave Martissant by sunset. Armed civilian gangs, known as kò (corps) or zenglendo, patrolled the zone and enforced a curfew. Payment in money or sex was required for safe passage. Regardless of these threats, the residents of the zone had to take their children to and from school. They were obliged to continue their work in petty trade, construction, or other occupations and for the most part to work in other areas of the capital. Return by nightfall was considered essential. Residents also spoke of the increasing boldness and desperation of homeless children and young adolescents, who had begun to attack women and commit robberies in broad daylight. Gangs of young men frequently highjacked cars and accosted women near the beny (public fountain) where women laundered clothes (both for pay and for their own families) and children sought water for their households.

The new Haitian National Police force made efforts to rid the area of organized gangs between 1997 and early 2000. Their use of excessive force only contributed to the ensekirite, while their motives for incursions into Martissant were often in doubt. In fact, corrupt police officers had fought with gangs for control over the flow of drugs and other illegal activities in the area. In many cases, the ongoing battles over territory in Martissant and other urban areas had been the unintended consequences of postconflict interventions to restore Haiti's democracy. When the international community imposed an embargo on Haiti between 1991 and 1994, the de facto regime cultivated an occult economy in fuel, weapons, narcotics, and other goods through its control of borders and customs. Members of the coup apparatus policed areas like Martissant.[5] Both the embargo, with its unintended effects of impoverishing the poor[6] while inadvertently strengthening the terror economy, and the limited disarmament and peacekeeping programs contributed to the growth of Haiti's political economy of trauma. In the prevailing climate of ontological ensekirite in Martissant, Chanm Fanm became another space of security for women.

CHANM FANM

I traveled to the Chanm Fanm clinic daily with Emilie Datilus, a young nurse who managed the clinic's day-to-day operations and graced my trip to work with her cheerful presence. She picked me up at my hosts' home in the Bois-Verna section of Port-au-Prince about two miles from the National Palace. First, we made our way by taxi, squeezing ourselves into dilapidated cars, usually with at least four other passengers. Eventually, we arrived at Portail Léogâne,[7] a transfer station not far from the Dessalines road that was notorious for its thieves, gangs, and appearance of chaos. Elaborately decorated *tap-tap* (local pickup trucks, remodeled with benches and seats, that served as mini-buses) battled for space with the large secondhand school buses and trucks that transported passengers from the capital to the provinces north and south of the city. Because the city so rarely had electricity at this time, the traffic lights did not work. When they did work, drivers respected them (or not) on a whim. Consequently, crossing the dangerous intersection on foot in order to reach the tap-tap that would take us to the clinic was always a challenge. Members of the HNP did what they could to guide traffic through the intersection, but they were not entirely successful: the two streams of traffic from the main commercial sector of the city and from the area of the National Palace merged at this juncture. Adding to the mix of this political and economic crossroads, the USAID headquarters rested tranquilly on Harry Truman Boulevard at this time, just a few blocks from the busy intersection.

Emilie was deft at positioning us in such a way that we could scramble onto a tap-tap that had space. I was more accustomed to waiting patiently in line for public transportation, but for these private services the driver's caprice or the ruthlessness of other travelers stood between us and arriving at work. I quickly learned to gather my skirts, make the dash onto the awaiting vehicle, and have my fare ready—one and a half gourdes, at the time about ten cents. After riding through the pungent, chronically flooded streets of the Bolosse section, we turned briefly onto the Carrefour road and then once again into the heart of Martissant before reaching the neighborhood of the clinic.

Chanm Fanm was located in the heart of a residential area of Martissant. It occupied a home rented from a landlord who continually inflated the rent, based on the knowledge that the clinic received support from an international organization. (This exploitation of humanitarian aid is another occult economy that operates in relation to the political economy of trauma.) Like most homes in the capital, the Chanm Fanm clinic had a small *lakou* (courtyard). The house was walled to provide some structural security for the physical plant; although as I discuss later, it would prove ineffective when the clinic was attacked by the HNP in 1998.

Figure 6. Harry Truman Boulevard. Photo credit: Erica Caple James.

On entering the house, there was a *galeri* (anteroom or veranda) where women would wait. Passersby would call out their hellos to those inside. Local market women often entered, selling water, *bonbon* (sweets), boiled eggs, or other sundries. Our neighbors across the street watched the coming and going of people as much from interest as from a need to survey the neighborhood for their security. From the galeri one entered the main waiting area—a space lined with wooden benches. A desk, the doctor's scale, and messages on the chalkboard on the wall behind it faced the benches. Invariably there were posters with information in Kreyòl that encouraged breast-feeding and other beneficial health practices. Off a corridor leading from the waiting room were the pharmacy, two examination rooms, a third room with beds, and an exterior space that was remodeled into a lab after the clinic first opened.

In the first few months of its existence the clinic had a color television set that worked a few hours a day, when there was electricity. There were also some electric fans in the examination rooms that stirred air heavy with dust, mosquitoes, and the anxiety of waiting patients. MAB and its supporters equipped the clinic with medicines and supplies that were stored in the "pharmacy," a small room that also served as a lounge for the nurses and me. From the room we could hear the crying of the infant in the house next door and the sounds of busy day-to-day life outside the walls. My "office" was the last room on the left. In this small space I listened to poignant stories of suffering and loss, of struggle and patience, but also of fortitude and resistance.

WOMEN'S BODIES

In general, my client base in Martissant was considered the "poorest of the poor." In addition to malnutrition, hypertension, and sexually transmitted diseases or other vaginal infections, they reported pain or illness for which there was no corresponding "physical" cause that could respond to biomedical treatment. Despite their efforts to find cures, biomedical practitioners often viewed these women's afflictions suspiciously, as "psychosomatic" or emotional rather than the result of a physical cause. In 1996 Nurse Emilie, as she was called, explained to a patient that she could not buy just any pills from the pharmacy to heal what ailed her. Emilie complained to me, "They want medicine for every symptom, fatigue, or slight pain." I wondered, How do you medicate poverty? Many of these patients with chronic, "psychosomatic" pain were referred to me by the staff physicians and nurses for Trager sessions, about which a brief discussion follows.

The Trager Approach is a method of "movement education," created and developed over a period of sixty-five years by Dr. Milton Trager. It affirms a model of embodiment and subjectivity that perceives the individual as a "body/mind." Chronic somatic conditions are viewed as patterns in the body/mind that can be "released" through Trager work: "Utilizing gentle, non-intrusive, natural movements, The Trager Approach helps release deep-seated physical and mental patterns and facilitates deep relaxation, increased physical mobility, and mental clarity. These patterns may have developed in response to accidents, illnesses, or any kind of physical or emotional trauma, including the stress of everyday life."[8]

Customarily a practitioner conducts an intake interview before commencing with a session in order to determine the client's history of illness or injury. In many respects this method echoes what Robert Desjarlais (2003) calls a "sensory biography." I asked clients about their pain, its location, intensity, and duration, as well as its impact on daily life. I also asked about the client's understanding of its cause. These questions elicited a narrative of what Thomas Csordas calls "somatic modes of attention":

Somatic modes of attention are culturally elaborated ways of attending to and with one's body in surroundings that include the embodied presence of others. . . . To attend to a bodily sensation is not to attend to the body as an isolated object, but to attend to the body's situation in the world. . . . Because we are not isolated subjectivities trapped within our bodies, but share an intersubjective milieu with others, we must also specify that a somatic mode of attention means not only attention to and with one's own body, but includes attention to the bodies of others. (1993: 138–39)

Through the interview process, I began to understand my clients' embodied self-awareness and the way they experienced their "situation in the world." The physical work with my clients added another dimension in which the somatic mode of attention was communicated and perceived through touch.

Following the intake interview there are two components of the work that are usually part of each session: manual therapy using a massage table and instruction in independent movement exercises. In the first component the client is passive and receives what is called "tablework." Sessions usually last from sixty to ninety minutes and are conducted without oils or lotions. The client chooses the level of dress with which they are at ease—usually a minimum of shorts or undergarments. She is also draped with sheets or blankets as needed. The client lies on the massage table and allows the practitioner to manipulate the body to assess range of motion and the "quality of the tissue." This diagnostic technique is a combination of the client's self-report of tightness or rigidity, "tension" or pain, and the practitioner's perception of inflexibility in the soma as he or she applies compression or traction.

The practitioner monitors the degree to which the client trusts him or her to manipulate the body during a tablework session. A client's deepening of breath, willingness to ask for repetition of certain gestures, verbal communication of approval, or even falling asleep indicates trust or the work's efficacy. "Resistance" might appear during the session as involuntary flexion of muscles or as unconscious movement in order to "help" the practitioner. Clients might also flinch, display minor or major muscle spasms when touched, or verbally express discomfort with the sensation caused by a particular movement. Clients at Chanm Fanm frequently reported that certain gestures or moves caused them to remember their experience of victimization. Such memories provoked tears in some but passed without visible displays of affect in others.[9] The client could at any time suspend a session voluntarily due to discomfort. Generally, however, practitioners make every effort to ensure that the quality of touch offers nothing to induce resistance. They will reduce or increase the level of compression, the speed of rocking, or the intensity of traction of the client's body in response to the client's voluntary and involuntary movement or verbal direction during the session.

In the second component of the work, the client is active and learns meditative exercises called Mentastics. These exercises help the recipient of the work recover a feeling of ease and create greater range of movement. They also enable the client to maintain and sustain the freedom of movement achieved in the manual therapy. Mentastics "have the same intent as the tablework in terms of releasing deep-seated patterns" and are ways to reinforce the new patterns of movement that are inculcated in the tablework. During this instruction the practitioner continues to evaluate the client's patterns of movement through space, the range of motion, and the limits of motion.

When I initially worked with women in 1996, it was difficult to extract a sensory biography given their distressed emotional and psychological state and my unfamiliarity with Haitian sensory experience. Eventually I developed a clinical practice that was efficacious therapeutically and as a research method by combining structured interviews using the CAPS, participant observation with viktim in other therapeutic institutional settings such as the Fund, and manual therapy with my clients at the women's clinic in Martissant.

One factor that was helpful in translating cross-culturally was that the Trager method used touch as the primary vehicle of communication. The use of touch and palpation of the body to assess symptoms is a common feature of traditional Haitian healing practices. As noted in a description of these practices:

> Folk healers use three diagnostic techniques. They may first inquire about the history of the illness: the length of time the person has been sick, the location and characteristics of the pain, whether it is acute or periodic, what the patient has eaten. A folk healer may also examine the patient's eyes, hands, and skin color for indications of the state of the blood. The third technique, man-yin (touching), consists of palpating various parts of the body to ascertain whether a displaced bone or internal organ needs to be placed in proper position. . . . Folk healers commonly massage the patient with either burned alcohol or hot oil to treat a dislocation or sprain; sores and inflammations are treated with compresses, poultices, or baths. (Laguerre 1984: 128–29)

In many respects the methodology that Trager employs was close enough to Haitian traditional practices that my work was categorized as *masay* (massage), and I was considered a person who knew how to *rale moun* (give massage; lit., "pull people"). After indicating that I did not use oil in my work and that there were no prohibitions on bathing afterward or eating a particular diet, as might be the case with Haitian traditional practitioners, the sessions proceeded without any superficial difficulties. For clients who were extremely traumatized, however, decoding the language of the body required a deeper understanding of notions of embodiment and cultural idioms of distress.

EMOTIONS, BODY, AND SPIRIT

Throughout both my fieldwork and my therapeutic work, the subjective experience of emotion, illness, or suffering was most often articulated through the epistemology of Haitian Vodou. This was the case even though many individuals were active practitioners of Evangelical denominations that have proliferated in Haiti.[10] As conceived within Haitian Vodou, the person or individual is situated at the crossroads of relationships that include not only the living but also the ancestors and the divine spirits, the lwa (Brown 1989: 257; 1991). Within each relational web, there are reciprocal sets of duties and obligations that maintain balance within the individual, family, and larger community. For those who are ritual practitioners of Vodou, personhood and identity are indelibly tied to the lwa (Dayan 1991: 50).

> Everyone has a personal *loa* as his protector; he is identified with the Catholic guardian angel. This protector is inherited either on the father's or the mother's side. Every family, the family (*fanmi*) being a large bilateral group of kin, worships its own spirits. . . . The family is the group within which the spirits have power and exercise authority; they do this mainly by "catching" a member of the group, meaning causing him some kind of affliction. The *loas* act only within the family. They may manifest themselves in many ways; in dreams, by assuming a human or an animal form . . . and finally in a privileged manner by possessing a member of the family. (Larose 1977: 92)

The social relationships between the lwa, the ancestors, the family, and the individual are multifaceted. To some extent these relationships can be described as embodied. However, the concept of the body and suffering in Haitian Vodou challenges Western conceptions of trauma (Young

1995), and even of chronic pain (Jackson 2000), that locate suffering in the discrete, embodied individual.

Generally, the embodied "person" as historically conceptualized in Haiti comprises multiple parts. The *gwo bonanj* is a nonmaterial force, consciousness, or energy that shadows or doubles the physical being. It is able to detach itself from the body during sleep (Brown 1991: 351–52; Dayan 1991: 51; Deren 1970 [1953]: 25–26; Larose 1977: 92; Métraux 1972 [1959]: 120, 303). It also detaches itself during the course of possession by the lwa and returns after the lwa has completed its intended action (Bourguignon 1984: 247). Located in the head *(tèt)*, the gwo bonanj is vulnerable to magical attacks, especially at death, when it may become a "disembodied force wandering here and there," known as a zonbi (Larose 1977: 93). The immaterial zonbi, like the lwa, can possess the individual as a malevolent spirit who seeks a permanent home, until it is dispersed by ceremonial means. But before the ritual dispersal has occurred, it can also be sent by a relative to avenge a wrong or injustice (Larose 1977: 95). A sorcerer can also capture the gwo bonanj when a person is alive. In this case, it is also called the zonbi. It can be used to force the material person to whom it belongs—literally, the living dead—to labor for the sorcerer. The *ti bonanj* is an energy or presence that is deeper than consciousness but can enervate the individual in times of stress (Brown 1989: 265; Larose 1977: 94). The *kò kadav* is the material body that is separable from the spiritual essences and subject to decay and dissolution (Brown 1989: 265–66; Dayan 1991: 51). Finally, the *nanm* is the animating force of the body that disappears after the death of the individual (Brown 1989: 264).

Conceptions of the emotions and their effect on health are also related to the notion of the individual's tèt, the repository of the gwo bonanj and the seat of the lwa who is its master. When an individual is emotionally distressed, he or she may describe that experience by saying that the "big guardian angel" is upset (Brown 1989: 264). Furthermore, "when an individual is worried, his or her head is said to be 'loaded.' In excitement, the head heats up; when the head cools, the individual becomes calm, also sad" (Bourguignon 1984: 262). *San* (blood) is the mechanism that regulates heating and cooling in the body. The balance of hot and cold in the body directly affects an individual's susceptibility to illness (Laguerre 1987a: 70). The state of equilibrium of hot and cold is determined by the foods that one eats, action on behalf of the individual, or environmental factors (Laguerre 1987a: 70–71). The relationship between the interior and exterior of the body, the blood, and the emotions is dynamic. Thus when one considers the impact of local behavioral ecologies on mental health, the bounds of the self must be viewed as extended or permeable.[11]

Subjectivity in these contexts is complex. The embodied subject is one whose social relationships and environment are constitutive aspects of the person. However, the consequences of the complex self/soul mean that disruptions in the relational webs between the individual, community, ancestors, and the lwa may result in disorder, illness, or other material and spiritual problems, not only for the individual, but also for the extended family.[12] Relational obligations are sometimes sources of threat to the self, even as they are also sources of blessing and healing. Failure to uphold these obligations can result in illness or misfortune for the person who is directly guilty or for others within the community (Métraux 1972 [1959]: 256). Likewise, sources of embodied pain and suffering extend beyond the material and temporal boundaries of the discrete corporeal individual to the environment—both physical and metaphysical—and to ascending and descending kinship and spiritual networks.

In my physical therapy work with Haitian women, the sensation and interpretation of acute and chronic suffering was frequently articulated as "full body pain." As Michel Laguerre (1984: 125–26) affirms, full body pain often has complex roots: "Because of a belief among Haitians that when one is ill, the whole body suffers, the location of pain at a particular moment is not particularly important, especially since diseases may shift position. In addition, the causes of pain that are suggested by patients do not usually comport with biomedical ideas of causation ('gas,' for example)." Indeed, the notion of *van* (wind) or *gaz* (gas) was one I would become familiar with. Some of my clients described the sensation of chronic pain as having gas or wind in a particular organ or vessel such as the "stomach" or "head." Laguerre writes, "Gas can occur in the head, where it enters through the ears; in the stomach, where it comes in through the mouth; and in the shoulder, back, legs, or appendix, where it may travel from the stomach. . . . When gas moves from one part of the body to another *(gas kap maché nan do-m)*, pain is produced" (120). Furthermore, *van nan tèt* describes a feeling of heavy-headedness or *tèt fè mal* (headaches). One client asserted that the sensation of pressure in her head had made her whole body pirèd (rigid or stiff), but the feeling disappeared after the Trager session. In addition to this, my elderly clients typically described the feeling of *tay fè mal* (low back pain), sciatica, or forms of joint pain associated with old age. Many clients for whom the work was effective immediately reported the sensation that the gaz shifted or moved during a session and dissipated at its conclusion.

In conducting bodywork with my clients, I was able to "sense" the pain that they carried within; however, this awareness was sometimes difficult to sustain. In her work on language, violence, and the contested politics of gender in the partition of India, Veena Das (1997) refers to Wittgenstein's contention that one's own pain may reside or be sensed in another's body.[13] The intersubjective nature of the work—in which I adjusted my movement or the placement of my hands in accordance with how a client responded to the same—meant that my own somatic mode of attention was necessary to the therapeutic process. At times I was successful in assisting a client's "healing," despite the persistence of a chronic injury, by gently offering another experience of her capability to move freely. By way of explanation I want to return to Csordas (1994) and his description of the practice of "leg-lengthening" in the "laying on of hands" healing process in the Catholic Charismatic community.

Csordas (1994: 65–67) describes the way in which individuals are able to maintain a sense of embodiment through the awareness of their own posture, and the structural relationship of the embodied self to the external world, as the "postural model." The Charismatic practitioner works with his client's posture in order to influence the individual's self-orientation, which results in the perception of a change in leg length, as well as an empirical shift in posture. The conscious process by which one is aware of these changing relations is an alteration in the "somatic mode of attention" (58–73). For some individuals the working relationship between Trager practitioner and client can alter the client's "habitual posture"—the "persistence of a sensory impression" (66) of the body, that may be deeply influenced by the accumulation of somatic stressors over time—as well as the attention to chronic or habitual patterns of tension through the intersubjective medium of touch.

Through the movement of a client's body, Trager practitioners may be able to sense and perhaps intuit the range of motion that a client is accustomed to permitting, as well as suggest new possibilities for motion that may rest beyond the client's self-orientation. Within a space of security viktim trusted me to alter the habitual posture and somatic tension that had accumulated in their bodies not only after recent shocks but also after distal traumas. I call this effort to adjust their mode of being in the world "embodied remoralization" (Frank and Frank 1991; Kleinman 1988, 2006), in which the method of the verbal sharing of experience and emotion in the interview process followed by the Trager session permitted us to attempt to restructure or "remake" (Das et al. 2001) the experience of suffering in the embodied realm. Such an approach parallels that of other manual therapies and is by no means exclusive to the Trager work.

If I was able to alleviate my client's somatic complaints, even temporarily, the space of security created in the course of the work could enable her to experience emotional and physical relief. When successful, it was sometimes difficult to extract myself from clients' repeated requests for physical therapy. For many survivors of torture, however, this work—like that of many Haitian traditional healing methods—provided only limited physical and emotional relief for their disability. This was especially the case given the ongoing risks that my clients faced in their everyday lives of ensekirite in Haiti.

WOMEN'S STORIES

Marie Grand-Pierre

Marie is the woman I met at the Women's Rights under Haitian Law workshop who asked whether the physical therapy I had practiced could do anything for her infections and other complaints. At Chanm Fanm she became one of my clients for Trager bodywork and had many sessions to assuage the frequent, severe headaches that she suffered. Once aware of my interest in understanding the situation of women in Haiti, she asked if she could give me an official statement about her life. Our previous conversations concerned her physical health and the emotional and psychological problems she faced as a direct result of having been raped and beaten by members of the civilian militia.

In our official taped interview Marie told me the story of her life, an archetypal story that resonated with many of the life histories that I received. She told of struggling to work and survive as a vulnerable woman faced with forces beyond her control. In her trauma narrative rape was the culmination of a long series of misfortunes and exploitation by others—one of which was sexual abuse in the export assembly sector. But this narrative was also intended as persuasion. Marie requested that when I returned to the United States I try to broadcast her story on Haitian-American radio stations, with the hope that her family members and other Haitians living abroad would rescue her or provide her with material support.[14] Such desires demonstrated another aspect of Haiti's political economy of trauma: in addition to attracting the attention of international humanitarians, stories of crisis that emerge from Haiti's unremitting ensekirite might return and intensify the gaze (and remittances) of Haitians living abroad.

Marie was born in March 1957 in Jacmel, a city near Haiti's southern coast, just a few months before François Duvalier became president. Her parents grew up together in Jacmel and eventually became involved in a relationship, although they did not marry. Her father's family thought her mother's social status was too low. Marie lived alone with her mother until she was seven years old. During that period her father entered Duvalier's army. While in the army he had other soldiers intimidate her mother to force her to relinquish Marie into his custody. After she complied, he placed Marie in his own mother's care. It was at this point that Marie began to attend school.

Marie's father later married a woman of higher social status and subsequently became embroiled in the affairs of the army. Marie asserts that he essentially abandoned her to the care of his new wife. She used Marie as a *restavèk*, a child servant with a status that has been likened to that of a slave (Cadet 1998). Her stepmother severely mistreated her while her father pursued the money that service in the Duvalier army offered at that time. The mistreatment was such that Marie eventually had to escape the household and went into hiding. She described her flight using the same term, *mawonaj*, that depicts the flight of escaped slaves in the late eighteenth century. While in hiding, Marie could not continue her studies, so she tried to contact her father for financial support. He refused and left her desperate and homeless. Marie said that she went to live in another town in the southern region but did not explain how she survived there.

Marie's story of her mother's choice demonstrates the constraints placed on both women and men during the Duvalier period and the way force had become a means to exercise sovereign power (see chapter 1). Her description of childhood exploitation demonstrates further how within the prevailing climate of repression nearly any individual could mistreat and exercise power over others. Her statement also illustrates how women have historically had less ability to make choices in their lives. On the other hand, her choice to flee a situation of abuse suggests that even in the most dire circumstances resistance is possible.

As a young adult Marie joined the rural-to-urban migration of thousands of other women hoping to ameliorate their situations through formal employment in the assembly factories in Port-au-Prince. Contrary to her expectations, however, conditions in the factories made survival nearly impossible: as a minor, she only made six and a half gourdes per day, the equivalent of about $1.30 in the late 1970s to early 1980s.[15] As she could not depend on either her mother or her father for assistance, she had to survive on this wage—an insufficient sum to provide food, a place to stay, and transportation. It is at this point, Marie indicated, that her employer "took advantage" of her situation in a manner that "ate her courage" *(manje kouray-m')*. She implied that she had been coerced into engaging in sexual relations with her boss in order to make the money she needed to live. Realizing that she could not continue in such a state, she decided to work elsewhere.

Marie chose to work in the informal market as a madanm sara. She entered into a relationship with a young man she had met who was interested in her and whom she also liked. The union began to change her situation. Soon after leaving the assembly sector, Marie and her partner established a plasaj relationship. Her "husband" worked sporadically as an artisan while she engaged in daily commerce selling fruits, vegetables, fish, and other items. She became pregnant almost immediately. They had the first of fourteen children that she would bear over the course of their relationship, eight of whom would tragically die for unspecified reasons. Marie said that, unfortunately, many marital problems began when her husband was unable to find work to help support the family financially. Although she contemplated finding another man who could help her with expenses, she stated that she did not do so. She believed that children should have two parents in the home. The consequence of her decision to remain with her partner was that she bore the burden of providing for their daily needs alone:

> I was working so hard, but it wasn't enough to keep the house and send the children to school. I was waking up early and going to bed late to make money for school. I didn't want the children to grow up stupid. When many of the children died, I buried them. The mister is an artisan, but he didn't do anything. But I wanted the children to leave the home knowing both their parents so that they would be prepared for tomorrow. So I worked and sold all kinds of things, but it was never enough to send them to school and to eat.

Marie strongly endorsed the dominant gender ideals of the woman as a faithful partner and mother and the man as an involved husband and father. She stated that she continued to work as a market woman during the sixteen years of her relationship without entering into any other conjugal union. Toward the end of their relationship, the couple married legally, but tragic events later ended their marriage.

On February 4, 1994, members of FRAPH and the coup apparatus invaded the households of the poor pro-democracy neighborhood where she lived. This was the date when the majority of my clients were raped during a single night of terror and debauchery. When I asked about the date's significance, some of my clients said that it was a sinister commemoration of the anniversary of Jean-Claude Duvalier's ouster on February 7, 1986; others, that it commemorated the date of Aristide's inauguration, February 7, 1991. Members of the de facto regime had driven through the market warning residents of the zone that retribution was coming. This mass punishment was an exercise in necropolitics serving as a reminder that the poor pro-democracy forces would not be free anytime soon. I learned later that the date, perhaps coincidentally, marks the bicentennial of the legislative abolition of slavery by the French on February 4, 1794. It is possible that this widespread attack on the community as a whole was an effort to remind the nation in bodily ways of its "enslaved" status.

Marie asserted that after a night of partying, drinking, and taking drugs, gangs of armed men entered each household to terrorize the community. The assailants beat her husband. Six men raped her in front of two of her children. They took all her money and material possessions and destroyed the house. In the aftermath of rape, she was afflicted with sexually transmitted diseases that she could not afford to have treated. From shame at her violation and fear of future violence, her husband left her with the children to support as best she could. Having been abandoned by her husband, she was unable to send the remaining children to school, and she was plagued with nightmares, depression, and fear. Marie attributed her plight to the negligence of the Haitian state "that doesn't recognize her as a person with rights." Nonetheless, despite a socioeconomic situation in Haiti that left few alternatives for the poor, Marie's narrative also illustrated the possibility of agency and courage despite exploitation. By the time I left Haiti in early 2000, Marie had rebuilt her business in Martissant and was quite successful. Her receipt of assistance from several agencies and agents in the aid apparatus was in no small part integral to her triumph over the scourges of past violation.

Caroline Antoine

Caroline Antoine, a tall woman who was forty-five years old at the time of the interview, lived in Martissant. I met Caroline in one of the Rehabilitation Program's therapy groups that had a psychological orientation (discussed below). She also spent time at Chanm Fanm and occasionally helped clean the facility. She had a wiry build that came from labor as a madanm sara and from infrequent meals. Haitian journalists and activists and their American counterparts interviewed her several times in the years following the coup. She was very willing to tell me her life story.

Caroline began by lamenting, "I am a victim, and I have always been a victim." She explained that she was born in Bizoton, in the western Carrefour area, the product of a sexually exploitative union. Her mother had been working as a domestic servant for a wealthier family. The son in the household "had gotten her pregnant" *(vin ansent li)*. Once her mother's pregnancy was revealed, the family expelled her from the house. Caroline was born while her mother was on the streets. Her mother gave her to a merchant woman's family when she was no longer able to care for her, and Caroline worked as a restavèk. She said that from the moment she was born she was abused, beaten, and enslaved: "They didn't send me to school. I used to get up early to sell cloth for her. She was a cloth merchant, and I sold her fabrics. . . . [T]hat has always stayed in my character, that since I was born I've been abused."

Over time, Caroline plotted her escape. In 1977 a woman friend whom she had known for years gave her twenty Haitian dollars (100 gourdes) to help her start her own business. She left the home where she worked as a servant and stayed with this woman while building her small-scale trade. She eventually rented her own house and became quite successful at marketing. Caroline stated, "When you have money, men see you." Many men sought her attention. She chose one and married him in 1979. Unfortunately, in 1992 this same husband abandoned her after she became a victim of gang rape. Between 1979 and 1992 Caroline received other "shocks" that contributed to the persistent anxiety and somatic distress that she routinely experienced.

Although Caroline did not remember the exact date, she told me that in 1986, at about the time of the departure of Jean-Claude Duvalier, she was robbed at gunpoint. Her business had grown to the point where she had saved H$4,000—nearly U.S.$800—at that time the equivalent of three years of earnings for the average Haitian. After a day's labor in the central market in downtown Port-au-Prince, she was returning home with a valise containing her money and remaining wares when some armed men threatened her with a gun. They told her to give them everything that she had, including her wedding ring. One of the men was dressed in an olive-colored military uniform, but she couldn't see a face. They told her, "The moment you raise your head we will shoot you." Caroline complied, but one of them still cut her with a knife. She gave them the suitcase and her wedding ring. Afterward she felt that she had lost everything she had painstakingly built in the preceding nine or ten years of her life. She repeated to me her lament: "Since I was born, since I was born, I have suffered" *(Kounye-a se depi-m' fèt, depi-m' fèt, m'ap pase mizè).*

Caroline "went crazy" *(vin fòl)* from the shock of losing her entire livelihood. In Haitian culture unexpected losses or violence can render a person *sezi* (shocked).[16] The term is also used to describe being "taken" or "seized" by the lwa in Vodou. When a traumatic event occurs, the shock can cause an individual's blood to rise to the head. If the balance of blood is not restored in the body, the afflicted individual can suffer physical stress and violent emotion. In extreme cases of *sezisman,* the afflicted person undresses and runs naked in public.

Caroline said that she does not remember this period very well but knows that she ran naked through the streets compulsively and became homeless. During her protracted illness her brother Ronald took care of her baby daughter, but at times Caroline returned to take her daughter away into the streets with her. During this time the baby suffered a head injury, but Caroline did not remember how. Ronald had to hospitalize the baby to keep her safe. For more than a year Caroline was on the street but gradually felt more herself. Nevertheless, she said that she didn't feel completely normal until 1992. That feeling of ease was short-lived: the same year members of the military attempted to assassinate her brother for his activism in the pro-democracy movement.

In the late 1980s Ronald had been a community organizer in the ti kominote legliz, the grassroots ecclesial movement for democracy. He had been galvanizing poor residents of Carrefour and Martissant to protest Jean-Claude Duvalier's bloody repression and to support former Father Aristide's mission. Both Ronald and Caroline attended the masses that Father Aristide said not far from their home at the Saint Jean-Bosco church. After the 1991 coup d'état members of the coup apparatus recognized Ronald for having attended the church. He was accused of being a Communist partisan of Aristide. The prospective assassins pursued him until he reached the safety of Léogâne, a small town west of the capital. After some weeks Caroline and Ronald regained contact. Caroline traveled back and forth to give him funds and supplies from a Haitian development organization in order to help him resume the work of organizing young adults. Caroline supported Ronald until he was recognized by a chèf seksyon, one of the section chiefs who were part of the Duvalier police apparatus that had been reactivated during the coup years. Ronald fled once more and found asylum in Jacmel, on the southern coast.

Caroline continued to transport goods and money between Jacmel and Port-au-Prince until November 1992, when her work promoting democracy in Haiti was halted. On these risky evening journeys she often dressed as a man and pretended to be an advocate for Jean-Claude Duvalier's return to power. She would tie up her hair, wear a military cap on her head, and place a red-and-black Duvalier flag in her front pocket. She hoped that these subterfuges would increase her chances of arriving safely. But on that fateful late afternoon in November, the *kamyon* (a large truck fitted for passenger travel between the provinces and the cities) on which she was riding broke down in Mariani, just outside the Port-au-Prince city limits.

The passengers were forced to disembark so that the kamyon could be repaired. While the driver worked on the vehicle, a military truck carrying soldiers in uniform and brandishing machetes stopped to investigate. The soldiers interrogated the passengers about the purposes of their voyage. When they came to Caroline and discovered that she was concealing her true sex and political identity, a group of the men dragged her off into the fields adjacent to the road. They beat her severely, breaking her ribs. What Caroline remembers next is waking up naked and alone in that field some hours later. She was covered in her own blood and had wounds all over her body. She believes that each man had raped her, but she did not know how many because at some point during the beatings she lost consciousness.

One of the passengers covered her and helped her to find a place to hide in the Carrefour foothills. While she was "out of her head," in a sort of fugue state of dissociation *(dekonpoze)* but still conscious, she managed to give her godmother's address in order for the helpful passenger to bring clothing and aid. Caroline was afraid to seek medical attention, as the coup apparatus pursued their targets in hospitals and clinics. While she was in hiding, her host brought a physician to treat her wounds. Dr. Andrea Baptiste, who became one of the staff physicians in Chanm Fanm, examined her. Atlhough Baptiste was able to treat her broken body, the process of healing Caroline's spirit is ongoing. Her ordeal has continued long after the rape.

Caroline gave birth to a daughter the next year. She is not sure exactly when she became pregnant, because her memory of those events is not very good. With the uncertainty about paternity and the shame of having been a victim of gang rape, her husband abandoned her and her two daughters. He alleged that she was now *fanm kadejak,* wife of the rapist. As a victim of rape she was shamed *(wont)* before her family and society. Those who knew her plight sometimes taunted her in the neighborhood. In the years after the rape, her children were also ashamed of her. And she felt ambivalent emotions toward them, especially her youngest daughter.

Caroline's sorrowful narrative was typical of the way Haitian women lamented their trials and sufferings. In the Rehabilitation Program's therapy groups, she spoke of the disgrace that her daughters felt knowing that their mother had been raped instead of focusing on her own feelings of "demoralization" (Frank and Frank 1991). She wanted to find psychological counseling for them to help them cope. She also expressed her desire that someone might help her youngest child come to terms with how she probably had been conceived. Eventually, she connected with staff at the Mars/Kline Center for Psychiatry and Neurology and received assistance for her children.

Much of Caroline's shame, like that of other viktim, arose from feelings of powerlessness and the inability to fulfill the Haitian ideals of gender and kinship. Caroline had difficulty regaining her livelihood as a market woman, in part because of Haiti's dire economic problems and in part because her emotional distress left her feeling anxious, depressed, and even suicidal. She mourned her lost ability to contribute to her children's care. She had left both of her daughters with her brother Ronald. He had returned to Carrefour after the restoration of Aristide. The girls were fortunate to have received scholarships to attend a parochial school in Carrefour and were moving forward. Caroline sometimes felt socially isolated and disconnected from her community. She remained frightened by the sight of any partially clothed man, a common sight in the zone among men who performed manual labor. Over time she regained contact with the husband who had abandoned her, but the relationship remained limited.

In my intake interview with Caroline in preparation for commencing the Trager session, she had told me that she continued to feel a nagging, irritating pain in her ribs where a callus had formed when the bones mended. Like a poisonous demon in her system that she needed to scratch compulsively to release, the skin over the callus was scarred from the times when she had reopened her flesh. Her wounded body had become a weapon of torment long after her torturers had finished with her. As we worked together, Caroline would giggle at times in recognition that her body remained guarded against even the gentlest therapeutic touch. Each time we spoke about her past traumatic experiences she told me that she would sometimes need to numb the pain with alcohol or other substances. But she insisted on sharing her experience through these verbal and nonverbal means of communication. Over time she reported that she no longer had the same involuntary startle responses or other fight-or-flight reflexes, but the ensekirite of Martissant only reinforced her embodied fear.

Sylvie Saint-Fleur

Sylvie was a woman with whom I had a complicated working relationship between 1996 and late 1998, when our collaboration ended quite abruptly. Like her mother before her, she was an activist and advocate for women's rights. At the time I knew her she had six children who ranged in age from four to eighteen. Some of the children resided with their fathers or had been fostered with her extended family when she was unable to provide for their care. Originally from Jacmel, Sylvie had come to Port-au-Prince to seek her fortune, as so many residents of the Martissant bidonvil had also done.

In 1992 she had been the target of egregious violence. One evening in August she had gone into labor, and Sylvie and her husband were desperately attempting to reach a hospital despite the military's imposed curfew and the dangers that circulation on the street posed after the de facto apparatus occupied Port-au-Prince. When a pickup truck carrying military men began to pull over, she debated whether to continue to go toward the hospital or to run into her home. She ran into her home. The soldiers entered her home and beat her and her husband, despite her full-term pregnancy and the throes of labor. They took her husband. He was never seen again and is presumed dead. Despite broken bones and head trauma, Sylvie fled to another section of Martissant and gave birth to her child. When that area was no longer safe, she went into hiding in the provinces with her other children. She returned to the Martissant area after the October 1994 restoration of Aristide to Haiti.

When I elicited her sensory biography and conducted bodywork with her, Sylvie was still plagued with flashbacks. She described *vizyon* (visions) of the 1992 attack that she sometimes saw as a "film" or "movie" playing in her field of sight. She was profoundly grieved by the disappearance and probable death of her husband and had other classic symptoms of PTSD. In our Trager work she was only able to receive limited compression on her upper left torso because her broken ribs had healed poorly. My ability to rotate her left arm at the shoulder was restricted by her unconscious "protection" of and resistance to movement of the limb. I was aware as I worked with her that the lingering effects of the injury meant that any lifting, pulling, and even pushing with her left arm might bring the injury and the memory of its acquisition to her attention.

Outside the clinic space, Sylvie remained "hypervigilant," especially given the climate of ensekirite. We spoke often about the continued "occupation" of the Martissant zone by the zenglendo—armed "assassins" in her words—who continued to steal and to rape women, children, *and* men in the neighborhood. They also extorted funds from its residents with impunity. In early 1996 Sylvie's family was once again victimized when her daughter Natasha was gang-raped in the same area. Nonetheless, these incidents did not deter Sylvie from activism.

In summer 1996 Sylvie and I documented cases of human rights abuses in the Martissant area and agreed to work together when I returned to Haiti. After my departure that summer, Sylvie organized groups of viktim in the Martissant area into an association whose membership was composed of women, men, and their families. Her work contrasted with the approach of the DRC and HWA, which at the time worked exclusively with women viktim, and she began to build a reputation as an activist and human rights advocate among the national and international NGOs working in this domain.

Marie's, Caroline's, and Sylvie's stories demonstrate how gender is inextricably linked to local and national politics. Ensekirite engenders a climate of risk and peril that is especially threatening for those who are vulnerable to everyday violences in local realms but especially for viktim. It is in this context that the continuing trauma of victimization can be seen. That having been said, the way extreme suffering, loss, and grief manifest in Haitian culture—mental illness, disturbances in the sense of embodiment and emotional distress, among other "symptoms"—can be compared with the trauma that may be manifested in the aftermath of terror and repression cross-culturally.

While many women recognized their victimization during the 1991–94 coup years as extremes of humiliation, violation, and loss, these ruptures in the fabric of their moral lives have become routine in the uncertain transitional climate. In many respects the way gender ideals and practices constrain women's lives—whether in times of political conflict or under ensekirite—makes the notion of victimization much more complex. The therapy groups at the Human Rights Fund Rehabilitation Program provided another space of security in which viktim testified about experiences of victimization in the hope of attaining healing and redress for their complex losses.

HUMAN RIGHTS AND CIVIL RIGHTS
AS THERAPEUTIC DISCOURSES

The America's Development Foundation building where the Rehabilitation Program operated had provided asylum to pro-democracy activists during the coup years. During the time of my research the program's therapy groups offered another space of security that permitted viktim to recount and review critically their past experiences. Their participation in the groups challenged a prevailing perception among Haitian mental health professionals that "talk therapy" is beyond the comprehension and capacity of poor Haitians and that psychotherapy is, therefore, superfluous. Many health professionals felt that the priority for viktim was satisfaction of "basic needs" rather than existential exploration of the psyche or mind. That these clients of the Fund went to great lengths to participate in the groups, to share their experiences with others, to give voice to their moral angst, and to learn tools to seek justice negated these stereotypical views.

Because I wanted to know more about what motivated participation in the groups, I took part in five biweekly therapy groups of four months' duration between fall 1998 and spring 1999.[17] One group comprised six men and four women and had a psychological orientation. Program staff members had diagnosed the participants as suffering from prolonged somatic stress and other acute psychological symptoms stemming from their victimization. Dr. François Verrette, a psychiatrist at the Mars/Kline Psychiatric Center, co-facilitated the group with John Medeus, a massage therapist who had training as a pharmacist. Medeus treated beneficiaries at his private office. Another facilitator was Marie-Claire Émile, a young psychology student in clinical training who interned with the program. Dr. Christine Thomas attended to check on the group's progress and to explain HRF bureaucratic procedures as needed.

The second therapy group had a legal counseling orientation. It also comprised six men and four women. The group was facilitated by Dr. Thomas, Marie-Claire Émile, and Mèt Lucienne Darius, a woman who was both an attorney and a registered nurse. Although I do not have statistical data that confirm my observations, it appeared that the legal counseling approach was the most effective in enabling its participants to regain a sense of empowerment and agency to change their circumstances on their own initiative.

The third group was for women only and focused on education. Most of these women had been raped during the coup years. While this was intended to be a support group, the information it disseminated was primarily in the form of reproductive health and nutrition counseling. By fall 1998 Nurse Emilie Datilus had left Chanm Fanm to join the staff of the Human Rights Fund. She co-facilitated this group with her colleague from HRF, Nurse Louise Gilles. Two psychiatric nurses from Mars/Kline who had participated in the Boston training also facilitated this group.

Dr. Thomas reiterated in each therapy group that their purpose was to "work" on the memories of the past *(travay sou memwa)* by recounting their trauma narratives. She emphasized that if a participant did not air the details of past human rights abuses, the memories would remain within them "like a poison in their minds." She expressed hope that they would not relive nightmares and intrusive recollections of their violation throughout their lives. She also stated that the act of narration within a group of individuals who had suffered similarly and who could empathize with the experiences of their peers would reduce feelings of isolation and shame. The ultimate goal was for viktim to attain a subjective position no longer oriented to or framed by the "identity" of victimization. Given how many militan became viktim by protesting the routine ruptures in their lives, and how many continued to live with risk, uncertainty, and the dangers of ensekirite, this task proved challenging. Many viktim viewed themselves as martyrs for the cause of democracy and considered this status honorable and deserving of acknowledgment. Viktim status was one means to attain political recognition, ankadreman, and at least intervals of security.

At the commencement of each meeting, Dr. Thomas and the other therapeutic staff "checked in" with each participant and inquired about the intervening two weeks since the last session. Often the daily struggle to subsist was a focus of discussion at the start of each group. After that, facilitators asked one or two persons to recount the narrative of what brought them to the Fund, so that by the third or fourth meeting most participants had been given time to introduce themselves and their trauma narratives. Facilitators also discussed their own experiences assisting Haitians in the domain of human rights and health. Thus the meetings were not solely performances of beneficiaries for a clinical audience but rather a group dialogue among people with diverse histories and experiences. Admittedly, the group's participants had unequal power and authority.

For many men in the groups, Haitian politics was a perpetual subject of interest that provoked heated discussion. The therapeutic staff decided to keep the focus on individual experience rather than foreground the broader political and economic situation, a strategy that countered the human rights frame in which the Fund operated and produced double binds for participants. HRF's programs were concerned with the community and extended family in terms of justice and human rights education efforts. The attention to individual experience in the therapy group setting encouraged the creation of an individual subjectivity that may not have been customary for the participant but aligned with predominant Western conceptions of human rights (An-Na'im 1992; Mutua 2001). Limiting discussions of the broader political framework in the treatment of individual trauma contributed to the transformation of militan to viktim.

In the group with the psychological orientation, viktim first recounted their trauma narratives and then were asked to describe their past. The operative question was, "Who were you before you became a victim?" In more than one case the question elicited nostalgic laments for childhoods spent in the provinces, where "one could at least live and eat from the land," whereas life in the city was harsher, more perilous, and fragile. Generally viktim described leaving the routines of the extended family and agricultural production for the "depravity," "risk," and "lawlessness" of urban life. Their experiences of threat, assault, and humiliation during the coup years forced many to flee an mawonaj. In some cases, their flight was to natal homes in the provinces and to pasts that no longer existed. Having to flee compounded their sense of shame and feelings of failure to succeed. Regardless, recollections of idyllic lives in rural areas were most likely inaccurate representations of the past. The provinces were generally acknowledged to be the poorest areas in Haiti and those least maintained by the centralized state. However, they were also viewed as less vulnerable to the waves of political and criminal ensekirite that have become routine in Port-au-Prince.

The intent of the question, "Who were you before you became a victim?" was to elicit stories that encouraged the participant to recall and even enact or perform an identity that existed prior to the presumed instance of degradation and humiliation. The implicit assumption appeared to be that the transformation from militan to viktim had been recent, arising from experiencing or witnessing a grave psycho-physical threat. The view that viktim status resulted from recent "state-sponsored" human rights violations in some ways forced participants to reinterpret their past and present experiences according to conventional conceptions of trauma, which attributed it to isolated events rather than ongoing routines of rupture in the context of ontological insecurity.

This approach also paralleled emphases in human rights discourse on abuses of civil and political rights, that is, on instances of extreme repression rather than the less visible, ongoing violations of economic, cultural, and social rights. While the framework of PTSD was not explicitly deployed or taught in these groups, the presumption was that victim status could and *should* be transcended in an ordered series of stages. The culmination of successful "memory work" was expected to be reinsertion or ankadreman in the community.

MEN'S STORIES

Some of the group's participants felt that viktim status was an aspect of their political subjectivity and symbolized their status as "martyrs" for the democratic cause. In some respects the physical and psychological scars acquired from waging the battle for democracy were badges of respect or honor, especially for men in the groups. They were also tangible and intangible emblems of loyalty to the original Lavalas platform and to the person of President Jean-Bertrand Aristide.

Phillippe Jonassaint

Phillippe Jonassaint, an activist in his early thirties from the Carrefour-Feuilles section of Port-au-Prince, stressed that he had been targeted more than once in his service to the democratic cause. He had been involved in local literacy and voter registration activities at the request of Aristide's campaign representatives. Phillippe framed his life history in terms of having come to Port-au-Prince from Jérémie to attend secondary school and, once in the capital, having experienced a political awakening or epiphany. While observing the tumultuous spread of activism before and after the 1986 ouster of Jean-Claude Duvalier, he felt compelled to become active in politics. In 1988 he put together a small theatrical group *(animasyon)* in order to perform consciousness-raising pieces for youth in his zone. His brother-in-law, a prominent militan in the National Front for Change and Democracy (Front National pour le Changement et la Démocratie, FNCD),[18] recognized his success. He invited Phillippe to work with the Aristide campaign and to continue promoting literacy in affiliation with Misyon Alfa, a church-sponsored movement using Haitian Creole that was inaugurated just after the ouster of Duvalier. Phillippe's group was successful in teaching more than 750 people to read and write. The group also coordinated cooperative rotating credit schemes in order to promote economic opportunities for small-scale merchants. These political activities made him a threat to antidemocratic forces in the nation.

On October 1, 1991, a pickup truck carrying a group of FAD'H soldiers disembarked in the area where his organization held its meetings. They asked residents in the zone for the location of the organization. Phillippe was fortunate to have been absent at the time, so he was not immediately apprehended. The following day he fled to Léogâne and remained in hiding for several months. However, members of the coup regime located him in 1992. He was caught by five men and beaten severely. His stomach and testicles were damaged to the extent that he needed surgery. He was treated at CITYMED through aid from the PIRÈD program. Phillippe lamented the material and symbolic attack on his masculinity. He was unable to service an outstanding debt of H$18,000 because of his internal displacement and persistent unemployment. In addition, he regretted being unable to take care of a child whom he had fathered after the attack. Group members of both sexes were quite critical of this admission and felt that he was making excuses for abandoning his responsibilities.

Phillippe's laments also reflected feelings of having been overlooked for his role in the democratic struggle. He was an associate of Alphonse Montina and Henri Claude, who at the time were HRF staff members who had sheltered with David Hunter while internally displaced during the coup period. Throughout the four months of the therapy groups, Phillippe was unrelenting in requests that the Fund give him a job, as it had done for Montina and Claude. In my interview with Phillippe he protested that he had also been with ADF as early as these two staff members and should be recognized as "different" from other viktim in that he was well educated. At the same time he expressed feelings of betrayal by President Aristide, saying that Aristide had not done more to ankadre those who risked their lives to support his administration before the coup and after his restoration to office. Phillippe took risks to promote democracy and assist poor Haitians in part from the alliances with and loyalty to Aristide. On some level the democracy movement was both personal and political, but it was not blind, nor was it free from self-interest. Phillippe wanted to be honored publicly and materially compensated accordingly, if not from Haitians or the Government of Haiti, then from the Human Rights Fund.

Christian Dieusibon

Among some participants, the focus was not on nostalgia for the past or a public political identity but on feelings of fear, persecution, and guilt for having been unable to honor the obligations to family, both living and dead. The inability to bury the dead properly was often a source of deep remorse and grief for survivors of violence or unexpected catastrophes in Haiti (James 2008). Christian Dieusibon, a young man who resided in the Artibonite department of Haiti, had lost both of his parents during the coup years, but the body of his father had never been recovered. He was left as the sole support of his siblings and had been feeling the pressure of failing to fulfill his familial duties. After listening to his story, Dr. Thomas and a psychiatrist from Mars/Kline suggested that he hold a "symbolic" funeral for his father in order to restore the relationship between the living and the dead (mete an plas moun ki mouri ak moun ki vivan). They suggested that once having completed the rite, all involved—both living and dead—would be at peace (tèt yo pli trankil). Dr. Thomas asserted, however, that the funeral would enable him to make a change in his own personal circumstances in order to move forward. Christian then asked if the Fund still provided assistance for funerals; unfortunately, by this stage such assistance had been discontinued.

In subsequent weeks, however, Christian was able to find the resources to hold a ceremony for his father and by doing so was relieved of some of the guilt that he experienced in failing to meet his obligations to family and community. In addition to receiving this advice, he was also able to consult with a lawyer about his specific case to learn the process by which he might be able to pursue a claim for justice (revandikasyon) through the Haitian judicial system. I was not party to these private legal counseling sessions, but Christian made an interesting comment at the end of the therapy groups. He said that before participating in the Fund's programs, he did not know that he was a "person." It was through his participation in the group and the support he received to resolve his relationship with his extended family that he was able to recognize himself *"kòm moun"*—as a human being or person. His description also suggested this was the first time he viewed himself as an "individual" in the Western sense—as a discrete subject with human and civil rights. This neomodern frame of subjectivity was counter to but not incompatible with "traditional" conceptions of the self. Viktim appropriated and translated their own suffering, in addition to adopting new subjectivities, according to the context in which care and ankadreman were sought, much like what Paul Brodwin (1996) has described in his ethnography of care-seeking practices among rural Haitians. Christian later entered the Fund's training program to become a field agent to identify and assist "local" viktim in his province.

Thus far I have discussed how gendered trauma narratives reveal a victim's feelings of lost hope, betrayal, and abuse. Trauma narratives portray melancholic losses and ontological mourning. Viktim live with the fragmentation and "natal alienation" (Patterson 1982) of urban, neomodern violence. In some cases, like Christian's, the narration of trauma in prescribed settings reframed or remoralized the victim. In others, the intersubjective sharing of traumatic stories did not inculcate a sense of self and identity that transcended victim status.

Yves Brutus

Yves Brutus, a man in his mid-forties, told a poignant story of his days in a Catholic mission school in his ancestral *peyi* (homeland), Jérémie. His instructors encouraged him to learn, but he was a mischievous boy who enjoyed pranks. Sometimes he was physically punished for his behavior. He did not express feeling maltreated by such beatings; rather, he described the corporal discipline with humor, portraying it as a demonstration of the priest's care for his personal development and achievement.

He journeyed to Port-au-Prince as a young man with a visceral, hopeful sense of *chans* (chance, luck, or opportunity to seek a new life) and eventually found employment as a tailor.[19] In this respect his tale paralleled those of other viktim who had to *chèche lavi* (seek a life or survival) in the capital to support themselves *and* family members who remained in the provinces.

On February 16, 1993, however, after a memorial service in Port-au-Prince for victims of the capsized *Neptune*, FAD'H soldiers apprehended him and beat him severely. There was no apparent reason for the attack, apart from his having participated in a public assembly. Over time he joined a victim advocacy group with more than fifteen hundred members, the Òganizasyon Viktim Koudeta (Organization of Coup Victims, OVKD). Mèt Camille Leblanc, the future minister of justice, provided legal representation to this group and managed its aggregate trauma portfolio. Where once Yves and others like him considered themselves militan, victim status and membership in groups such as OVKD had become means of political recognition.

Yves was one of the participants in the therapy groups most adamant about retaining the status of viktim. Underneath what appeared to be a subdued exterior he was perpetually cho (angry, hotheaded). At the slightest indication of injustice or inequality, he reacted quite vociferously and at times without warrant. Special sources of frustration were alterations in the Rehabilitation Program's services. One of the complaints commonly expressed by viktim was a decision made by program staff to begin regulating their medical prescriptions directly and prescribing generic drugs because of a decreased budget. Yves and other therapy group participants who were also members of OVKD grumbled at the opening of the sessions about the injustice of this practice. "I'm a victim!" Yves exclaimed in order to demand what he felt was equitable medical treatment. Others in the groups complained of having negative side effects from the medications they had been given. When Dr. Thomas was out of hearing range, Yves and other OVKD members said that if the program did not change its policies on prescriptions they would demonstrate publicly against the Fund. Yet these beneficiaries received a level of care that was unusually good for Haiti, and even for the United States.

The desire for recognition and the feelings of entitlement to equal and even privileged treatment in comparison to other Haitians because of their past suffering were things against which Dr. Thomas struggled in the therapy sessions. It is possible to interpret such protests as displaced aggression: viktim may have directed anger about their experiences of victimization against the therapy group staff rather than against the perpetrators of their suffering. The Fund might also have been seen as a surrogate for the United States. Such public displays of protest could also be gendered forms of posturing, similar to those Michael Herzfeld (1985) observed among Cretan shepherds. In most cases men in the groups discussed their public personae and loss of prestige, wealth, or political and economic status. They were also those most likely to confront the Rehabilitation Program staff members or the general staff at HRF and ADF.

The dynamics of this group contrasted with another therapy group that had a legal orientation. The approach of Mèt Darius as primary facilitator was instructive and disciplinary, as well as palliative. As each participant narrated the events of his or her victimization, she discussed how the "facts" of humiliation could be documented to create a legal claim against the perpetrators or the state itself. Implicit in the group discussion, however, was acknowledgment of the weakness and corruption of the judicial system (LCHR 1990; NCHR 1995). Nonetheless, at moments when an individual narrator of a horror story expressed grief or rage at his or her powerlessness, Mèt Darius interrupted the story—also disrupting the intensity of the intersubjective affect that had been generated—in order to demonstrate the process by which that person could begin to compile a case for prosecution. She taught us the benevolent arts of bureaucraft: how to transform the receipts for medical treatment, the testimonies of witnesses, the photos of wounded bodies, and other affidavits documenting participants' cases into dossiers or trauma portfolios that had potential to engender justice and reparations. Some of the participants met with her privately or with other members of the legal referral system and reported feeling satisfied, even if their cases did not have enough supporting evidence to move forward. The act of having been heard—of having been addressed as an equal with civil rights under Haitian law and with human rights according to international law—was therapeutic or healing on some level as a step toward restitution.

Mèt Darius also taught us the meaning of citizenship under Haitian law and how to resolve disputes by means of dialogue and negotiation rather than aggressive confrontation. Her mediation was crucial at the moment when the participants in many of the groups expressed frustration with the changes in the Rehab Program's benefits. In this group the provision of concrete information and assistance to "reframe" the experience of victimization and to "craft" citizens from viktim appeared to be empowering. Her overall approach demonstrated the beneficent and therapeutic side of the professional transformation of suffering. Raw, unmediated pain was crafted into something potentially productive of long-term justice in Haiti, even if the "citizenship" that this process engendered was limited to this space of security.

WOMEN'S HEALTH AND ENSEKIRITE

The women-only therapy group did not have the same overtly political, performative character as the predominantly male groups. In contrast to the other therapy groups, in the women's group there was little or no emphasis on recounting trauma narratives. Like the seminar on women's rights under Haitian law, the group provided education and emotional support to participants as they struggled with everyday gender inequalities. In many respects, however, the reproductive and nutritional health approach disseminated in this group inadvertently reinforced the ideal gender ideologies against which its participants were struggling—namely, that women had primary responsibility for the care of the household and children. The four participating nurses offered instruction on reproductive health and nutrition. They acknowledged the reality that Haitian women are predominantly in charge of child care. Nonetheless, the therapeutic team felt that the women would be empowered by information that promoted their ability to protect themselves from sexually transmitted disease and to control their fertility.

A general point of similarity between the narratives of men and women was their concern about being able to fulfill their obligations to family and society. In public speech, however, women viktim tended to focus on the daily pressures to maintain the domestic sphere. There were a couple of women in this group, however, who expressed grief over the loss of their fertility when, in the aftermath of rape, they had to undergo hysterectomies. One woman had been shot in the vagina. She still had bullet fragments in her womb that required the removal of her uterus in order for her to heal fully. She grieved in advance its loss and the loss of her identity as a woman. Other women in the group consoled her and encouraged her not to think of herself solely in terms of her sex or her physical body, telling her she would retain her value to her children and community regardless of her injury. For some participants in this group, however, the injuries sustained in the aftermath of being physically and emotionally assaulted would more than likely result in death: they had been diagnosed as HIV positive or were suffering from AIDS.

As I spent time with some of the women outside these institutional settings I learned how these devastating, gendered afflictions were in some senses only a minimal part of the ensekirite they faced. By coincidence, the majority of the fourteen women in this group were residents of Martissant, some of whom I met at the 1996 women's rights seminar. In 1997 I reconnected with many of them at the women's tribunal (see introduction). I continued to associate with them at Chanm Fanm before participating with them in the Rehabilitation Program's therapy group. My encounters with women viktim within and outside spaces of security organized by the humanitarian and development apparatus revealed an expanding occult economy within the political economy of trauma.

THE WOMEN'S TRIBUNAL

In the absence of a functioning, transparent, and accountable judiciary, Haitian civil society organizations created other spaces of security in which the truths of victimization could be heard. A coalition of feminist organizations sponsored the highly visible International Tribunal against Violence toward Women, held in Port-au-Prince on November 24–26, 1997. It was modeled on the International Criminal Tribunals of Rwanda and the former Yugoslavia. Its goal, however, was to analyze the spectrum of violence perpetrated against Haitian women in times of both peace and overt conflict. I attended the tribunal as an international guest and a representative of the Human Rights Fund. Oxfam and other Canadian development organizations funded the tribunal. Representatives from UNIFEM, the U.N./OAS International Civilian Mission, the U.S. Embassy, and USAID also attended. Also participating were Haitian and international human rights groups, international human rights medical missions, Haitian victims' organizations, representatives from the Haitian Ministry of Justice, and others.

A Haitian feminist organization made the following statement in its introduction to the event: "Whether in periods of political conflict or periods of calm, repression never stops for Haitian women." This declaration asserts that violence occurs along a continuum from peace to conflict that is disproportionately gendered (Moser 2001). It also marks the contested, interconnected relationship between individuals, institutions, and the state in human rights and women's rights discourses. This perspective highlights the challenges of categorizing types of victimization. The slogan for the conference, "N'ap wete baboukèt la" (We're taking the muzzle off), signaled the intent to open a space of security in which women could move from silence and shame to speak about the persecution that they had endured on a daily basis. Explicit in the introduction to the tribunal was the acknowledgment that while the Haitian state seeks political recognition in the international realm through the ratification of international human rights conventions, its domestic practices of justice are sorely lacking. A panel of international women activists served as judges and a large audience comprising viktim and the aid apparatus acted in some ways as a chorus.

Women testified regarding their vulnerability to domestic, political, and sexual violence, as well as other forms of exploitation. To protect their identities, complainants were hidden behind black sheeting that enclosed an area of the conference room. The majority of these speakers

were poor. After each woman spoke she was questioned by the judges
about the details of her presentation so that they could render a judgment
at the conclusion of the two days of hearings. To some extent hearing the
disembodied voices of women reveal publicly the horrors of rape, gang
rape, or daily humiliation and physical abuse was shocking, even having
worked with many viktim in face-to-face encounters. In my discussions
with viktim at its conclusion, however, many reported feeling empowered
by their participation in the event. It had been broadcast nationally on the
radio and was recognized publicly by state representatives as a contribution to the processes of justice. Despite these successes, it is the structure
of the tribunal, the performance of suffering, and the elision of some of
the complexities of violence and its representation that concern me.

Although the tribunal was a collective effort sponsored by many
women and victims' organizations, it was also a theatrical showcase for
one Haitian women's rights group in particular. One of the directors of
this organization interrupted the proceedings in dramatic fashion and
asked for a moment of silence to acknowledge a crisis that was unfolding
as we participated. We were told that a thirteen-year-old girl had been
living with her mother, who was unable to care for all of her children. At
some point her mother gave the girl away to live with a man, and the girl
was now pregnant with his child. She was raped just before the tribunal,
and the perpetrator was in prison, but unfortunately the baby died inside
her. The women's rights organization was helping her receive care at the
General Hospital in downtown Port-au-Prince. One of its representatives
said we would receive postings throughout the day on the girl's progress.

After a couple of hours the leader of the women's organization sponsoring the tribunal interrupted a woman's testimony to provide a second dramatic update on the young girl's condition. We were told that
the fetus had been removed from the young girl, but the situation was
one of life or death. The testimonies, judges' responses, and general proceedings then continued. Eventually, there was a third interruption, and
we were told that the young woman had survived.

On one level, presenting the case of the thirteen-year-old girl as the
crisis unfolded highlighted the desperation of women in Haiti. The
drama of each interjection increased the heightened emotion and indignation among the participants. Nevertheless, the presentation was also
an appropriation of another's suffering for the purpose of dramatizing the organization's commitment to the struggle for women's rights.
It was also a means to demonstrate its work to current and potential
international governmental and nongovernmental donor groups whose

representatives were in the audience. Indeed, the circulation of wealth in the humanitarian assistance apparatus was one of the factors at stake.

At the conclusion of the tribunal, a leader of a women's victim advocacy group whom I knew from my work at the Fund lamented that her organization had been the first formed during the coup years but also the one that had made the least progress in terms of "sustainability." Most of its members were nonliterate and poor, and they lacked access to the donors that other national feminist organizations with middle- and upper-class members and international connections had attracted. She affirmed, however, "They always call us when they need us to testify about our suffering in front of others." She complained that these organizations did not share the funds acquired from their performances of suffering.

A prominent member of a competing multiclass feminist organization echoed this perception of the disparity in access to resources. She complained that in the initial planning of the tribunal and the solicitation of funds from Oxfam, her organization had been invited to the meeting but was subsequently excluded. They still participated in the event and drafted recommendations for the judges' consideration, which articulated what must be done to change Haitian law and society, but there remained lingering frustration with the process afterward. The hidden complexities surrounding the organization of the event and its funding were not the only occult economies.

Although the identities of many "plaintiffs" were kept anonymous, I was surprised to recognize the voices of some of the women I knew from the Martissant clinic who testified about their own experiences or those of others. One woman with whom I had worked in Martissant was Sylvie Saint-Fleur, who at the time was a leader of a new victims' advocacy group. She spoke on behalf of her daughter, Natasha, the deaf-mute young woman who had been gang-raped by four men in Martissant. A document provided by the sponsors of the tribunal stated that in the Haitian Vodou belief system the rape of a disabled woman was purportedly a means by which perpetrators acquired *pwen* (power) or *chans* (luck)—something that I was not able to confirm after many requests for information about this supposed practice. Natasha suffered health problems after the rape, especially recurring vaginal infections. The family never found formal justice because of the difficulty of pursuing rape cases in the Haitian judicial system.

I had learned through my ethnographic work, however, that the context of Natasha's case was more complicated than what was presented in the tribunal. The perpetrators of this rape were well-known residents of the Martissant neighborhood, part of a gang that had risen to power during the coup years. The mother of one perpetrator made financial restitution to Sylvie in the amount of H$800 to resolve the transgression in the local moral community. Sylvie's presentation of her daughter's story did not mention local efforts to mediate the dispute and to procure damages for the crime. In the context of the tribunal, her testimony was a means by which she gained recognition as an advocate within the viktim community, even as she revealed the terrible vulnerability of women in general and, more specifically, of the disabled living in poor enclaves.

The selectivity of public testimony and the uses of trauma narratives as presentations of a political self are important issues that emerged in other contexts throughout my fieldwork, much as had Liliane's testimonies that I discussed in the introduction. For example, it was in the public realm that Sylvie demonstrated charisma as a leader among viktim. She offered a model of how to appropriate experiences of victimization and suffering and transform them into something empowering and materially productive. Sylvie was becoming an "expert" (Fortun 2001; Mitchell 2002; Shore and Wright 1997) on human rights, justice, and violence who was sought for her ability to articulate the challenges of Haiti's ensekirite. Always outspoken and assertive, Sylvie was among the few in her neighborhood who could read and write well. These skills attracted to her organization several hundred viktim in the greater Martissant area.

The performance of public charisma did not always engender greater security. I learned at the tribunal that Sylvie had been the target of yet another human rights violation in 1996. A group of young adult men had threatened her for her activism. They stole the collection of dossiers she had been compiling for viktim from her neighborhood. I was not able to determine if this event was connected to the rape of Natasha. This second attack was also more complicated than was initially revealed, and I did not learn more details until I returned to work at Chanm Fanm in 1998 while attending the Rehabilitation Program's therapy groups (see chapter 5). Between our first meeting at the women's rights workshop and the November tribunal, Sylvie had also joined several other women and victim's advocacy groups, not only to promote interventions on behalf of victims, but also to improve her personal circumstances. At the 1997 tribunal I introduced her to Dr. Manata, who at the time was directing the Human Rights Fund, in order that Sylvie and those in her organization could receive assistance. I also introduced Dr. Manata to Dr. Andrea Baptiste at the Martissant clinic with the hope that they might collaborate after I had left to return to my university.

In my ongoing work with Sylvie, I learned more about how victimization, trauma, embodied suffering, and ensekirite are gender-specific in local communities that lie outside of the institutional spaces of security. Viktim had complex subjective experiences. For both women and men, experiences of victimization occurred as acute episodes within routine violence, poverty, and other forms of ensekirite. As they moved from institution to institution, seeking assistance, ankadreman, and other forms of social support, they struggled with disordered sensory as well as social experiences. They were plagued by bodily sensations and pain that were phantom traces of past victimization. The ghosts of the dead haunted them, as did the specters of loved ones who had disappeared. Their experiences led me to question the use of the concept of posttraumatic stress, especially to describe the experience of living in areas like Martissant. If ruptures had become routine, what possibility was there for hope or for a sense of the future? What interventions could promote human and civil rights, healing, justice, and reparations for those whose lives were ruptured during the years of de facto rule but continued living indefinitely with routines of rupture? For these individuals, there was no "post-" to their trauma, only a constant present.

The spaces of security offered by organizations and events within the aid apparatus were vehicles by which raw, unmediated suffering could be shaped through the technologies of trauma employed in benevolent forms of bureaucraft. The discourses of feminism, human rights, psychiatry, women's reproductive health, and law crafted multiple types of public testimony. The act of testimony was another form of labor. Whether recounted in private or public settings, trauma narratives had plots meant to persuade an audience or a listener to accept a narrator's self-image as victim, martyr, innocent, betrayed, worthy, or failed. The styles and contexts of narration reproduced and reinforced prevailing gender ideals, even as they also encoded particular professional languages and bureaucratic practices. The performance of suffering and its material representation in the trauma portfolio were integral aspects of economies of compassion within the political economy of trauma. But practices of rehabilitation in the humanitarian and development assistance domain also generated multiple occult economies and perversions of "truth" within and without the institutions of benevolent aid. The effort to craft citizens from viktim would be just as challenging in the daily operations of the Human Rights Fund.

CHAPTER 4

Double Binds in Audit Cultures

The Human Rights Fund no longer exists. During its brief tenure in Haiti, it occupied the liminal space between the U.S. government and the Government of Haiti, between victims of human rights abuses and perpetrators, and between the transnational media and "local" arbiters of truth and knowledge. Given its nodal position in the aid apparatus, the Fund was an intermediary vehicle through which the messiness of social experience—inequalities of power, poverty, violence, victimization, and ensekirite—could be rationally assessed, calculated, and managed. In its malleability, impermanence, and mobility, the institution was characteristic of humanitarian assemblages. It was a vehicle through which interveners applied technologies of trauma in order to craft democratic citizens from viktim in a society deemed transitional.

While in operation, the Fund resembled other intermediary advocacy institutions called funds *(fondy)* that Adriana Petryna (2002) describes in her ethnographic work with the survivors of the Chernobyl nuclear disaster. These Chernobyl "funds" surveyed and cared for the health of individuals living with bodily and social contamination (18, 54–55, 143–48). They acted at times like nongovernmental organizations and at times like small businesses. Chernobyl funds had the political, material, and institutional support of the Ukrainian state, as did the victims of the disaster. The postsocialist Ukraine government permitted funds to import and sell goods without regulation (144). In addition to providing access to health care, legal representation, and economic support for their members, funds generated a form of biological citizenship for the legal categories of persons called "disabled" and "sufferers."

In much the same way, the Human Rights Fund, like other "Haitian" institutions described in this book, acted as an advocacy organization and as an institutional broker and dispenser of humanitarian aid. As this chapter makes clear, there was only limited ankadreman, or support, for viktim, which had also been the case in earlier disasters. The concept of traumatic citizenship that I previously suggested (James 2004) to describe the situation of victims of manufactured, industrial, or natural disasters in Haiti no longer seems adequate. This is especially true because of the very limited recognition and support that the Haitian state and other actors in the aid apparatus were capable of providing in the aftermath of such incidents. While ruptures in routine ensekirite created new victim clients who became targets of intervention, these individuals' dire plight emerged only temporarily from the sea of suffering and ensekirite experienced by other impoverished, vulnerable Haitians.

Furthermore, the Human Rights Fund was vulnerable to institutional insecurity. The Fund and its institutional host, America's Development Foundation, operated in what might be thought of as the *grant economy.* Kenneth E. Boulding (1981: 1) describes a grant as a "one-way transfer, which is a change in ownership of economic goods from a donor to a recipient." Grant economies are situated between the practices of direct and reciprocal exchange between givers and receivers in gift economies (Mauss 1950) and the indirect transfer of currencies for crafted objects in commodity economies (Appadurai 2006: 19). Gift exchanges are frequently based on relationships of affect, alliance, or kinship and may encode implicit obligations of a return gift over time (Godelier 1999). Grants frequently entail greater formalization or rationalization of the relationship between givers and receivers, as well as the expectation that grant recipients will perform or fulfill explicit tasks or services over time, whether at the individual, organizational, or governmental level.

Like gift and commodity economies, grant economies are based on and generate particular cultures. U.S.-funded postconflict humanitarian and development assistance, like many other forms of aid, is structured by an audit culture (Strathern 2000). Institutions that receive grants or other conditional aid perform services on behalf of the donor, usually for third parties. Although the transfer or resources is one way, there is an expectation that certain outcomes or "deliverables" will be achieved.

The fruits of gifts or grants of aid are frequently assessed by formal and informal audits. Therefore, the ability to demonstrate a continued demand for the services an institution supplies—as well as the efficiency, productivity, and quality of services—is intrinsic to ensuring the institution's, program's, or project's survival.

Humanitarian and development aid organizations operating in the publicly funded grant economy often compete against other organizations for scarce resources. Federally funded aid institutions such as ADF must meet a narrow or restricted set of goals while also undergoing ongoing assessments of productivity that may affect future funding when compared with those of competing organizations. However, the constraints on a project's activities, the limits placed on the flow of its resources to local grant recipients, and the requirements of accountability are not solely examples of top-down external regulation. The ADF Human Rights Fund's activities sparked contests over power, knowledge, and ethics in Haitian civil society, as well as in the foreign aid apparatus. Like all formal political economies and structures of power, grant economies may generate resistances, subcultures, and occult economies.

As Haitian actors within and without the aid apparatus confronted both the etiology of traumatic suffering and the unequal distribution of aid in its aftermath, such perceived inequities generated accusations of witchcraft and even "bureaucraft." At times, hidden or occult bureaucratic procedures accompanied the distribution of grants within Haiti's political economy of trauma and were perceived as nepotism, favoritism, or graft. Such distributions of aid occurred in an environment in which political and criminal violence ebbed and flowed, aggravating the sense of risk and uncertainty of everyday survival, especially for viktim. Haitian victims' frustrations with ensekirite, which gave rise to intermittent ankadreman from the aid apparatus offered after episodes of natural or human-caused disaster, also had unanticipated consequences for both aid givers and aid receivers.

As discussed in chapter 2, I define *bureaucraft* as a process that emerges from the way opaque, bureaucratic technologies and practices resemble realms of ritual secrecy. Bureaucratic techniques to document, authenticate, and circulate trauma portfolios in the compassion economy were employed to secure the interests of the intervening agent or agency, even as they were intended to affect their targets of intervention in benevolent or therapeutic ways. Such practices generated rumor, gossip, and accusations of malevolent or occult activity that sometimes culminated in threats or violence. Intrinsic to these accusations were anxieties about truth. Suspicions of the hidden motives or practices of those perceived to have accumulated power or resources through occult means—that is, the exploitation of others—proliferated in the environment of scarcity and indirectly sparked a succession of new episodes of ensekirite, with profound consequences for the actors promoting Haiti's postconflict transition.

The questions that loomed over the Human Rights Fund's day-to-day operations were the following: Who would be responsible, ultimately, for the needs of Haitian citizens? Would attempts to rationalize or make more efficient the management of care for traumatized viktim, and for new victims of human rights abuses perpetrated by the Haitian National Police, substitute for efforts to limit and eradicate ensekirite? Could a single program create a rational plan for the mediation of psychosocial cleavages? If the program operated at the interstices of disjointed and sometimes competing international, national, and local governmental and nongovernmental humanitarian interests, could it be successful? Would such an interstitial program produce results that were predictable, transparent, and accountable to its donors, its host nation, its institutional base, and the communities and individuals that it served?

This chapter documents the inauguration of the HRFII Rehabilitation Program. After outlining the accounting technologies that the Fund was required to implement in the grant economy, I discuss two critical events that revealed the underlying conflicts inherent in the humanitarian and development assistance apparatus in the overall political economy of trauma. The first event was crafted: on May 29, 1997, the Fund sponsored the National Colloquium for the Rehabilitation of Victims of Organized Violence. The event created a space of security for civil society organizations and victims' advocacy groups to debate the work of the CNVJ. The second event was an example of routines of rupture, or episodic crises: on September 8, 1997, a local Haitian ferry, *La Fierté Gonâvienne*, capsized. The Fund was asked to intervene. HRF staff members investigated the accident, assessed numbers of victims and survivors, and attempted to identify parties within the local government who could channel emergency assistance effectively and accountably. Both events highlighted the dilemmas posed by neomodern methods of governance. Efforts to control, regulate, or manage "crises" that emerged in the Fund's postconflict development work were sometimes thwarted by occult economies.

THE HRFII REHABILITATION PROGRAM

The Rehabilitation Program got under way in April 1997 as a project of HRFII, the Fund's second incarnation. HRFII was controversial because of its design and because, at the urging of the U.S. Congress, it gave priority to the needs of victims of the HNP over the needs of viktim from the coup years. With the addition of new ADF consultants, Dr. Christine Thomas and Dr. Raphael Manata, who in 1996 had been ousted from the MICIVIH Medical Unit, the Fund's institutional mandate was revised. Instead of focusing on rehabilitating victims of the HNP, its scope of work returned to its original mandate of assisting victims from the 1991–94 coup period; however, it continued to aid individuals who were targets of human rights violations perpetrated by the HNP. Over time, victims of human rights abuses perpetrated during the Duvalier dictatorship (1957–86) were eligible for assistance.

In spring 1997 I met with a former director of the Human Rights Fund, an American human rights activist and sociologist, to request access to victims' case files for research purposes, just as I had previously done with the directors of MICIVIH. I specifically asked to examine what these trauma portfolios revealed about the way violence had been perpetrated during the coup and postcoup years. The HRF director encouraged me to study the case files but asserted that as many as 50 percent of the more recently documented cases of police abuse were of questionable veracity. The files compiled by the PIRÈD program during the coup years, he said, were more reliable.[1]

As an institution operating in a grant economy regulated by audits, the need for administrative transparency, accountability, and certainty regarding the authenticity of victim status influenced the bureaucratic procedures required for prospective beneficiaries of the new Rehabilitation Program to gain eligibility. To meet its grantors' bureaucratic requirements of fiscal responsibility, Dr. Thomas and Dr. Manata suspended certain practices that had become routine during the early years of the Human Rights Fund. Whereas in 1994 beneficiaries of HRFI had been able to receive stipends as individuals, the new consultants decided to discontinue direct financial aid, except for emergencies. Viktim resented these changes. The original HRFI staff members also resented the new regulations, and some chose to leave the Fund in the first two months of the new program.

It is possible that the uncovering of financial irregularities at ADF contributed to these resentments and the resulting personnel changes.

When USAID audited ADF in spring 1997 the new consultants learned that prior to their joining ADF, former staff members had written several checks to personnel and others outside the Fund without supporting documentation. This movement of funds without proper paperwork could have been in part an administrative oversight during the time of crisis. But it might also have been graft or other covert channeling of funds, supporting the suspicions of the American and Haitian political left. Another factor in the decision to suspend most forms of direct financial payment to beneficiaries concerned the short-term viability of the program and the long-term goal of establishing a Haitian center for survivors of violence that would be independent and sustainable. Such an institution could not make grants of aid to its victim clients for indefinite periods. The new consultants made other administrative changes to bring HRFII's practices in alignment with the requirements of its major donor, USAID.

On learning that the validity of some of the HNP cases was in doubt, Thomas and Manata required that prospective beneficiaries of the new Rehab Program arrive with a written referral from a "recognized" human rights organization, civil society institution, or representative of the Haitian state. The motive for this request reflected the need for transparency: the ADF Human Rights Fund program was accountable to USAID/Haiti, USAID in Washington, D.C., and ultimately to the U.S. Congress. According to the cooperative agreement between USAID and ADF, USAID/Haiti assisted with the design of the ongoing work of ADF in Haiti and monitored its progress. Thus accounting practices to document activities and expenditures were instrumental to the daily work of the new HRFII Rehab Program.

The bureaucratic requirements of accountability resulted in part from recent shifts within USAID's administrative structure. These changes gradually trickled down and were implemented through its international aid portfolio in many developing countries. Between 1993 and 2000 Vice President Al Gore's National Partnership for Reinventing Government (NPR) worked to improve government functioning and to reduce the inefficiencies in bloated U.S. government bureaucracies. The NPR initiative focused "on transforming the culture in major agencies with the most public contact to be more results-oriented, performance-based, and customer-focused" using "technology and new approaches in employees' roles as key levers." The NPR plan "created a network of results-oriented partnerships across agency lines with states and local governments, and changed the relations between regulatory agencies and business."[2]

In the mid-1990s USAID's worldwide missions were "reengineered" toward a new corporate model called "management for results" or "result-oriented assistance" as part of a broad effort to restructure federal bureaucracies. USAID had to demonstrate "accountability for achieving results" in its programs abroad to the U.S. Congress. USAID viewed itself as an organization that provided an aid "product" or package to its "customer," the host country in which it worked. With the implementation of results-oriented management, the goal was to transform USAID from what some perceived as an overgrown, unregulated bureaucracy into an institution that was more "efficient" and could measure its outcomes or "outputs" in a systematic and even scientific manner. A September 1994 on-line document titled *Creating a Government That Works Better and Costs Less* outlined the rationale for reengineering USAID:

> One of the keys to reinventing USAID is reengineering the way we do business. This reengineering builds on the ongoing development of an integrated, Agency-wide information system, but goes far beyond. It represents a commitment to assuring that all of USAID's business functions focus on meeting customer needs and achieving results; that they fully empower staff, while enhancing accountability; and that they reflect core Agency values of participation and teamwork.
>
> USAID's reengineering encompasses procurement reforms, financial management reforms, and budget reforms. It embodies new ways of managing our human resources to clarify responsibilities and accountability, reward teamwork and appropriate risk-taking, and develop and expand knowledge and skills to fully utilize everyone's capacities.[3]

In addition to creating an innovative, motivated staff and institution, results-oriented management addressed concerns about measuring, assessing, and reporting the achievement of its performance goals. USAID, through its satellite offices abroad, worked in partnership with its customers—developing host nations—to define a series of strategic objectives (SOs) to be fulfilled in any strategic plan within a specific time frame. As I argue below, SOs can be considered domains of neomodern governance: they are symbolic, ideological, and material terrains of intervention. Through their implementation, USAID attempted to craft neo-Enlightenment polities from so-called fragile, failing, and failed nation-states.

USAID itself, however, was not the principal agent that implemented these SOs. "Development Partners"—institutions such as ADF that also had satellite offices in developing or transitional nations—received funding to execute the Agency Strategic Plan while local USAID personnel monitored their work.

> Achieving results at the output level and the outcome level is very much the responsibility of the Development Partner (Recipient). The core Strategic Objective (SO) Team orchestrates the alignment of the various contributions of the different Development Partners to the Agency Strategic Plan. . . . Planning results-oriented assistance . . . will require teamwork within the core SO Team and between the core SO Team (USAID technical, procurement and support staff) and the expanded SO Team (Development Partners, stakeholders, and customer representatives). (USAID 1998)

USAID acknowledged that a strategic plan for a customer nation was designed at different levels because of the multiple stakeholders involved. In theory, plans should reflect convergences among stakeholders' goals and visions:

> Ideally, the strategic planning process includes the participation of customer representatives, stakeholders and Development Partners. At the same time, Development Partners also have organizational Strategic Plans, mission statements, goals and objectives. These will not always match those of USAID or any other individual donor. Nevertheless, in the process of mutual consultation between USAID and Development Partners there will often be a convergence of objectives representing a shared commitment to customer-focused, results-oriented assistance that will contribute to sustainable development and the Agency's . . . goals. . . . The challenge is to seek mutually desirable alignment of objectives and mechanisms for "managing for results" between USAID and Development Partners. (USAID 1998)

The relationship between these institutional actors is depicted in table 1. Each arrow links activities that must be performed by the development partners, satellite USAID missions, and USAID/Washington and indicates the flow of accountability from one stakeholder level to the next. It is important to emphasize here that accountability flows up to Congress rather than down to the level of citizens in the countries in which USAID works. USAID acknowledges, however, the potential for divergence between stakeholders' goals, missions, or visions at the various levels of design and implementation, as well as in the relationships between the development partners, international USAID missions, and USAID in Washington, D.C. Moreover, in assessing the development partners' results in host nations, USAID stresses the need to determine the "distinction between unforeseen or external challenges, and real performance deficiencies within the Recipient's reasonable control" (USAID 1998).

TABLE I. RELATIONSHIP BETWEEN
DEVELOPMENT PARTNERS AND USAID
OPERATING UNITS. REPRODUCED FROM
USAID, RESULTS-ORIENTED ASSISTANCE,
MARCH 10, 1998.

Development Partner	→	USAID Missions and Operating Units	→	Agency
Organizational Strategic Plan	→	Country Strategic Plan / Operating Unit Strategic Plan	→	USAID's Strategic Plan (1997–2007)
Results Package (activities funded by USAID)	→	Results Framework	→	Agency Strategic Framework
Performance Monitoring and Evaluation Plan	→	Performance Monitoring, Evaluation, and Research Plan	→	Agency Performance Plan and Congressional Presentation
Organization's results that can be incorporated in the Annual Results Review and Resource Request (R4)	→	Annual Results Review and Resource Request (R4)	→	Annual Performance Report to Congress

Risk, uncertainty, and unpredictability are intrinsic to humanitarian and development efforts, especially in "postconflict" environments. It is crucial, therefore, for USAID to be able to take credit for successes but also to delegate fault or blame when its projects are perceived to have failed, especially because it is ultimately accountable to the U.S. Congress. Intermediary development partners implementing USAID's strategies around the globe, such as ADF, serve as examples of USAID's successes and as scapegoats for its failures, often at the same moment. In my research at the ADF Human Rights Fund and later at USAID/Haiti, I learned how the relationships between USAID/Washington, USAID missions abroad, development partners, and their "local" staff, customer nations, and even members of Congress were undermined by disconnects, resistances, and conflicts. As I discuss in chapter 5, USAID/Haiti's administrative supervision of the Fund's Rehabilitation Program ranged from advocacy to sabotage, all of which raises questions about exactly how USAID conceived the work of postconflict development in Haiti.

USAID's Strategic Objectives for Haiti changed from year to year in the postconflict period as a result of the collaborative process between the multiple stakeholders involved in planning the transition. After the 1994 restoration of democracy, the Strategic Objectives for Haiti were aimed at achieving "a successful transition to a democracy based on the rule of law . . . through election assistance, the demobilization of the military and their replacement with trained police" (USAID/Haiti 1996: 1). The United States recognized the devastating impact of the embargo and the years of fiscal mismanagement by the de facto regime. Other assistance interventions had the goals of "stabilizing the country through a local governance transition program, balance of payments support, short-term jobs, Haitian Skills Bank, rehabilitation of health infrastructure, intensified feeding program (Title II and III funds) and tree-planting" (USAID/Haiti 1996: 1). In 1995 the SOs were amended to promote democratic institutions and community action; economic growth; public health, food security, and education; and environment and agricultural productivity.

In early 1997 USAID revised the SOs for Haiti once again when Phyllis Dichter-Forbes joined USAID/Haiti as its new mission director. Forbes (as she was called by members of the aid apparatus) had been the architect of the reengineering of USAID in the mid-1990s, and the new model of results-oriented development assistance was instituted in Haiti. The Strategic Plan was redesigned under one broad goal: "Reduction of Poverty in a Democratic Society." This objective was subdivided into several SOs,[4] each SO encompassing a number of intermediate results (IR) to be achieved by a selection of "indicators."[5] Indicators were measures or "signs" that displayed how well USAID and its development partners were implementing the overall plan.

The specific interventions that the Fund was expected to complete fell mostly under USAID/Haiti's Strategic Objective 1 (SO1): "foster more effective and responsive democratic institutions and empowered communities" (HRFII 1997: 1). Under SO1, USAID/Haiti's IRs were to achieve a "more effective, self-sustaining judicial system and improved legal advocacy," a "well-established electoral process," a "more effective and responsive legislature," a "redefined and circumscribed government," and Haiti's "increased capacity to address and resolve community issues at the local level" (USAID/Haiti 1997: 3). The Fund focused on promoting the first and last of these IRs (HRFII 1997: 1), which accorded with its mandate "to support Haitians in their efforts to redress human rights abuses and provide assistance to victims" and "to contribute to the growth of a society based on nonviolent, democratic principles" (HRFII 1997: 1).

At the local level the specific service or "product" provided to the customer (host nation) was called a "results package." Results packages were specific activities that would implement the Agency's intermediate results. They were also "outcomes" that USAID assessed, in this case when the Fund's work was audited. Each development partner had a USAID results package team leader, a USAID/Haiti staff person who was the liaison between the "local" development partners implementing each intermediate result and the Agency. The results package team leader worked with the development partner to design the "Results Framework," a work plan that was aligned with the overall strategic plan for the customer nation and the goals of the U.S. mission. Through the Results Framework, the local development partner was given a blueprint for "activities" or "outcomes" that it needed to demonstrate at the conclusion of a project or an institution's grant. The Human Rights Fund's Results Packages are presented below.

RESULT PACKAGE 1: INCREASED CAPACITY TO ADDRESS AND RESOLVE
HUMAN RIGHTS ISSUES AT THE LOCAL LEVEL

Result 1.1: Increased (and increasingly responsible) public participation in identifying, resolving, and potentially preventing human rights abuses at [the] local level in selected communities.

Result 1.2: Improved monitoring and documenting of human rights abuses by community-based groups in selected communities

Result 1.3: Improved advocacy by community groups in selected communities.

Result 1.4: Police and informed communities come together to identify and resolve human rights issues at [the] local level in selected communities.

Result 1.5: Emerging models for increasing community capacity to address and resolve human rights issues at [the] local level through police/ community liaison that might be replicated in other communities.

RESULT PACKAGE 2: INCREASED ADVOCACY AND PUBLIC CONFIDENCE IN THE
RULE OF LAW AND JUSTICE

Result 2.1: Improved and appropriate assistance provided to direct victims of current abuse.

Result 2.1.1: Improved medical treatment and legal referral provided to victims of current abuse.

Result 2.1.2: Increased public awareness of and GOH attention to assistance to victims of human rights abuse.

Result 2.1.3: Emerging models for more effective and efficient assistance to victims of current abuse.

Result 2.2: Improved psychological and psychiatric care provided to traumatized victims of organized violence and human rights abuses.

Result 2.2.1: Increased capacity to diagnose, treat and refer for treatment traumatized victims of organized violence at the local level.

Result 2.2.2: Increased public awareness of and GOH attention to the traumatic impact of organized violence and human rights abuse on victims and their families, and its importance as a public health problem.

Result 2.2.3: Emerging models for more effective, culturally appropriate and efficient rehabilitation of victims of organized violence. (HRFII 1997: 3–4)

This list of objectives depicted organized violence and its traumatic long-term effects as public health problems that affected the individual, family, and community, as well as Haiti's capacity for developing democracy, justice, and the rule of law. The results packages were "indicators," or social signs, to be inculcated with "effectiveness and efficiency" in order to promote "public confidence in the justice system" and "the advent of a reliable rule of law in Haiti" (HRFII 1997: 2). What is ironic and even jarring about the results packages is the explicit expectation that psychosocial trauma can be treated or rehabilitated through rationalized, bureaucratic processes in a delimited time period. Given the legacies of necropolitical violence, the culture of impunity, and the ongoing ensekirite, the expectation that psychosocial ruptures could be redressed and ontological security or trust established in a matter of months was unrealistic. Ultimately, the results packages were less about facilitating Haiti's sociopolitical and economic rehabilitation or transformation and more about providing USAID headquarters and Congress with measurable signs of change that indicated improvements in security at multiple levels. While the results packages were designed to create "empowered communities" that possessed a "sense of justice" by means of support from both government and international donor activities, implicit in the objectives is a neomodern subtext that the Fund would craft rational, nonviolent citizens from victims.

As I observed the conflicts between ADF, the Fund, and USAID/Haiti regarding the best way to implement the results packages when working with traumatized communities and individual viktim, the emphasis on efficiency in implementing justice, the rule of law, and psychosocial rehabilitation was problematic. The disputes illustrated the tensions inherent in the chain of institutional accountability from ADF to USAID and from USAID to the U.S. Congress. These dilemmas were not merely the result of limits imposed by donors on recipients of grants or aid, whether those recipients were governments, international organizations, medial institutions, or local individuals. Nor were such challenges solely the "fault" or responsibility of the so-called fragile, transitional customer state.

On a practical level competing bureaucratic time frames structured the Human Rights Fund's administrative functioning and its provision of services to viktim. The calendars that shaped the Fund's "activities" were many. Of greatest priority was USAID/Haiti's strategic plan and objectives. USAID/Haiti needed to account for funded activities during the fiscal year to USAID in Washington, D.C., and to Congress. The calendar of next importance was the finite period of ADF's cooperative agreement and then the HRFII's scope of work between October 1, 1997, and June 30, 1998. Additional calendars that indirectly influenced the Fund's work were the grant cycles of ADF's other civil society project in Haiti (see chapter 5) and those of ADF's democracy promotion projects in other countries. Haiti's "local" context of unceasing ensekirite confronted all these institutional cycles.

The bureaucratic framework described above became an additional means to rationalize rehabilitation for traumatized "victims" at the HRFII Victim Assistance and Rehabilitation Program. In this respect institutional development partners *and* their institutional and individual grant recipients in local realms had to demonstrate accountability and transparency, as well as their competence to accomplish set tasks. Requirements of transparency and accountability also shaped the "relationships" that developed between ADF/HRF and the Haitian state. Furthermore, there was a trickling down of constraint that influenced the interaction between HRF therapeutic staff members and their viktim beneficiaries that concerned which victims HRF was authorized to recognize for intervention.

The HRF Rehabilitation Program operated using a limited and limiting definition of *victim*. The criteria for recognizing victim status reflected U.S. policy, as well as the Fund's obligation to complete its work in a transparent, accountable manner. The U.S. mission and USAID/Haiti recognized "victims of human rights violations" as persons subjected to violence that was "politically motivated" or perpetrated by an agent of the Haitian state. In alignment with the U.S. position on international human rights covenants, the definition did not acknowledge economic, cultural, and social rights. Rather, the emphasis was on redressing abuses of civil and political rights.[6] According to HRF's institutional mandate, it was necessary to determine whether a prospective beneficiary was indeed a "victim of a human rights violation" and not a victim of interpersonal violence or everyday ensekirite. Given the complexities of categorizing violence in Haiti as either state-sponsored or interpersonal, this requirement proved challenging.

Under such constraints, the draft documents for the Rehab Program defined candidates eligible for intervention according to the World Health Organization's (WHO's) 1986 definition of a human rights violation:

> The interhuman infliction of significant, avoidable pain and suffering by an organized group according to a declared or implied strategy and/or system of ideas and attitudes. It comprises any violent action which is unacceptable by general human standards, and relates to the victims' feelings. Organized violence includes inter alia "torture, cruel, inhuman or degrading treatment or punishment" as mentioned in article 5 of the UN Universal Declaration of Human Rights (1948). Imprisonment without trial, mock executions, hostage taking or any other form of violent deprivation of liberty also fall under the heading of organized violence. (Ministry of Welfare, Health and Cultural Affairs 1987: 9)

Victims were categorized as persons who had, among other criteria, been threatened, arbitrarily detained, forced to flee from persecution, or sustained losses to property or goods in a politically motivated context. HRF consultants themselves acknowledged that distinguishing between types of "victimization"—whether stemming from political and economic factors or arising from interpersonal conflict—was difficult.

The Human Rights Fund had limited capacity to investigate human rights abuse cases that had occurred during the coup years. It was necessary, therefore, for the Rehabilitation Program staff to carefully ascertain the "truth" of a potential beneficiary's victim status, especially because this would influence how and for whom U.S. tax dollars would be spent. It was also crucial to verify a victim's status as legitimate in view of potential audits of the whole project in the future. In effect, each potential beneficiary needed to "prove" that he or she was a victim of a human rights abuse.

When an individual or family first came to the Fund in search of assistance a specific intake procedure was begun. The Rehab nursing staff or HRF case managers interviewed prospective beneficiaries about their experiences and reviewed any supporting documentation of the claim. A team of field investigators and consultants authenticated more recent cases of alleged abuses, such as violations perpetrated by the HNP. Violations that had occurred in years past were more difficult to corroborate. If supplicants did not arrive with documentation of their cases in hand, they were asked to provide letters of reference from a recognized human rights organization, a corresponding civil society organization, or a legal bureau that had documented cases of human rights violations in the past. Witnesses could also corroborate a person's testimony as valid in cases where no such documentation existed. In addition, various institutions were able to refer "victims" to the Fund. Members of the Haitian government—such as the minister of justice, or other ministry staff, the staff of the Office for the Protection of Citizens, members of Parliament, or representatives of local government throughout the nation—were entitled to do so. Furthermore, international human rights organizations and medical missions, such as the National Coalition for Haitian Rights, the U.N. International Civilian Mission, or Médecins du Monde, referred the trauma portfolios of individuals and their families. Finally, Haitian civic organizations, such as the Justice and Peace Commission, the TKL, other church groups, and popular organizations in urban and rural areas, also gave viktim referrals.

Over time, a group of community health workers who had formerly been beneficiaries of the Rehab Program assisted with the verification process. These individuals had completed training to coordinate investigative and outreach services in other departments in Haiti, much as had viktim working with other victims' advocacy institutions, such as M'AP VIV, which had been instituted by MICIVIH and MDM, and the Fondasyon 30 Sektanm, which was established by the former president of the National Commission for Truth and Justice and a state employee who was also a former member of M'AP VIV (see chapter 2). The HRF staff then met as a group to determine which supplicants would be granted eligibility.

The Fund had two categories of eligibility. "Direct" victims were defined according to the WHO standard, mentioned above. Once those conditions had been met, the Rehab Program accepted that "victims" sometimes included those persons who were indirectly affected by a human rights violation, such as relatives or household members of an individual who had been a direct target of violence. For example, if a woman had lost an immediate family member who had supported her financially or if a child had lost a parent, the prospective beneficiary could become eligible for aid once her or his case had been documented and validated. Acknowledging that Haitian households do not always conform to the model of the nuclear family, the program was initially able to provide resources to all dependent members of a beneficiary's household.

The Rehab Program staff gave eligible beneficiaries written referrals that authorized their access to a network of Haitian and international caregivers. The services provided were primarily medical assistance, psychological counseling, and legal counseling. In some cases, however, individuals were given temporary housing for emergency asylum. Beneficiaries were able to receive reconstructive surgery, dentistry, ophthalmology, obstetrics and gynecology, pediatric care, and psychiatric treatment, among other services. Institutions and individuals providing these benefits billed the costs directly to the Fund. Beneficiaries were also referred to a network of pharmacists and private laboratories that specialized in various medical diagnostic testing technologies. Psychological counseling occurred in one-on-one sessions between viktim and Dr. Thomas, the ethnopsychiatrist, as well as with other Haitian mental health providers and in the new therapy group counseling sessions as previously described.

The regimentation and bureaucratization of the Rehab Program's therapeutic practices became standard in the U.S. development assistance audit culture. These practices can also be viewed as examples of the exportation of "managed care" abroad. Managed care is a strategy to regulate the fiscal and therapeutic relationship between patients and health care providers in order to cut costs. It became prevalent in the United States after passage of the 1973 Health Maintenance Organization Act. Independent organizations, some of which are for-profit, largely implement these practices in the United States. These health maintenance organizations (HMOs) act as gatekeepers—between patients and providers and between providers and the medical technologies that physicians and other caregivers would ordinarily select for patients in a fee-for-service plan. In controlling the process by which viktim patients received care and regulating the frequency and duration of treatment and other forms of assistance, the Rehab Program worked very much like an HMO. In this respect and others the Rehab Program was an example of neomodern governance.

The demand for a letter of reference or institutional referral before a new beneficiary gained admittance to the program was reminiscent of historical forms of medical care in cosmopolitan settings in the United States. For example, in the early nineteenth century trustees controlled admissions to municipal facilities like the Massachusetts General Hospital. In order to gain admittance, a prospective patient needed to be referred to a trustee for approval. At times a letter of recommendation or other formal documentation was required to verify the patient's "worthiness" to receive care.[7] At issue was whether the provision of treatment would result in an implicit return on the investment—namely, that the patient, once healed, would become a productive member of society. The regulation of care at the Human Rights Fund likewise incorporated implicit assumptions about the "worthiness" of beneficiaries, in this case judged in terms of the political roots of their victimization as verified by powerful political institutional and individual actors.

In practice, the Fund's criteria for eligibility were narrow. At times the need to circumscribe the boundaries of eligibility undermined the institution's stated humanitarian, charitable foundations, thereby creating double binds for both staff members and beneficiaries. For the medical staff, the institutional location of the Rehab Program under the ADF umbrella challenged efforts to treat "patients" under conditions of political neutrality, especially considering ADF's controversial background in promoting democracy abroad. ADF operated explicitly to implement U.S. political development strategies to promote democracy (and reduce poverty) in Haiti. Like USAID/Haiti, ADF was not ultimately accountable to local Haitians. Even as its Rehab staff members treated patient-clients, HRF also worked to promote democracy and the growth of civil society as defined by the United States.

One of the means by which the Rehabilitation Program promoted civil society that may have impeded the "rehabilitation" of viktim was through additional forms of governing the psychosocial treatment process. Because formal recognition as legitimate viktim was necessary in order to receive services to mitigate suffering, viktim were encouraged to organize, join, and incorporate victims' advocacy organizations that the Haitian state legally recognized. This measure was intended to create sustainable support systems for viktim prior to receiving services and fulfilled USAID's request that ADF/HRF conduct work to promote democracy, human rights, and "capacity building" within civil society. Thus, in addition to its provision of humanitarian aid, the Fund gave technical assistance to victims' advocacy, human rights, and other civil society organizations with which it collaborated to create sustainable local institutions. However, the process of obtaining official recognition for such organizations was time-consuming and lengthy and required a measure of fluency with bureaucratic procedures that the majority of the Fund's beneficiaries did not possess. Prospective beneficiaries frequently had to rely on the patronage of "brokers" with the political and social capital to facilitate these processes. As discussed below, these brokers were able to employ the benevolent practices of bureaucraft to create opportunities for viktim but also to manipulate bureaucratic procedures for illicit personal and institutional gain, thereby generating the negative dimensions of bureaucraft.

At best, these technologies of trauma were compassionate means to provide appropriate assistance to Haitian "victims" given the institutional constraints and the requirements of accountability. At worst, they were forms of "discipline"[8] or regulation that prescribed specific behaviors and practices to authenticate, document, and even perform suffering under conditions of duress. This was another aspect of the grant economy. The power relations between the program staff and its supplicants were highly unequal, which influenced daily encounters between victims and Rehab Program staff, especially if there were suspicions about the truth of a victim's trauma narrative or if prospective clients' narratives of trauma did not fit the narrow criteria for eligibility. The ambiguities raised by such categorical uncertainties interfered with the interactions between prospective beneficiaries, caseworkers, and therapeutic staff members.

For example, despite the comprehensive nature of the Rehab Program's services, rape cases that occurred after the restoration of democracy on October 15, 1994, were problematic in terms of the HRF mandate. With the blanket amnesty given to members of the coup apparatus (see chapter 2) and U.S. ambivalence about recognizing rape as a state-sponsored abuse (see chapter 1), the political motivation for sexual violence still needed to be proven. The validation of suffering by an external authority as political in origin was especially challenging given that many of the perpetrators were civilian affiliates of the coup apparatus. In addition, the MNF had never disarmed the atache and zenglendo who continued to police the communities in which viktim lived. Therefore, the Rehab Program was limited in its capacity to assist survivors of sexual violence who could not prove the political motivation underlying their victimization. Usually the Fund referred these women to other civil society groups and health organizations for assistance.

Rape survivors from the 1991–94 coup years whose cases had been documented previously by civil society organizations or who were referred by Haitian state officials or known to the ADF/HRF staff continued to be eligible for care. However, these cases were challenging for other reasons. The case of one woman who requested assistance from the Rehab Program suggests some of the reasons for this. Marianne Pascal was a resident of Martissant with whom I had worked at

Chanm Fanm in summer 1996. In October 1998 she came to the Fund seeking aid for herself and her family, as she was one of the viktim whose families were targeted by FRAPH members while the Governors Island Accord agreement was being negotiated. On July 31, 1993, six armed individuals had entered her home in search of her husband. They beat him, and some of the men took him out of the house. Each man then raped Marianne in turn. They trampled her nine-year-old son. The FRAPH members left Marianne and her son behind and took her husband away with them. He was never seen again. Her son died three days later from the injuries that he sustained. Marianne told me in our work together that she nearly died from the grief. She explained that she had been "out of her head" for years. Only in early 1996, when she bore another child, did she feel some relief from her *chagren* (sorrow). She continued to mourn her losses in the years afterward, even as she received medical care and some financial support through the DRC and the HWA.

One of the Martissant community agents who had been trained by the Rehab Program referred Marianne to the Fund. A witness who corroborated her testimony accompanied her. Marie-Claire Girard, a young woman finishing a degree in psychology at the time, conducted the intake interview. After Marianne recounted her trauma narrative, Marie-Claire asked her how her losses continued to afflict her. Marianne complained of ongoing vaginal infections, chronic headaches, back pain, and weakness. In order to be eligible for care, however, she still needed to provide a "medical certificate" from a physician to validate her injury and health problems. While that certificate was pending, the Rehab Program staff deliberated her case. In light of the urgency of her need, Marianne became eligible for care a week later.

Nevertheless, there was still something troubling about Marianne's case for the young woman who had conducted the intake interview. In the notes Marie-Claire added to Marianne's trauma portfolio—the case file completed during the course of the interview, along with supporting documentation—she expressed doubts that *eight* men raped Marianne rather than six. However, Marianne herself had testified to being violated by six men, as was recorded accurately a few pages earlier in the same report. I have wondered why Marie-Claire would question the number of men who had committed the rapes but then mistakenly inflate the estimate to eight. Was the enormity of Marianne's abject suffering unthinkable, implausible, and therefore deniable or even exaggerated, as Marie-Claire imagined and recorded the event? Why was the extremity of the sexual violation a focus rather than the disappearance of her husband and the death of her young son?

Marie-Claire's doubts about Marianne's trauma narrative may have reflected the general concerns about the truths of horrific suffering that humanitarian actors operating in Haiti frequently expressed. Questions about patient or client eligibility frequently arose from the pressures on agencies and agents to rationalize and justify rehabilitation, especially since decisions made on the basis of the report could be questioned during a subsequent program assessment. But Marianne's doubts might also have been the sign of "compassion fatigue," "burnout," or "secondary" (Figley and Kleber 1995; Stamm 1995) or "vicarious traumatization" (Pearlman and Saakvitne 1995). The routine hearing of victim's testimonies of trauma might have precipitated countertransference reactions of being overwhelmed, denial of the egregiousness of abuses, or indifference (Bustos 1992).[9] These reactions recall Scarry's (1985) discussion of the difficulties of signifying or translating into language the experience of torture and pain.

In addition to the difficulties of determining a beneficiary's eligibility, Rehab Program staff members were pressured by viktim to provide additional assistance and insisted that HRF give perpetual gifts and grants of humanitarian and development aid. Such requests entangled the staff and the institution in a messy set of obligations clouded by the questions of torture, trauma, and truth. But entanglements also arose from the peculiar relationships among ADF, HRF, the Rehab Program, its beneficiaries, and the aid assemblage in general as it operated Haiti in the postconflict period.

The complications of past and current therapeutic and institutional relationships became clear when the Human Rights Fund presented the Rehabilitation Program to the Haitian public as part of its effort to gain support for a sustainable center for victims of organized violence. The Fund sponsored several roundtable discussions with members of the Haitian medical community and public health department regarding how to create a sustainable victim assistance institution. The most notable event was the May 1997 rehabilitation colloquium. A key issue for debate was the status of the relationship between the Haitian state and civil society: Given the Government of Haiti's limited infrastructural capacity and its predatory past, to what extent could it be a vehicle for reparations, reconciliation, and truth for victims of organized violence?

REHABILITATION FOR VICTIMS OF ORGANIZED VIOLENCE

The moral stakes in reputed state failures and the politics of victim assistance in general became clear during the May 29, 1997, HRF National Colloquium for the Rehabilitation of Victims of Organized Violence. The event was an occasion when opaque bureaucratic practices for assessing truth and promoting justice and rehabilitation became clouded by accusations about the motives, authenticity, and practices of actors in the aid apparatus. The pattern of accusation and counteraccusation and of intimations of hidden or occult action to exploit the suffering of others was a negative dimension of bureaucraft.

The colloquium was intended to explore long-term approaches to the rehabilitation of victims of organized violence in Haiti through the creation of a network of professionals with expertise in the medical, psychological, and legal dimensions of victim assistance. Notable members of Haitian governmental and civil society organizations participated in the event, as did international humanitarian missions, representatives of victims' organizations throughout the country, international and Haitian human rights and women's rights organizations, and others. The colloquium was moderated by the activist and economist Michèle Pierre-Louis, founder and executive director of the Fondation Connaissance et Liberté (Open Society Institute Haiti).[10] Françoise Boucard, president of Haiti's National Commission for Truth and Justice and cofounder of the Fondasyon 30 Sektanm, agreed to present her experience with the CNVJ. Madame Florence Elie, the widow of Guy Malary—the former minister of justice who was assassinated in broad daylight in 1993, three days after the *Harlan County* debacle (see chapter 2)—represented the Ministry of Justice. Another featured presenter was Mèt Camille Leblanc,[11] an attorney who coordinated a group of lawyers that had documented more than eight hundred cases of human rights abuses perpetrated against viktim. Although the colloquium was criticized for being conducted primarily in French, excluding the full participation of the majority of Haitians, who spoke only Haitian Creole, crucial segments were in Creole.

After presentations on violence, trauma, and justice in cross-cultural postconflict settings, Boucard's talk on the work of the CNVJ sparked tremendous debate about the functioning of this institution, which continued throughout the day. The CNVJ was heavily criticized because of the secrecy with which it reportedly conducted its work, for its inaccessibility, and for delays in disseminating the final report. Its bureaucratic failures and the opacity of its practices reinforced the image of the Government of Haiti as incompetent, corrupt, indifferent, and unwilling to combat impunity.[12] The opacity and secrecy with which the CNVJ operated and controlled information was a source of ongoing frustration for Haitian human rights activists as well.

The CNVJ was inaugurated by presidential decree on March 28, 1995, just a few months after President Aristide's return to office. While its purpose was to reveal the truths of what had occurred in Haiti during the coup period, in many respects it could be viewed as another example of the failure of the Haitian government to be accountable, responsible, and transparent to its citizens. The CNVJ was composed of seven commissioners, three of whom were foreigners who did not maintain a consistent presence in Haiti during the time of the investigation (CNVJ 1997: 8). In addition to the commissioners, there were six data analysts, eight temporary "collaborators" with special expertise in data processing, and a team of forty-four investigators who had received special training in recording testimonies of human rights abuses (8). Their charge was to "solicit the participation of the majority of citizens to establish the facts of human rights abuses committed during the period of reference [September 29, 1991, to October 14, 1994], while guaranteeing the security of the plaintiffs, victims, and investigators in the field" (8).

The commissioners began to hear cases of human rights violations between June and October 1995. Investigators spent considerable time in the West and Artibonite Departments in Haiti. The International Centre for Human Rights and Democratic Development (Centre International des Droits de la Personne et du Développement Démocratique), based in Montreal, forwarded some testimonies of Haitian refugees in exile in Canada (CNVJ 1997: 8–9).[13] The CNVJ also accepted documentation from other human rights and nongovernmental organizations, such as MICIVIH, the IACHR, the Platform, and the JPC (9).

Boucard had asked the American Association for the Advancement of Science (AAAS) for technical support to manage the data.[14] The report of AAAS team members on their assistance to the CNVJ indicated some of the troubles that plagued the institution.

> The CNVJ team took 5,453 interviews. In all, they identified 8,667 victims who suffered 18,629 violations. The CNVJ interviewing was quite good by scientific standards. A data processing group of eleven of the interviewers applied standard definitions to the raw interview data and produced detailed regional analyses, incorporating qualitative material from the interviews, as well as historical, economic and demographic analysis.

> Unfortunately, in the last stages of the process, *the commissioners discarded almost all the work the field investigators did* and substituted a chronology of the de facto regime. The commissioners never informed the AAAS of their reasons for not using the regional data; *although the statistical analyses were present, the tables omitted most of the content and the translations into French were inadequate.* (Ball and Spirer 2000: 27; emphasis added)

The discarding of the regional data was alarming, especially given the continuing questions about the truth of human rights abuses in Haiti and whether or not there had been a systematic campaign against pro-democracy activists between 1991 and 1994. As discussed previously, these debates included U.S. government challenges to the credibility of MICIVIH's human rights documentation, as well as the difficulties of documenting the plight of victims in Haiti.

The fate of the report after the commissioners had concluded their work was equally disturbing. The AAAS team stated that although the CNVJ's final report was forwarded to President Aristide in February 1996, "because of policy disagreements in the Haitian government, it was not published until September 1996, and then in a printing of only 75 copies. A second edition was published in February 1997" (Ball and Spirer 2000: 27). Many viewed the limited release of the report as an indication of a lack of commitment to combat impunity on part of the Government of Haiti. The process by which the CNVJ report was disseminated was subjected to a devastating critique that appeared in *Le Monde Diplomatique*. The article alleged that the final CNVJ report

> was hidden in the files of the minister of justice, M. P-Pierre-Max Antoine [sic], for many months. After many protests, only small parts of this report were published. The public and the many victims still wait for its publication in Creole. The majority of the final recommendations were never enacted. Former perpetrators occupied positions in the new national police or as prison guards: one of them was even in the security guard of the national palace even though his name appeared in Appendix 4 of the final CNVJ report. (Roussiere and Danroc 1998, cited in Ball and Spirer 2000: 27–28)

In an interview with a former Justice and Peace Commission executive who later directed the Community-Police Relations Program of the Human Rights Fund, I was told that there was also controversy about the timing of the report. The CNVJ completed its mandate in fall 1995 but only submitted a partial report on February 5, 1996, the last day of Aristide's first term. The timing was such that the Préval administration was not obligated to act on its recommendations, nor could the outgoing

Aristide administration hold the Préval administration accountable for the perceived failures of the CNVJ. After the CNVJ released the summary report, access to the full report was limited, even as late as spring 1997.

When given the opportunity to participate in the debate at the rehabilitation colloquium on victim assistance and justice for past human rights abuses, the primary concerns viktim expressed were criticisms of the CNVJ. Viktim and their representatives asked both Boucard and Elie why the CNVJ had not done more to document cases in all parts of the nation, why the report was still unavailable to the majority of the public, and when there would be justice. The responses to these queries provoked accusations of blame and intimations of corruption for the perceived failure of the CNVJ. These ethical discourses marked the emergence of negative dimensions of bureaucraft in the aid apparatus that increased in frequency and intensity over time. Boucard answered sharply that fifteen months after the submission of the final report, the Ministry of Justice must be the one to whom questions were asked about its intent to distribute the report and to pursue the CNVJ's recommendations. She lamented, however, "I remember that the National Commission for Truth and Justice, the commissioners, the technicians, the personnel in general, everyone worked with the firm conviction of accomplishing an historic work, a useful work. Today . . . I admit that I am ashamed to see that all of this work will have been for nothing." Boucard went on to insist that it was not the responsibility of the state alone to address the question of rehabilitation of victims and repairing past wrongs. Justice, rehabilitation, and reparations—including the dissemination of the CNVJ report—must also be the responsibility of civil society. Her statements worked to deflect sole responsibility for the Commission's failures from herself by implicitly accusing others of not taking greater responsibility for the effort.

Elie then spoke, passionately affirming her position as a representative of the Ministry of Justice, as well as her position as viktim. She stated that the ministry had made available the recommendations chapter of the report as an early step and that it was ready at that moment to distribute 1,500 additional copies of the full text (minus the names of alleged perpetrators).

The public debate, accusations, and innuendo continued when a member of the Haitian Women's Association (one of the sponsors of the Chanm Fanm clinic) criticized Boucard and her desire to place more responsibility for promoting justice on Haitian civil society.

Madame Boucard has insisted much upon the responsibility of civil society. I, what I think is that civil society has always taken charge of certain things in Haiti. Since 1986 civil society has tried to lead certain activities with the aim of the construction of the country. Since 1986, we have been saying the same thing, we are trying to distance ourselves from the state, and we . . . are trying, somehow or another, what we can. But it is high time that the state takes charge of its responsibilities. We are not able to substitute for the state. The state is there. It must also fulfill its duties toward its citizens. We have spent a long time fulfilling . . . the state's own obligations. We say that we have a "democratic" state, but if we are able to collaborate so that this state is more effective in its achievements, we will do it, but we are not able to substitute for the state.

This woman's perspective highlighted the political and economic fact that civil society could not replace the state—however limited its capacity might be—and that the state must be accountable to its citizenry. Her statement was also a plea for the Haitian state to "parent" its populace responsibly as the nation continued on a democratic path.

In contrast, Pierre-Louis compared the CNVJ to the South African Truth and Reconciliation Commission, noted for offering amnesty to perpetrators of human rights violations in exchange for full disclosure of the truth of the abuses (Gobodo-Madikizela 2004; Hayner 2001: 98–99; Wilson 2001). She questioned whether the Haitian government had truly intended to shed light on the many crimes of the coup period. She argued that in contrast to the transparency of the South African commission, the CNVJ was "established nearly in secret. No one knew what it was doing and nothing was rendered public." For her, the issue was whether the long-term effects of the egregious repression of the coup years had made members of civil society grant the state impunity. An unstated issue was the extent to which civil society had been collectively silenced or traumatized and whether the CNVJ had the will or capacity to address the enormous problem of organized violence. In broader terms, it might be asked, to what standard should an embattled, failing state without the capacity to provide for its citizens' welfare be held as it progresses along a democratic path?

These issues of trauma, truth, and transparency, as well as of state capacity, accountability, and the role of civil society, were echoed in Mèt Leblanc's presentation. He emphasized the need for victims to make public testimony in order to establish personal and collective truths concerning the past and to determine the possibilities for formal justice. In his view the CNVJ failed to accomplish these goals. Leblanc also responded broadly to a question Dr. Thomas had previously posed regarding how the notion of justice could be integrated into the Rehab Program's therapeutic process for viktim, as one part of the more general judicial reform movement in the nation. He stated:

> Personally, I wished that the Truth Commission were a place that would have permitted an answer [to this question]. I mean by this that the fact that things are spoken is important symbolically for those who have lived that situation, because that permits the public, those who have not lived it, to be able—for at least an instant—to experience [viv] with the victim what had happened. But the fact that this approach had not been possible and that the Truth Commission contented itself solely with hearing the victim [without public testimony], a point of question remains: did this truly happen?

For Leblanc, establishing the facts or truth of the past, and categorizing who was a victim and who was a torturer, was therapeutic. The public recognition of the victims' suffering was equally important in order to validate their experience. But a public, transparent process for eliciting the truth was also essential on the national level to document the government's predatory history, which was still contested by actors in and outside Haiti.

Boucard, who by this time was quite emotional, spoke in Haitian Creole in her response to Leblanc's condemnation of the CNVJ. Viktim and others in the audience noted the shift in language. It was an example of code switching that signaled the authenticity of speech, heightened emotion, and the speaker's willingness to take the gloves off in self-defense. It also indicated Boucard's desire to be understood clearly by everyone in attendance. She exclaimed that the CNVJ's perceived failure to incorporate civil society in public hearings was partially the fault of President Aristide. She accused the National Palace of having undermined or "sabotaged" the CNVJ. She claimed that there was a parallel effort to document and make public incidents of human rights violations that originated within the National Palace under Camille Leblanc's own direction. One possible implication was that such covert efforts were intended to cultivate and reaffirm viktim as a loyal political base, as well as to create a "shadow" judicial process.

The public trade in accusations about hidden or occult activity to determine the truths of the coup years and the suggestion of nefarious intent on the part of the executive office were public charges of malevolent bureaucraft. An underlying point of contention concerned the politics of advocacy for viktim. While many international aid organizations recognized victims of human rights abuses on the basis of their suffering, in national politics viktim were becoming influential civil and political actors. Victims' advocacy associations symbolized a powerful source of value or political legitimacy for those who represented them, even if their members had little social and political capital outside the realm of aid. As stated above, Leblanc represented hundreds of viktim and managed their trauma portfolios. His experience and visibility as a victim's advocate cannot be discounted as a factor in his appointment as minister of justice in early 1999.

The debates over the CNVJ's success or failure to document the violence of the coup period were contentious, not only for viktim, but also for other actors in the realm of victim assistance. They reflected the challenges of implementing postconflict reconstruction and transitional justice efforts in insecure states. At issue were perceptions of Haiti's need for judicial reform and state accountability, the need for formal recognition of viktim as targets of state-sponsored human rights abuses, victims' need for healing, and the role of Haitian civil society in these efforts. The individual political rhetoric and accusations also arose from each person's desire to demonstrate accountability to and encourage the political allegiance of viktim.

Despite its perceived inadequacies, the CNVJ made comprehensive recommendations aimed at transforming Haitian society and providing reparations to acknowledged victims. It urged the establishment of a special reparations commission that would fulfill the Haitian state's obligation to protect and serve its citizens according to international law. The new reparations institution, it was hoped, would be important for the "collective memory of the Haitian people" in order that "those who had given their lives or lost their physical integrity [would] not [be] forgotten either at the symbolic, moral, or material levels" (CNVJ 1997: 85). The CNVJ suggested that the proposed commission pay special attention to the problem of sexual violence. It should work toward reclassifying such offenses in the Haitian penal code from crimes against virtue *(atteinte aux bonne moeurs)*, which "attracts attention to the status or honor of the victim," to crimes against the victim's "physical integrity or well-being" (85). Other major focuses of the proposed special commission included judicial reform, revision of the laws prohibiting Haitians from holding dual citizenship, and the demilitarization of the armed forces.

* * *

The National Colloquium for the Rehabilitation of Victims of Organized Violence permitted members of Haitian civil society and their international partners to deliberate on issues of truth, justice, reparations, and accountability in both government and civil society. Through the presentations by international and national spokespersons, the event created the opportunity for diverse segments of Haitian citizenry to discuss Haiti's fate, albeit within the structural frame the Human Rights Fund had provided for the occasion. It was also significant for the participation of prominent Haitian human, civil, and women's rights activists who formerly would not have participated or collaborated with a U.S. government–funded project.

In this respect, it is possible to analyze the colloquium as an indicator that fulfilled HRF's intermediate results as part of USAID's overall strategic objectives. The conference was a vehicle by which psychosocial trauma was approached in a rationalized, bureaucratic manner. Indeed, that such debate occurred in a moderated format, in front of an audience of participants, demonstrated to USAID that the HRFII project was a success. HRFII was able to bring together opposing factions of Haitian civil society to participate in its activities, whereas such participation would have previously been difficult if not impossible. Furthermore, for the ADF Human Rights Fund, the event was an important indicator of institutional achievement that contributed to ADF receiving additional funding and an extension from July 1, 1997, to June 30, 1998. Thus the successful demonstration of institutional capacity and competency through the achievement of measurable, quantifiable results translated into gains in the grant economy.

RUPTURES AND RESPONSES: THE SINKING
OF 'LA FIERTÉ GONÂVIENNE'

In 1997 another critical event highlighted how HRF's medial position between governments, institutions, associations, and individuals permitted it to act as a surrogate for the U.S. government and, indirectly, for the Haitian state. The Fund was asked to intervene during a crisis: the capsizing of the *Fierté Gonâvienne* ferry. This event was critical for two reasons. First, the international and national responses demonstrated the failure of results-oriented management techniques to confront routines of rupture—unforeseen occurrences that emphasized the ongoing ensekirite in Haiti. The inability to control the responses to the disaster using rational, bureaucratic practices generated ambivalence about responding to and taking responsibility for the victims of this crisis. The sense of bureaucratic insecurity contributed to the withholding of both gifts and grants of humanitarian and development aid that were desperately needed. Furthermore, the incident signaled how ensekirite exacerbated local conflicts about the distribution of humanitarian and development aid, which in turn contributed to "witchcraft" discourses and practices, as well as bureaucraft. Ensekirite was felt not only by victims of circumstance and victims of human rights abuses but also by those who assisted them.

Second, the processes that unfolded during the event mirrored in microcosm the transactions in the political economy of trauma that subsequently contributed to the demise of the Human Rights Fund Rehabilitation Program between 1998 and 1999 (see chapters 5 and 6). I tell this story using a "processual" (Moore 1987; Farmer 1992) analysis to enable an understanding of how the sequence of events highlighted and reinforced a visceral "sense" of ensekirite in those affected by the the tragedy, which was linked to local unrest and long-standing grievances at the community level. It was also related to historical incidents of state failure to protect Haitian citizens from ensekirite—whether economic, political, or infrastructural.

In evaluating the evolution of this disaster, Stanley Tambiah's (1996: 81) concepts of focalization and transvaluation are useful. Tambiah analyzed how collective ethnic and nationalist violence erupted in riots in South Asia in a variety of historical contexts in the twentieth century. These incidences of collective violence were "purposive and instrumental in their logic rather than simply or solely an expression of crowd mentality run amok in the context of anomie, widespread hardship, or incidental provocation" (80–81). He states that "focalization progressively denudes local incidents and disputes of their contextual particulars, and transvaluation distorts, abstracts, and aggregates those incidents into larger collective issues of national or ethnic interest" (81). These concepts are also useful for analyzing the responses to disaster. As a crisis unfolds, conflicts that erupt in a local moral world (Kleinman and Kleinman 1991) are detached from the immediate context in which they occur. Then the meaning of the crisis is linked to broader social, political, and economic interests that are only indirectly related to the original issue or event. Through a processual analysis of this notorious ferry disaster, I track the outwardly spiraling way in which the central event became a trope or vehicle for Haitians to articulate frustrations and injustices about the state. Discourse about the event was also a means to lament the ontological reality of ensekirite. This catastrophe demonstrates how the political economy of trauma flourishes in Haiti but also how bureaucraft can generate rumor, gossip, and accusations of secrecy and occult or illicit accumulation of resources that may culminate in violence.

Catastrophe

On September 8, 1997, at about 5:00 A.M., *La Fierté Gonâvienne* (the Pride of Gonâve), a sixty-one-foot fiberglass triple-decked ferry, capsized while transporting passengers from the island of La Gonâve to Montrouis, a town on the coast northwest of Port-au-Prince. Early reports indicated that as many as four hundred people had drowned, but these reports could not yet be verified. USAID Mission Director Phyllis Forbes asked the Human Rights Fund to conduct an inquiry into the accident. The goal was to determine the best way to allocate an initial offer of $25,000 in humanitarian assistance to the survivors and their families.

Given its collective staff experience with victim assistance and its local "expertise" in La Gonâve, the HRF program seemed a natural choice to determine the extent of the tragedy and to provide the United States with an estimate of what kind of long-term humanitarian investment would be needed. At the time the Fund had a caseworker on staff, Claude Oscar, who was a native of La Gonâve. He had been hired before the establishment of the Rehab Program at ADF in 1997 and had been authenticating alleged cases of human rights abuses perpetrated by the new HNP on the island. Two other HRF team members, Alphonse Montina and Henri Raphael, also investigated the capsizing of *La Fierté Gonâvienne*. Montina and Raphael were Haitian activists who had formerly received development assistance from ADF's other civil society project for their popular organization. David Hunter, the controversial former ADF employee who had worked to establish the Rehabilitation Program as a component of the Human Rights Fund (see chapter 2), had provided them with asylum when they were threatened during the coup years. Montina and Raphael eventually became permanent paid staff of HRF and served as advisers to USAID on its political strategies in the democracy sector (as did Françoise Boucard).

On September 9 Oscar began the inquiry in La Gonâve while Montina and Raphael traveled to Montrouis on the mainland to document the crisis and locate the recovered bodies of the deceased. The dead had been transported to at least five funeral homes in different towns on the mainland. On September 10 the Montrouis team returned to

Port-au-Prince with Father Paul, an African priest from the Scheut Mission who was affiliated with the Justice and Peace Commission. For a year Father Paul had been based in one of La Gonâve's small towns, Anse-à-Galets. He had been in Montrouis counseling families and assisting them to find the bodies of their deceased loved ones.

On the morning of September 11 Father Paul, other HRF staff members, and I flew by charter plane to La Gonâve to continue the investigation. An unknown woman accompanied us on the small plane. By the end of the day she would play a role in the unfolding drama that we witnessed on the island. As we began our descent the size and beauty of the island was striking. Thirty-seven miles long and nine miles wide, the island is located in the Gulf of Gonâve, just twelve miles northwest of Port-au-Prince. Surrounded by coral reefs, turquoise water, and sugar-sand beaches, the semiarid island appeared as mountainous as the mainland. We landed in a small clearing on a vast stretch of land that served as the runway. On our arrival Oscar led us on motorbikes to a modest home so that we could interview survivors and other residents of the community about the accident.

We learned that *La Fierté Gonâvienne,* one of a few boats that provided transport from La Gonâve to Montrouis, served a total population of about 110,000. The Haitian American man who owned the vessel was described as having returned to Haiti from Miami to establish his business and try to develop the island. The boat had left La Gonâve at 4:30 on the morning of September 8. As it neared the unloading point in Montrouis, it began to sink. Though less than 60 meters from shore, the boat sank very quickly in about 110 feet of water.

The reasons why the boat sank are not clear, and many of the witnesses and survivors speculated about the causes. Residents of La Gonâve told us that the service had been in operation for only ten days when the accident occurred. Apparently, in order to capitalize on high demand, the captain of the boat had allowed too many passengers to board with their luggage, merchandise, and other items. While 276 tickets were sold, children under fifteen were allowed on board for free, and some early media reports estimated the number of passengers at 500 to 800 persons, most of them residents of Anse-à-Galets, although this estimate was later revised downward to just over 300. The number of passengers was high because of a local soccer tournament between the island and mainland teams. Among those who perished were the local soccer team and police officers from the Anse-à-Galets district. Apparently the boat had been certified in the United States to carry only 80 passengers, although even this claim is not clear: some reported that it was able to transport as many as 260.

Confusion and speculation about the cause of the accident circulated feverishly. Witnesses and survivors felt that the captain, a Cuban man, was not properly trained to pilot the boat. They told us that as he prepared to drop anchor (the wharf begun years before by the Haitian state still not having been finished), he turned too sharply, and there was a wrenching sound. The passengers ran to one side to see what was happening, and their weight turned the boat on its side. According to media reports, the passengers were too eager to disembark into the waiting rowboats to make it to shore. Their rush toward the small boats tipped the ship. Regardless of the cause, as the boat began to fill with water, passengers on the lower decks were unable to open the cabin doors and drowned. Some estimate that more than one hundred people were trapped inside.

Rumors circulated among the survivors that the captain, who was eventually arrested but then set free, had actually locked the cabin doors. Other survivors we interviewed insisted that the doors had not been locked. They said that the force of the water rushing into the ship prevented those inside from opening the doors to escape. Those passengers on the boat's upper deck were able to get free, but most never reached land. Although it was a modern, air-conditioned vessel equipped with a television and other luxuries, it carried no life jackets. Of the more than 300 men, women, and children on board, at least 170 drowned, all within sight of their awaiting friends and family. Official counts listed just 62 survivors.

By four o'clock that afternoon, two Canadian U.N. divers arrived to help recover bodies. With the strong ocean currents, however, many of the bodies had immediately drifted out to sea. Those that washed ashore or were brought up from the depths of the sea were transported to local morgues. The divers worked steadily for two days to bring the decomposing bodies to the surface but soon needed hospitalization for decompression sickness. Crowds of weeping family and friends who waited for news lamented the failure of the state to recover the bodies quickly. At this stage the processes of focalization and transvaluation unfolded as individuals, families, and the community began to blame the Haitian state not only for this tragedy but also for its failure to address the many societal problems Haiti faced at the time.

For many Haitians, the state's failure to respond indicated not just bureaucratic indifference but also its fundamentally predatory nature as an entity dedicated to accumulating and consuming the resources of its citizens rather than protecting their welfare. As the days passed, many protesters burned tires and linked the tragedy to the problem of *lavi chè* (inflation) and ensekirite. They also accused President Préval and Haiti's political leaders of creating obstacles to block the struggle for development ("Ministè Edikasyon, Konsèy Inivèsite, Jwèt Pou Nou" 1997: 1). The disaster raised questions about public security and the state's obligation to protect its citizens. As one person told us, "It's a right for people not to have to drown in the sea." The catastrophe seemed even more senseless because the sinking of *La Fierté Gonâvienne* was not the first maritime tragedy that Haiti had suffered in recent years. In addition to the desperate flight of Haitian boat people who died tragically in sight of U.S. shores, survivors were reminded that in February 1993 the *Neptune* had capsized and sunk off the coast of Jérémie, in the south. Nearly 1,000 people were thought to have perished. And a decade before, on November 11, 1986, the *Okelele* capsized on the same route between La Gonâve and Montrouis, killing more than 260 people. After the 1986 accident the Haitian state apparently committed to building a proper wharf at Montrouis but abandoned the effort shortly afterward, a failure with devastating consequences for those in La Gonâve who required such services to reach the mainland. Another report stated that in March 1996 a ferry had sunk on the Montrouis route and 100 people died.

In addition to exacerbating frustrations regarding the state's incapacity to provide security for citizens, the tragedy highlighted the state's dependence on international interventions in the midst of national crises and the way the prevailing culture of impunity fomented vigilante justice. On September 11, as tensions mounted among the survivors and families of victims, the recovery effort was taken over by the U.S. Navy's Mobile Dive and Salvage Unit under Operation Restore Dignity, and the U.S. Coast Guard joined in recovering the bodies as they drifted out to sea. Unfortunately, at least thirty bodies were not recovered. Back on La Gonâve, the accident precipitated an eruption of grievances that had long festered in the community, resulting in attempted vigilante justice. Just before our arrival on the island, angry residents of Anse-à-Galets burned another ferry, the *Tinodio Express,* a wooden sailboat owned by a man of the same name. Apparently Tinodio had made public threats against *La Fierté Gonâvienne* and its owner ten days before, when the ferry first began operation. Residents accused Tinodio of witchcraft: allegedly, he used sorcery to curse the boat. One witness reasoned, "Why else would it sink just before reaching the shore?" Tinodio and a man known as Calypso, the owner of another boat, the *Épreuve de la Vie* (Proof of Life), were in hiding when we arrived. They were later reported to have fled to Miami. No one we interviewed that morning, however, blamed the owner of *La Fierté Gonâvienne* for the accident. He was described as a good person who only wanted to give back to the community and for that reason was a victim of jealousy.

In the attempt to make sense of the tragedy and allocate blame, rumors, gossip, and accusations flowed freely. Allegations that malevolent forms of magic had been employed to sabotage the ferry revealed the underlying tension between the boat owners who competed for limited passenger revenues. Accusations that Tinodio had used occult means to assuage his feelings of jealousy were highly charged. That these accusations culminated in the burning of his boat was a sign that the community needed an object on which to vent its anger for the accident, regardless of the truth about Tinodio's alleged nefarious activity.

After finishing the morning interviews, we went to have lunch at the Scheut parish in Anse-à-Galets, which was located just off the town square. Crowds of grieving and frustrated island residents gathered to await news. Father Paul did his best to console those he knew in the crowd and to temper the group's heightened emotions. Although he encouraged people to go home, his efforts met with limited success. At around 1:00 P.M. some of the crowd went on the offensive and attempted to murder Tinodio's wife by "necklacing" her—placing a tire around her neck and setting it on fire. The police rescued Madame Tinodio by putting her in protective custody. The HNP commissioner pleaded with the crowd: "It's not a solution to kill the Madame and to destroy her home. We must find the person who is responsible for the accident." Just a couple of hours later another incident occurred while we were still at the Scheut Mission. Members of the assembled group attempted to attack an employee of Tinodio who had also been accused of having performed malevolent magic to capsize the boat. After some time the crowd dispersed from the square, and we spoke with the local HNP officers about the violence, the relationship between the police and the community, and local security. We learned that those who precipitated this violence belonged to a gang that had fomented conflicts with another group in the Anse-à-Galets area earlier that year, suggesting these events had a complex history. The details of the conflict could not be ascertained during the short duration of our fact-finding mission. As it turned out, we would not leave the island without one more unexpected incident. The woman who had flown with us on the

plane that morning had traveled to La Gonâve to retrieve Tinodio's wife
from the volatile situation and intended to bring her on the afternoon
flight to Port-au-Prince. Although Tinodio's wife did not leave with us
because she was still sequestered in the police station, knowledge of the
planned rescue would prove difficult for us as we attempted to return
to Port-au-Prince. As we readied to leave on motorbikes and once again
approached the dirt runway, we found that a small group had barri-
caded the runway with bushes and other debris to prevent the plane
from taking off. Tensions were high, and given the events of that day, I
worried that the group's frustration and anger would now build toward
violence directed against us. We were very fortunate that Father Paul
and Claude Oscar, who were both well known to residents of the island,
were accompanying us. The two men suggested to the irate group that
their blockade was no way to resolve the crisis and they should let us
depart peaceably. After much palliative discussion, the group removed
the brambles and departed from the scene. We took off to continue the
investigation of the effects of the catastrophe on the mainland.

In addition to demonstrating the processes by which critical events
can precipitate collective violence, the sequence of events described
above demonstrates the relationship between embodied emotion, grief,
and social protest in Haiti. According to some interpretations, the com-
munal anger and eruptions of mob violence following the disaster could
be interpreted in terms of conceptions of heat, cold, and blood. As discussed in chapter 3, many Haitians experience situations of shock and
unexpected loss as a disruption of the body's equilibrium of hot and
cold and as imbalances in blood. Many of the survivors with whom we
spoke during this crisis were suffering from shock. As an example, one
man exclaimed that his legs had collapsed under him on reaching shore
and that even days afterward his whole body still felt "weak" or "loose"
(kò lage). He told us that it was still dangerous for him to bathe his head
because it had not yet been restored to balance. He required a healer to
ritually wash his head (lave tèt) with herbal infusions (rafrechi) in order
to regain balance. Furthermore, in my studies at the Mars/Kline Center
for Neurology and Psychiatry, one psychologist with whom I worked
closely stated that his Haitian patients tended to display "depression"
through aggressive or irritable behavior rather than lassitude or impair-
ment of functioning, sleep disturbances, or changes in weight—symptoms more common in the United States. In his formulation, many
forms of social protest became violent because participants were actually chronically depressed.

I am wary, however, of offering what could be interpreted as an evolutionary, psychobiological theory to analyze how ruptures in routine can culminate in violence in Haiti. Contemporary analyses of crowd behavior and spontaneous mobs frequently invoke the late-nineteenth-century theories of the physician and political philosopher Gustave Le Bon (1999) as intellectual antecedents (Tambiah 1996). Less discussed is Le Bon's theory of the psychologies, or "national characters," of social groups in which a group's reputed "mentality" and supposed position on the "ladder of the races" directly influenced its capacity for rationality. In his 1894 work, *The Psychology of Peoples,* Le Bon presented Haiti and Haitians as examples of black/African "incapacity" for governance. This reputed racial flaw arose from a psychobiological defect that prevented control of the body, passions, and "instinct" in favor of "discipline" and reason. As discussed in chapter 1, such racialist stereotypes strongly influenced U.S. foreign policy toward Haiti in the early twentieth century. Furthermore, as the HRF results packages demonstrate, traces of such negative stereotypes informed postconflict development strategies proposed by USAID for Haiti. While the political development rhetoric did not suggest that Haitians are inherently violent, the way this discourse linked violence, trauma, and the prevailing sense of injustice that many Haitians feel implied natural or cultural rather than political and economic roots to Haiti's challenges with ensekirite.

Documenting the disaster as it unfolded and witnessing the psychosocial sequelae experienced by survivors of the catastrophe also provided me with a lens through which to interpret the experience that many viktim suffered during the de facto period. By tracing the psychosocial effects of the disaster on the island and the mainland, however, I became aware of how the chaotic situation permitted some institutions and individuals to profit from the vulnerability and traumatic suffering of the afflicted. Such profiteering in times of ensekirite was a hallmark of the political economy of trauma.

Bereavement and the Appropriation of Suffering

The heartbreaking case of another Haitian ferry survivor demonstrates how shocking losses could destabilize self, family, and community on an ontological level, rendering them even more vulnerable socially, politically, and economically. This case also revealed the contours of occult economies that intersected with the political economy of trauma in

Haiti. The wife of one of La Gonâve's deputies, whom I will call Rose-Marie, was traveling with her son and daughter and members of her extended family when the ferry capsized. Rose-Marie, who had been on the upper deck, was able to begin swimming to shore with her children holding onto her back. Despite her efforts to save her family, another passenger who could not swim grabbed her eight-year-old son to stay afloat. Both of them disappeared underwater. Rose-Marie reached shore with her daughter but could not find her son. Once on land, she began searching for his body but was unable to locate him. To compound the confusion, she heard a rumor that someone had seen him alive; then the ordeal of trying to find him truly began. Was he alive, or was he dead? Although she knew he had perished, she could not yet accept her loss.

What would be confirmed was that nearly twenty members of her extended family drowned on that day.[15] Claude Oscar spoke with Rose-Marie on September 9. He reported that she was suffering from visual and auditory hallucinations. She both saw and conversed with her son at length. Father Paul told us that on that same evening Rose-Marie attempted suicide. She was hospitalized at a private facility in Port-au-Prince for two days after this attempt. On the evening of September 11, after finally being able to leave La Gonâve for Port-au-Prince, the HRF team went to Rose-Marie's home with Father Paul to pay respects and to offer assistance to the family. Members of the extended family and close friends had gathered in the living room to await further news while Rose-Marie's husband searched for their son's body. Her husband eventually was able to locate his body at one of the morgues in the area. Other families were less fortunate.

As is common in many cultures, the completion of culturally sanctioned funerary rites is necessary to maintaining proper relationships, and even boundaries, between the living and the dead (Douglas 1966). Given the inability to recover many of the bodies that had floated out to sea—or to identify badly decomposed corpses that floated to the surface in the days after the disaster—many survivors and family members of the deceased were unable to grieve and to memorialize the dead properly. As previously discussed, traditional Haitian religious culture requires the performance of burial rites in order for the nanm, or soul, of the deceased to be at peace. Families that were unable to lay their loved ones to rest could be subject to torment and persecution by their disembodied souls. These desperate losses reminded us of the fate of the murdered and disappeared persons during the coup years whose absence continued to traumatize many viktim.

The importance of properly observing funerary rites to honor kinship obligations between the living and the dead became a means by which suffering was transformed and appropriated for others' material gain. Such processes revealed negative dimensions of the political economy of trauma. When the funeral home directors learned that international assistance was going to be available to the families of the deceased, they immediately raised the price for storing the bodies from H$3,000 to more than H$5,000. The fee did not cover funeral costs. The unexpected loss and suffering of families thus became an occasion for others to *pwofite* (profit) from the disaster.

Other attempts to benefit from the disaster revealed the desperate poverty and fragility of this poor community. Individuals attempted to falsify victim status to "pwofite" from the emerging compassion economy. Like efforts to assist coup victims, enumerating true victims would become essential. Oscar informed us that at least five hundred children were orphaned by the shipwreck. Nevertheless, he was aware that in the aftermath of the accident some families that anticipated potential financial assistance had added the names of children whose parents had died years before to the victim census the Fund had been compiling. They did so with the hope that they might become eligible for the aid that would eventually arrive. Confirming a "true" list of victims would take a few weeks after the initial field assessment. In the interim period the Haitian government sponsored a memorial service in Montrouis to commemorate the tragedy.

The Montrouis memorial was yet another example of Tambiah's concepts of focalization and transvaluation in that the local tragedy was linked to national and international concerns about political economy and to a desire for the state to demonstrate its competence and accountability to citizens and international observers. Of special concern was the state's responsibility to promote and protect the welfare of Haitian citizens and questions about whether international governmental and nongovernmental interveners that promoted postconflict development and democracy in Haiti were obligated to assist with this local crisis. On the morning of September 16 a mass funeral was held at the site of the shipwreck in Montrouis, since many of the recovered bodies had decomposed too far to be identifiable. (There were no efforts to solicit the assistance of forensic anthropologists or specialists in DNA technologies to identify the bodies of the dead.) At the ceremony the Haitian minister of public health reassured local residents that the bodies posed no health risk, as they had disinfected the area. The Haitian

Senate also announced that the Japanese government had pledged U.S.$80,000 to improve the ports in La Gonâve and Montrouis. They informed the community of other international pledges of assistance to the victims' families. The $25,000 pledged by the United States was later increased to $80,000. France offered 120,000 francs, and Taiwan pledged U.S.$15,000 for the parents of victims.

Despite the limited international resources to assist victims of the disaster, the state still had to demonstrate accountability to its citizens through a stated intent to rehabilitate the infrastructure between Montrouis and La Gonâve. On Friday, September 19, President Préval and a number of diplomats attended another memorial service in Anse-à-Galets for victims of the ferry residing on La Gonâve. The Canadian defense minister, who was in Haiti to discuss the impending withdrawal of the U.N. peacekeeping force, also attended. The minister offered U.S.$12,000 for victims' families and expressed his solidarity with the Haitian people. Préval then announced that the wharf in Montrouis would be closed but that the beachfront residence· of former President-for-Life Jean-Claude Duvalier would be available as a docking site. The state would provide two boats to transport travelers between the island and the mainland. While expressing condolences to the hundreds of families and residents in attendance, Préval was careful to assign blame for the accident elsewhere: "It is difficult to overcome thirty years of dictatorship that had a policy of squeeze and suck dry. But we will rebuild, the way a bird builds a nest, little by little." The state absolved itself of responsibility for the accident by referring to the Duvaliers' predatory practices of repression and extraction of resources from citizens. At the same time the state's response to the local emergency signaled to international donors its intent to develop Haiti with accountability and sustainability.

Historically Haitians have not had many opportunities to hold state officials accountable, so the memorial provided another means to link local suffering to issues of state responsibility. At this same commemoration, the deputy from La Gonâve who lost his child and many members of his extended family asked that docks be constructed in Anse-à-Galets and Pointe-à-Raquette, the island's second largest city. He also requested that interior roads be built on the island to facilitate development. His own suffering and the anguish of local survivors and families of the deceased provided a window of recognition that placed the gaze of the international community and the Government of Haiti on the everyday insecurities that the community suffered. Collective experiences of suffering also provided a platform for articulating chronic frustrations with state neglect and indifference. At the same time the national and international assistance that flowed from this event were means by which the democratic state attempted to show its responsibility and legitimacy in the postdictatorship period and the international community could unequivocally express its "solidarity" with Haiti.

In the weeks after the accident a major point of contention would emerge concerning how to distribute the limited aid to the victims' families. In meetings between La Gonâve's two mayors and representatives of the national and international humanitarian assistance organizations channeling their respective nations' funds, there were disputes over which community should receive the bulk of the assistance. The IDB, France, Canada, Taiwan, Japan, and the United States had pledged funds through the Office for Disaster Assistance and the U.S. Embassy. Haitian businesses and civil society organizations abroad had all pledged money, food, school supplies, and medical assistance to the survivors. They also promised infrastructural development assistance. Given the political discord that more than likely would accompany the distribution of aid to La Gonâve, the Human Rights Fund declined to take on the responsibility. The Fund advised the United States to avoid what could become a morass of difficulties if it became involved further.

As the fall progressed, disputes over who had the right to represent the victims increased, much as Das (1995) has described in the aftermath of the Bhopal disaster in India. The Haitian crisis, however, did not evolve into a large-scale victims' social movement. I was told that much of the aid promised to families was "appropriated" by the agencies responsible for coordinating the relief effort. External offers of assistance also seemed to fade or disappear in the weeks after the accident. The Japanese government had initially pledged infrastructural assistance for long-term development of the wharves. Representatives later stated that such an effort could only be undertaken after a "thorough assessment" had been conducted to determine what needed to be done. In another example, the 1997 fiscal year report of the USAID Office of the U.S. Foreign Disaster Assistance Bureau for Humanitarian Response stated that $25,000 was divided among the families of the survivors, which amounted to $125 for each person lost. I was informed, however, that even this small sum did not reflect the actual amount given since some of the relief funds were actually allocated to the Human Rights Fund to cover the cost of its investigation.

In the aftermath of this calamity, accusations and blame directed against the Haitian state continued in the media. The Haitian daily

paper, *Le Nouvelliste,* reported on September 21 that the accident had
delivered a fatal blow to the local fishing industry because people were
afraid to eat fish that might have consumed the lost bodies of those
who perished in the ferry disaster. Fishing, a subsistence activity for the
majority of Montrouis's residents, was described as a cursed *(maudite)*
activity, revealing how "marginal [the residents] were in the chain of
production in the fish industry" ("L'Actualité en question" 1997: 1).
The article criticized the state for having failed to mount a systematic
campaign to dispel fears about consuming fish from this region. State
negligence was described as a sign of the division in government:

> Whereas the [population] weep for their dead and the [fishermen] ask only
> to survive, behind the scenes in the State media, the director general and the
> director of information would nearly come to blows after having shown
> face-to-face their conflict over the treatment of the Montrouis case. [It is]
> a dirty affair that passes judgment on the National Palace. . . . Politics: to
> find a happy aspect to the crisis, President Préval announced that he has
> already opened discussions among the political sector of the country in the
> context of designating a new Prime Minister. (1, 40)

At this point, the tragedy was explicitly used to evoke the failures of the
state to protect its citizenry. But in linking the disaster to widespread
perceptions of Préval's inability to resolve the political crisis, these discourses are additional examples of focalization and transvaluation:
the micropolitical dynamics of the ferry disaster were generalized and
extended to macropolitical conflicts.

For many months preceding the capsizing, an ongoing macropolitical and economic conflict was the debate over the designation of the
new prime minister. On June 9, 1997, Prime Minister Rosny Smarth
had resigned after six months of general strikes, protest marches by
"popular organizations," bomb scares, and widespread social unrest.
The resignation was the culmination of intense criticism focused on the
Haitian government for its inability to resolve the April 6, 1997, elections. Seven of twenty-seven Senate seats and one deputy's seat were in
dispute. Members of Smarth's Lavalas Political Organization (OPL),[16]
the opposition party to Lafanmi Lavalas (the Lavalas Family, the new
party of former President Aristide), alleged that Lafanmi won a majority
in government fraudulently. They claimed that the Provisional Electoral
Council had ignored election irregularities. The dispute also stemmed
in part from the OPL's support of Préval and Smarth. The president
and prime minister had agreed to implement fiscal austerity and privatization plans that the United States and the international financial

institutions had proposed as the path to Haiti's economic recovery and development. Lafanmi held that the state's industries were part of its patrimony or national heritage, and their control should thus not be ceded to international organizations or private corporations. With the election in dispute—and amid international concern that Lafanmi wanted to operate as a one-party state—the United States, the United Nations, and multilateral donors alleged that the electoral process was not democratic. They chose to withhold financial assistance from Haiti until the elections could be resolved. As the dispute dragged on, President Préval's appointees for prime minister were not ratified by the legislature. Préval began ruling by decree in January 1999 (but here I am getting ahead of the story). All these arguments and accusations occurred against the backdrop of ensekirite.

Later during that 1997 fall, new rumors about the *Fierté Gonâvienne* shipwreck circulated that linked the tragedy to party politics. In mid-October an article appeared in *Haïti-Observateur*—a newspaper known for its anti-Aristide line—claiming that the ferry was actually carrying a shipload of weapons. The hidden cache of weapons supposedly prevented the doors from opening on the lower decks, trapping the passengers ("Une cargaison d'armes" 1997: 18). These "phantom" weapons were reputedly intended for partisans of former President Aristide. The newspaper further alleged that individuals "close to" the U.S. Coast Guard had revealed that its divers had observed different types of weapons in the boat's interior where it lay underwater. Supposedly, once that knowledge reached U.S. authorities they abandoned efforts to raise the boat (18). The article then reminded readers of President Préval's "nonchalance" in his management of the crisis and reluctance to help finance the effort to raise the ferry and castigated President Aristide for his "indifference" to the plight of the victims and their parents in the current tragedy, when in 1993 after the *Neptune* capsized he had pledged U.S.$100,000 in aid and offered words of encouragement. Underlying some of these accusations were insinuations that Aristide was undermining Préval's presidency and allowing him to "sink" in terms of public opinion in order that he himself could appear as a savior when he ran for reelection in 2000. Beyond this question of electoral politics, however, many rumors circulated throughout the period of my research that Lafanmi was arming its partisans in preparation for any further coup attempts by former Duvalierists.

The loss of *La Fierté Gonâvienne* was invoked again in the media to criticize the state after yet another shipwreck on the La Gonâve-Montrouis route that occurred in December 1997. This boat was a thirty-five-foot vessel bearing the name *Kris Vivan* (Living Christ). Once again the number of passengers, the amount of cargo, and the number of the deceased were uncertain. According to a *Libète* editorial, the calamity repeated nearly the same pattern described above ("Sispann bay lanmò ochan" 1997: 1). The editorial would go on to state:

> There are many signs that show that human life is losing importance a little more each day in Haiti. A cluster of phenomena can justify this: *ensekirite, zenglendo*, the drug phenomenon, the high birthrate of children in poor conditions *[timoun k'ap fèt san kontwòl nan move kondisyon]*, corruption and lack of State responsibility that should be there to protect people's lives. Accidents happen on the national routes every day. There isn't a shred of control over transportation in the country. . . . And what is more serious still, in the manner that the Justice and Peace [Commission] said in a meeting last week, with the new politics that threaten to swallow up the country, everything is going to become merchandise, even people's life and dignity. (1)

The Justice and Peace Commission had met from December 12 to 14 to discuss the problems that the state had not yet resolved: ensekirite, *chomaj* (unemployment), and illiteracy—conditions said to "torment" the population. The organization asserted that this "disgusting situation created the conditions for more corruption, waste and insecurity within the State," and that there were practically no morals in society any longer. The meeting's slogan: "san jistis pa gen lape, san lape pa gen lavi"—"Without justice, there is no peace; without peace, there is no life" (Konfidan 1997: 5)[17]—highlighted the way that security, state accountability, and livelihood were linked in political and human rights discourses. At the same time the comment that people's lives and dignity were susceptible to commodification pointedly critiqued the political economy of trauma in Haiti.

The *Fierté Gonâvienne* disaster was also invoked as a reminder of the plight of viktim from the coup years. The capsizing occurred just a few weeks before the commemoration of the sixth anniversary of the September 30, 1991, coup d'état. Since the 1994 "restoration of democracy," viktim had mobilized in public demonstrations to demand justice and reparations for their suffering, especially on the anniversary of the de facto regime's usurpation of power. As the anniversary approached, the Government of Haiti made repeated public statements of accountability for the victims of the shipwreck. Viktim demanded that the state complete making restitution to *them* for their losses between 1991 and 1994 and begin reforming the judiciary.

On September 30, 1997, the Haitian media reported that at a mass at the Sacré-Coeur Church, Minister of Justice Pierre Max Antoine assured viktim that the ministry was establishing a fund "in order that justice be rendered to the Haitian people, in particular the most weak in Haitian society" ("Le Ministre de la Justice" 1997: 1).[18] Minister Antoine emphasized, furthermore, that Haitian institutions of justice had been corrupted by "the complicity of certain foreign countries within local sectors" of Haitian society, referring to the rumored covert interventions of foreign polities in Haiti's political and economic affairs. On this same occasion, MICIVIH coordinator Colin Granderson saluted the work of victims' advocacy organizations. He added that by its action, the Ministry of Justice was "taking an important step in acting on the recommendations of MICIVIH as far as the improvement of the functioning of the judicial system, and pursuing the cases of the crimes and abuses perpetrated during the coup period" (24). The U.N./OAS approval that Granderson gave Minister Antoine was striking, especially given the anti-U.S. sentiment implied in Antoine's statement. It signaled that the international human rights monitors allied themselves with governmental and nongovernmental Haitian actors to position themselves as potent political forces in a highly charged postconflict environment. Despite the rhetoric of state accountability and desire to promote justice and the rule of law, however, Minister Antoine would later be accused by Haitian human rights groups of thwarting one of the first trials of alleged perpetrators of political violence during the de facto period: the Raboteau trial.[19]

* * *

The capsizing of *La Fierté Gonâvienne* demonstrated the processes of focalization and transvaluation when the meaning of the disaster was abstracted from the local politics of La Gonâve and linked to past and current perceptions of the state as predatory rather than accountable. It was also a diagnostic event revealing social cleavages and inequalities of power at not only local but also national and international levels. The incident further highlighted the politics of the truth of suffering and the processes by which traumatic suffering could be commodified and exploited through a variety of professional, bureaucratic practices at all levels. Multiple actors sought to ensure their security and to demonstrate accountability and competence by intervening in the disaster's wake. The pattern of rumor, accusation, counteraccusation, and violence in the context of scarce aid and overall ensekirite would be repeated as the Haitian state and its national and international partners attempted to promote rehabilitation, reparations, justice, and the rule of law for viktim. Perceptions that some individuals and institutions were profiting from the suffering of others would generate more accusations of both witchcraft and bureaucraft among those who interacted with agencies and agents in the grant economy.

   The events described in this chapter, one manufactured and the other accidental, also revealed the intense politicization of suffering in Haiti. Both generated debates about truth and the competence, incapacity, or failure of the Government of Haiti to protect and sustain the majority of its citizens. As it unfolded, each event also displayed features of bureaucraft and illustrated the work of occult economies. In the first case, the National Colloquium for the Rehabilitation of Victims of Organized Violence, the existence of such practices was implied. In the case of the ferry disaster, the traces of occult transactions were more easily discernible in the contests over the distribution of humanitarian aid. Both occasions were means by which the Human Rights Fund and, indirectly, ADF demonstrated their competence and accountability. The successful management of trauma interventions and the suggestion of nonintervention in the case of the ferry disaster gained HRF material and political capital—features of the political economy of trauma.

CHAPTER 5

Bureaucraft, Accusations, and the Social Life of Aid

Nou pa labank, nou pa leta, nou pa Bondye
"We're not the bank, we're not the state, and we're not God."

In fall 1998 I interviewed Phillippe Jonassaint, a beneficiary of the Human Rights Fund Victim Assistance and Rehabilitation Program and a participant in one of its therapy groups. While lamenting the challenges of finding employment and rebuilding his life after victimization, Phillippe observed, "We can speak, but we can't eat." His frustration about hunger in Haiti arose from the reality of ensekirite. Although there might be "democracy," along with, in theory, the ability to speak freely that democracy ensures, there was little "security." His words also evoked a political slogan often repeated within the Haitian prodemocracy sector: "Lapè nan tèt, lapè nan vant" (Peace of mind, peace/ bread in the belly).[1] The slogan suggests that without a full stomach, there can be no peace. It also suggests that without ontological security, there would be no end to conflict.

At the same time, Phillippe's words were a pointed critique of the postconflict humanitarian and development aid apparatus in general and of the ADF Human Rights Fund in particular. Of what use were civil and human rights if the poor Haitian majority could not feed themselves and their families? Of what use was psychotherapy for viktim if daily survival was in doubt? By extension, of what use was democracy if there was no security? Phillippe's comments highlighted the double binds facing both the Rehabilitation Program staff and its viktim clients who grappled with multiple forms of social, political, economic, and institutional insecurity as the postconflict period wore on.

In this chapter and the next, I trace the social life of humanitarian assistance from 1998 to 1999, from the Fund's Rehab Program to Martissant and back to the Fund. I illustrate controversies over the definitions of democracy, rights, and security. Issues of politics, class, and status saturated rehabilitation work with victims of organized violence at both the individual and institutional levels. In each setting the use of humanitarian and development gifts (Mauss 1950) or grants of aid was debated. Most important, I argue that the competition for resources and the desire for status and recognition *within* the humanitarian and development aid apparatus trickled down to foment conflicts over aid in local communities. Like the discourses about witchcraft discussed previously, these contests reflected negative aspects of bureaucraft—both as hidden or secret practices and as accusations of bureaucratic secrecy, or occult activity, regarding the distribution of resources, contracts, and alliances in the compassion economy. Such discourses and practices also concerned the truths of individual and institutional identities. Amid the climate of ensekirite, strife was omnipresent among the donor assemblages, as well as between and among institutional and individual grant recipients.

The scarcity of resources influenced the social life of humanitarian and development assistance. Outside the institutional efforts to rehabilitate and craft disciplined citizens from viktim, gifts or grants of aid were inserted into existing local moral worlds (Kleinman and Kleinman 1991). These insertions of aid sometimes reinforced occult economies or generated new ones. Bureaucraft practices and accusations in institutional settings also paralleled "witchcraft" accusations in Martissant. The combination of both "crafts" culminated in the termination of the Rehab Program in May 1999 as the institution and its personnel came under attack from within and without the aid apparatus.

The anxiety, frustration, and anger produced by the escalating ensekirite and the decline in ankadreman provided the ontological quicksand for these disastrous events. On November 30, 1997, the U.N. peacekeeping forces withdrew, leaving behind a smaller civilian mission (MIPONUH) that continued to work toward professionalizing the Haitian National Police.[2] The HNP assumed greater responsibility for providing security but without much success. Gang violence increased, as did political violence, and sometimes the two were in distinguishable. At the height of a wave of ensekirite between late fall 1998 and spring 1999 President Préval—who had grown weary of the failure of Parliament to ratify four successive prime minister appointees in seventeen months (because of electoral disputes between political parties)[3]—dissolved Parliament and began rule by decree. Humanitarian aid also grew scarce, as promised aid remained suspended because of the crisis in government. Aid to coup victims also diminished, as international donors no longer viewed the period as one of "crisis" or emergency, and therefore warranting international military and humanitarian intervention, but rather as one of long-term democratic consolidation. Victims' advocacy organizations responding to the fluctuating number of institutions aiding them scrambled desperately for assistance. Given the limited aid provided by the Haitian state, viktim sought to strengthen connections to institutions such as the Fund.

Many viktim maintained concurrent memberships in several victims' advocacy groups as a strategy to improve their chances of receiving support. As these groups developed, they splintered off, regrouped, and reformed their mandates. Furthermore, victims' advocacy groups shapeshifted in response to fluctuations in the humanitarian market and changes in the supply of local, national, and international resources to rehabilitate viktim: as new client categories were recognized or defined as objects of intervention or development (i.e., "trafficked women" or "women and microfinance"), these groups transformed themselves accordingly to meet the new criteria for aid. At the same time, politically and criminally motivated ensekirite escalated. The insecure climate captured viktim and those who assisted them in its web. These constraints pitted grantors against grantors, viktim against viktim, and grantors and viktim against each other.

"CHÈZ YO PA POU NOU!"

The tension was thick at the stately gingerbread manor that had once housed America's Development Foundation/Haiti when I returned to conduct ethnographic fieldwork on the Human Rights Fund Rehabilitation Program in summer 1998. One reason for the friction stemmed from the institutional uncertainties and temporal fluxes of working in the grant economy. Historically ADF operated with a small staff in its Virginia headquarters in the United States. When faced with budget constraints, whether at headquarters or in its regional programs, ADF tended to cut overseas expenditures in order to preserve the overall functioning of the nonprofit company. The ADF office in Port-au-Prince was badly crowded because of these budgetary constraints. In 1997, just after the Rehabilitation Program got under way, ADF decided to put the

Fund (formerly housed elsewhere) into the same limited space occupied by a civil society project called ASOSYE.[4]

ADF's ASOSYE program was funded by USAID and implemented as part of the Democracy Enhancement Project. "ASOSYE," which means "associate" or "partner" in Haitian Creole, was the name chosen to promote the effort as a "local" project. Georges Duval, a Haitian American anthropologist, joined ADF as its chief of party in August 1997 and initially managed both the ASOSYE and HRF programs. Duval had worked in development for many years and was a close friend of USAID Mission Director Phyllis Forbes from his previous work with her overseas. After a year of directing ADF/Haiti, however, Duval for the most part began to conduct his work at home in Pétionville, a suburb of the capital. As a result it was difficult for both ASOSYE and HRF program administrators to manage personnel and institutional finances without his on-site oversight of daily affairs.

Other challenges the Fund program faced reflected Haiti's cultural and structural inequalities. There were disputes between the HRF and ASOSYE staff that were related to class and political orientation. The majority of the Fund's personnel could be described as pro-democracy supporters of former President Aristide who were concerned about Haiti's transition to democracy. They came from lower- to middle-class backgrounds and had a range of levels of education. The perception among the HRF staff was that the generally wealthier ASOSYE team was politically conservative and in some cases even reactionary. One HRF staff member alleged that the brother of one of the female ASO-SYE employees was among the worst torturers during the 1991–94 coup period. While this did not necessarily reflect on the personal politics of his sister, the Fund staff was wary of her, even though she had assisted viktim under the PIRÈD program. Over time the rumors and speculation about each staff member's identity, socioeconomic status, and political position generated negative aspects of bureaucraft that closely resembled witchcraft accusations. Integral to the proliferation of these accusations was an underlying environment of social, political, and institutional ensekirite that generated fear, suspicion, and even paranoia.

There were additional sources of friction exacerbating the social, economic, and political divergences between the two ADF project staffs, because the Fund expanded between 1997 and 1999 in terms of budget, programming, number and rank of personnel, and program resources (i.e., vehicles, communications equipment, security personnel, etc.). After two previous directors left the Human Rights Fund,[5] Dr. Manata became the interim director and was confirmed as director in November 1997. From that point forward he interacted primarily with the U.S. headquarters of ADF, the U.S. Embassy, and USAID/Haiti. During the same period, Dr. Thomas became director of the Rehab Program, a permanent staff position. Early in 1998 two Haitian nurses, Louise Gilles and Emilie Datilus,[6] joined the Rehab Program. In addition to this, the Community-Police Relations pilot program that was inaugurated in November 1997 by Julien Duverger, a highly respected Haitian human rights leader, was made a permanent project within the Fund with Duverger as director. Duverger was affiliated with the Justice and Peace Commission and had rejected any participation with ADF and HRF after the scandal of the leaked U.S. cablegram in 1994 (see chapter 2). The addition of this prominent Haitian statesman to the permanent staff was considered a coup for ADF. A third project was also added: the Human Rights Education Program. ADF headquarters had hired Bernard Jerôme, a French anthropologist and former MICIVIH observer, to direct this program.[7] Finally, René Ibrahim, a journalist from a central African nation who had resided in Haiti for nearly two decades, also joined the Human Rights Education Program.

Uncertainty and tension existed also because ASOSYE had formerly been the largest project in the ADF/Haiti portfolio but lacked sufficient funds for daily operations in fall 1998 as it neared the end of its grant. ASOSYE was not assured of future funding, even though ADF/USA intended to bid for the newest USAID/Haiti civil society proposal. Thus the Fund's budget covered the largest part of expenses related to the maintenance of the physical plant. Nevertheless, the ASOSYE staff members refused to relinquish any space to the HRF program. There was a widespread belief among Fund staff members that ASOSYE staff perceived the Fund and its largely pro-democracy staff as poachers encroaching on their territory. Frustration and resentment built. To diffuse some of the tension, a running joke among the HRF staff was, "*chèz yo pa pou nou*" (the chairs are not for us).

In addition to the infrastructural, management, and fiscal problems as the ASOSYE grant waned, the rising status of the Human Rights Fund program among international and national actors in the aid apparatus provoked jealousy or resentment between ASOSYE and HRF personnel. In 1997 the Fund had enjoyed tremendous success building bridges to Haitian activists, nongovernmental advocacy groups, and state officials who were implementing postconflict transition initiatives through the National Colloquium for the Rehabilitation of Victims of Organized

Violence and the assessment of the *Fierté Gonâvienne* disaster. HRF had also demonstrated accountability in "rationalizing rehabilitation" and promoting USAID's Strategic Objectives. HRF was rewarded for these public relations and management gains,[8] and by August 1998 the program grew from its initial status as a subgrant under the auspices of the ASOSYE civil society program to become a separate project in the Justice and Democratic Governance sector of the USAID/Haiti portfolio.[9] When the Fund was upgraded as a separate project with the new extension, all the Fund support staff received raises that increased their salaries beyond those of their generally higher-class counterparts in the ASOSYE group. Given the restrictions on the ASOSYE budget, there was no way to raise the salaries for its staff. As can be expected, jealousy and resentment began to fester.

The bureaucratic procedures by which HRF was upgraded to an independent project in the JDG sector merit further discussion as examples of bureaucraft. After evaluations that are routine in the audit culture of publicly funded humanitarian and development assistance, the Fund was judged to be performing at a "world class" level.[10] While I do not challenge the quality of the work that the Fund provided, other scholars have criticized USAID's evaluations of its democracy assistance projects (e.g., Carothers 1996). Independent audits and assessments are often limited in scope and duration. Auditors may possess appropriate skills and expertise to assess a project's scope of work but not necessarily its appropriateness for the cultural context in which the work is performed. They also share the institutional language, rationality, and cultural practices of development. Auditors of USAID programs may have close ties to the network of institutional actors in development whose work they are to assess, making critical assessments challenging for political, professional, and personal reasons. Thus negative critiques of such programs and actors are difficult. According to Thomas Carothers:

> The persons who conduct evaluations for USAID, though independent of USAID itself, are often part of a relatively close community of development professionals who work as contractors for USAID on a regular basis. As such, they are likely to share many of the basic assumptions of USAID staff about the methods and goals of foreign assistance and to produce evaluations that reflect rather than question these assumptions. (1996: 5)

Furthermore, actors in the federally funded aid apparatus frequently solicited the expertise of individuals who had assessed the work of other USAID programs as consultants. These individuals also assisted with strategic planning and design of activities that achieved "results" during the course of a project grant. They also contributed to processes of competing for future grants. Although these contractors possessed expert knowledge in their respective fields, they were frequently dependent on opportunities to assess the work of a variety of institutions—whether at the donor or development partner level—to gain access to employment and other professional opportunities in the future.

While observing these tensions at close range, I became aware of how bureaucratic procedures to mobilize, circulate, and assess the expert knowledge of other agencies and agents could generate political and economic gain for the actors involved. To offer one example, one of the members of the Eval team (as it was called) that gave HRF a world-class ranking was a former executive with Amnesty USA and a close friend of the chief of party of the prime development partner of the USAID Administration of Justice Program, a group called Checchi and Company.[11] This individual was also a longtime friend of USAID Mission Director Forbes, having served with her in the Peace Corps decades before. In fall 1998, as staff planned to commemorate the fiftieth anniversary of the Universal Declaration of Human Rights, the Human Rights Fund hired this former Amnesty executive as a consultant.

The work of these mobile experts, often contested, implied to some actors in the aid apparatus the existence of hidden transactions to consolidate and increase bureaucratic power for those with strong political connections. For example, some members of the Eval team possessed extensive training and experience in law and human rights and had previously worked in Haiti with MICIVIH or Haitian civil society organizations. In spring 1999 the expertise and practices of these individuals became controversial when USAID released the new Administration of Justice request for proposals for a new "rule of law" project that was currently being implemented by Checchi and Company. On reviewing the proposal, the Checchi and Company chief of party made accusations that the former MICIVIH Eval team member who had assessed Checchi's work in January 1998 had influenced how the design team drafted the new proposal. He charged the assessor with "spying" and unfair influence in the design. In addition, he complained that the same individual was listed as a potential staff person in a competing company's proposal for the new project. In his view there were several conflicts of interest, and ultimately Checchi and Company lost its bid for the new proposal. Its chief of party's allegations about the former MICIVIH

Eval team member's covert motives and practices are an example of bureaucraft accusations in the scarce grant economy.

Just as witchcraft accusations arising between closely related actors over the causes of fortune and misfortune can lead to retributive attacks, bureaucraft accusations regarding perceptions of illicit accumulation of resources by closely affiliated actors in the aid apparatus led to what can be interpreted as retributive attacks. As discussed below, accusations against ADF and the Fund as institutions, as well as against individual staff members, were generated from within and without the aid apparatus and culminated in multiple forms of violence. What became clear over time was that some within and outside ADF perceived that the Human Rights Fund program had made unfair gains. For example, after the January 1998 Eval team's positive review of the Fund's work, the Fund received a fourteen-month extension, to August 1999. Its budget was increased to U.S.$2.2 million. Each improvement in HRF's status exacerbated interpersonal relations at ADF/Haiti but also sparked greater criticism of and resistance to ADF/HRF within the broader U.S.-funded political development realm. Then in spring 1999, the entire ASOSYE project mutinied, after using what were rumored to be covert business strategies to bid successfully for the latest civil society request for proposals. Ultimately, USAID removed ASOSYE from ADF and housed it within a competitor's development portfolio, the for-profit Washington, D.C.-based Management Systems International (MSI).

The processes by which ASOSYE was removed from ADF were complex and involved negative aspects of bureaucraft. The perceived failure of HRF staff members to fulfill tacit expectations to distribute gifts and grants of aid at both individual and institutional levels was an important component of these dynamics. Breaches of unstated obligations to reciprocate a gift or grant—whether in kind or through indirect means—were a source of conflict. For example, by fall 1998 the Fund was a newly independent project fulfilling the goals of USAID's JDG category. The USAID mission director's spouse requested employment at the Fund. Manata, who had recently been promoted to HRF chief of party, turned down his request. Manata was concerned that there was a potential conflict of interest. This was an important issue as ADF also intended to bid for the USAID "rule of law" proposal that would be released in spring 1999. If the USAID director's spouse was an employee of the institution that won the grant, there could be accusations of favoritism or nepotism. Instead, ASOSYE chief of party Georges Duval chose to hire the mission director's husband as a consultant, and among other tasks, he conducted an unsuccessful mediation seminar between the staff of ASOSYE and HRF.

The implicit or unspoken obligations between agencies and agents in the aid apparatus in Haiti could influence the gains and losses of both institutions and individuals. In December 1998, after the failure to resolve the friction between the two programs, Duval informed Manata that ASOSYE staff members were not going to honor an exclusivity agreement with ADF to apply for the new USAID civil society project proposal. Rather, they intended to be listed as potential staff both for MSI and ADF. It is unclear if the strategy of aligning a program and its staff with multiple development partner proposals to increase the chances of securing future employment and institutional resources is a routine development practice. By late spring 1999 ADF learned that MSI had won the bid, though its proposal was scored nearly identically to the one submitted by ADF. Apparently, from what ADF president Michael Miller said to the staff, USAID had given MSI two extra points for the identical ASOSYE staff members listed on ADF's proposal. Miller lodged a formal protest to stop the process from moving forward. His administrative complaint against the USAID/Haiti team that had reviewed the proposals was met with hostility, and it may also have contributed to the decision to cut HRF's funding in 1999.

The discourses employed to explain the loss of ASOSYE evoked dimensions of bureaucraft that resembled practices of divination, as well as the diagnosis of the etiology of misfortune in witchcraft. As previously discussed, bureaucratic discourses and practices are secular theodicies that can be employed to explain one's own misfortune and the suffering of others. During this period of conflict and uncertainty, rumors circulated among the remaining ADF staff, as well as the staff of other USAID-funded projects, alleging that the USAID mission director and her spouse were founding members or partners in the for-profit MSI.[12] The covert negotiations by the ASOSYE staff and the "voodoo economics" that gave the MSI proposals two extra points to thwart ADF and the Fund were markers of what some perceived as negative bureaucraft practices, as were the allegations that the USAID mission director and her spouse were founding partners of MSI. ADF staff members were desperate to divine what had gone wrong. How had they lost ASOSYE? The truth did not emerge until after the Rehabilitation Program was shut down.

'DEBLOZAY,' THREATS, AND ETHICS

The institutional practices described above paralleled hidden strategies and tactics used by viktim to increase flows of aid by maintaining memberships in multiple victims' advocacy groups and by forms of "graft." As in the ASOSYE case, hidden tactics to ensure institutional (and personal) gain could be interpreted as justifiable forms of resistance to ADF policies and procedures. Bureaucratic conflicts about how aid should be distributed at the institutional level also paralleled conflicts and attacks at the organizational and interpersonal levels. These individual, organizational, institutional, and even governmental uncertainties occurred amid escalating ensekirite and were additional factors that influenced the frequency and severity of attacks against the Fund.

From fall 1998 to spring 1999 the daily presence of viktim at ADF headquarters proved another source of discord between ASOSYE and HRF staff members. When the PIRÈD staff had begun assisting internally displaced Haitian activists at ADF/Haiti during the coup years, many viktim, sometimes hundreds, had sought refuge in the rear of the lakou—the gated courtyard surrounding the manor. During the subsequent tenure of the original Human Rights Fund (HRFI), the formal victim assistance program moved to a small suite of offices in Pacot, a beautiful residential area in the foothills of the mountains overlooking Port-au-Prince, home to a number of national and international NGOs. This site was less accessible by public transportation for the viktim who needed its services but provided privacy and security for clients. The subsequent relocation of the Fund back to ADF/Haiti headquarters in 1997 made the Fund more accessible and reduced infrastructural costs. However, the ADF manor, while grand, could not easily accommodate a treatment program for traumatized survivors of violence who required privacy, security, and recognition from all ADF staff as legitimate participants in democratic political processes. In particular, ASOSYE staff members expressed negative perceptions and attitudes toward the predominantly impoverished and nonliterate Rehab Program beneficiaries that mirrored the class and political judgments between HRF and ASOSYE staff.

From the PIRÈD period during the coup years to the early years of HRF and between 1997 and 1999 under the new Rehab Program, there were multiple changes in victim assistance policies that strongly influenced the frustrations viktim clients felt and expressed to ADF staff as a whole. In 1997 Rehab staff members had set a limit of one year of eligibility for complete medical care and other forms of support for each beneficiary and his or her dependents. At the conclusion of the year, beneficiaries of the program were expected to have found other resources, especially since the project was intended to develop into an independent Haitian-administered institution. In particular, there were two incidents involving viktim that disturbed the working environment and threatened the staff that resulted from perceived injustices regarding how the Rehab Program administered and distributed victim assistance funds.

The first incident occurred early in June 1998, just over a year after the latest change in victim assistance policies. Julie Dorville, a forty-one-year-old beneficiary of the Fund, had an argument with Dr. Thomas about the impending termination of victim assistance to her family and herself. Originally from Jacmel and a seamstress by trade, she had been living in Cité Soleil at the time she became a target of violence. On May 25, 1991, Julie was at home when some atache stormed the house looking for her husband, a known activist. When they did not find him at the home, all six of these men raped her. Her husband was arrested at the radio station where he worked and disappeared. Around the same time her sister was assassinated in Jacmel, leaving Julie responsible for six children, her own and her sister's. In order to find aid and justice for her suffering she joined Fanm Viktim Leve Kanpe (Women Victims Mobilize, FAVILEK), one of the first female victims' advocacy organizations, and she received emergency assistance from PIRÈD when the program was providing direct financial stipends to viktim during the coup years.

Under the new Rehab Program all former clients were reauthenticated as legitimate beneficiaries (see chapter 4). Julie thus became eligible for additional services in June 1997, receiving one year of victim assistance for herself and the children under her charge; however, no further financial stipend was granted. In June 1998 her year of benefits was ending, which undoubtedly contributed to her frustrations with the program. On the day the altercation occurred, Dr. Thomas had chastised Julie for adding powdered milk for her children to a prescription authorized for payment (for which the pharmacy had in turn billed the Fund for reimbursement). Dr. Thomas viewed her actions as an attempt to pwofite through her affiliation with the Fund, a charge that would also be leveled at the Haitian medical network in the months that followed.

There were other reasons for the altercation. In addition to Julie's protest about the suspension of services and the confrontation concerning her "delinquency," Julie disliked the way that Maxine Ambroise, another physician working with the Rehab Program, had spoken to her earlier that day. Between 1998 and 1999 Dr. Ambroise became the object of many beneficiaries' frustrations because of her role as a gatekeeper to medications and medical services outside the Fund. Dr. Ambroise had been an employee of the local Médecins du Monde office. She had worked with Dr. Thomas and Dr. Manata through the link between MDM and the MICIVIH Medical Unit. A year after the Medical Unit was terminated and victims' trauma portfolios were transferred to MDM, Dr. Ambroise lost her job because MDM was compelled to streamline its operation in Haiti as donors became less receptive to providing long-term assistance to viktim. HRF then hired Dr. Ambroise to provide basic medical care to viktim, make referrals to the network of Haitian care providers, and eventually prescribe medicine under the Rehab Program when it became a grant recipient of generic essential drugs supplied by the World Health Organization's PROMESS (Program for Essential Medications in Haiti). After viktim received evaluations from physicians working in the referral network, Dr. Ambroise determined whether any cheaper substitutions could be found for the brand-name medications favored by the physicians in the private health care sector. To explain the change in policy, the Rehab staff met with viktim, emphasizing that the generic replacement medications were essentially the same as the brand-name ones. Despite these efforts to be transparent about the change in administrative practices, Dr. Ambroise's administration and distribution of these medications became increasingly controversial.

On the day of the incident in June 1998, Julie lamented that she could not take care of her family without the Fund's assistance. She wept before the two nurses on staff. Despite their efforts to calm her down, she became more and more aggressive. To diffuse the situation staff members went to get Dr. Manata. In the meantime Julie tried to hit Nurse Gilles and then threatened to kill Dr. Thomas. Her violent tirade, called a *deblozay* in Haitian Creole, disturbed other beneficiaries who were waiting patiently in the lobby of the building to be seen by the Rehab staff, as well as the ASOSYE staff members working nearby. Some of the waiting clients were sister members of FAVILEK, who ended up taking Julie away from the building. Concerned with maintaining good relations with the Fund, the FAVILEK women returned later that day to apologize. Dr. Manata decided to suspend Julie's services and told her that she needed to write him a personal letter of apology. He said the medical team would consider readmitting her to the program after things had calmed down. Because of the upsetting nature of the encounter, however, the Rehab team did not readmit her for almost a year, not until just before the program's unexpected demise.

In many ways Julie's actions accorded with traditional gender ideals of a responsible Haitian mother, the potomitan of Haitian society. At stake was her ability to obtain resources to care for her dependents and herself. The resort to threats to force a change in what she perceived as indifferent bureaucratic policies (Herzfeld 1992) could be interpreted as an act of desperation, although, as discussed below, these acts paralleled the way other viktim used aggression to resolve disputes when other alternatives had failed. Julie's behavior may have arisen from depression and misery, as well as anger. I would like to suggest, however, that the attempt to extract additional benefits from the Fund through "delinquent" acts, as Dr. Thomas called them, could also be interpreted as resistance to the Fund's policies. To some degree Julie's protests were a pointed critique that echoed throughout my work at the institution: Why should the Fund provide medications and medical treatment when its beneficiaries could not eat?

Many therapy group clients who had previously received direct financial aid from PIRÈD echoed Julie's complaints. In frustration over the continued demands for direct financial gifts, Dr. Thomas forcefully rejected such claims: "Nou pa labank, nou pa leta, nou pa Bondye"— "We're not the bank, we're not the state, and we're not God." She stated in more than one therapy group that other charitable organizations or missionary groups—for example, CARE, UNICEF, or Feed the Children—had programs that would provide for daily subsistence. It was clear, however, that viktim preferred that a single institution meet all their needs.

In late July 1998 a second incident occurred involving a dispute about the Fund's benefits between another viktim beneficiary and Dr. Thomas. After an argument with Dr. Thomas, Jean Belzor was yelling as he exited her office. Within earshot of staff and other beneficiaries, he threatened to pour gasoline on her car and burn her to death. Dr. Manata, Alphonse Montina, and another staff member of the Community-Police Relations team, Henri Claude, came out into the main office area to try to calm the situation. They threatened to call the police if Jean did not leave the premises. He was escorted out of the building to the gate of the lakou by one of the Fund's security officers. The Fund alerted Dany Fabien, director of the Bureau Poursuites et Suivi, about the threats against Dr. Thomas.[13] A couple of days later Jean returned to the Fund with lawyers affiliated with MICIVIH. He accused the Fund staff of attacking him and depriving him of his human rights. To resolve the dispute, HRF staff members referred him and his lawyers to another lawyer who worked with the Fund's legal counseling program.

That Jean employed the services of lawyers affiliated with MICIVIH was significant on many levels. Soliciting the support of lawyers was a tactical improvement on making threats to resolve disputes. His choice of lawyers affiliated with MICIVIH was politically astute: given the factions and disputes within the aid apparatus—and the pattern of rumor, suspicion, and accusations that flowed through it—persuading members of a competing human rights assemblage that former MICIVIH staff members at the Fund had violated his rights was shrewd. Over time good working relationships were reestablished between Jean and the Fund but not without his committing to dialogue and negotiation as a way to manage conflict. What was at stake?

Although the issues motivating Jean's threats related specifically to the distribution of victim assistance funds, they also concerned personal and institutional power. Jean was one of the spokespersons and leaders of the Organization of Coup Victims, a group of nearly fifteen hundred victims.[14] Attorney Camille Leblanc, the future minister of justice, provided legal representation. Thus OVKD claimed privileged status as one of the earliest victims' associations and because of Leblanc's advocacy on its members' behalf. OVKD members argued that many of the victims' organizations that had emerged in the postcoup period were not composed of "real victims." They alleged that politicians were manipulating some victims' organizations in order to promote their own agendas. One group that Jean had accused of political collusion was the Fondasyon 30 Sektanm. He also criticized Dany Fabien himself, who was managing the approximate sum of U.S.$4 million that the Government of Haiti had allocated to the BPS to provide aid to victims.

Jean appeared to have other motives for making public accusations against other actors in the victim assistance apparatus: political identity, status, and the performance of masculinity. He was notorious in the international and national aid apparatus for his aggressiveness in advocating for his rights and those of fellow OVKD members. During an interview he informed me that he wanted to expand OVKD into a national organization with technical and infrastructural assistance from the Fund. Furthermore, his accusations about the public accountability of institutions and the authenticity of viktim, as well as his desire that OVKD receive "political recognition," were to some extent gendered according to ideals of public masculinity. In many respects Jean was concerned with maintaining his status as the "patron" of a large base of viktim "clients." As discussed in chapter 3, many of the men who narrated their suffering in the therapy groups were concerned with their loss of status and honor because of their victimization. On the one hand, aggressive, threatening actions and overt forms of coercion and corruption indicated a gendered form of desperation. These acts also displayed victims' feelings of having been thwarted in their struggles to attain personal and political goals (Moore 1994). On the other hand, the public, highly charged displays of aggression were also performances of responsibility and accountability for those to whom one was obligated, in this case, a large political organization.

Apart from using interpretive lenses of gender and political culture to explain these disputes, it is possible to interpret Jean's acts from the perspective of ethnopsychiatry. Among the mental health professionals that I observed at the Mars/Kline Psychiatric Center and in the therapy groups, biomedical theories operated alongside Haitian traditional conceptions of the interrelationship of depression, anxiety, and injustice. Some Haitian and international mental health caregivers who knew Jean felt that his behavior typified that of "bipolar disorder." Such speculation about Jean's personality and behavior was characteristic of Western biomedical theories of mood and behavior. However, the Haitian nurses characterized viktim exhibiting agitation, anger, and sensitivity to slights or perceived injustices as part of a state of being cho, or hotheaded. This organic state of distress resulted from the prolonged, cumulative imbalances of hot, cold, and blood that accumulated in the body after having been victimized (see chapter 3). That being said, Haitian traditional and biomedical theories did not solely medicalize suffering; rather, they acknowledged the clinical effects of routine psychosocial stressors on patients' health.

Interestingly, HRF staff members felt that Jean and Dr. Thomas were both responsible for the fight, and they categorized Dr. Thomas's behavior in terms of the same frame of "embodiment" used for both Julie and Jean, treating it as the result of long-term frustrations. In addition to these frustrations, it is possible in her case that over time compassion fatigue or secondary trauma may have provoked irritation, skepticism, or indifference to the needs of Haitian victims. Dr. Thomas's history of work with Haitian refugees, as well as her own experiences of victimization and dechoukaj, cannot be discounted as possible causes of her brusque treatment of viktim. Such conflicts led me to wonder about the possibilities for ethical, compassionate, and egalitarian relationships between providers and beneficiaries of services, especially when regulated by neomodern forms of rationalized rehabilitation. I also considered such questions personally. What should be the ethical relationship between anthropologists and those with whom they work, especially if one adopts a subject position of advocate, confidante, or therapist?

The multiple roles that anthropologists adopt in advocacy settings can lead to persistent double binds regarding the ethics of gift giving and the practices of compassion, especially when conducting research about these same social dynamics. For example, HRF staff members often complained to me about Dr. Thomas's tendency to lose her temper with staff or viktim. I experienced this firsthand when Dr. Thomas accused me of causing strife in the Rehab Program. She held me responsible for some of the delinquent behavior of the beneficiaries and the medical network care providers in Martissant, presumably because I had facilitated their admission into the program after the November 1997 International Tribunal against Violence toward Women. Dr. Thomas also accused me of undermining her authority when she learned that I provided personal funds to one of the Fund's beneficiaries on one occasion when the Rehab Program was unable to do so expediently. She asserted that giving money directly would continue the pernicious cycles of inequality and dependency between donor and recipient of aid and between the victim and the agent of rehabilitation, an argument reminiscent of critiques of welfare and other "reparations" programs. In response to my somewhat naive assertion that I just wanted to help or "do good," Dr. Thomas stated that I could not help viktim indefinitely. After a period of reflection I agreed with many of her points, but I was disturbed by the problematic dynamics of power occurring between givers and receivers of aid.

During the course of my fieldwork, I also tried to interpret Dr. Thomas's motivations for doing this kind of work. She occasionally joked that for her the job was about *"le quinze, le trente"*—referring to the biweekly salary payments that the ADF program staff received—and that she was not there to save others, to help, or to "do good" beyond the requirements of the job. Yet she had worked under great personal duress to provide assistance—material, psychological, and sustainable—to the viktim she served. Questions that Dr. Thomas raised in the therapy groups are relevant here: To what extent should a past traumatic history justify or rationalize present behavior? What obligations are there to viktim, and are they entitled to benefits in perpetuity? The ongoing presence of ensekirite made answering these questions difficult.

ENSEKIRITE, MILITARIZATION, AND RETRIBUTION

In the aftermath of the two incidents described above, Dr. Thomas said, "These types of threats are the ones that must be watched. The first one is a warning of sabotage. Any further warnings are too late. The Haitian pattern is that something random can occur when we are engaged in other work." Indeed, the pattern of seemingly random violence, with motives ranging from criminal to political, added to the frustration and nervousness already present in the building. ADF staff members were in fact being attacked outside the institution. For example, in August 1998 the ASOSYE staff woman whose brother was alleged to have been a torturer during the coup years was carjacked, a crime that was occurring with increasing frequency in Port-au-Prince. As word spread in the ADF building of the incident, it increased the sense of uncertainty felt by many staff members. Another rupture in routine occurred a few weeks later. René Ibrahim, the new Human Rights Education staff member, was driving his car when it broke down unexpectedly. Soon afterward someone riding on a motorbike pulled over and offered assistance. René refused the help, but then the would-be samaritan pulled out a gun and robbed René of his briefcase. The briefcase happened to contain documents from the Fund. The staff classified the robbery as a crime rather than a politically motivated incident, but its characteristics were peculiar and signaled what was becoming known as a pattern of attacks that could not be easily categorized.

This new pattern was one of the features of ensekirite. In a similar situation, Dr. Andrea Baptiste, one of the directors of the Chanm Fanm women's clinic, was traveling by car earlier that year to a meeting with the Préval administration. Baptiste was a prominent member of President Aristide's first administration and a Lavalas supporter with long-standing commitments to the democratic struggle. While en route with her sister to the meeting with Préval to discuss an April 1998 raid on the clinic by the Haitian National Police, her car broke down. An unknown man pulled over to offer assistance. Dr. Baptiste declined. The motorist pulled out a gun and demanded the briefcase in her possession. She gave it to him. Unfortunately, the case contained the clinic staff's paychecks and other documentation relevant to the HNP attack.

This pattern of violence occurred with more frequency in relation to the shifting political context, especially in late 1998 and in early 1999, when ensekirite peaked. On the surface such crimes could be interpreted as merely criminal; however, there was always a measure of uncertainty.

The motive could also have been political. For example, when I spoke with her later about this incident, Dr. Baptiste did not attribute a political motivation to the attack. Only in retrospect was it significant that it occurred just as she was on her way to an important political meeting, especially considering how this type of crime occurred in other contexts. Such acts are the benchmarks of ensekirite. The gossip, rumors, and speculation that these incidents engendered also reinforced the sense of risk and ensekirite in daily life.

Furthermore, the speculation about the origins of such nefarious acts, combined with the actual attacks on the institution, characterized negative dimensions of bureaucraft in an overarching environment of ensekirite. Like contexts in which misfortune is divined as caused (and remedied) by witchcraft, ADF members made continual attempts to divine whether these attacks were the work of occult actors who were orchestrating efforts to sabotage the institution and its staff members. Significantly, in the weeks after the attack René began to wear dark sunglasses and a style of dress reminiscent of the tonton makout, perhaps as a measure of self-protection or as a warning to others that was suggestive of malevolent occult power. Such measures were also related to insecurity and trauma in the workplace. A few weeks afterward, René lost his position because he was unable to function at work. Nonetheless, his deployment of symbols of Duvalierist necropolitics for self-protection paralleled similar strategies to increase security at the ADF institutional level.

The ADF Human Rights Fund, comprising foreign managers and staff members and Haitian "experts" in human rights and democracy, employed militarist tactics that in some ways evoked historical predatory political practices. The ADF management responded to the deblozay inside the Fund and the ensekirite outside by hiring more security officers. ADF already retained the services of the Citadelle private security firm, as did most U.S.-funded projects at the time. HRF added the services of a well-connected, freelance security officer who was armed but wearing civilian attire. He was a mobile sovereign, much like the individuals making up the Duvalierist makout apparatus. In addition to this, HRF staff members paid market vendors on the street to act as unofficial informants to keep track of individuals who regularly approached the institution's gates. ADF could do little to provide security for its staff outside of headquarters, but key personnel were given walkie-talkies to communicate with ADF and one another. All the staff with radios had code names, as did persons and locations in Port-au-Prince they routinely visited. The Fund communicated on its own frequency, as did other projects of this sort. In case others were listening, staff members took care not to reveal details about the location of ADF personnel and their daily activities. ADF also hired armed security guards for the homes of key program officers.

Institutional attempts to create additional security had the unintended consequences of further provoking viktim. As another precaution after the incidents with Julie and Jean, the Rehab Program suspended the therapy groups and victim assistance for one week to assess the best way to protect ADF and HRF staff. The suspension of services was a warning to beneficiaries of the negative consequences that would be meted out to *all* as the result of any further threatening protests against the Fund's staff or the project as a whole. After these incidents HRF management met with a broad assemblage of victims' organizations to reinforce the need for "civilized" expressions of dissent between its patient-client beneficiaries and ADF/HRF, their patron.

These protective measures only served to increase beneficiaries' frustrations and their specific grievances against the Fund. During the suspension staff members considered alternative spatial arrangements in the ADF physical plant that would permit the Rehab Program to provide confidential assistance to its beneficiaries while containing the potential "insecurity" that viktim represented. The first solution was to create "offices" in the storage depot in the lakou behind the building. The second strategy was to have viktim enter through another entrance, not the main one that led to the HRF and ASOSYE reception area. To reach this entrance viktim had to pass by the armed, uniformed security officers. Many viktim who visited ADF were uncomfortable around these guards. The presence of the new freelance security person also heightened the perception of covert and overt threat, should the Fund's beneficiaries transgress acceptable boundaries of interaction. Moreover, the "segregation" of viktim exacerbated their feelings of being treated as second-class citizens.

It is deeply ironic that the Fund resorted to practices of militarization in order to protect a program intended to heal, educate, and advocate for victims of human rights violations. Although its security practices arose from the intent to protect staff members, in effect, all beneficiaries were punished for the threat posed by a few, enacting patterns of discipline reminiscent of those during the Duvalier dictatorship. In many respects staff members and the institution adopted sovereign forms of power and authority to protect themselves against the very repression and intimidation they were working to eradicate. For example, later that fall the Fund rented a small suite of offices a few blocks away that had been used by the Medical Unit under MICIVIH. Eventually the Rehab Program relocated to this suite of offices, known as Base 2. The Human Rights Education and Community-Police Relations staff members protested the move. Some felt that receiving independent program space was an undeserved benefit rather than banishment, especially because Dr. Thomas had allegedly mismanaged the program's budget. The details of the fiscal shortfall surfaced in the aftermath of the aforementioned irruptions of routine practice.

Whereas the physical separation of the programs calmed some of the tensions in the ADF building, the transfer of the Rehab Program failed to solve the ongoing problems of communication between the program and its beneficiaries and between HRF and ASOSYE regarding the just and ethical distribution of aid resources. The grievances that arose during this time reflected perceptions of breached alliances or obligations between aid givers and receivers, as well as between actors of more equal status in the aid apparatus. Such disputes raise the question of the "tyranny of the gift" as aid flows through social networks of unequal power.

> Giving . . . seems to establish a difference and an inequality of status between donor and recipient, which can in certain instances become a hierarchy: if this hierarchy already exists, the gift expresses and legitimizes it. Two opposite movements are thus contained in a single act. The gift decreases the distance between the protagonists because it is a form of sharing, and it increases the social distance between them because one is now indebted to the other. . . . It can be, simultaneously or successively, an act of generosity or of violence; in the latter case, however, the violence is disguised as a disinterested gesture, since it is committed by means of and in the form of sharing. (Godelier 1999 [1996]: 12)

The transactions that I have described thus far range from gifts to grants and encoded either implicit or explicit expectations of reciprocal gifts or the indirect fulfillment of bureaucratic procedures by a grant recipient. Such exchanges occurred between institutions, between institutions and individuals, and between individuals. The respective power and status of givers and receivers of gifts and grants engenders perceptions of these exchanges as either generosity or violence. The power and status of those who gain or lose in the course of such transactions is also integral to whether bureaucraft is viewed as productive or repressive and malevolent. In the next section I discuss how concepts of alliance, obligation, and exchange arising from Haitian culture influenced these dynamics.

'MOUN PA': PATRONS, CLIENTS, AND STATE SURROGATES

It is possible to interpret the way viktim approached the Fund—for health care, employment, housing, or other forms of ankadreman—as the reproduction of historical client-patron patterns. As discussed earlier, the patron-client relationship was exploited to an extreme under the Duvalier dictatorship (Lundahl 1979: 350–59; 1992: 384–97). Agencies like the Fund acted as surrogates for the Haitian state. In the one-on-one relationships between the ADF manager and prospective beneficiaries of HRF's Rehab Program, the chief of party was approached much in the same manner as the *"gwo nèg"* (big man) in the local realm.

This relationship of obligation and reciprocity was frequently invoked in the interaction between the Fund and its beneficiaries, which both parties described using the terminology *"moun pa-m'"* (my partisan or follower). Viktim and some of the support staff at HRF often referred to the chief of party as moun pa-m', or *patwon-mwen* (my patron), especially when describing how he advocated on their behalf with USAID, the U.S. Mission, and the Government of Haiti. In Martissant I witnessed how beneficiaries of the Rehab Program wore that status almost as a badge of honor or recognition. This was a form of "identification" or alliance with the institution. Indeed, one of the complaints that arose from the physicians in the medical referral network was that Fund beneficiaries, with their authorization letters or cards identifying them as clients of the Fon Dwa Moun (Human Rights Fund), demanded to be seen before other patients. Such expectations of favored treatment were sometimes disruptive in the workplace.

When I inquired further about the *moun pa* relationship, I was told that it entitled one to favored treatment, especially in situations like marketing or business. It also encoded expectations of loyalty and fulfillment of other reciprocal obligations. If the perception was that one had reneged on an unstated *angajman* (agreement or contract), then the results could be quite negative. Retribution for a patron's perceived breaches of the relationship could involve subtle or overt resistance on the part of the client. For example, by fall 1997, when *La Fierté Gonâvienne* capsized, I had begun to recognize a pattern in the behavior of individuals and families who solicited victim assistance that I had already witnessed the previous summer at Chanm Fanm. It seemed to replicate the violent protest that Julie demonstrated. At this time many beneficiaries of the Fund and their dependents were especially anxious to receive further benefits and even direct financial assistance because they needed to enroll their children in schools in October (see James 2004). Even after having received benefits, they were persistent in pressuring the staff to assist them, financially or otherwise. In justifying their demands, clients invoked personal relationships—in much the same way it should be acknowledged that Dr. Manata had been asked to hire Mission Director Forbes's husband. Relationships of mutual assistance and obligation between patrons and clients were integral to the politics within the aid apparatus and between aid organizations and their beneficiaries.

The disputes over emergency aid following the ferry crisis and the processes of auditing, designing, and bidding for USAID proposals demonstrated how patron-client networks could generate subtle forms of what some might interpret as corruption in the Haitian *and* American nongovernmental and governmental humanitarian assistance apparatuses. Such processes were also contested. For example, by early fall 1998, when the Rehab budget shortfalls had been identified, Dr. Thomas criticized beneficiaries or clients who believed the U.S.-funded institution had unlimited resources that were "owed" to them. She felt that they "profited" unjustly from their affiliation with the Fund outside of her management and control. One of the problems that arose for the Rehab Program beginning in summer 1997 was that several viktim who had received eyeglasses through the medical network claimed to have lost them and demanded new ones. I learned in discussions with viktim in Martissant, however, that some of these beneficiaries had in fact pawned their eyeglasses, using them as collateral to secure high interest loans to start small businesses or supplement their incomes.

As it turned out, the Rehab Program's beneficiaries were not the only ones who exploited the Fund's financial resources. At the first staff meeting after these disruptions, we were informed that even as the fourteen-month extension was just beginning, half of the Rehab Program's budget had already been exhausted. Some of the health care providers in the referral network had submitted invoices months after the provision of care to beneficiaries. These costs had not been included in the previous HRF budget before the end of June 30, 1998. Dr. Thomas complained that many of these invoices totaled tens of thousands of dollars but did not list the exact services provided. For example, a physician was caring for my research assistant Sylvie's son, who had been hospitalized for complications relating to sickle-cell anemia. During the child's stay of approximately three weeks, the doctor charged for sixty-five separate visits, at U.S.$75 per visit. Other physicians were also accused of graft. On some level there was little possibility of controlling the Rehab budget because of these "unforeseen circumstances," unless the Fund and programs like it were to rationalize rehabilitation assistance to a much greater degree.

In the broader context of political, economic, and other forms of insecurity, as well as limited state capacity to protect the welfare of citizens, accumulating scarce humanitarian and development aid was a strategy for combating insecurity at both the institutional and individual levels. For example, the pharmacies in the health care network also profited from their affiliation with the HRF program. On receipt of a prescription, they tended to supply the most expensive brand-name drug and to bill the Fund accordingly. For their part, viktim attempted to maximize the financial opportunities that the Fund's services provided by adding items to their prescriptions, which the pharmacists honored. Viktim would then sell these goods outside the institution. As viktim maintained membership in multiple victims' organizations, some were able to *"double"* (duplicate) services by taking advantage of the confusion over which group sponsored their beneficiary status. In effect, they received medical treatment and medications from more than one assistance organization, for the *same* illness, in more than one health facility. Dr. Ambroise confirmed that while working with Médecins du Monde, she had treated some of the same individuals who were receiving care from Chanm Fanm in Martissant *and* at the Fund. These patients had presented themselves as members of other victims' advocacy organizations.

There were other ways in which beneficiaries were able to pwofite from their affiliation with the Fund. Because of its budgetary constraints, the program was unable to provide financial aid apart from reimbursing each beneficiary's travel expenses for attending the therapy groups or when viktim needed urgent medical care. Over time the Fund staff realized that even the activity of visiting the Rehab Program became a means of generating income. For example, in June 1998 Claude Oscar, the field investigator who had helped coordinate the intervention in the aftermath of the *Fierté Gonâvienne* disaster, left his position after the Fund helped him receive a multiyear, multiple entry visa to the United States. Oscar had been with the HRFI program before the new Rehab Program was placed in ADF in 1997. Only after his departure did the new management learn that in constructing the price list for reimbursing beneficiaries' travel from the various rural departments to Port-au-Prince, he had significantly inflated the fares. While employed under HRFI Oscar had also made arrangements with local hospitals and pharmacies to refer patients to them, for which they would bill ADF/HRF. He received a commission for his work as a broker for these deals. It also became clear that Oscar must have instituted similar patronage practices with his hometown community in La Gonâve, since the numerous individuals from this region who had solicited assistance nearly disappeared after Oscar's departure from the Fund. When I spoke with the nurses about this situation, they acknowledged that for some viktim, the bimonthly visits to the Fund for therapy groups and additional visits for their dependents for medical care were means of supplementing their incomes. As I recalled Dr. Ambroise's assertions that viktim also received care at other institutions, presumably reimbursed for travel or other expenses, it became clear that attaining and maintaining client or beneficiary status was literally an occupation. Gaining client status required labor and bureaucratic expertise, but once attained such practices could generate currency through the transformation and commodification of suffering in the political economy of trauma. Such processes were the unintended consequences of humanitarian assistance.

MOUN PA, ALLIANCES, AND RECOGNITION IN MARTISSANT

As I traced the social life of humanitarian assistance to Martissant, I learned much more about the politics of aid, contests over victim status, and the political economy of trauma. The meaning of democracy, rights, justice, and accountability was debated at the community level, and by extension at the national and international levels. Viktim in Martissant highlighted the importance of security, alliances, and loyalties. I witnessed how communities of responsibility constrained and compelled action in this social space. The question of loyalty arose not only in my relationship with the residents of Martissant but also in my ongoing affiliation with the Chanm Fanm staff. With the change in my position from volunteer manual therapist and researcher in 1996 to unofficial staff person with ADF that 1998 summer, I was placed in the role of advocate, gatekeeper, and mediator between the Rehab Program, viktim, and members of the medical network. This position taught me much about the political economy of kinship and alliances in Martissant and the way the perceived breaches of patron-client relationships could culminate in violence.

After settling into a routine with the biweekly therapy groups at the Fund, I had decided to return to work at Chanm Fanm on Tuesday and Thursday mornings to alternate with work at the Mars/Kline Center for Neurology and Psychiatry. In this phase of my research, my intent was to continue to learn about the long-term effects of victimization on the lives of my informants. I also wanted to determine how they adopted, resisted, or transformed the category of viktim into something else in daily life. At the same time I continued to work as a Trager practitioner at the clinic as a service to its clients but also to interact with women in the area who had not yet become entangled in the advocacy networks established in the zone.

In addition to participating with women *viktim* in the Rehab Program's therapy groups, I associated with some of the same women as well as others at Chanm Fanm. Ginette Charles was a participant in the women-only therapy group (see chapter 3). She also worked as a receptionist at Chanm Fanm and was a local representative of the HRF Rehab Program in the zone. She had been a target of organized violence on two separate occasions. In November 1993 men in civilian garb assumed to be affiliated with the coup apparatus had threatened her for unknown reasons. Then in April 1998 she was threatened because of her membership in the Haitian Women's Association. But there were also some positive changes in her life as Ginette's role at the clinic expanded to incorporate managerial duties after nurse Emilie Datilus's departure to the Fund earlier that year.

Another therapy group participant whom I saw in Martissant was Denise Jules, a market woman in her late fifties to whom I had provided physical therapy in 1996. In fall 1998 Denise and her daughter-in-law, Marie-Rose, were also in the women-only therapy group. Both women had been gang-raped on February 4, 1994, when FRAPH members attacked nearly every household in the area. In my prior interviews and bodywork with her at the clinic, Denise, the mother of seven sons and one daughter, expressed her suffering and shame at having been raped. In 1998 she still suffered physical complications that she attributed to the attack, including chronic pain where she had been beaten in her left thigh and frequent urinary tract infections. I did not know Marie-Rose well but learned that she was suffering from full-blown AIDS that was attributed to her rape.

I returned to work at the Chanm Fanm clinic on September 1, 1998, and that first day of fieldwork emphasized how during the course of its social life humanitarian aid extended to both givers and receivers had become contested outside institutions such as ADF and the Human Rights Fund. When I arrived that Tuesday morning Sylvie and Denise were waiting for me, along with other participants in the Fund's women-only therapy group, to catch up on events that had occurred since the November 1997 Tribunal. I asked these women to give me a few minutes to greet one of the clinic directors, Dr. Andrea Baptiste, and Ginette Charles before meeting. After exchanging pleasantries with the two clinic staff members, we then quickly discussed the April 1998 HNP attack on the clinic, an attack that occurred because of debates over the form and distribution of international aid in local communities. As with the allegations about *La Fierté Gonâvienne,* the HNP accused Mothers Across Borders, the U.S.-based women's rights organization that sponsored the clinic, of sending weapons in the shipment of medications earlier that year. Some parts of the clinic were still in shambles. The police had destroyed the pharmacy, bathroom, and rear section of the clinic.

But there were other rumors about the cause of the attack. Health professionals affiliated with the clinic told me that a former Chanm Fanm caretaker who had been fired made false accusations against the clinic to the police in retribution for the loss of his job, but this rationale for the attack was not publicly circulated. Nothing was found during the raid. In protest of the police raid, HWA members and a delegation from MAB paraded in the streets, claiming that the true motive for the raid had been to intimidate HWA members and clinic staff. The women's network also claimed the attack was intended to prevent women from organizing against the problem of violence and the lack of justice for victims. Thus in order to display the evidence of the attack against the organization, the clinic staff had not cleared away all the rubble. For the most part, the building had been restored to order, but it still bore these physical scars.

After Dr. Baptiste and I discussed the progress the clinic had made and the dangerous events of the previous months, other aspects of the politics of aid emerged as the conversation shifted to the Fund. In the days before my return to the clinic, Dr. Thomas had quite vociferously expressed her frustrations with the Martissant beneficiaries, the Chanm Fanm staff, and me. The situation was still tense, and now Dr. Baptiste and Ginette gave me another version of the dispute about how resources were being distributed and used in Martissant. Apparently Dr. Thomas had accused Dr. Baptiste of graft. After the conclusion of the November 1997 International Tribunal against Violence toward Women, Dr. Manata asked Dr. Baptiste if she would conduct medical exams of the members of Sylvie's organization so they could gain beneficiary status. Dr. Baptiste agreed and began to see these individuals early in 1998, some of them more than once. She billed the Fund several times for each person at ten times the clinic's normal rate of H$3 per person.[15] Dr. Thomas, who had not yet become medical director at the time these arrangements were made, resented not having been consulted in the decision. Dr. Thomas also complained that the Fund's beneficiaries' attempted to double. Many of the individuals in Sylvie's organization were already receiving assistance from the Fund through their membership in the HWA. They had also been seen at Médecins du Monde.

Dr. Baptiste was irate at being accused of corruption: "Why does Christine [Thomas] only choose physicians who were trained in Europe or France to facilitate the therapy groups? They are all her personal friends. Why should they receive $100 [U.S.] for an hour of work [facilitating a therapy group], and I cannot charge her for the work that I am doing on my own time as an individual doctor?" Dr. Baptiste protested what appeared to be a devaluing of her training and expertise. Ginette echoed Dr. Baptiste's outrage and castigated Dr. Thomas for favoritism, adding the complaints about the Rehab Program's decision to prescribe generic rather than brand-name medications. Ginette said, "We deserve to have the medications that the physicians prescribe for us." For her, receiving higher status medications was a similar matter of equal treatment and political recognition, as was the issue of fair compensation for Dr. Baptiste's expertise.

These disputes emphasized how ethnographic fieldwork can transform into "circumstantial activism" (Marcus 1998: 98–99) while at the same time generating ethical challenges and double binds. I was in a difficult position because I could see both sides of the problem. I explained the discovery of the existence of false beneficiaries and the problem of forged prescriptions. I also emphasized that the budget was already half gone before the fiscal year had begun. I told them that I would speak to Dr. Manata about the issue and that I was sure it would be resolved but that they needed to keep in mind the bureaucratic limitations that HRF faced.

The exchange of accusations and counteraccusations of corruption or occult activity were negative characteristics of bureaucraft that operated between aid institutions, victims' advocacy organizations, and their members. Dr. Baptiste's indignation at Dr. Thomas's accusations of dishonesty reflected concerns for her status, reputation, and political and professional recognition. In some respects she performed for her Chanm

Fanm staff her dedication to the clinic and, indirectly, the HWA against a perceived injustice perpetrated by a foreigner—and a French one at that.

Such accusations were not solely lodged against persons in positions of power; they were also made against viktim. When I told Dr. Baptiste that Sylvie, Denise, and the members of Sylvie's organization were waiting for me so that I could meet the extended victims' group in another area of Martissant, Dr. Baptiste warned me to be careful about working with either Sylvie or Denise. Both women had recently been expelled from the HWA, along with other members of Sylvie's organization, for conflicts with the general membership (among other reasons that I was never told). Similarly, Emilie Datilus and Stephanie Joseph, the international lawyer who had conducted the seminars on women's rights under Haitian law earlier in 1996, also warned me about working with these women. Both felt that the Martissant women were not above treachery.

Once again these accusations concerned perceived breaches of patron-client relationships and the distribution of aid. Emilie told me that some of the Martissant women accused her of having changed toward them over time. They implied that she was less accommodating to their needs—especially after she left the clinic to work at the Fund. She also said that before leaving Chanm Fanm to work at the Fund, she arrived at the clinic one morning and found that a fine white powdery substance had been spread in a line across her personal workspace. She told me that it was poison. She attributed the threat to members of the rape survivors' group that had been established by the HWA. Emilie expressed fear for my safety if I spent much time in Martissant, as did other HRF staff. In the same way that I had reassured Emilie I would be careful, I told Dr. Baptiste that I was sure I would not have problems and exited the clinic to rejoin the group of women for our short walk to the meeting spot.

The first meeting with the Martissant beneficiaries of the Fund highlighted the politicization of aid and victim identities in the course of social life in Martissant. A group of about twenty of us walked to meet at a home in another area near the clinic. On the way, however, one young woman with whom I had participated in a therapy group at the Fund took me aside and warned me about Sylvie. She told me that the larger group had split recently because of a dispute over funds. I thanked her for the information and suggested we discuss it on another occasion. Then someone else in our party spoke aloud and said that I needed to tell Dr. Thomas that Bernadette César had been threatening to have some of the Fund's beneficiaries in the zone expelled from the

Rehab Program. I knew Bernadette as a beneficiary of the Fund and patient at the Mars/Kline Center. She was in her early forties. Bernadette's case was unusual because President Aristide's office had referred her to the Fund. During the coup years a FAD'H officer had shot her five times—including in the neck—but almost miraculously she had survived. In rendering their charges against her, the Martissant women had named Bernadette "Kòkòt" (someone sweet or flirtatious; or pejoratively, "female genitals"). They alleged that Bernadette was not a "true victim" like them because she was actually plase—in a common law marriage—with the FAD'H officer.

The women charged further that the shooting was the result of nefarious activity and that Bernadette was a *lougawou,* a vampirelike entity able to transform from a material form into a disembodied force. Lougawou shed their skin and leave their homes through the roof in noncorporeal form. On their night journeys they seek the souls or blood of the weak, especially those of children, to *souse* (suck) or *manje* (eat, consume) (Métraux 1972 [1959]: 300–305). The group told me that the officer had shot Bernadette on recognizing her as a lougawou. She did not die because lougawou cannot be killed when they are in immaterial form.

Although the anthropologist Alfred Métraux (1972 [1959]: 300–305) claimed that lougawou are usually women, in discussions with my clients and others, I was told that both men and women become lougawou. The "male" counterparts of the "female" lougawou are men who participate in *sanpwèl, zobop, bizango,* or other mystical secret societies in Haiti (Davis 1988; Laguerre 1980). I met some of these men in August 1995 when a friend took me to a Vodou ceremony in the Tabarre area outside Port-au-Prince. The sound of drums beat in the background while they drank rum, smoked, and enjoyed the festive atmosphere. These men told me stories of their ability to shape-shift and of their Tuesday and Thursday night patrols of the neighborhood. The group had a hierarchical order and required a special pass from nonmembers if they wished to circulate on the streets without interference. I was sure that such tales were meant to inspire awe and respect, or to tease me, as one would do by telling ghost stories to a child.

It was with incredulity, therefore, that I heard these witchcraft accusations against Bernadette. I was not quite sure how to interpret them. Were they means to resolve disputes over scarce resources among peers, as had been described in the anthropological literature, or was something more going on? Were their accusations attempts to make sense of Bernadette having survived five bullets, any one of which could have caused her death? To my knowledge these women did not know how she had been referred to the Fund. I had already observed, however, the extent to which connections claimed with President Aristide, Mèt Leblanc, or other prominent Haitian political figures were status markers among viktim. If they were aware of Bernadette's political connections, this may have provoked jealousy or conflict.

It is possible that such accusations of aberrant status related to perceptions of Bernadette's emotional state. Bernadette was a tiny woman with ill-fitting glasses who had a gaze that did not track directly when she looked at you, leaving the impression that other things in her field of vision distracted her. I had never felt any threat from her, but I knew that those who were considered *foul/fòl* (crazy) were feared, ridiculed, and marginalized in Haitian communities. While she was always pleasant toward me in our limited encounters, admittedly she had the comportment that I had come to associate with the schizophrenics the Mars/ Kline staff treated. The fear and stigma that surrounded the mentally ill in Haiti (and perhaps the administration of pharmaceuticals to tranquilize ward residents) made the Mars/Kline Center a space of security or asylum in Haiti. Indeed, a security officer known to the Fund staff once remarked that during times of ensekirite "only the mad are safe," in that people tended to avoid them. However, I never heard of any attempts by disgruntled viktim to terrorize Bernadette in order to resolve the threat they supposedly felt from her. I recognized that the zone's residents had to negotiate the perils of ensekirite to the best of their ability and that the stakes for survival were high.

The pattern of accusations and complaints about inauthentic victim status that permeated the Martissant research revealed the complicated relationships between viktim and their patrons. However, I did not expect that my own attempt to employ Sylvie and Denise as research assistants would unveil some of the deeper cleavages within the victim community. Earlier that fall I had asked both women to work as my research assistants, each for different reasons. Sylvie, an experienced, literate activist, had always been outspoken in her critique of the injustices perpetrated by the Haitian state. She had made quite a career as a "professional victim" and was often called to give testimony. The Rehab Program had also trained her to work as its local representative, as it had Ginette. When the budget was reduced drastically, only Ginette received a paid position as a local representative. I knew that Sylvie had three children at home to support, including her disabled daughter, Natasha (see chapter 3). Denise, on the other hand, had been a resident of

Martissant for almost twenty years. She was nonliterate, as were most of my clients, but she was successful in marketing. Her children were grown, and all but two were out of the house. She had friendships with a different group in the neighborhood from Sylvie's partisans. I thought that I would be able to get a different sense of life in the bidonvil by working with individuals with different expertise and social networks.

At the close of my first day back in Martissant, the group of women escorted me back to the clinic and I began arranging appointments for therapy and interviews in subsequent weeks. Sylvie then took me aside to say that if I chose to work with Denise publicly she would be unable to take me to meet viktim in the area neighboring the clinic. I was surprised, and given the pattern of accusations that had permeated that day's activities, I expected that the dispute concerned financial resources. I knew that the two women sometimes had been in conflict in the past, but since I knew Sylvie better than Denise I made the decision—perhaps a mistaken one—to work with Sylvie first and arranged to work with Denise later that fall.[16] I knew that a few years before, Denise had caused her to lose a job. Both of them had worked for a woman from the Dominican Republic in the neighborhood who ran a laundry service. They washed clothing for her at the beny, the public water fountain nearby. Although I do not recall the details of the disagreement, Sylvie was fired from the job and continued to harbor resentment about the loss. The Dominican woman eventually left the area, abruptly leaving the women she had employed without resources. The loss of income forced residents of the zone to choose riskier activities to generate their livelihoods unless they were able to find other means expediently. Sylvie and other women sometimes employed the strategy of "going with someone" in order to supplement their income; however, she admitted this only indirectly (James 2008). The loss of the laundry position was thus a devastating blow.

Over the course of the fall, however, I learned that this dispute had much more complicated roots. Denise and her family had joined Sylvie's victims' advocacy organization to seek justice and "reparations" from international organizations. Because Sylvie could read and write well and had learned the craft of grassroots organizing from her late mother's work in Jacmel, she was able to act as a broker with the humanitarian assistance apparatus. Sylvie was able to receive technical assistance and other microfinancial support from the Haitian Ministry of Women's Affairs, the Aristide Foundation for Democracy, UNICEF, and the Canadian Fund, not to mention the extensive personal support her family and she received at the Human Rights Fund. Grants from some of these institutions were to be held in common among the members of her organization. The goal was to develop a permanent *kès* (treasury). All members could borrow short-term loans to restart their businesses or other occupations lost or damaged during the coup years.

A crucial feature of these cooperative ventures, however, was trust. Each member was to contribute a small amount regularly in order to maintain the treasury. When it was Denise's turn to borrow, she did not repay her loan, nor did she continue to contribute to the *kès*. Eventually the collective venture collapsed, and the ensuing argument that arose was one of the factors that caused the group to splinter in two. Denise and her family were expelled from the organization. What surprised me, therefore, was Sylvie's continued association with Denise. The need to maintain cordial relationships within communities of responsibility also stemmed from the past.

Both women's families were forced into hiding during the coup years; however, the circumstances under which they returned to Martissant differed. As I discuss below, these differences of circumstance contributed in part to the disparities in their respective social positions, as well as to their respective security in the zone. As Sylvie and I mapped the community and I began to recognize many of the Human Rights Fund beneficiaries living in the zone, she made sure that we greeted certain men as we walked by them. She explained that a number of them were members of a *kò*, or gang, that controlled the zone. At times they prohibited the circulation of its residents at night unless they were compensated. Single women were especially vulnerable, unless they fell under the patronage of one of the *kò*'s members or manifested respect in tangible and intangible ways. This did not preclude these men from sexually assaulting those whom they chose, as happened to Sylvie's daughter, Natasha, in 1996.

The politics of the gang and its significance in the local political economy of trauma unfolded over time in discussions with my clients outside the clinic. One October morning Sylvie, Liliane, and I discussed Denise's position in the community at the home they shared. The two asked Liliane's daughter, Monique, to join us and tell me about "Granpye" (Bigfoot), the code name they had given Denise, and "Jiraf" (Giraffe), the nickname given to her younger son, David. Because Denise's home was next door and they were concerned about being overheard by neighbors, all three women spoke in hushed tones. They chuckled a little about the code names and then told me, quite solemnly, about a family that had been expelled from the community in 1996. They alleged that Denise and her sons had forced the family to flee.

After Hurricane Gordon devastated the area in November 1994 and the road leading through the bidonvil was washed out, Denise's family and others banded together to reconstruct a road using their own manual labor. In the interim period between the disaster and their efforts to reconstruct the community, a family had built a house where the road had been washed away. The reconstruction group wanted the family to leave, but they refused. Finally, Denise's group threatened the family, seized the house, and forced them into hiding. At the time that this story was told the family was still hiding in Léogâne.

Friends alerted the police about the clash, and state investigators came to evaluate the circumstances surrounding the land dispute. The *jij de pè* (justice of the peace) asked for Denise's son David and attempted to take him into custody for questioning. Sylvie and Liliane affirmed that Denise physically attacked the justice in order to protect her son. Overwhelmed by the opposition, the investigators fled the area. The justice issued a warrant for Denise's arrest, but to my knowledge she was never arrested.

Denise's family's willingness to use threats and physical force was not the only cause of fear and mistrust. Sylvie, Liliane, and Monique argued that Denise and her family should not be considered real victims in spite of the fact that they were the targets of attacks during the coup years and had been forced to flee. According to them, when Liliane and her sons returned from the Dominican Republic where they had fled an mawonaj, they initially seemed to be as they had been before, partisans of Aristide who were in search of assistance to rebuild their lives. After a short period, however, they assumed the role of neomodern "overseers" who patrolled the bidonvil. Their control included functioning as brokers or gatekeepers to the domain of humanitarian assistance when patrons in the aid apparatus authorized Denise's family to organize victims' advocacy groups after other residents of the area began to return in 1995.

On some level brokerage of access to the humanitarian assemblage was a form of speculation, an investment in the potential value of commodified suffering and trauma when circulated within the realm of governmental and nongovernmental humanitarian assistance. It was consistent with the marketing activity that had been the main form of livelihood for women like Sylvie, Liliane, and Denise in particular but also of many other small-scale entrepreneurs. Denise and her sons eventually acted as brokers facilitating access for others to aid NGOs or programs *or* blocking it through intimidation. For example, members of the family first received scholarships for school-age dependents in their family from ATD Quart Monde (Fourth World), a French organization dedicated to the eradication of persistent poverty that was based in the Fontamara section west of Martissant. It provided aid to viktim throughout the coup period. "Ka Monn" (Fourth World) or "Kay Monn" (World House), as my informants mistakenly called it, provided medical care, housing assistance, tuition support for children, and job training for its beneficiaries. By the time I was able to interview its director, a French physician, later that fall, its victim assistance program had been discontinued. I told the director about some of the challenges the Human Rights Fund faced with victim assistance, and he admitted, somewhat reluctantly, that ATD Quart Monde had also had difficulties with viktim because they pressured it to provide financial assistance beyond its capacity. He added that there had also been problems with graft and competition among its clients that evolved outside of the organization.

The extent to which David/Jiraf and his compatriots were both physically coercive and financially exploitative in their role as brokers emerged in another interview with a woman named Danielle Marcia. Danielle was desperately haunted by the ghosts of murdered family members and had to resort to prostitution to support her remaining children (James 2008). Since 1996, after the murder of her husband and two sons, one of whom was a member of the new Haitian National Police, she had no protection or support. With Sylvie in attendance, I asked what Danielle most needed to survive. During the discussion she mentioned being intimidated by Denise's son David when she sought international aid for her children's tuition.

DM: I need everything. At the same time that I need help for my
        health, my children . . . are forsaken like good-for-nothings.
        Because other children get up in the morning, find some other
        little friends, they get dressed right away. They are very clean.
        They go to school. Mine are abandoned. I feel that in the end I'd
        like them to go to school. . . . But it's when you're in the house
        with a bunch of kids, that they [neighborhood gang members]
        unleash a plot against you [mare konminezon] . . . when they see
        that there is no family to take care of you . . .

EJ: But the problem with David, can you explain what happened?

DM: Yes. There was a school that they had over there—what was
        it called? "La main ouverte"—that's it right?

SSF: Yes.

DM: [David] told me that the director [of ATD Quart Monde] used to give opportunities [scholarships], and if I gave him some money he'd go talk to him. I could give him H$60 for them to take two children, because they don't take all of them . . . for them to give uniforms and shoes. I wouldn't have to go to the school—and the school was one where you had to pay each month—and I wouldn't have to pay when I didn't have the money for it, so I agreed. I sent the kids in October. As soon as November came they had to stop because I didn't have money to pay [David]. I made them withdraw. I didn't want the young man to hurt me. I let them keep the money.

David demanded ongoing payment for brokering her access to the scholarship program. Even though the organization assisted with the tuition and supplies, access was the key issue. Danielle was expected to · continue to pay David for his mediation. Indeed, David's role as trauma broker extended beyond mediation to physical coercion. The fear of crossing him was so great that Danielle had sacrificed her children's education rather than risk their collective safety.

Danielle and Sylvie explained that even after the "restoration of democracy" the neighborhood gangs controlled their lives.

DM: [When] you see them coming for you, you have to give them [money] or they'll crush you to the ground. . . . [Whether] you are at home, if I'm down the street . . .

SSF: It's a command [yon manda]. They could shoot you.

DM: . . . if I'm not inside, or where I sent the children, they'll come for you. If you say something or betray them, selling them out could mean your life [yo kapab frape ou atè]. Because when they're out at night, you don't know. . . . That's why since I came into this quarter, I respect them. I warned my children too for them to not say anything about it because I don't want them to hurt them.

During the conversation about the threat Denise and her children posed as overseers in the zone, Sylvie, Liliane, and Monique stated that some of the family members had returned to Martissant armed after the reinstallation of President Aristide. Sylvie alleged that Denise's sons and a group of other youths returned from the Dominican Republic spouting anti-Aristide rhetoric and boasting that the group to which they belonged would carry out a coup d'état against Aristide should he be reelected. At that time, however, neighborhood residents did not know that members of Denise's family had shifted from the pro-Aristide position they had once espoused. As time passed and the zone remained excluded from the reconstruction efforts in other parts of the city, Denise's sons operated in the bidonvil much as had members of the coup apparatus years before.

Many residents of the zone also did not consider Denise and her family legitimate victims because they were doing well financially in comparison with their neighbors. Marie-Rose's husband, Alain, who was one of Denise's older sons, owned a small boutique in the bidonvil. Denise owned *two* houses, albeit tiny structures poorly constructed of cinder blocks with tin roofs. Her relative wealth sparked indignation among other women besides Sylvie and Liliane, as did their move to take land whose true owner (I was told) was an absentee landlord residing in the Dominican Republic. Apparently he was too afraid to come to the neighborhood but collected rent through a third party.[17] Another source of resentment was that Denise's group allegedly received state funds to establish a community health center in the area. In 1998 a formal sign designated the spot where a building was going to be constructed, although the center had not been built by the time I left Haiti in 2000. Sylvie and Liliane charged that Denise and her kò had pocketed the state funds.

Sylvie and Liliane also made disturbing accusations about the HWA and DRC initiative to form rape survivors' groups in the area. Liliane and Sylvie claimed that one of the local spokespersons for the HWA had exploited them before the arrival of the MAB international lawyers and women's rights activists. The international women's group was preparing to present their cases to an investigative team of the Inter-American Court of Human Rights. They claimed that the HWA representative asked them to pay her a fee for the opportunity to testify about their victimization to the international women's delegation. I confirmed this claim with other survivors who were in these groups.

Sylvie and Liliane's bureaucraft accusations against the HWA member and their expressions of resentment and frustration did not go unchallenged. While Sylvie and Liliane accused the HWA and Denise's kò of corruption, Ginette and other members of the HWA approached me at Chanm Fanm to level charges against Sylvie. They wanted to make sure that I was aware of the "gray zone" (Levi 1989 [1986]) in which she operated as a victim advocate. As discussed previously, Sylvie was the victim of a second "human rights" violation early in 1996, when four young men in the Martissant zone threatened her for documenting human rights abuse cases in the area. Ginette alleged that Sylvie's second attack actually was not a human rights violation but something that she deserved. According to Ginette, Sylvie had arranged to share with neighbors some of the goods that were given to local HWA members from the depot that had been established in the zone in the postcoup period. The goal was to distribute some of these donated goods for resale, another example of how compassion economies can generate occult economies as aid develops a social life. Ginette accused Sylvie of reneging on the agreement and implied that this broken angajman justified the threats and second assault against Sylvie. Sylvie had filed a complaint with the police over the incident. The HNP issued a *manda* (subpoena) to compel the men to appear in court, but they were able to bribe the judge to have the charges dropped.

Another accusation that Ginette, Denise, and even Dr. Baptiste leveled at Sylvie concerned whether she had embezzled funds from her victims' group. Ginette claimed that Sylvie was withholding the medical certificates that Dr. Baptiste provided for viktim until they paid her 100 gourdes (H$20). They implied Sylvie kept the money for herself. Moreover, Ginette and Denise accused Sylvie of acting as a broker who prevented or facilitated access to me at the clinic or in the neighborhood.[18] The charges leveled at Sylvie were disturbing and followed a pattern that had begun on my return to the clinic earlier that September.

Sylvie had heard about Ginette's and Denise's charges of illicit accumulation of resources from the compassion economy. When I next met with Sylvie, I chose not to confront or accuse her but rather to present the allegations and to interview her formally about them. Interestingly, her response resembled the bureaucratic rationale to which I was becoming accustomed at the Fund and that I increasingly witnessed in my interaction with the USAID development community. As previously discussed, institutions receiving U.S. government funding through USAID needed to demonstrate accountability and the completion of results in formal and informal reporting and audits. Sylvie's testimony had some of this bureaucratic character. She presented a biographical narrative in which she performed her status as authentic militan, viktim, and victims' rights advocate. After reiterating her history and all that she had done to help women in the community, Sylvie explained her logic for requiring members of her organization to contribute financially to the kès. In her words, her organization would only have long-term security and stability with a *depo* (storehouse, deposit) of funds and goods, like an endowment, that members of the group could rely on in difficult times. Each person needed to contribute to the collective organization before Sylvie would facilitate his or her access to other charitable organizations. When I asked about the allegations that she herself consumed these funds, she stated that she needed to pay for the formatting and printing of the organization's official documents and for a trustworthy copier. The information in the documents was sensitive and could not be circulated freely. She also needed to pay for her transportation to the capital and back from Martissant. The remainder went into the organization's emergency fund. She reminded me that with one child who was regularly in the hospital and others at home, she was not profiting from this work. I could not be sure of the truth and knew that it would be beyond my capacity to determine it. However, I felt that her presentation accorded with what I had known of her circumstances and her behavior with individuals in the community with whom we had worked.

In the days after the interview, however, Sylvie began to pressure me for more financial aid. I reminded her that we were coming to the end of our agreed-on "scope of work" and that I would be commencing with Denise shortly. Sylvie protested and suggested that we just continue as we had been, but I maintained that I needed to honor the arrangement that we had made earlier that fall. But before this could happen, another critical event (described below) occurred in the zone that prevented me from working with Denise. In some ways it confirmed Sylvie's and Liliane's claims that Denise and her family were resented in the neighborhood. I had assumed, wrongly, that apart from the periodic incursions into the zone by the Haitian National Police to round up zenglendo, as gang members were usually referred to, residents of the neighborhood had little recourse to resist gangs. Rather, collective defense could be used as a means of resistance with the risk of reproducing predatory forms of extrajudicial discipline in enclaves such as Martissant.

'BRIGAD VIJILANS': NEIGHBORHOOD WATCH OR VIGILANTE BRIGADE?

In this section I reconstruct a crisis in which members of Denise's family were targeted with collective violence. The account raises several issues regarding the ambiguous relationship between perpetrators and victims and between terror and compassion economies as collective groups attempt to resist repression. The story also demonstrates how acts of group violence such as dechoukaj can be means to resist oppressors, but they can also have the character of lynchings. Similarly, *brigad vijilans* can be neighborhood watch associations like the groups that resisted the de facto regime during the 1991–94 coup years, but they can also transform themselves into vigilante brigades—collective retributive mobs that engage in witch-hunts. Given that Haitian judicial and security apparatuses have historically been predatory, corrupt, or weak, the absence of an accountable, responsible state permits extrajudicial, paramilitary, gang, and retributive violence to flourish. The ensekirite that results makes the determination of "victims" and "perpetrators" even more difficult.

I have reconstructed the sequence from Sylvie's initial statements of what had transpired. She did not witness them herself but elicited the details from neighbors the evening they occurred, November 19, 1998. In the days after the attack I also spoke to some of Sylvie's partisans to confirm the details. In early 1999 I was able to interview Denise and one of her sons about what had happened. Their narrative follows the first version below. The event demonstrated the unpredictable irruptions of collective violence that characterized routines of rupture in Haiti. Like the example of *La Fierté Gonâvienne,* scapegoating and outbreaks of group violence were fully enmeshed in recent histories of competition, violence, vengeance, and chronic conditions of frustration. They also had distal roots in other forms of necropolitical victimization, a culture of impunity, and Haiti's "(un)rule of law" (Méndez, O'Donnell, and Pinheiro 1999).

On November 20, 1998, Sylvie came to the Fund. I was surprised because I normally met with her at the clinic and her home. She was agitated and excited to tell me what had happened in Martissant after I left the previous day. She said that it was a "glorious day" and a "true victory" in the zone. On the afternoon of Thursday, November 19, David/ Jiraf had threatened a young adult in the zone but had been thwarted by another young man in the neighborhood. The events escalated into what could look on the surface like an incident of mob violence but were actually much more complex. As we sat in one of the Fund's offices, Sylvie began telling the tale.

> Members of Denise's family acted. They tried to take a television from a family for themselves. A young man in the home tried to prevent them from doing so. David pulled him by the neck and forced his head down on a rock. He then took his machete and started to strike him on the neck with it. Fritzner Masson [a young adult man in the neighborhood] stopped David from cutting him.

Other residents of the zone then joined Fritzner and all of them attacked David with machetes *(yo rache sou li)*. Sylvie continued:

> They told me that they decapitated him near his right eye *[yo di-m' yo dekape-l' bò zye dwat]*. They broke through the skull *[tèt li pèse]* and cut his whole body and foot.

One of David's brothers who had come to protect him was seriously injured. At some point *leta* (the state) came and took David to the hospital. In Denise's version of the story, an ambulance came and took him away. In another version of the story that I heard days after the incident, the police had saved him. As other Martissant residents developed and elaborated the story, I was told that the unit that retrieved him consisted of members of CIMO—the Compagnie d'Intervention et de Maintien de l'Orde, a special operations unit trained in riot control—rather than the regular corps of HNP officers that sometimes patrolled the zone. The Martissant residents who gave this version alleged that the officers were associates of Ginette's husband, but I chose not to pursue this line of inquiry with her. If true, it raises further questions about victim status, divisions within the police force, the entrenchment of alliances within state institutions, and the continued presence of retributive justice as a means to resolve disputes.

Sylvie told me with some satisfaction that she thought David was at the General Hospital, but she wanted to see him with her own eyes to be sure. She then said that after David had been taken away, Denise and the rest of her family threatened the residents of the community. They claimed that they would call in "reinforcements" from Cité Soleil to retaliate by burning up the neighborhood *(yo pral' konsonmen zònnan)*. I had been told previously that David/Jiraf's gang was affiliated with a larger gang in Cité Soleil that controlled organized crime and the flow of narcotics and that policed the poor residents of that neighborhood.[19] The Martissant residents against whom threats of retribution were made would not have taken them lightly.

I suspect that the Cité Soleil group with which they worked were collections of individuals who evolved into organized groups of criminals/terrorists now known as *chimè* (chimaera). The chimè, named after a mythical dragonlike monster,[20] were linked to the pro-Aristide sector after his reelection in 2001 (Fatton 2002). However, Robert Fatton (2002: 24 n.) states that in 1997, when a senior member of the Fanmi Lavalas party described encountering these groups in Cité Soleil, the chimè seemed to be politically independent. The chimè can be likened to the mobile sovereigns or "war machines" (Deleuze and Guattari 1987) of earlier historical periods. As discussed earlier, such groups use neo-modern forms of necropolitics to terrorize others. Their alleged political allegiance to Aristide might have been a "new" partnership, but their loyalty was most likely temporary and could have been procured by other interests offering multiple forms of capital. While there might have been some sort of linkage between these organized criminals and political parties, it was not purely political, given the shifting, ambiguous, and elusive nature of the criminal bands. Occult groups such as the chimè generated power through intimidation, which fomented ensekirite, thus reproducing and reinforcing the economy of terror in Haiti's political economy of trauma.

Sylvie said that not long after Denise and her family made threats against residents of the zone, the HNP stormed the neighborhood and attempted to round up the remaining members of the gang, forcing the ones they caught to lie face-down in the middle of the crossroad. The police then beat the alleged members of the kò with batons. Denise and her family managed to flee the area and were not caught. When the residents of the neighborhood told the police about the threats of retribution, the police encouraged them to form a brigad vijilans to defend themselves against potential incursions by other gangs. Earlier the same month Minister of Justice Antoine asked the Haitian people to form brigad vijilans to combat ensekirite and to prevent the "delinquency" of criminal youth. Thus such groups had implicit if not explicit state sanction.

Sylvie said, furthermore, that Fritzner had been collaborating with the HNP to rid the neighborhood of David and Denise's family as a whole.

> Fritzner had already gone to the police to discuss the problem of the family and they had given him a document that said that they recognized that the family was one accustomed to beating *jij de pè* [justices of the peace], beating police officers, and pulling guns on residents of the zone. So the document authorized him to kill David and to bring the body to them.

Apparently, on arriving in the zone, the police chastised Fritzner publicly, saying that he had not kept the terms of their agreement.[21] Without a guarantee of their protection, Fritzner was vulnerable and fled the area the morning of November 20, 1998.

Before the events concluded on November 19, the group of angry residents—who at this point could be called a state-authorized brigad—expanded their efforts to *dechouke* (uproot) neighborhood oppressors. They demolished both of Denise's homes and Alain and Marie-Rose's home and boutique. The group leveled these cinder-block structures to their foundations. That same evening Sylvie joined the group in patrolling the borders of the zone from 5:00 P.M. until 2:00 A.M.

When I returned to Martissant the following Tuesday, I saw that the homes and property of Denise and her family members had indeed been destroyed. Denise remained in hiding. I did not see her again until February 1999, when she came out of hiding to be interviewed at the Fund with her second youngest son, François, who was then in his late teens. Denise began her narrative with the events of November 19, noting that she had just finished with the marketing and returned home. While she was finishing her household chores, a neighborhood child came to tell her that someone was yelling at David and that a group of young men was attacking him *(aji sou li)* near the market. She asked the reason for the fight but did not receive an answer. Denise told me:

> You know how near where I live they like to rape a lot nowadays. I am against rape, because I am an activist *[se yon fanm òganize ke mwen ye]*. Do you understand me? Because I have suffered rape myself, and I am against it. So by the time I arrived I intercepted them trying to assassinate my son. They were beating him, torturing him *[matirize-l']*, and crushing him. Then I ran and yelled for help. While I ran, they took him and went down [the mountain] with him. I ran to find his [older] brother, but when I arrived he wasn't yet at home.

Later in the interview she said that the young men dumped David close to the main road, assuming that he was dead. Denise arrived at her son's side and realized that in fact he was not dead, as she had feared. Then two *chèf* ("police chiefs" who were patrolling the neighborhood) called an ambulance. The medics were able to provide on-site emergency care and then took him to the hospital.

Denise said next that they had attacked David because of the "good" he had done in the neighborhood. He had tried to reconstruct the road and helped to get the health center established. Moreover, he simply had "spirit." She insisted that she got along with everyone in the zone and had no disagreements with anyone. She repeated that she had been an advocate for protecting rape victims and had testified to assist a women's organization to prosecute a case that had transpired in the area the previous May. The implication was that she had not done anything for which retaliation was warranted.

At this point I shared the accusations I had heard about Denise and her family thus far, including their controlling presence in the neighborhood, their attack on the justice of the peace, and their taking land from others. I said I did not know the truth, but I wanted to hear their side of the story. Denise frowned angrily. François took over the conversation to explain the history of the problem between Fritzner and David. He said that it began during the coup years. Many of the young adults had worked in community theater to organize youth and the community to struggle for democracy. With the escalation of attacks in popular areas in 1993, Denise, François, David, and an elder son had fled across the border to the Dominican Republic. A group of fifteen youths from the zone, as well as Fritzner and two young women joined the family in a camp of refugees.[22]

When they returned from exile the divisions began within their group. François continued:

> When we returned there was FRAPH and they offered rice and cabbage. . . . Fritzner and Jacques joined FRAPH as trainers.[23] But on our part, we said that we went into hiding for one regime [Aristide], and thought that we needed to stay loyal to that regime. So they began to show off in front of me [because of their status with FRAPH], but I said that what they were doing was acting like *makout*, if they were stealing in order to eat, among other things. . . . So we waited for Aristide to return.

François explained that his family chose another route to financial *ankadreman*. Before their return to the area at the end of 1993, they had heard that the National Office for Migration was offering aid to returning Haitians. François said proudly that their family fought to be recognized as political refugees and "unblocked" a substantial sum that they felt obliged to share with others who had been with them in exile. François claimed, however, that Fritzner was jealous and wanted all the money for himself. He took a "Qaddafi"—a semiautomatic gun—that he had borrowed from one of the other young men and aimed it at them in order to take the money.

François next named all the members of the youth gang who were the "real perpetrators" in the zone. He emphasized the good that his family had done to combat the impunity that permitted these "real" gang members to commit *kadejak* (rape) at will. François implicated Fritzner in this group of youths who violated young women. He claimed that his family members had been targeted on November 19 because of these struggles for justice. He emphasized that they had not deserved their victimization and said "there was an organization called Dekamo [ATD Quart Monde] that they had asked to help children in the neighborhood to attend school."

François claimed, furthermore, that even the February 4, 1994, attacks on Denise, Marie-Rose, and their family property and households were somehow connected to Fritzner, in his capacity as a FRAPH trainer. Indeed, on a previous occasion Sylvie hinted that the rape of these two women might have been an act of vengeance, even as the crime fit under the criteria for "human rights abuses." At the close of the interview François alleged that all the young men associated with Fritzner used drugs, as did Sylvie herself, and that the problem was that as soon as money was offered to them it was used to feed their drug problem. He claimed that Sylvie even resorted to prostitution to feed her habit. Denise and François then asked me if I might be able to help them get visas to the United States. I told them that I was unable to do so but asked them to stay in touch.

By the time François had presented the last piece of information regarding Sylvie's alleged personal "habits," I had no means to definitively verify his allegations. I was already aware that Sylvie would do whatever was necessary to ensure the welfare of her children. Early in December, while the Human Rights Fund prepared to commemorate the fiftieth anniversary of the Universal Declaration of Human Rights, Sylvie pressured me again to continue working with her. I said that I could not do so, despite the fact that Denise had fled Martissant. By this time I was fatigued with the challenges of working in the zone and wanted to learn more about the practice of community policing and political development assistance strategies employed in ADF's other programs.

Sylvie decided to write to Dr. Manata and me at the Fund to protest my decision to suspend her "aid." In her letter she stated:

> It's my right. When you were in danger, I always took you out of it. It's my right, my obligation [se dwa-m', se devwa-m'], because you're my friend. As a friend I am working with you. I could lose my life at the very moment that I don't have money to pay the criminals in the zone for passage.

Sylvie used the discourse of rights and responsibility that was employed in many human rights training sessions for victims and linked it to the obligations of reciprocity and personal alliances that were encompassed in angajman and moun pa. I did not have time to respond to her formally. The following day, Sylvie came to the Fund to see me but instead spoke with Dr. Manata about our conflict. During their conversation she became quite aggressive and told him that if I did not continue to support her she could no longer guarantee my safety in the zone. The implicit threat was not one that I could ignore, especially given what I had learned about how conflicts escalate in the zone. After discussions with the Rehab staff and others working in Martissant, we determined that it would be better for me to discontinue my research there temporarily and not risk her revenge or retaliation, or that of the individuals whose suffering she may have appropriated as a gatekeeper for her own ends. Once I had received word from the clinic staff a few months later that Sylvie had moved out of the zone, I returned to my work at Chanm Fanm.

* * *

These stories of the social life of humanitarian assistance in Martissant demonstrate how postconflict aid to "insecure" or "transitional" states can become enmeshed in local politics, violence, retributive justice, and everyday ensekirite. Stories like these are disheartening at best and horrifying at worst. By the time the accusations were made that the women in Martissant or their family members had problems with drug use, resorted to "prostitution," or even committed violence, I distrusted accusations viktim made against other viktim. I was also no longer shocked (or easily moved) by horrific trauma narratives. What was most distressing was the way the scarcity of resources—local, national, and international—encouraged some of these individuals to use predatory practices to survive. Not least among those scarce resources was the humanitarian and development aid made available to these "poorest of the poor" by the international, national, and local organizations that targeted them for interventions.

The patterns of accusation, counteraccusation, and strategic control of information were complex in Martissant, just as they were in the U.S. development realm. The contested truths of victim, perpetrator, and activist status remained difficult to determine. The complexity of identity recalled another passage in the leaked April 12, 1994, embassy cablegram. The point was titled "Lavalas and FRAPH: Same M.O., Overlapping Membership" and concerned the difficulty of distinguishing the authors of violent acts during the coup years.

> In addition to having many of the same "members," FRAPH has essentially the same modus operandi as the Lavalas "comites de quartier" [sic] that were sanctioned, and encouraged, during the Aristide presidency. The key difference is that the amorphous repression of popular discontent that is FRAPH is an instrument of the military, whereas the "comites de quartier" [sic] were the instruments of the executive. FRAPH is already grooming candidates, and wooing/terrorizing potential voters, in anticipation of local and parliamentary elections scheduled for this December.

The *comités de quartier* were the same as the brigad vijilans. President Aristide urged that pro-democracy activists protect themselves against the coup apparatus by forming these groups. For the U.S. Mission, however, defining the indeterminate and sometimes overlapping categories of "villains" was instrumental to determining how it should respond to incidents of "human rights abuses." As previously discussed, U.S. agencies were ultimately concerned with accountability to the U.S. Congress rather than to Haitians and the Government of Haiti. Thus U.S. strategies to facilitate postconflict reconstruction and justice in contexts where the roots of conflict are complex, historical, and opaque tend to favor U.S. interests by demonstrating discrete results that promote U.S. national security rather than the interests of the transitional nation in which such strategies are implemented.

Furthermore, François's account indicated how FRAPH was viewed by some as an aid organization that could ensure security and survival, regardless of how its members terrorized and tortured thousands of individuals during the coup years. The National Office for Migration was another vehicle of social reinsertion after victimization and displacement, as was ATD Quart Monde, MICIVIH, Médecins du Monde, HWA, MAB, the Human Rights Fund, and numerous others. These agencies could be placed along a political continuum that offered a selection of financial aid but never complete ankadreman. Their various political orientations and sources of funding did not pose ethical dilemmas for some viktim, especially when the latter were struggling not only to survive but also to gain political recognition of their plight.

But what about the assertions that Denise's family members and associates had been recruited while in the Dominican Republic to participate in a future coup d'état against Aristide, should he be reelected? How is it that desperately poor viktim returned from exile armed with semi-automatic weapons? Some have alleged that the United States financed the training of anti-Aristide rebel forces in the Dominican Republic by channeling funds through the International Republican Institute, the development arm of the U.S. Republican Party.[24] Indeed, members of Denise's kò were able to intimidate others, to demand ongoing "commissions" for brokering access to assistance, and to act as "overseers" in this bidonvil because of their weapons, however acquired. What other kinds of occult interventions have occurred that remain in the shadows?

Sylvie had acted as a trauma broker and gatekeeper to the local, national, and international domains of humanitarian actors. She used several strategies to achieve revandikasyon for viktim: testimony and the performance of suffering, investigation and documentation of past abuses, and discourses of rights and obligation, among others. These were technologies of trauma and truth that had been inculcated by years of exposure to rationalized efforts to rehabilitate Haiti's viktim. That these efforts did not fully succeed in permanently changing her status and access to resources increased her frustrations. Perhaps, as a last resort, she decided to use threats, an oral form of dechoukaj, to achieve her goals, much as had occurred in the Rehab Program earlier that fall 1998. Nevertheless, I have often wondered whether I was obligated to do more in Martissant, or to continue to provide aid to Sylvie. Given Haiti's structural challenges and the limitations of aid, what should be done, and who or what institution is responsible? The same questions underpinned the sequence of events that contributed to the closing of the Rehab Program.

CHAPTER 6

Sovereign Rule, Ensekirite, and Death

In early 1999 a series of incidents occurred that indicated how negative dimensions of bureaucraft—the pattern of rumors, gossip, and accusations of occult activity lodged against agencies and agents in the humanitarian and development aid apparatus—could culminate in violence. The events described in this chapter occurred against a backdrop of waves of political and economic insecurity in Haiti and increasing tension in the victim advocacy assemblage. As had occurred during earlier crises described in this book, contests over resources and political power were waged in the print and visual media, as well as in social space. The disputes were linked to macropolitical issues regarding Haitian sovereignty and sovereign rule. At the national level President Préval's rule by decree was one form of sovereign rule. At the micropolitical level brigad vijilans became state-authorized vigilante brigades that employed collective violence to combat the repression of gangs. As these processes unfolded, interactions between viktim and the Human Rights Fund and between other aid agencies and the Fund were increasingly contentious and generated discourses and practices of violence that precipitated the closing of the Rehabilitation Program. Following the termination of the program, the links between discourses of torture, trauma, and truth and practices of bureaucraft would be reaffirmed as both ADF and Human Rights Fund Rehabilitation Program clients promoted their respective collective and individual trauma portfolios to seek additional sources of aid from donors in the compassion economy.

In November 1998 Minister of Justice Antoine asked citizens to form brigad vijilans to combat the rise in political and criminal violence in the capital. An editorial in the anti-Aristide newspaper, *Haïti Observateur,* criticized the minister's request because some groups had already unleashed "extrajudicial" forms of retribution. Between November 9 and 15 the General Hospital morgue registered fifteen murder victims. There were twenty-five other murders between November 16 and 22 ("Insécurité et banditisme" 1998), the week when David/Jiraf, a son of Denise Jules, was nearly executed by a mob in Martissant. The mounting tally of deaths signified an alarming intensification of ensekirite. The article criticized Felder Jean-Baptiste, Haitian National Police spokesperson at the time, for attributing these murders to the "delinquency of youth" rather than to the prolonged political and economic crisis, the "ineptness" of the HNP, and the lack of any security function offered by MIPONUH ("Insécurité et banditisme" 1998: 11).[1] Another newspaper challenged negative representations of the Haitian state's capacity to promote security and justice by a foreign intervener whose own institution had failed to maintain peace and security in the nation. The Argentine lawyer Rodolfo Mattarollo, MICIVIH deputy director of the Human Rights Unit, reacted publicly to the call for the formation of brigad vijilans as a solution to the growing problem of ensekirite by chastising Haitians as a whole about their failure to uphold their civic duties. He stated that as the brigad vijilans were not instruments of the state established under the 1987 Constitution, promoting them encouraged the spread of vigilante justice. As reported by the pro-Aristide newspaper, *Haïti Progrès,* Mattarollo urged that Minister Antoine should be "reprimanded severely" for his suggestion to revive these watch groups.[2] The *Haïti Progrès* article questioned why Mattarollo should arrogate to himself the responsibility to remind Haitians about their Constitution or the duties of the minister of justice. His reported comments were considered paternalistic or neocolonial, especially when neither MICIVIH nor MIPONUH provided any form of security in the nation.[3]

Ultimately, these media discourses concerned state sovereignty and the negative legacies of international military, economic, and humanitarian interventions. Another editorial in the same *Haïti Progrès* issue, titled "La Micivih: des airs de sainte nitouche" (MICIVIH: Hypocritically Pious), criticized not only Mattarollo but also the interventions of international and bilateral institutions to promote (but not protect) human rights in the country. An extended quotation from the statement

highlights that political development assistance to Haiti was viewed as
superficial if not disingenuous.

> With the approach of the fiftieth anniversary of the Universal Declaration
> of Human Rights [on] December 10, 1998, the directors of MICIVIH and
> other organizations have exhorted the population to respect human rights
> at all levels. Reflection sessions have been organized in the provincial towns
> . . . on the means by which to protect these rights. For the past two weeks
> banners on which have been reproduced the articles of the Declaration
> have been placed on Lalue [Avenue John Brown]. The group ASOSYE [sic][4]
> financed by USAID (which is mixed up in all of it) and OCODE[5] partici-
> pate in these activities in producing notably the [pro-democracy] murals in
> the metropolitan area—efforts that will remain a dead letter, serving only
> as deceptions [poudre aux yeux], while the end of impunity will never serve
> as a concrete example of the real will to respect these human rights.
>
> In parallel, the Secretary General of the UN, Kofi Annan, must submit
> to the General Assembly the request for the extension of the MICIVIH
> mandate formulated by President Préval. . . . The UN/OAS International
> Civilian Mission has been charged with supervising the respect for human
> rights in the country since 1993. . . . For its part the National Episcopal
> Justice and Peace Commission . . . asks, when will the principles enunciated
> in this Declaration become a concrete reality?[6]

The editorial accused the executive branch of government of failing to
reestablish the sovereignty of the country as prescribed by the Constitution, as demonstrated by the presence of U.S. military troops in
Haiti, "whose function is unknown." The article also denounced rich
countries that "extol the globalization of the economy, whereas the
external debt of poor countries never ceases to climb,"[7] then exhorted
the international financial institutions to cancel poor nations' external debt, especially Haiti's. Finally, the statement accused the "Préval
regime" of having a penchant for "emptying the treasury, for dismiss-
ing civil servants, for selling off the national patrimony, and for divest-
ing the national coffers in order to satisfy the international creditors."[8]
As discussed in chapter 4, Préval's political party was heavily criticized
for accepting international neoliberal economic strategies to implement
structural adjustment and privatization in Haiti. The disputes expressed
in this editorial ultimately concerned the capacity for a developing
nation to wield political and economic power in the neomodern era.

Of critical importance for this chapter, however, is the way the America's Development Foundation ASOSYE project was accused of "superficial efforts" to promote human rights in Haiti—while the United
States was considered to be actively undermining Haitian political

Figure 7. MICIVIH and OCODÉ human rights murals, Port-au-Prince. The OCODÉ mural in French on the left reads: "Those who do not respect the law will be punished by the law." The MICIVIH mural in the center promotes human rights for all humanity. The OCODÉ mural in Haitian Creole on the right reads: "Respect the law. Respect the country. Respect human life." Photo credit: Erica Caple James.

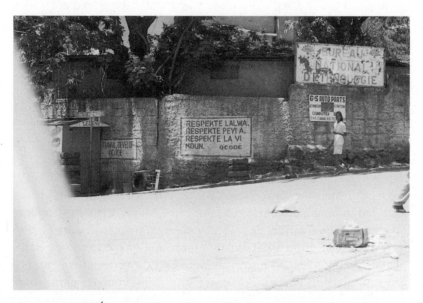

Figure 8. OCODÉ mural, Port-au-Prince. The Haitian Creole text of the center image reads: "Respect the Law. Respect the Country. Respect Human Life." Photo credit: Erica Caple James.

and economic sovereignty. These allegations are integral to analyzing how witchcraft and bureaucraft practices and accusations escalated into scapegoating and even violence directed against ADF and it staff members. Although the ADF Human Rights Fund was actually the project responsible for coordinating and implementing USAID's strategic objectives in the realm of human rights in Haiti, the subtle differences between the political orientations of its political development aid programs were not evident from the outside. It was in this context that the Fund came under attack in spring 1999, soon after the ASOSYE project moved to a new institutional procurement structure, the for-profit company Management Systems International.

Despite the rise in vigilante violence across Port-au-Prince, the Fund carried on activities to promote human rights, justice, and the rule of law through its commemoration of the fiftieth anniversary of the Universal Declaration of Human Rights (UDHR) on December 10, 1998. The Fund sponsored free public concerts in Port-au-Prince, Jacmel, and Les Cayes at which prominent Haitian bands performed and which drew thousands of Haitians. Between musical acts Fund staff members read the UDHR. The Fund also sponsored public banners spanning one of the most highly traveled roads, on which the articles of the UDHR were printed in Haitian Creole. In addition, the Fund sponsored radio programs in which prominent Haitian activists discussed human rights in Haitian history. The Fund held events for children, especially beneficiaries of its programs. These activities commemorating the anniversary of the UDHR generated positive press for the Fund, which was still widely perceived as another Haitian civil society organization. At a meeting of the USAID AOJ Programs, Mission Director Forbes congratulated HRF staff on these successful outreach projects to local Haitians; however, the positive response by Haitians and actors in the aid apparatus would soon end, overshadowed by another wave of ensekirite brought on by the ever-changing political and economic climate.

Once again, the process by which violence occurred and was analyzed in public discourse was much like Tambiah's (1996) descriptions of transvaluation and focalization, in which discrete events were abstracted from a particular context and linked to more general political, economic, and historical events. As the series of violent incidents unfolded in Port-au-Prince, the media and human rights groups and other actors in the aid apparatus linked these seemingly random events and related them to the broader context of political and economic ensekirite.

On January 11, 1999, President René Préval dismissed the embattled parliament and began ruling by decree.⁹ The social climate was hypervigilant because of the reported rise in violence at the close of the previous year. A new series of violent crimes followed Préval's decision to act as a sovereign. In the afternoon of January 12, 1999, Préval's sister and secretary, Marie-Claude Préval Calvin, was shot in the chest, neck, and leg. A motorcyclist drove alongside her vehicle and fired a gun, killing the driver and critically injuring Calvin. At first examination the attack resembled those that were "purely" criminal. In this case, however, the motive for the attack was labeled political. The shooting had a character similar to "arbitrary" crimes that were subsequently attributed to the nefarious work of the chimè, the mobile sovereigns that in later years were accused of working for President Aristide.

In response to these events, the Platform of Haitian Human Rights Organizations issued a statement that decried both the suspension of parliament and the increase in insecurity. Following this release, human rights activists and organizations, whether national or international, were also threatened. In the afternoon of March 1, 1999, Pierre Espérance, spokesperson for NCHR and a member of the secretariat of the Platform, barely survived an assassination attempt. Espérance had also been a former grantee of the Human Rights Fund. Four assassins in a white sedan followed Espérance's car as it approached NCHR headquarters. As they sped alongside his vehicle one of the passengers fired a machine gun into the car, hitting Espérance in the shoulder and leg. He was hospitalized at the General Hospital and later went with his family into exile in the United States to recover.

In addition to this, the murder of two physicians further blurred the line between political, criminal, and retributive violence. Dr. Jimmy Lalanne was killed on February 27, 1999. On March 1 Dr. Yvon Toussaint, a senator, was killed. Both murders were linked in public discourse to the escalating insecurity in the nation as a whole. In the first case news reports alleged that a family was disgruntled over the death of one of its members who was a patient in Dr. Lalanne's care at the General Hospital. Reputedly, the family murdered Lalanne in retaliation. The murder sparked a general strike by the hospital staff in protest against the new vulnerability of social sectors that ideally should be immune from politics and criminal acts. In the second case, Dr. Toussaint was killed in front of his home in the lower Delmas section of Port-au-Prince while working on his car. At first the murder was thought to have been merely

criminal, but gradually people concluded that Toussaint was assassinated for having been a prominent member of Préval's OPL party.

On March 2 the Platform released a statement that connected
the murders to a campaign of intimidation and terror that had been
unleashed after the August 3, 1998, killing of Pè Ti Jan (Fr. Jean Pierre-
Louis). The Platform had received threatening *trak* (political leaflets)
that targeted the association and its members. But more broadly, the
release asked:

> How can the Platform rest tranquilly in front of the situation of impunity,
> the liquidation of public enterprises, the occupation of the country, [and] the
> deterioration of the situation of the masses who are sinking in malnutrition
> and the darkness of ignorance? How can the Platform rest quietly before the
> worsening of the political situation, society, and diverse institutions such that
> students are obliged to protest to ask their directors to be responsible? How
> can the Platform remain silent before the corruption that spreads through-
> out public administration? How can the Platform remain at peace when the
> human rights situation continues to deteriorate? (Platform 1999: 1)

On March 12, in this pervasive atmosphere of ensekirite, the Human
Rights Fund's Community-Police Relations Program held a roundtable
discussion on community policing and public security. The Port-au-
Prince event was organized in cooperation with the Office Protecteur du
Citoyen (OPC), the Government of Haiti's Office for the Protection of
Citizens. Members of Haitian civil society—human rights groups, victims
advocacy groups, the chamber of commerce, artisan groups, women's
rights groups, and others—attended the conference. Minister of Justice
Antoine and the director general of the Haitian National Police, Pierre
Denizé, gave presentations, as did other prominent members of the Min-
istry of Justice and Public Security. Each of them examined the challenges
that faced the HNP as it sought to root out corruption and create better
relationships with the communities served by the police. Of note was
a cordial exchange between Dr. Andrea Baptiste and Director General
Denizé regarding the timetable for reparations to the Haitian Women's
Association and Chanm Fanm for the April 1998 attack on the clinic.

By most accounts the event, thought to be one of the first occasions
when a head of the Haitian armed forces was available to answer questions posed by Haitian citizens, was judged a success. In the weeks after
the discussion, however, there were negative repercussions. Human
Rights Fund staff members Henri Raphael, Alphonse Montina, and
Alice Pierre-Richard of the Community-Police Relations team began
receiving death threats at home by phone. These calls provoked intense

anxiety and fear among Fund staff. Once again staff members attempted to divine the source of these overt threats and to read the signs of escalating ensekirite for their potential to bring misfortune and suffering down on them.

The Rehab Program was also receiving threats but with different motivations. Viktim were frustrated by the program's inability to meet all their material needs. Despite attempts to explain the budgetary crisis, some viktim continued to resent the reduction of services. They were also angry about the way that Dr. Ambroise administered the PROMESS essential drug program. In the second round of therapy groups, for example, beneficiaries claimed that Dr. Ambroise had begun to treat them rudely. They alleged that she said that the reason Haitians are always sick is because "they live in their shit." After their complaints reached the ADF managerial level, Dr. Manata asked Dr. Thomas to put Ambroise on leave for a couple of weeks to take a break from the daily demands of her clients.

Viktim also leveled charges against the Rehab Program for their perceived exclusion from international and national assistance to which other groups had access. Many of these accusations stemmed in part from perceptions of political and economic gains that the Fund and its associates made when President Préval began ruling by decree. Préval had formed a new government and named former Minister of Education Jacques-Édouard Alexis the new prime minister. Alexis began functioning in that role in January and announced his new cabinet on March 25, 1999. He appointed Mèt Leblanc the new minister of justice and public security. With the human rights lawyer in this position, viktim were anxious to have their individual and collective needs for justice, reparation, and rehabilitation met. Minister Leblanc had invited a number of civil society groups—including the Human Rights Fund, FAVILEK, M'AP VIV, the Justice and Peace Commission, and the Fondasyon 30 Sektanm—to participate in a series of meetings to create another committee that would explore implementing the recommendations of the National Commission for Truth and Justice. Leblanc had also begun meeting with a collective of victims' advocacy groups that he had represented before becoming minister, the majority of which were directed by men. In response to this perceived gender inequity, in an April 5, 1999, press conference twelve women victim's organizations announced that they had formed the Groupe de Concertation des Associations de Femmes Victimes du Coup d'État (GCAFVCE)—the Consultative Group of Associations of Women Coup Victims.[10]

As certain groups and not others gained access to these meetings, conflict and competition over alliances and resources again emerged, and disputes occurring outside the Human Rights Fund were eventually directed toward the Fund. Since January 1999 the Fondasyon 30 Sektanm had publicly accused Dany Fabien, director of the BPS, of having mismanaged the U.S.$4 million that the BPS administered. In one respect these accusations were a means by which the organization's spokespersons performed their accountability to their constituents. The debate between Pierre-Antoine Lovinsky of the Fondasyon 30 Sektanm and Fabien remained quite heated and public over the course of the spring. At the same time, another smaller victims' organization protested that OVKD, a large victims' advocacy group that Minister Leblanc had represented legally before his tenure as minister of justice, had also received preferential access to the BPS funds and greater assistance than other victims' advocacy groups. The debacle ended in Leblanc's request for an audit of the BPS and the eventual dismantling of the office.

In late April and early May 1999, as the threats against the HRF staff continued, individual Rehab Program staff members began to be accused of corruption through a combination of scandal publicity and overt threats. A new victim's advocacy organization had formed called the Mouvman Viktim 30 Sektanm (September 30 Victims' Movement, MOVI-30), composed of beneficiaries of the Rehab Program. MOVI-30 pasted anti–Human Rights Fund leaflets on the outer gate of ADF, on walls throughout the city, and on the gates of other aid organizations in Port-au-Prince calling for justice for perceived breaches of obligations to viktim. This public protest occurred at the same time that a press release denouncing the Fund appeared in one of the pro-democracy newspapers. In an article titled "'Nou pa manje, manje bliye': Deklarasyon Mouvman Viktim 30 Sektanm" ("We don't eat, food is forgotten": Declaration of the September 30 Victims' Movement), the newspaper printed MOVI-30's statement outlining a series of complaints that ranged from the personal to the political. The statement began by charging that the U.S. government planned the 1991 coup d'état. It next accused the U.S. government of stealing the FRAPH documents to hide its role and the role of greedy *(patripòch)* members of the Haitian bourgeoisie in implementing the coup.[11] The statement went on to denounce Human Rights Fund staff members Ambroise, Thomas, and Alphonse Montina for having "decided to wipe out *[pete fyèl]* victims by changing their prescriptions and giving them whatever they [the accused] wished." (Montina, who was actually not part of the Rehab

Program, was accused on the basis of misinformation; however, he had helped victim advocacy organizations to write grant proposals in the past.) This last point referred to the decision to change beneficiaries' prescriptions from brand-name to generic medications. The declaration went on to request that all three be expelled from the Fund.

The U.S. government and the Human Rights Fund were not the only targets. MOVI-30's declaration also accused the Haitian state of protecting the rich by exploiting the poor and criticized the implementation of imported economic plans that "destroy the environment, and engender hunger, misery, unemployment and insecurity in the country." The MOVI-30 press release next denounced the Préval administration for pursuing a neoliberal economic program intended to privatize the national industries: the cement factory, the airport, the ports, and other institutions. Préval was accused of having cast the people aside and of failing to involve them in the processes of government until after decisions had been made. In 1994, when the Fund was originally instituted, the Platform made a similar argument against the United States. MOVI-30 linked all these political and economic processes to the plight of viktim.

> It's the same as the *viktim* question. Instead of the heads of state arresting the assassins that repress us, they'd rather separate victims' organizations by means of the Office of Proceedings and Follow-up [BPS], and in the scattering of a few crumbs here and there that can't resolve anything for victims[,] . . . which causes trouble between victims' organizations and demoralizes them, leaving them confused. We ask on behalf of all victims' organizations that are not involved in following behind these crumbs of money *[ti tchotcho]*, which causes them to lose their dignity, to unite in order to find true justice and reparations.

The statement then lists MOVI-30's demands:

1. That Minister Camille Leblanc give victims a deadline by which the BPS would present a public, transparent report on the victim assistance fund.
2. For the Minister to give a good explanation of the Human Rights Fund's activities in the country. The Minister must also make a statement on the way Dr. Thomas, Dr. Ambroise, and . . . Alphonse Montina have changed prescriptions.
3. For the minister to have arrested all makout and the greedy bourgeoisie who financed the coup of September 30, 1991.
4. That the American government remit the more than 160,000 pages of [FRAPH] documents, audio- and videocassettes without any names or images erased.
5. That Emmanuel (Toto) Constant be judged in Haiti.[12]
6. Justice and reparations for all *viktim*.

The declaration concluded with the cry, "Down with Dr. Thomas and Dr. Ambroise! Long live good living conditions for *viktim!* Long live justice and reparations for *viktim!*"

Like the media press release, the political leaflet that was pasted throughout the city was highly professional. It had the organization's letterhead next to a hand-drawn illustration of the scales of justice balanced by a man and a woman. The title of the tract was "Apre 8 Lane, Viktim Yo Toujou Anba Soufrans" (After 8 Years, Victims Still Suffer). Its contents contained much the same information as the declaration but did not name Alphonse Montina. The demands differed slightly, in that MOVI-30 asked for Drs. Thomas and Ambroise to be expelled from the Fund. It also accused them of trying to murder viktim by changing to generic drugs. In part, such accusations may have reflected an issue discussed in the therapy groups regarding the strong negative side effects that accompanied the ingestion of certain medications without adequate food. The implication of the leaflet, however, was that Thomas and Ambroise were intentionally poisoning viktim, much as had been feared historically of those who have practiced malevolent magic in Haiti.

In the aftermath of these shocking events, Human Rights Fund staff members began to speculate about what hidden actor was truly behind MOVI-30's action, given the highly professional leaflet, the press release, and the statement's reference to national political processes. An implication of these divinatory discussions was that viktim were not the sole authors of the documents but the puppets of hidden actors. The failure to attribute the capacity for independent political action to viktim was ironic given the Fund's provision of technical assistance to victims' advocacy groups as civil society organizations. In this respect the leaflet and press release were also interesting in the way they combined demands for political recognition and justice with personal grievances with individual agents of humanitarian and development assistance. Both texts revealed the intermingling of rumor, gossip, and misunderstandings about bureaucratic practices that arose within the scarce victim assistance grant economy. Both leveled bureaucraft accusations implying covert activity on the part of the Rehab Program, the Human Rights Fund, the Haitian bourgeoisie, the Haitian state, and the U.S. government. Moreover, the political leaflet demonstrated the relationship between bureaucraft and classic witchcraft accusations, in which anxieties and even paranoia about secrecy, power, and bureaucracy intermingled with demands for justice and reparations. The allegation that Thomas and Ambroise were "poisoning" Fund beneficiaries incorporated suspicions that these professionals had hidden identities and engaged in occult, baneful actions—perhaps to enrich themselves from the surplus funds that the change to generic medications reputedly produced.

That these two forms of communication appeared in public space and in the print media provoked fear among the Rehab staff but not yet a sense of panic. Then, in early May, a young man who had been hired as a courier to take messages between ADF headquarters and the Rehab Program at Base 2 was threatened at gunpoint while in transit between the two institutions. After this assault it was clear that similar attacks would escalate in frequency and severity and that greater security measures had to be taken. Dr. Manata chose to shut down Base 2 and ordered Drs. Thomas and Ambroise to remain at home. A few days later the security guard who had remained at Base 2 reported that a mob bearing weapons and handcuffs had come looking for the two doctors. The mob was disappointed to find only the guard at the office. When Dr. Manata reported the attacks to Mission Director Forbes at USAID, she suggested that the Fund shut down operations until the situation could be assessed for future security risks.

The increased sense of institutional and personal insecurity that Fund staff members experienced as a result of these attacks intensified the fear and anxiety with which other U.S.-funded development aid actors were struggling. During the same period another violent incident occurred that had the ambiguous character of ensekirite and exacerbated the growing sense of panic among USAID's medial development partners. In contrast to the U.S. Embassy and USAID in Haiti, which provided private security for many of the foreign service officers in their employ, development partners such as ADF generally lacked the resources to provide private security to staff members. Security was of heightened concern because this latest incident was thought to predict a shift in the pattern of ensekirite. Whereas in the past Haitians had been the primary targets of ensekirite, in this case violence was directed at one of the expatriate associates who worked with USAID/Haiti. Just days before MOVI-30 members attempted to use collective violence to enact retributive justice against Drs. Thomas and Ambroise, a former ADF staff member and consultant for USAID, Marcus Belmonte, was murdered. Belmonte had worked with David Hunter to install the Rehab Program in ADF after meeting Thomas and Manata in 1996 at the Haitian Studies Association Conference in Haiti (see chapter 2). Late one evening, unknown assailants shot Belmonte in the head at point-blank range in front of his wife just outside their home.

The news circulated quickly in the early morning hours after Belmonte was murdered, and in the days afterward rumor, speculation, and suspicion swirled as actors in the U.S.-funded aid apparatus attempted to divine the cause and to make sense of their loss. Was Belmonte's murder a random killing? Was it politically or criminally motivated? Who was to blame? The murder prompted an emergency meeting of the USAID/Haiti Strategic Objective Team to discuss security. I attended the May 4, 1999, meeting at USAID headquarters. There was considerable hushed discussion about Belmonte's death and tremendous concern for Hunter and his wife, who had been close personal friends of Belmonte and his family for many years. To the surprise of many in attendance, Hunter came to the meeting looking visibly shaken. To the consternation of some of the development partners in attendance, the USAID Strategic Objective Team staff members did not seriously address their apprehensions about their institutional and personal security as agencies and agents that operated in the liminal space between USAID/Haiti and its Haitian customers. In fact, there was little to no discussion of security issues. Rather, after a few words acknowledging Belmonte's tragic death, the conversation focused on what contingency plans USAID/Haiti needed to make should it be unable to implement the strategic plan in light of the escalation in ensekirite.

In the days after the meeting there was also little discussion between USAID/Haiti and ADF regarding the future of the Rehabilitation Program. Thus in May, a few weeks before the end of the HRFII fourteen-month extension, the Victim Assistance and Rehabilitation Program shut down. Given the Fund's uncertain future and the greater interest at USAID/Haiti in implementing political development assistance through judicial reform and community policing rather than rehabilitation of viktim, the management team at ADF headquarters in the United States decided not to renew the contracts of Thomas and Ambroise. Beneficiaries of the program were abruptly left without other apparent institutional means to address their health care needs. For weeks afterward, many viktim continued to approach staff members to learn when, if ever, services would resume.

As debates about the future of both the Rehab Program and the Fund once again ensued, the issue of truth emerged from questions regarding the causes of institutional and personal gains and losses in the aid apparatus, bureaucratic rationales for policy changes, and victim identities. The question of the truths of victimization surfaced a couple of weeks after the Rehabilitation Program closed down when I received another trauma narrative from a victim of human rights abuses. The story depicts the intricate relationship between torture, trauma, and truth in Haiti. Caroline Antoine, whose sensory biography I presented in chapter 3, told me that a woman who had been a beneficiary of the Fund wanted to be interviewed about traumatic events in her life history using the CAPS diagnostic interview schedule (for which I provided H$20 in compensation). She implied that the woman's history was similar to her own and hoped that either the Fund or I could still help her. I agreed to the interview, and Roseline Jerome, with Caroline at her side for support, came to see me.

The details of her victimization were tragic, much as they were for others who had shared their testimonies with me. I will only recount here the aspects of her story that reinforced the power of the political economy of trauma and its related occult economies. During the coup years Roseline and her entire family were targeted for politically motivated violence. She reported being gang-raped in Port-au-Prince, then fleeing to the provinces. She revealed that during the rape she had conceived a child. While in hiding in the provinces, she gave birth to a daughter, whom she had since abandoned. Roseline gave the child to her extended family because she could not bear the memories of how she had come into existence.

What was striking about the tale was not what was stated in the interview. Rather, it was the discrepancies between what Roseline revealed to me and the content of her official trauma portfolio at the Rehab Program. According to the narrative in Roseline's dossier, a younger girl in the household had been raped, not Roseline. Perhaps for the first time Roseline had revealed the source of her deep shame—her own rape, her pregnancy, and her child's birth. I asked one of the Rehab nurses still on staff to listen to a portion of the interview to determine if I had understood Roseline correctly—that she herself and not the young girl had been raped. Although I worried about the potential violation of a confidence, it seemed necessary to do so in order to understand this case and determine the best way to assist this woman.

The nurse listened to the segment of the tape and confirmed that Roseline admitted to the rape and pregnancy. She too was stunned by the discrepancies between the stated narrative and what was documented in Roseline's trauma portfolio. Assuming this new story was true, it suggested that viktim might have revealed only that which was necessary to become eligible for services. In some cases they may have omitted, altered, or even falsified the details, much as had Liliane, whose trauma narratives presented these ethical dilemmas in the introduction to this book. Viktim may have adopted others' trauma narratives as their own in order to gain political and therapeutic recognition, mirroring the accusations against the famed Guatemalan human rights activist and Nobel Peace Prize winner, Rigoberta Menchú (Nelson 2001; Stoll 1999). In other cases like this one, the actual trauma of viktim may have been far worse than what was reported. Ultimately, the full truths of the experiences of viktim may never be known.

Despite the continued suffering of viktim like Roseline, ameliorating the ongoing vulnerability of Haitians was no longer considered a priority of USAID/Haiti's strategic objectives, even though providing aid to torture survivors worldwide was an important goal of USAID and the U.S. Congress. That there were conflicts regarding Haitian trauma portfolios was evident in the weeks after the closing of the Rehabilitation Program when ADF president Michael Miller continued to lobby for support for the program with the Latin America and Caribbean portfolio manager at USAID headquarters in Washington, D.C. He also solicited USAID support to extend ADF's cooperative agreement, despite the loss of the ASOSYE Civil Society project. With regard to the Rehabilitation Program, the USAID/Washington desk person told Miller that USAID/Haiti had informed him that "there were no more victims in Haiti." This declaration occurred at nearly the same moment that USAID/Washington presented the Human Rights Fund Rehabilitation Program to Congress as one of its success stories in providing treatment to torture survivors (U.S. Congress 1999a, 1999b).

Some of the reasons underlying the ambivalence about the Human Rights Fund reflected tensions in USAID regarding its overall mission. Actors outside its sovereign domain frequently describe USAID/Haiti as a "state within a state." However, the disconnect between USAID/Washington's desires and policies and those of USAID/Haiti and its local actors should be seen as refutations of arguments that pose the domain of postconflict transition solely as a top-down imposition of power by external interveners or as examples of neocolonialisms against which there is no resistance. Furthermore, the way that USAID/Haiti employees were able to suspend a program to aid Haitian victims of human rights abuses that USAID/Washington promoted as an example of its achievements abroad demonstrates the extent to which USAID had been successful in decentralizing power through its global network of aid missions. While to some degree these satellite USAID missions were sovereign actors limited in practice only by the authorization of their host nation customers, the Haiti example demonstrates that such institutions were nonetheless fraught with conflicts over the implementation of strategic objectives.

In many respects the ADF Human Rights Fund Victim Assistance and Rehabilitation Program was destined to fail, given the competing local, national, and international demands that it was asked to fulfill and the ambivalence the program evoked among USAID/Haiti staff members. For example, in March 1999 I interviewed a member of the Justice, Democracy and Governance office about USAID's history of democratic development. She expressed unease with the HRF Rehab Program and lamented, "We are used to dealing with crops, not this kind of development. . . . It would be better for a charity to do this sort of work." This woman was an anthropologist who had worked for USAID for at least twenty years. Her statements echoed the discomfort that many development practitioners felt with the explicit political trajectory that USAID was following in the neomodern period. As Carothers writes:

> The great majority of USAID officers were wary of direct involvement by the agency in political development assistance. They thought that USAID— being an economic development organization—was ill prepared to influence the political life of other countries through aid programs. Attempting to do so, they feared, could jeopardize its other programs and involve it in foreign policy controversies and undertakings better left to the State Department and the intelligence agencies. (1999: 26)

USAID and its staff members faced ethical questions and double binds regarding the extent to which the agency should engage in the slippery, unpredictable realm of political development assistance in the context of changes in its own institutional paradigm. Providing aid to victims of human rights abuses was even more troubling, despite the way it could be framed according to conventional forms of humanitarian assistance or development. Thus the Rehab Program faced challenges negotiating the morally ambiguous external and internal politics of the ADF procurement structure and its major donor, USAID, while simultaneously working toward establishing a sustainable program to assist "victims of organized violence" in Haiti.

These structural tensions were not the only ones that contributed to the backlash against ADF, the Human Rights Fund, and the Rehabilitation Program. While tracing the allegation that there were no longer victims in Haiti, further evidence of malevolent forms of bureaucraft emerged that provided additional causes for ADF's misfortunes in the U.S. domain of political development assistance. Whereas USAID headquarters considered the Rehab Program a success, Mission Director Forbes told ADF president Michael Miller that the USAID/Haiti JDG office staff members had not actually chronicled HRF's progress and successes. In fact, USAID/Haiti staff members had reported that HRF was recalcitrant and uncooperative and had failed to implement USAID's desired results packages. Thus the refusal to create knowledge and to use bureaucratic procedures and technologies to document "truth" was one means to limit or withhold access to resources in the compassion economy. Furthermore, at the same time that HRF's work was depicted as successful to Congress, USAID/Haiti accused the Fund of being too closely aligned with Haitians and of being a "Lavalas political organization." Forbes also revealed to Miller that Georges Duval, the former ADF chief of party who had mutinied with the ASOSYE staff to MSI and who had hired her husband as a consultant, told her that the HRF staff members were uncooperative with his program and staff and declined to participate in joint activities. From my observation of the two projects' activities from 1997 to 1999, such an allegation is difficult to support. Nonetheless, this negative portrayal of HRF's performance provided justification for reconsidering ADF's cooperative agreement with USAID. In this respect, Duval's actions, if true, are another sign of bureaucraft. There is another indication of these processes: when I spoke with Hunter about the fate of HRF and its Rehab Program, he affirmed that Miller should have known that he was not going to get any more funding in the short term, given the negative sentiment against Miller and the ADF institution in the federally funded aid apparatus. These statements confirm how accusations, blame, and information control were forms of bureaucraft used in the competitive business of political development assistance to influence the distribution of aid resources. Such practices paralleled the treachery and competition in the victim assistance apparatus and in local communities as aid developed its social life.

Thus a little more than a year after the closing of the Rehab Program, the Human Rights Fund also ceased to function. Although its services never resumed, in 2003, during the period of unrest that preceded President Aristide's second controversial ouster—one fomented as much by international nonintervention as by direct action—USAID funded a new victim assistance program within another institutional procurement structure like ADF. Dr. Thomas eventually became the chief of party of this institution, and former ADF staff members joined her.

CHAPTER 7

The Tyranny of the Gift

The practices and accusations of bureaucraft, like those of witchcraft, reflect moral contests about identity, sociopolitical power, and the disparate distribution and consumption of economic resources, especially under conditions of ensekirite. They also demonstrate the "irrationalities" that remain embedded in bureaucratic practices. Moral disputes about power continue to be regulated in informal, personal ways, even as they arise within institutions that promote efficient, transparent, and productive technologies of political and social engineering. Thus bureaucraft discourses and practices are means by which actors operating in the compassion economy articulate ambivalences about institutional and individual identities and interventions. While bureaucraft could be restrictive and even destructive—especially when deployed in retributive fashion in response to perceptions of illicit or unjust accumulation of resources—it could also be productive through the use of professional technologies that transformed trauma into portfolios, thereby generating multiple forms of capital for both aid givers and aid receivers. The continuum of bureaucraft discourses and practices was evident at multiple levels, whether at the level of privately funded grassroots organizations, the bilateral domain of U.S. political development assistance, or the international sphere, which included the multilateral U.N. and its International Civilian Mission.

As I have described in this book, the processes by which Haitian suffering was devalued, revalued, and once again devalued stemmed

cycle

[handwritten margin notes: bureaucraft in aid apparatus v. political economy of trauma]

from the articulations between bureaucraft in the aid apparatus and the political economy of trauma. The contradictory positions regarding the worth of Haitian trauma portfolios recalls Appadurai's discussion of how the value of things can be unstable in the course of their social lives. Initially, the trauma portfolios of Haitian victims became a commodity whereby USAID/Washington demonstrated to the U.S. Congress its accountability and competence in promoting democracy and human rights abroad. However, when such evidence was no longer needed or had the potential to be harmful, USAID/Haiti devalued this Haitian currency, rendering the commodified suffering generic once again. Indeed, one of the rumors that circulated about why the Rehab Program had not been renewed was that the continued presence of Haitian viktim would be a potential point of tension for the Democrats in the 2000 presidential elections. The perceived success or failure of the U.S. mission to restore democracy and to support Haiti's "transition"—and the billions of dollars spent directly or indirectly to facilitate this mission—would certainly be issues for debate.

Other general problems that these cycles of valuation reflected were conflicts in both the governmental and nongovernmental aid apparatus regarding how to manage the "unforeseen circumstances" that confront donors, their development partners, and "local" staff in implementing the programs that their "customers" desire. When faced with threats to the immediate, efficient, verifiable, and demonstrable success of aid programs, grantors may prefer to suspend activities rather than risk their security or make long-term commitments to assist those who resist their development strategies in any way.

[handwritten margin note: Competitive human]

Despite intentions of "doing good," humanitarian and development aid may only be able to apply a superficial bandage to psychosocial wounds that are deep and that recur from time to time. In no small part, an indisputable fact was that conflicts over scarce humanitarian and development aid pitted community members against one another in Haiti and impeded the success of these interventions. This was the case both in the donor community and as aid trickled down to various actors in local communities during the course of its social life. The overt and covert grant economies that I have described flowed from international and national governmental and nongovernmental donors to local actors in Haiti. These transactions contributed to the proliferation of occult economies of terror *and* compassion within the political economy of trauma. The complex cycles described in this book highlight the uncertainties, ambiguities, and perils facing aid actors who work in the interstitial spaces between these terror and compassion economies. The disastrous events leading to the termination of the Rehabilitation Program occurred at the nexus of unintended bureaucratic failures but also covert and overt malevolent acts. What lessons can we take from this ethnography?

In many respects, the disputes described here concerned Haiti's sovereignty and the right to administer its own affairs. Interventions in Haiti have ranged from covert interference undermining the state to overt intercession to heal its beleaguered citizens. Many of the institutional interveners implementing such work are NGOs of varied political perspectives. NGOs operate at the interstices of governments and their citizenry. They are not easily characterized as international, national, or local in origin, especially given the diverse individuals in their employ. The ambiguous, liminal position of these institutions and actors provides both flexibility and insecurity when working in a "host" country or challenging the excesses of a state. Their work may be misrepresented and easily misunderstood both inside and outside the aid apparatus. Humanitarian and development assistance, furthermore, remains a contested domain, in which patrons and clients clash at the institutional and interpersonal levels.

More generally, institutions operating in the aid apparatus in Haiti could have done more to coordinate their resources to meet their clients' needs in a more efficient and transparent manner while preserving compassion. For example, at the programmatic level the victim assistance services might have been more successful had the Human Rights Fund Rehabilitation Program been able to provide limited food security along with its other comprehensive services. Perhaps other steps could have been taken to assuage the growing frustrations viktim directed at those who intended to "do good," despite many institutional constraints. Some problems may have been inevitable because of the Human Rights Fund's liminal position between viktim, the aid apparatus, and the Haitian and U.S. governments. The Fund became a surrogate against which long-standing grievances and frustrations over disempowerment were leveled.

Agencies and agents that promote postconflict transitions to states of democracy, rule of law, and security must also consider carefully how to address the psychosocial routines of rupture that may underlie complex histories of violence and cultures of ensekirite. One could interpret the circulation of rumors and gossip that escalated into threats and thwarted

violence as a form of cultural pathology or as the reenactment of psychosocial trauma. Indeed, as it evolved over time with the overt and covert
support of many actors within and without Haiti, the terror apparatus
did much to undermine any sense of ontological security in the nation.
At the same time the specter of the Haitian past always hovered over the
terror apparatus, which evolved along a path that was historically contingent as much as it was culturally shaped. However, such a perspective
does not mean rationalizing interpersonal and collective ruptures in the
social fabric by privileging discourses of structural violence over those
of individual agency and responsibility for injustice. The Duvalier dictatorship was explicit in promoting state fetishism by way of privatized
necropolitics. The makout apparatus disciplined the nation not only
through sovereign forms of violence but also through the manipulation
of religious power and moral norms. As Trouillot reminds us, a good
Duvalierist was prepared to sacrifice his own mother. Such ritualistic
killings were directed toward the Haitian body and "were so many sacrificial offerings, confirming the permanence of power, a reminder to the
people of their smallness in regard to the state, a reminder to the executioners of the omnipotence of their chief" (Trouillot 1990: 169). The
terror apparatus employed a literal, occult economy with roots in the
historical political economy of extraction. The effects of terror produced
a population whose cheap, docile labor could be alienated, appropriated,
and circulated in the export assembly sector.

Determining effective approaches to promoting democracy in fragile or failed states does not mean minimizing the way individuals can
enact sovereign power through violence, even as such acts may have
been ordered to confirm the authority of predatory regimes or may have
historical and cultural roots in long-embedded structural inequalities.
The relationship between extraction, necropolitics, and state security
was most visible during the 1991–94 coup years. Duvalierist modes of
sacrificial torture were deployed once again in order to confer legitimacy on the de facto regime and to increase the power or fecundity of
the individual rapist, murderer, or torturer. But the manner in which
these acts were perpetrated—styles of violation that enacted the worst
abuses and humiliations from the period of plantation slavery—under-
lines the extent to which the traumatic legacy of the past remains a
specter riding the tèt of the Haitian social imaginary. Is the resurgence of
these forms of violent repression a form of *dominasyon* by a collective
"ghost" (Gordon 1997) or zonbi yet to be mourned properly? Are these
necropolitical forms of torture merely aspects of a global repertoire of

violent methods for repressing the population? How does one rehabilitate this past?

Postconflict assistance is one means by which to aid nations seeking
to transform predatory polities. As I have argued in this book, the politics embedded in such aid can produce unintended consequences that
exacerbate existing social, economic, and political cleavages. Postconflict development efforts must also confront the legacy of prior interventions—whether overt or covert, military or humanitarian—as they
seek to craft new policies and practices at the international, national,
and local levels. Interventions across and within national borders can
both challenge and support the authority and security of the state, as
well as the security of other institutions, organizations, and individuals.
However, the activity of intervention is rarely undertaken without some
measure of self-interest on the part of the actor, whether that actor is an
individual agent, an agency, or a government.

In order for such interventions to occur, a condition of need or a
particular "crisis" must be recognized that precipitates action. Nongovernmental actors mobilized scandal publicity, rumor, and accusations to
condemn more powerful governmental actors' perceived indifference
to Haiti and Haitians' plight. These actors circulated horrific stories
about torture, trauma, and truth to generate action. The dissemination of traumatic images and narratives through multiple media ultimately sparked interventions to transform suffering. The humanitarian
and development actors responding to such conditions viewed their
target populations as general clients needing assistance. The bureaucratic technologies that accompanied these interventions transformed
the raw experience of misery through many forms of labor, whether
implemented by grassroots, bilateral, or international actors. The product or package that was produced became a type of "extracted" power,
the trauma portfolio. When collected, these portfolios were circulated,
traded, and valued but ultimately devalued once again, like the currencies of many underdeveloped nations.

Such generalizing tactics erase the complexity of local moral worlds.
Viktim learned that benevolent aid is temporary, fleeting, and myopic,
and so they competed with one another to gain access to these finite
flows. They transformed, performed, and appropriated their own suffering in order to forestall the ravages of ensekirite. Victims' competition
for resources in local communities paralleled, and perhaps mirrored,
similar conflicts over resources and political power within the national
and international aid apparatus. These actors purportedly desired to

rehabilitate Haiti and its citizens, but bureaucraft within the aid apparatus impeded this goal. The practices of graft and the occult economies
that humanitarian and development aid generated within and without
the aid apparatus paralleled historical transnational practices of exploitation, extraction, and consumption in the global political economy.

As I have demonstrated, analyses of terror and compassion must
examine what motivates actors who are embedded in complex fields of
power relations to act in malevolent *or* benevolent ways, whether at the
individual or institutional level. In this respect analyses of Haitian realities that would posit only a structural determinant for the ensekirite of
everyday life negate the very real ways in which individuals and groups
may strategize to manipulate and to resist international and national
policies. Such practices are also means to bolster personal statuses, identities, and subject positions. Haitian "victims" act despite the broader
constraints of trenchant and enduring structural inequalities.

Terror economies and compassion economies, while opposed in
intent, are linked through economies of scarcity that engender political
and economic competition and strife. The U.S. government has been
but one overt and covert actor in this political economy of trauma. Its
agencies may act at cross-purposes, fomenting the endless circulation of
resources between terror and compassion economies that may generate further violence among recipients of such aid. The United Nations,
Canada, France, Taiwan, Japan, and other nations intervened in Haiti,
as did a plethora of institutions in the aid apparatus. These actors are
engaged in other theaters of conflict and humanitarian crisis throughout
the globe and will likely intervene to promote postconflict development
in Iraq, Afghanistan, Sudan, Palestine, and other sites of insecurity in
the future. They propose models of political and economic development
to rehabilitate governments and civilians that are similar to those that
have failed in Haiti.

Aid institutions such as the America's Development Foundation, and
the programs they implement in postconflict settings, emerge at the nexus
of economies of terror and compassion, in the space between gift and
commodity exchanges. They can never be divorced from the political-
economic relationships between secure and insecure states and from the
occult histories of repression and domination that the global capitalist
economy generates. Nor should these institutions be immune from critique for their tendency to inadvertently reproduce or generate inequalities
between governments, nations, and the people they serve in the process
of providing scarce aid. While these agents and agencies may inculcate

new political subjectivities based on secular theodicies of human rights, democracy, women's rights, law, and psychiatry, the overarching insecurities within their terrains of operation may also generate accusations of witchcraft, sorcery, and bureaucraft in the social life of aid.

In thinking through the broader grant economy of which humanitarian and development aid is a part and the ways that this economy evokes moral ambivalences for the donors and recipients within it, it is useful to recall Maurice Godelier's discussion of the "tyranny of the gift":

> Giving . . . seems to establish a difference and an inequality of status
> between donor and recipient, which can in certain instances become a
> hierarchy: if this hierarchy already exists, the gift expresses and legitimizes
> it. Two opposite movements are thus contained in a single act. The gift
> decreases the distance between the protagonists because it is a form of
> sharing, and it increases the social distance between them because one is
> now indebted to the other. . . . It can be, simultaneously or successively, an
> act of generosity or of violence; in the latter case, however, the violence is
> disguised as a disinterested gesture, since it is committed by means of and
> in the form of sharing. (1999: 12)

The provision of "aid" encodes the power inequalities between giver and receiver, whether at the individual, institutional, or governmental level. As currently structured, the U.S. federal grant economy and its bureaucratic ordering techniques leave few other possibilities for collaboration across boundaries between giver and receiver, especially when aid is filtered through the narrow lens of recognition of the other based on injury or vulnerable status. Furthermore, donors are often embedded in contested domains of power that make altruism and the disinterested gift a fiction.

In "The Trauma of Insignificance," the concluding chapter of a book that analyzes the work of the Haitian intellectual and political historian Dantès Bellegarde (1877–1966), Patrick Bellegarde-Smith makes the following observation about the relationship between social policy and foreign relations for small underdeveloped states:

> Under prevailing conditions, the policies of small states become defensive
> measures even, in a certain sense, when they pass to the offensive. The
> politics of small states are thus often a reflection of international condi-
> tions acting as vectors for domestic political situations. This relationship
> advances the feeling of powerlessness of the small state, since the crucial
> economic and financial decisions affecting it are made abroad in a decreas-
> ing number of loci of power. These traumata of insignificance affect indi-
> viduals and states alike. (1985: 176)

Bellegarde-Smith points to a reality that many nations and their citizens face as they contemplate or are forced to make the "transition" to forms of governance that are contested domestically and internationally. These states of insecurity receive selective recognition internationally. In Bellegarde-Smith's formulation, the trajectory of these uncertainties moves from the international level and trickles down to the domestic realms of sociality in small states.

Some scholars have even argued that the contemporary relationship between governments and organizations in the secure states of the "North" and the insecure states of the "South" is predicated on separation, containment, and management of disorder (e.g., Duffield 2001). According to these observers, the presumed order, rationality, and economic productivity in economic "centers" depend on corraling and channeling the reputed insecurity, irrationality, and economic stagnation in "peripheral" nations. Although I share many of these concerns about a north-south divide, I also believe that the mechanisms of containment and control are subtly reinforced by overt and covert interventions.

Moreover, I argue, the relationships between so-called stable and transitional nations are also structured through flows of humanitarian and development assistance. The aid apparatus distributes humanitarian and development assistance to the periphery, representing the benevolent face of an unequal global political economy. As Michael Fischer (2008: 262) suggests, "There is a dovetailing between first world governments' insistence [that] security [is] now more endangered by underdevelopment than by interstate conflict; and humanitarian aid organizations' shift to conflict resolution, social reconstruction, and transformation of societies into not just liberal economic market relations but also democratic, pluralistic, political institutions." It is in the context of these contested historical inequalities that contemporary military and humanitarian interventions and postconflict development must be evaluated.

As I have demonstrated in this book, however, theories of hegemonic, "neocolonial" relationships between large and small states appear too simple, especially in this moment of globalizing neomodernity. Rather, the fragility or failed character of states such as Haiti contributes to the government acting as a broker of privatized or imported resources for its vulnerable populations in ways that can range from predatory to compassionate. The state as broker is a phenomenon that also encodes and reproduces structural inequalities as stronger states employ sovereign political and economic vehicles to extract resources from those that are weak and weak states broker gifts and grants of aid for citizens that they cannot and may never be able to provide. As ongoing international debates on security attest, Haiti's challenges at times prefigure what the world at large is facing: manifest anxieties over political, economic, social, and ontological insecurity. Ensekirite can no longer be fixed in time and space.

Notes

INTRODUCTION

1. Conférence des Religieux Haïtiens 1990, cited in Rey and Stepick 2009.

2. *Lavalas* is a Haitian Creole term meaning "flood" that evokes biblical images of the deluge that cleansed the world of sin and evil. As used by pro-democracy activists, lavalas symbolized a movement to purge Haiti of the violence and exploitation (both domestic and foreign) that flourished during the Duvalier dictatorships. See Ives 1995: 44.

3. Throughout this book the contested meaning of concepts such as democracy, rule of law, justice, human rights, governmental accountability, and socioeconomic equality should be understood as implicit with each usage.

4. See Larry Rohter, "Mission to Haiti: Haiti's Attaches: Deadly Heirs to the Tontons Macoute," *New York Times,* October 4, 1994. http://query.nytimes.com/gst/fullpage.html?res = 9A0CE0DA143DF937A35753C1A962958260. Accessed February 2009.

5. In this book names of individuals are pseudonyms, except for when they are recognized public figures. In some cases I assured public figures of anonymity as a prerequisite to obtaining an interview and therefore use pseudonyms for these individuals and slightly alter identifying details in my descriptions of them. Throughout this text there are occasions when individuals are referred to with varying degrees of formality. The decision to refer to clients, colleagues, or other informants informally, or by first name only, is not intended to discount the knowledge and expertise that these persons possess. Rather, such usages reflect the sociopolitical and therapeutic dynamics of our encounters. I have chosen not to disguise the identities or locations of all the institutions in which

I worked, recognizing that my study represents a slice of their histories. If the institutions still exist, many of their staff members have moved on to other opportunities.

6. Jean Jackson, pers. com. See, e.g., Teresa P.R. Caldeira, *City of Walls: Crime, Segregation, and Citizenship in São Paulo* (Berkeley: University of California Press, 2000).

7. The embargo increased costs of basic goods and had a disproportionately negative effect on the poor. For a description of this period, see Gibbons 1999; Ives 1994; National Labor Committee 1994.

8. The term *dechoukaj* is derived from traditional, agricultural language. It denotes the complete uprooting of a tree in order to prevent future growth.

9. The research for this book is based on my dissertation; see James 2003.

10. For historical background on the revolutionary and immediate postcolonial period, see Bell 2007; Blackburn 1988; Dubois 2004; Fick 1990; Geggus 2002; Ghachem forthcoming; James 1989 [1963]; Nicholls 1996.

11. These rates vary according to region and other factors: at a May 2002 talk at the Boston-based Management Sciences for Health (MSH), Dr. Georges Dubuche, Reproductive Health and HIV/AIDS Advisor for the MSH/HS-2004 project, presented a rate as high as 13 percent in the Northwest Department (based on 1998 estimates).

12. International assistance was initially suspended in spring 1997 in protest against alleged irregularities in the April parliamentary elections; the disputed seats were put up for reelection in May 2000 in order to resolve the crisis in the government. On Aristide's reelection, opposition party leaders contested the results and accused Aristide's Lavalas Family party of voter intimidation. Many claim that the United States supported the opposition groups by channeling funds through the International Republican Institute. See Walt Bogdanich and Jenny Nordberg, "Mixed U.S. Signals Helped Tilt Haiti toward Chaos," *New York Times,* January 29, 2006, www.nytimes.com/2006/01/29/international/americas/29haiti.html?_r = 1&oref = slogin&pagewanted = print; last accessed January 12, 2009.

13. In 1948 the U.S. Congress approved what became known as the Marshall Plan. By 1952 the joint American-European endeavor had provided $13 billion to sixteen countries. In these countries the combined GNP increased by 30 percent, and industrial production increased 40 percent beyond prewar levels. The Marshall Plan was regarded as a successful intervention that saved desperate European nations and citizens from further suffering in the aftermath of conflict. See U.S. Department of State, Bureau of International Information Programs, *The Marshall Plan: Rebuilding Europe* (n.d.), http://usinfo.state.gov; last accessed October 2008.

14. See Michael J. Hogan, "Blueprint for Recovery," http://usa.usembassy.de/etexts/marshall/pam-blu.htm; last accessed March 2009.

15. See also Comaroff and Comaroff's vision of a "neomodernist anthropology," one that asserts "faith that the human world, post-anything and -everything, remains the product of discernible social and cultural processes. . . . It is in this sense that we affirm, by prefix and predilection, our commitment to *neo*modern anthropology" (1992: xi).

16. See Lev. 6:13: "A perpetual fire shall be kept burning on the altar; it shall not go out," referring to ongoing rituals of sacrifice or atonement through burnt offerings to make amends for past wrongs or to restore social ruptures.

17. See http://humanterrainsystem.army.mil/default.htm and the recent debate on anthropologists working with national security agencies and in the U.S. armed forces "Human Terrain Systems" in the wars in Iraq and Afghanistan. See also Network of Concerned Anthropologists, *The Counter-Counterinsurgency Manual* (Chicago: Prickly Paradigm Press, 2009).

18. In Haitian Creole nouns can be both singular and plural. Definite or indefinite status, singularity, and plurality are designated by modifiers in speech. Although other anthropologists have adopted the convention of adding an *s* to indicate the plural form of the noun (see Smith 2001), I have chosen not to do so here.

19. The Trager® Approach is a method of "somatic therapy, movement re-education and rehabilitation" (Juhan 1998) that was developed by Milton Trager in the late 1930s. The Trager work combines gentle manipulation of the physical body of the client while he or she lies on a massage table, as well as exercises called "mentastics" that assist the client to recognize and release long-held patterns of tension in the body. See www.trager.com.

20. At the suggestion of the organizations that funded my Ph.D. research, I also received training to use the Composite International Diagnostic Interview (CIDI), which enabled me to familiarize myself further with the categorization of psychiatric disorders in the DSM-IV (the fourth revision of the *Diagnostic and Statistical Manual of the American Psychiatric Association*) and the ICD-10 Classification of Mental and Behavioural Disorders of the World Health Organization. Ultimately, I did not use the CIDI instrument in my ethnographic work.

21. See the recent analyses of Daniels, Kettl, and Kunreuther 2006; and the collection of essays on the topic "The Impact of the Hurricanes of 2005 on New Orleans and the Gulf Coast of the United States," *American Anthropologist* 108, no. 4 (December 2006): 637–813.

22. Mission Civile Internationale en Haïti, OEA/ONU, the UN/OAS International Civilian Mission.

23. President Aristide instituted the commission on his restoration to office, but as I discuss later in this book, it was largely considered a failure.

24. In July 2006, however, the siyon failed to provide sanctuary: more than twenty men, women, and children who were praying at the church were massacred when caught in the crossfire of rival gangs.

CHAPTER ONE

1. See, e.g., Amnesty International, "Don't Turn Your Back on Girls: Sexual Violence against Girls in Haiti," report, Amnesty International, London, 2008.

2. As used here, the term *gender* refers to the social meanings or stereotypes ascribed to the differences between the biological sexes that "signif[y] relationships of power" (Scott 1999: 42). Gender ideals reflect changing cultural symbols, laws and morals, ideas of kinship, economic practices, politics, and religious beliefs, as well as understandings of the body.

3. In cases of domestic violence and marital rape, such distinctions are even more difficult to disentangle but are no less important to women's rights activists seeking to challenge the distinctions between interpersonal violations and human rights violations, whether in times of relative peace or conflict. See Plesset 2006 for a nuanced discussion of law and intimate partner violence in Italy.

4. Late-twentieth-century discourses about sexual violence continued to examine whether rape is "natural" or "cultural." Evolutionary psychologists and biological anthropologists have suggested that the propensity to rape arises from innate male drives or aggression rather than from learned behavior (Thornhill and Palmer 2000; Wrangham and Peterson 1996). For a refutation of arguments like these, see Stefan Helmreich and Heather Paxson, "Sex on the Brain: A Natural History of Rape and the Dubious History of Evolutionary Psychology," in Why America's Top Pundits Are Wrong: Anthropologists Talk Back, ed. Catherine Besteman and Hugh Gusterson (Berkeley: University of California Press, 2005), 180–205.

5. Foucault builds his poststructuralist conception of the "deployment of sexuality" on Claude Lévi-Strauss's structuralist theory of alliances contained in The Elementary Structures of Kinship (1969 [1949]). In the Elementary Structures, Lévi-Strauss describes women as objects of exchange or value that are "communicated" between men, kinship networks, and other small-scale collective social groups. He notes, however, that such exchanges are not free from desire and even violent desire, nor are women mere "signs," as they are depicted both as "the object of personal desire, thus exciting sexual and proprietorial instincts; and . . . as the subject of the desire of others, and seen as such, i.e., as the means of binding others through alliance with them" (496). In depicting women as communicated signs and objects of desire, Lévi-Strauss posits a political theory of gender and sexuality that can be extended to contexts in which women have become explicit focuses of national struggles for sovereignty and independence.

6. In subsequent chapters I discuss the infamous FRAPH and FAD'H documents that were seized during Operation Uphold Democracy by U.S. armed forces. It is suspected that such documents are evidence of how the terror apparatus recorded its violent practices through photography, audio- and videocassettes, and written materials. These documents may include personnel rosters, budgets, and other means by which the apparatus could be "audited."

7. Arjun Appadurai (1996) presents the concept of mobile sovereignties to signal the global movement of immigrants and refugees, the legal and illegal transnational flow of goods and services, the spread of disease across boundaries, the circulation of weapons, and the challenges such distributions pose to the nation-state. In his analysis, territoriality, while crucial for the integrity of the nation-state, is no longer the guarantor of "markets, livelihoods, identities, and histories" (49)—what some might call the foundations of security. For an application of this concept to the military-humanitarian apparatus, see Pandolfi's (2003) notion of "migrant sovereignties."

8. In the United States Haitians were held for processing for indefinite periods in the Krome Detention Center in Miami and other centers like it (Nachman 1993). They were also detained at the U.S. naval installation at Guantánamo

Bay, Cuba, that has attained notoriety for its imprisonment of suspected enemy combatants after September 11, 2001 (Farmer 2003).

9. In early 1992, as the coup regime accelerated its repression and thousands more boat people left Haiti seeking safety, the United States implemented an "in-country" processing strategy. Some Haitians attained asylum status; however, the majority were denied asylum before leaving Haiti. See HRW/A, NCHR, and JRS/USA 1993.

10. The Convention on the Prevention and Punishment of the Crime of Genocide entered into force January 12, 1951. The Convention defines genocide as

> any number of acts committed with the intent to destroy, in whole or in part, a national, ethnic, racial or religious group: killing members of the group; causing serious bodily or mental harm to members of the group; deliberately inflicting on the group conditions of life calculated to bring about its physical destruction in whole or in part; imposing measures intended to prevent births within the group, and forcibly transferring children of the group to another group.

11. See, e.g., Elaine Sciolino, "Embassy in Haiti Doubts Aristide's Rights Reports," *New York Times,* May 9, 1994.

12. The pattern of statement, accusation, and counteraccusation between the aid apparatus, pro-Aristide activists, the media, and U.S. government officials also resembles what Paul Farmer calls a "flow of speculation" (1992: 224). Farmer observed a similar kind of speculative economy in the context of accusations that Haiti and Haitians are the source of the AIDS crisis (208–28).

13. For a description of the conditions under which laborers worked, see Lynn M. Morgan's *Community Participation in Health: The Politics of Primary Care in Costa Rica* (Cambridge: Cambridge University Press, 1993).

14. See Drake 1991: 24–25. Drake cites Bruce J. Calder, *The Impact of Intervention: The Dominican Republic during the U.S. Occupation of 1916–1924* (Austin: University of Texas Press, 1984), 249.

15. See Trouillot 1990: 135–52 for a description of the electoral politics employed by Duvalier to ensure his victory.

16. In Haitian Creole the words *lapè, lapen,* and *lape* are pronounced similarly, thus *lapè* can also sound like the words for "peace" and "bread." While there are stories regarding the consumption of the flesh of the dead in the Vodou tradition, I cannot confirm whether the phrase "lapè simityè" suggests another double entendre regarding the literal consumption of others by the makout apparatus.

17. Trouillot cites Albert D. Chassagne, *Bain de sang en Haïti: Les macoutes opèrent à Jérémie en 1964,* 2nd ed. (New York: Cohen Offset Printing, 1977).

18. In the context of Vodou, the term signifies the central post through which the *lwa* (spirits) manifest in the material world in the *peristil* (the temple in which Vodou rituals take place).

19. See Maternowska 2006: chap. 3 for an overview of contemporary ideologies of gender and sex in Haiti, sexual practices and the conjugal household, and the way that political economy influenced the household during the period of de facto rule.

20. Cited in Rey 1999: 84.

Notes to Pages 65–79

21. Liberation theology is a movement in the Catholic Church that interprets theology from the perspective of the oppressed, a "preferential option for the poor." Christian doctrine is viewed as having revolutionary potential to liberate the poor, to eradicate social disparities, and to promote human rights. Liberation theology is sometimes controversial for its affinity with Marxism, especially in Latin America.

22. For more details on the reciprocal escalation of violence between Haitian state and nation and the international influence on Jean-Claude's departure from Haiti, see Farmer 1994: 105–25; Wilentz 1989: 15–95; Barthélemy 1992; NCHR and Americas Watch 1986.

23. For the role of U.S. foreign policy in the 1990 elections and more general information on the political climate before the elections, see NCHR and Americas Watch 1990: 65–71.

24. "Marronage" refers to a strategy of resistance employed during the colonial period in which slaves escaped plantations to form hidden communities in the mountains and in some urban areas of Haiti. From these hidden "cells" they organized guerrilla attacks on the plantations (see Laguerre 1989). During my fieldwork the term was used frequently to signify flight from persecution.

25. Titanyen is a small village in the north of Port-au-Prince that houses a "cemetery"—a mass grave site where the tonton makout dumped their victims under the Duvaliers—and that was used by the death squads of the coup regime. See Farmer 1994: 5, 319; Wilentz 1989: 101.

26. The public "spectacle" of death in Haiti is reminiscent of *la violencia* in Guatemala (Warren 1993: 30–31).

27. See Arnove 1995.

28. See McAlister 2002 for a description of these bands and the way in which they are embedded in local politics.

29. "Testimony, Woman #2," photocopy, n.d.

30. Haitian Platform of Human Rights Organizations, *Haiti: Resistance & Democracy*, Information Bulletin, Port-au-Prince, vol. 2, no. 36 (5/10/94–5/20/94): 1–3.

31. Index of Affidavits, Statements and Testimonies, provided to me from the International Liaison Office for President Jean-Bertrand Aristide, n.d., p. 4.

32. Beverly Bell, "Memorandum regarding rape and violence against women in Haiti," International Liaison Office for President Jean-Bertrand Aristide, June 30, 1994.

33. The *djak* is a form of torture in which the victim—usually male—is suspended in the air from a long pole *(baton)* by the knees; the arms are wrapped underneath the bar but then lashed around the knees, forcing a fetal position around the baton that leaves buttocks exposed. Victims are then beaten on the buttocks and sacrum, often hundreds of times.

34. See Irene Léon, "Haitian Rape Victims Take Action," *Caribbean Women: Issues and Insights* [Newsletter of the Caribbean Association for Feminist Research and Action] 9, no. 1 (January–June 1995): 21. See also Minnesota Advocates for Human Rights, *Another Violence against Women: The Lack of Accountability in Haiti* (Minneapolis: Minnesota Advocates for Human Rights, December 1995), 9.

CHAPTER TWO

1. See Christine J. Walley's account of the conflicting notions of "community" between international and national actors in chapter 3 of *Rough Waters: Nature and Development in an East African Marine Park* (Princeton, NJ: Princeton University Press, 2004).

2. In the Indian transplant industry, competing interlocutors employed "purgatorial ethics" (Cohen 1999; Rabinow 1999)—an ethics of alarm about the commodification of bodily tissue and organs—to mobilize public sentiment against such transactions. For recent analyses of the contemporary commodification of bodies, see also Scheper-Hughes and Wacquant 2002.

3. These documents have since been returned to Haiti; however, they have not been made public.

4. This section presents a limited sample of international, national, and local organizations, projects, and individuals assisting victims of violence in Haiti at the time of my research. There were many others agencies and agents in the aid assemblage that gave both formal and informal support to viktim, especially foreign and domestic religious organizations providing both "charity" and "development" aid. The actors described here were the ones I most frequently encountered while tracking the international, national, and "local" responses to victims in Haiti.

5. See, e.g., Ashforth 2005; Bornstein 2005; Comaroff and Comaroff 1999, 2003; Dolan 2002; Geschiere 1997; Moore and Sanders 2001; Stewart and Strathern 2004; Taussig 1980; West 2005; West and Sanders 2003.

6. See Merry 2006 and Riles 2000 for descriptions of networks of NGOs that promoted women's rights and human rights in other international contexts.

7. See www.un.org/rights/micivih/rapports/news.htm. Accessed October 2007.

8. See the instructions for MICIVIH observers at www.un.org/rights/micivih/rapports/manuel.htm. Accessed February 2009.

9. See "Haiti: A Start, at Least," *Economist,* February 20, 1993, 40.

10. See Hopgood 2006 for an analysis of race, ethnic, and gender disparities within Amnesty International. There are distinctions between individuals hired on the U.N. versus the OAS side of the Mission, but I do not know at this point the extent to which perquisites and status of the respective employees varied.

11. In terms of salary alone, the *Economist* reported that MICIVIH observers earned U.S.$6,000 a month (February 20, 1993, 40).

12. "M'ap viv," in Haitian Creole means literally "I am living/surviving."

13. M'AP VIV received international financing from the Quebecois Association for International Assistance (AQOCI), a consortium of 52 international aid organizations, and from Oxfam-Québec, MDM, the International Committee of the Red Cross (Le Comité Internationale de la Croix Rouge), Amnesty International–Montréal, and Save the Children–Canada (Aide à l'Enfance Canada). M'AP VIV received local funding and support from MICIVIH, the Soros Foundation's Open Society Institute–Haiti (La Fondation Connaissance et Liberté, FOCAL), and the Haitian Conference of the Faithful (La Conférence Haïtienne des Religieux et des Religieuses, CHR), among other institutions.

14. Nathan's approach to ethnopsychiatry and his work with refugee populations are controversial. See the dialogue between Didier Fassin and Tobie Nathan in *Genèses* 35 (June 1999): 146–71 and 38 (March 2000): 136–59.

15. The IRCT has elaborated a prescribed model of "rehabilitation" that it exports globally.

16. In 1995 the National Coalition for Haitian Refugees was renamed the National Coalition for Haitian Rights.

17. Interestingly, *relève* also connotes "changing of the guard."

18. On August 12, 2007, Pierre-Antoine Lovinsky was kidnapped after taking leave of a joint delegation of Canadian and American human rights activists. See www.amnestyusa.org/document.php?id = ENGAMR3600 32008&lang = e; last accessed February 2009. The responses to Lovinsky's disappearance have also been highly politicized. The Web site www.lovinsky.org/ (accessed February 2009) accuses HRW of paying insufficient attention to his disappearance in comparison to its attention to human rights violations in Latin America. The Web site also posted an editorial by Joe Emersberger of HaitiAnalysis.com that accuses HRW of failing to condemn U.S. military interventions abroad: "HRW has routinely ignored critics who have shown that it has increasingly become a tool of US imperialism."

19. In April 1994 alleged coup perpetrators massacred pro-democracy activists in the coastal Raboteau section of Gonaïves, northwest of Port-au-Prince. The BAI is a group of attorneys asked by the Government of Haiti to prepare the Raboteau trial in Gonaïves. The trial was one of the first prosecutions of these perpetrators.

20. The military had profited from the black market in oil and other contraband during the embargo period (Gibbons 1999: 13). The occult economies created during the coup period provided the financing for FRAPH, the "civil society organization" described in chapter 1 that terrorized the pro-democracy sector in Haiti (39).

21. The reporter Allan Nairn had uncovered the fact that both Constant and Michel François were on the CIA payroll and that FRAPH had received "assistance" from the U.S. Army during Operation Uphold Democracy. Apparently the U.S. Special Forces were instructed not to disarm FRAPH members but to view them as a "loyal opposition." Allan Nairn, "Haiti under the Gun," *Nation*, January 8–15, 1996, www.thirdworldtraveler.com/Foreign_Policy/HaitiJan96_Nairn.html; last accessed March 2009.

22. In Haitian Creole something that is *pirèd* is "harder," " more rigid," or "worse." The word can also mean "to endure" or "stand firm."

23. I discuss the type of partnerships between USAID and its contractors in chapter 4.

24. See www.adfusa.org/; last accessed March 2009.

25. GroupWatch, "America's Development Foundation," in *Profiles of U.S. Private Organizations and Churches*," http://rightweb.irc-online.org/gw/1576 .html; last accessed March 2009. GroupWatch cites USAID, Report of American Voluntary Agencies Engaged in Overseas Relief and Development Registered with the Agency for International Development, 1985–1986.

26. NRI is now known as the International Republican Institute (IRI).

27. GroupWatch cites Hemisphere Initiatives, Nicaraguan Election Update #2, "Foreign Funding of the Internal Opposition," October 16, 1989.

28. See www.adfusa.org/content/highlight/detail/645/; last accessed April 2009.

29. I discuss the ambiguities of his position below.

30. For an analysis of the early complicity of anthropology as a discipline in colonial projects, see Asad 1973; Fabian 2000. For discussions of ethics and the practice of anthropology, see Bourgois 1990; Goodale 2006; Scheper-Hughes 1995; Speed 2006.

31. See, e.g., Escobar 1995; Farmer 1992; Ferguson 1994; Fisher 1995; Gardner and Lewis 1996.

32. This proposal was one of a number that originated among former consultants and staff of the MICIVIH Medical Unit and Médecins du Monde. Among the most comprehensive of these early proposals was presented by Dr. Federico Allodi in collaboration with the Medical Unit for Amnesty International.

33. In the July 1993 Governors Island Accord, President Aristide had agreed to full amnesty for the coup leaders and their affiliates "within the framework of Article 147 of the Constitution of the Republic of Haiti, and 'implementation of other instruments which may be adopted by the Parliament.' Article 147 allows a presidential amnesty only for political matters 'as stipulated by law.' Thus, the amnesty would have covered the military's human rights violations only if Parliament defined those violations as 'political'" (Stotzky 1997: 33, citing Governors Island Accord par. 6). Because the de facto regime violated the accord with the *Harlan County* incident, the Haitian Parliament would not consider the fate of the coup apparatus until it was able to meet on October 7, 1994. Parliament gave Aristide the power to grant amnesty for political crimes but not for human rights violations (Stotzky 1997: 40, 119).

34. The guiding mandate of HRFII was as follows: "1. To support Haitians in their efforts to redress human rights abuses and provide assistance to victims, and 2. To contribute to the growth of a society based on nonviolent, democratic principles." Furthermore, "The specific objectives of the Fund are: a) to assist the victims of politically motivated violence and human rights abuse, and their families, by providing medical and trauma rehabilitation and lawyer referral services; b) to help prevent the recurrence of human rights abuses by the newly-deployed HNP; and c) to strengthen civil society institutions and initiatives, particularly in the areas of human rights monitoring, legal assistance, training and citizen involvement with the police in order to encourage a broad societal commitment to nonviolence and the rule of law and to create the local capacity required to realize such a commitment" (USAID 1998).

35. See the ADF 1997 memo, "Account of HRF's Contact with Time Magazine." No additional source information available.

CHAPTER THREE

1. The term *potomitan* also signifies the central post through which the lwa manifest in the material world in the *peristil* (the temple where Vodou rituals take place).

2. On plot, emplotment, and clinical narratives, see also Good 1995, 2001; and Mattingly 1998.

3. Fass (1988) estimated that in 1976, half of the Port-au-Prince population lived in one-story homes of varying levels of permanence. The population density was 600 persons per hectare, and one-third lived at a population density of more than 1,000 persons per hectare. Nearly 10 percent lived on the streets or slept on the doorsteps or "galleries" of homes because there was no room for each inhabitant (Fass 1988: 190). In 1976 the Saint Martin slum had a residential population density of 1,540 persons per hectare, which offered each resident approximately 1.2 square meters of living space within an average 5.1-square-meter household. At the time residential space in low-income areas in "Kingston, Panama, Bombay, Nairobi, Calcutta, and Hong Kong ranged from 0.6 to 2.7 square meters per adult" (192). Fass's calculations give an average household size of six. From my observations, the average home size in the Martissant bidonvil was approximately the same as the Saint Martin average but had an even greater number of residents.

4. In 2005 USAID provided funds to rebuild roads in Martissant that had been washed out during these and other tropical storms as part of its new Haiti Transition Initiative. See USAID/OTI (Office of Transition Initiatives), "From Dirt Road to Disarmament: The HTI Process at Work," May 2005, www.usaid .gov/our_work/cross-cutting_programs/transition_initiatives/country/haiti/ topic0505.html; last accessed March 2009.

5. When the U.S.-led MNF intervened in 1994, however, there was no systematic plan to disarm FAD'H, FRAPH, and other paramilitary groups. Instead, a voluntary "guns for cash" program was initiated, with minimal success. Nor was there a mandate for the MNF interveners to police Haiti directly. Instead, they were only to provide training and support to interim and civilian police forces. See Kathie Klarreich, "Haiti's Hidden Arms Are Worry as Cash-for-Guns Swap Starts," *Christian Science Monitor,* September 29, 1994, 1.

6. See Garry Pierre-Pierre, "As Haiti Embargo Tightens, Poor Children Get Hungrier," *New York Times,* July 3, 1994, http://query.nytimes.com/gst/ fullpage.html?sec=health&res=9E02E4D6103CF930A35754C0A962958260; last accessed January 2009.

7. See Kovats-Bernat 2006 on the plight of Haitian street children in Port-au-Prince. The author worked with orphans living in the vicinity of Portail Léogâne, the bus/taxi station area at the southwestern edge of Port-au-Prince, not far from the Bolosse section of town.

8. See www.trager.com. In this ethnography I cannot analyze the Approach's folk epistemology of embodiment; rather, I offer phenomenological observations from work with my clients, recognizing the cultural embeddedness of my biomedical understanding of anatomy and physiology.

9. I want to be cautious in the presentation of this material to avoid postulating a grand psychoanalytic theory of character analysis or of muscular armoring and affect, as has Wilhelm Reich (1991 [1945]).

10. Although none of my clients admitted to serving the spirits, the broad formulation of a sociocentric "self/body" (Becker 1991) that follows was commonly expressed regardless of their stated religious practice.

11. Brown (1979: 23) notes that "for the Vodou worshipper, each person is at the core of his or her being, a multiplicity of beings, a polymorphous entity and that it is only at the periphery of life, in areas less important to that person, that he or she adopts clearly definable, and consistent roles or modes of being."

12. For further discussions of how the expression of alternate selves through either spontaneous possession or multiple personality disorder can be viewed as creative presentations of self in everyday life, see also Antze 1996; Boddy 1988; Brown 1991; Lambek 1996.

13. Das (1997: 69–70) cites Wittgenstein's *The Blue and Brown Books* (London: Basil Blackwell, 1958): "In order to see that it is conceivable that one person should have pain in another person's body, one must examine what sorts of facts we call criteria for a pain being in a certain place. . . . Suppose I feel a pain which on the evidence of the pain alone, e.g. with closed eyes, I should call a pain in my left hand. Someone asks me to touch the painful spot with my right hand. I do so and looking around perceive that I am touching my neighbor's hand. . . .This would be pain *felt* in another's body."

14. I told her that I would try but that I couldn't promise this would happen.

15. Marie was not sure of the exact dates of her transitions, so I am estimating that she was in her late teens at this time, based on her choice of words to describe her age and date of birth *(demwazèl)*.

16. *Move san* (bad blood) is another illness caused by emotional distress that primarily affects women and can lead to *lèt gate* (spoiled milk) in nursing mothers. Farmer (1988a: 63) considers the "*move san/lèt gate* complex to be an illness caused by malignant emotions—anger born of interpersonal strife, shock, grief, chronic worry, and other affects perceived as potentially harmful." See Brodwin 1996 for additional analyses of embodiment and idioms of distress in Haiti.

17. I address selected highlights from three of these groups. A fourth had a therapeutic discourse based on Haitian traditional healing. The fifth had a psychological orientation. Both groups began late in 1998 and dwindled in attendance in early 1999. As I discuss in later chapters, ensekirite deepened after President Préval's January 11, 1999, dissolution of parliament and decision to rule by decree.

18. The FNCD was an umbrella organization of pro-democracy groups that aligned with the Lavalas coalition and elected Aristide president in December 1990.

19. I do not know if Yves received training and employment in the assembly sector or if he worked with independent artisans.

CHAPTER FOUR

1. The director did not explain the basis for these assertions. Chapter 5 explores the question of the authenticity of HRF clients' trauma portfolios.

2. See http://govinfo.library.unt.edu/npr/whoweare/appendixf.html; last accessed March 2009.

3. See http://govinfo.library.unt.edu/npr/library/nprrpt/annrpt/wrkcst94/create.html and http://govinfo.library.unt.edu/npr/library/status/sstories/aid3.htm; accessed March 2009.

4. In the FY1999 "Results Review Resource Request" (R4), designed in 1997, the following SOs were outlined for USAID/Haiti's 1999–2004 Strategic Plan: (1) sustainable increased income for the poor; (2) environmental degradation slowed; (3) achieved desired family size and health; (4) improved human capacity; and (5) more genuinely inclusive democratic governance attained.

5. I cannot discuss each intermediate result under each SO for Haiti; my discussion is limited to the way in which ADF/HRF attempted to complete certain intermediate results in its work.

6. For a general overview of the history of the Universal Declaration of Human Rights, the International Covenant on Civil and Political Rights, the International Covenant on Economic, Cultural and Social Rights, or the debates about their recognition and application in international law, see An-Na'im 1992; Donnelly 1989; Dunne and Wheeler 1999; Savic 1999; Shute and Hurley 1993; Steiner and Alston 2000.

7. Dr. David S. Jones, pers. com., December 5, 2007. For more information on ideas of charity and the "worthy" and "unworthy poor" in nineteenth-century hospitals, see Charles Rosenberg, *The Care of Strangers: The Rise of America's Hospital System* (New York: Basic Books, 1987); David Rosner, *A Once Charitable Enterprise: Hospitals and Health Care in Brooklyn and New York, 1885–1915* (New York: Cambridge University Press, 1982). For an analysis of discourses of indigence and malingering in mental hospitals, see Foucault 1988 [1965].

8. Foucault states: "The individual is no doubt the fictitious atom of an 'ideological' representation of society; but he is also a reality fabricated by this specific technology of power that I have called 'discipline'. We must cease once and for all to describe the effects of power in negative terms. . . . In fact, power produces; it produces reality; it produces domains of objects and rituals of truth. The individual and the knowledge that may be gained of him belong to this production" (1979: 194).

9. There are, of course, other possible countertransference reactions to working with survivors of egregious forms of violence, such as "rage, sadistic gratification, dread and horror, shame, viewing the survivor as a hero, and privileged voyeurism" (Vesti and Kastrup 1992: 356, citing Danieli 1984).

10. Michèle Pierre-Louis served as Haiti's prime minister from September 2008 until October 2009, when she was ousted because of alleged poor performance in promoting economic recovery in Haiti.

11. Camille Leblanc became minister of justice and public security in March 1999.

12. See also the complaints about the CNVJ in Human Rights Watch, "Haiti—Thirst for Justice: A Decade of Impunity in Haiti," vol. 8, no. 7B (September 1996).

13. See http://shr.aaas.org/haiti/cnvj/; last accessed March 2009.

14. See Wilson 2001 for an analysis of the use of this information database technology by the South African Truth and Reconciliation Commission.

15. Some reports in the media indicate that the deputy lost two sons in this tragedy; however, during our visits with Rose-Marie only her missing eight-year-old was discussed.

16. The original Lavalas Political Organization (Organisation Politique Lavalas) changed its name to the Organization of People in Struggle (Organisation du Peuple en Lutte) after the resignation of Smarth in June 1997.

17. The word *lapè* (also spelled *lapen*) can also mean "bread." I also discuss this double entendre in chapters 1 and 5.

18. This fund is discussed below and in chapter 5.

19. In a meeting that I attended in spring 1999 with HRF staff members and Antoine's successor, Minister of Justice Camille Leblanc, Antoine was heavily criticized for allegedly having "obstructed the processes of justice" in this trial. On the Raboteau trial itself, see Brian Concannon Jr., "Beyond Complementarity: The International Criminal Court and National Prosecutions, A View from Haiti," *Columbia Human Rights Law Review* 32 (fall 2000): 201–50; and the documentary film *Pote Mak Sonje: The Raboteau Trial*, dir. Harriet Hirshorn, prod. Christine Cynn (February 2003).

CHAPTER FIVE

1. As pronounced, *lapè* can also mean "peace" and "bread." As discussed in chapter 1, it can also mean "fear."

2. Mission de Police Civile des Nations Unies en Haïti (United Nations Civilian Police Mission in Haiti).

3. See chapter 4.

4. The project's formal Haitian Creole name was the Pwojè pou Bay Sosyete Sivil la Jarèt (Project to Strengthen Civil Society). I did not focus on the ASOSYE project during my research beyond the extent to which its staff interacted with those of the Human Rights Fund. For a description of this program, see www.adfusa.org/content/highlight/detail/647/; last accessed March 2009.

5. The original HRFII director left his position soon after the May 29 National Colloquium for the Rehabilitation of Victims of Organized Violence. His replacement, another former MICIVIH observer, in turn left the Fund in August 1997 because of severe emotional distress.

6. Emilie Datilus is the nurse with whom I worked at the Chanm Fanm clinic in 1996.

7. Ultimately, the management team at ADF/Haiti minimized his presence in the program because of a perception that he was not able to work well with the Haitian staff and ADF's Haitian collaborators.

8. On the basis of these and other successful activities, ADF received additional funds to expand and extend its overall political development assistance in Haiti. USAID extended the Human Rights Fund II program from July 1, 1997, to June 30, 1998.

9. The ASOSYE project fell within USAID's Civil Society section, a section that development partners implementing USAID's strategic objectives perceived as having lesser status than the Justice and Democratic Governance projects.

10. HRFII was judged successful in achieving the intermediate results outlined in the October 1, 1997, to June 30, 1998, Results Framework. In January 1998, at the midpoint of the contract, an "independent" assessment team evaluated all USAID-funded projects in the Administration of Justice Program

(of which the Human Rights Fund was a part), a practice that is characteristic of the publicly funded grant economy. As a result of the successful assessment, HRF was extended through summer 1999.

11. In November 1999 the AOJ program achieved infamy after a scathing portrayal by the CBS *60 Minutes* program.

12. I have not been able to corroborate these allegations.

13. The BPS (Ministry of Justice Proceedings and Follow-up Office for Victims) was implementing the recommendations of the National Commission for Truth and Justice and administered the Government of Haiti's reparation funds for viktim.

14. I was not able to interview Jean to learn what had led him to acquire beneficiary status at the Fund or to his having risen to leadership in this prominent victims' organization.

15. At the time the rate per visit was only H$3, but Dr. Baptiste had billed a total of up to H$90 per person.

16. I told Denise that I needed to postpone our research together for just a few weeks, and then I would be able to start her contract later in the fall. She agreed to wait until December, and I began working with Sylvie as my only guide in the community outside the clinic. I was still accessible, however, to women who came to see me for bodywork or to viktim who chose to meet me at the Fund.

17. I was not able to confirm this during the course of my research.

18. Among other sources of these allegations, my own research practices may have played a part. As is common in clinical research contexts, I paid individuals who were willing to test the CAPS H$20. Although these sessions were usually one-on-one and the transfer of funds was direct, it is possible that they provoked rumors specifically about this sum of money.

19. See Maternowska 2006; and *Ghosts of Cité Soleil,* the 2007 documentary directed by Asger Leth.

20. The Chimaera is a "fire-breathing female monster usually represented as a composite of a lion, goat, and serpent" (*American Heritage College Dictionary* 1993: 243). The name *chimè* also signifies the dreamlike, imaginary, or ghostly presence that these groups embody through their covert but very real use of violence.

21. I do not know if the problem was that David had survived the attack or that Fritzner had not actually been "authorized" to exercise sovereign power on behalf of the state to attempt murder.

22. I am not sure exactly where the family crossed the border or where they stayed during their time an mawonaj.

23. Jacques was one of the individuals whom Danielle Marcia accused of having participated in the killing of her son, Mathieu Marcia, the police officer.

24. See Walt Bogdanich and Jenny Nordberg, "Mixed U.S. Signals Helped Tilt Haiti toward Chaos," *New York Times,* January 29, 2006, www.nytimes .com/2006/01/29/international/americas/29haiti.html?_r = 1&oref = slogin& pagewanted = print; accessed May 2009. See also Paul Farmer, "Who Removed Aristide?" *London Review of Books,* April 15, 2004, www.lrb.co.uk/v26/no8/ print/farm01_.html; last accessed May 2009.

CHAPTER SIX

1. MIPONUH (Mission de Police Civile des Nations Unies en Haïti) was the U.N. Civilian Police Mission in Haiti. It was inaugurated in December 1997 to help "professionalize" the HNP. It had no military or peacekeeping function.

2. "Les aveux de Rodolfo Mattarollo?" *Haïti Progrès* 16, no. 38 (December 9–15, 1998): 1, 8.

3. Ibid., 8.

4. The Human Rights Fund, rather than ASOSYE, was actually responsible for the banners.

5. L'Office de Concertation pour le Développement—the Office of Dialogue for Development. OCODE had received USAID funding in the past and sponsored the painting of murals throughout Haiti's urban areas that contained French and Haitian Creole slogans promoting democracy and respect for human rights.

6. *Haïti Progrès*, December 9–15, 1998, 4.

7. Ibid.

8. Ibid.

9. One rationale for what many denounced as Préval's "coup d'état" was that the decision could resolve the ongoing electoral dispute and parliament's failure to ratify an acceptable prime minister. As discussed previously, Haiti had had no functioning government because of this protracted stalemate. Furthermore, the electoral dispute was a sign to international donors that "democracy" was failing in Haiti. Until the conflict was resolved to their satisfaction, they withheld nearly $500 million in development assistance from Haiti.

10. The GCAFVCE was inaugurated to provide better advocacy for female victims with human rights institutions, women's organizations, and other NGOs, the Ministry of Justice, and the Bureau Poursuites et Suivi.

11. As discussed in chapters 1 and 2, when the Multinational Force invaded Haiti to restore democracy in September 1994, U.S. and U.N. military forces seized these documents and other materials that reportedly record the administrative practices and methods of repression that the terror apparatus employed between 1991 and 1994 against the pro-democracy sector.

12. "Toto" Constant was one of the founders of the FRAPH organization. See chapter 2.

Glossary

angajman contract, obligation, agreement
animasyon theatrical group, community theater for development purposes
ankadreman support, structural framing, guidance, protection, security
an mawonaj hiding inside Haiti
atache attachés, paramilitary affiliates of the coup apparatus
beny public fountain or water source
bidonvil slum, shantytown
blan foreigner, white
bonanj angel
brigad vijilans neighborhood watch groups/vigilante brigades
chans luck
chèf chief
chèf seksyon section chiefs
chimè criminal terrorists, assassins
cho hot, angry, hotheaded
chomaj unemployment
deblozay violent tirade
dechoukaj uprooting, lynching, mob violence
dekonpoze state of dissociation
depo storehouse, deposit
ensekirite insecurity
fanm woman, common-law wife
fanm deyò "wife" or partner living outside the primary household
fanm saj lay midwives

fè jèn to fast
fou/fòl crazy
galeri anteroom or veranda
gason lakou yard boy, caretaker
gaz gas
gwo bonanj big guardian angel, nonmaterial force
gwo nèg big man
jij de pè justice of the peace
kadejak rape
kamyon large truck fitted for passenger travel
kès treasury, fund
kò body, corps, gang
kò kadav the body, as opposed to the soul or spirit
konbit large-scale, cooperative agricultural production outside the home
lakou courtyard
lapè peace, fear
lapè simityè fear or peace of the cemetery
lavalas flood; also the name chosen for the pro-democracy coalition (masc.,
    Lavalasyen; fem., Lavalasyèn)
lavi chè inflation
lèt gate spoiled milk
lougawou vampirelike spiritual entity that consumes the soul
lwa Vodou spirit
madanm sara (madansara) small-scale market woman
makout sack
manda subpoena
manje food, to eat
maryaj marriage
masay massage
mawonaj flight from plantation slavery, internal displacement in Haiti
met attorney, master
militan activist
moun person, human
moun pa partisan, patron-client relationship, favoritism, cronyism
move san bad blood
nanm soul
patwon-mwen my patron
plasaj common-law marriage
potomitan pillar
pwen verbal barbs, metaphysical power points
pwofite to profit, exploit
restavèk child servant or slave
san blood
sektè popilè popular sector
sezi shocked
sezisman affliction arising from shock or trauma
simityè cemetery

siyon sanctuary, church, Zion
souse to suck, suck the blood from a young child
tap-tap pickups serving as mini-buses
tay fè mal low back pain
tèt head
tèt fè mal headaches
ti bonanj little guardian angel, character, will
ti kominote legliz base ecclesial communities
tonton makout member of the Duvalier terror apparatus
travay work, sex work
travay fanm women's work
travay sou memwa work on memories of the past
van wind
van nan tèt feeling of heavy-headedness
viktim victim
vin fòl went crazy
vizyon visions
zenglendo armed bandit, criminal
zonbi disembodied aspect of the soul, the living dead

Bibliography

ADF. 1999. "Human Rights Fund Community-Police Relations Program Proposal." Cooperative Agreement No. 521–0236-A-00–1112–00, Technical Proposal Attachment 2, ADF Institutional Capabilities, July 9.

Agamben, Giorgio. 1998 [1995]. *Homo Sacer: Sovereign Power and Bare Life.* Trans. Daniel Heller-Roazen. Stanford, CA: Stanford University Press.

———. 2005. *State of Exception.* Trans. Kevin Attell. Chicago: University of Chicago Press.

Agger, Inger, and Søren Buus Jensen. 1996. *Trauma and Healing under State Terrorism.* London: Zed Books.

Albright, Madeleine. 1997. "The United States and Assistance to Post-Conflict Societies." Keynote address at USAID Conference: Promoting Democracy, Human Rights and Reintegration in Post-Conflict Societies, Washington, DC, Oct. 30–31.

Alexander, Jeffrey C. 1995. "Modern, Anti, Post, and Neo*." *New Left Review* 1 (210): 63–101.

Améry, Jean. 1980. *At the Mind's Limits: Contemplations by a Survivor of Auschwitz and Its Realities.* Trans. Sidney Rosenfeld and Stella P. Rosenfeld. Bloomington: Indiana University Press.

Amnesty International. 1992. *Haiti—The Human Rights Tragedy: Human Rights Violations since the Coup.* New York: Amnesty International.

An-Na'im, Abdullah Ahmed, ed. 1992. *Human Rights in Cross-Cultural Perspectives: A Quest for Consensus.* Philadelphia: University of Pennsylvania Press.

Antze, Paul. 1996. "Telling Stories, Making Selves: Memory and Identity in Multiple Personality Disorder." In *Tense Past: Cultural Essays in Trauma and Memory,* ed. Paul Antze and Michael Lambek, 3–23. London: Routledge.

Appadurai, Arjun. 1996. "Sovereignty without Territoriality: Notes for a Post-
national Geography." In *The Geography of Identity*, ed. Patricia Yaeger,
40–58. Ann Arbor: University of Michigan Press.
———. 2006. "The Thing Itself." *Public Culture* 18 (1): 15–21.
Appadurai, Arjun, ed. 1986. *The Social Life of Things: Commodities in Cultural
Perspective.* Cambridge: Cambridge University Press.
Arditti, Rita. 1999. *Searching for Life: The Grandmothers of the Plaza de Mayo
and the Disappeared Children of Argentina.* Berkeley: University of Califor-
nia Press.
Aretxaga, Begoña. 1997. *Shattering Silence: Women, Nationalism, and Political
Subjectivity in Northern Ireland.* Princeton: Princeton University Press.
Aristide, Jean-Bertrand. 2004. "President Aristide in His Own Words: DN!'s
Exclusive Interview, Part 1." In *Getting Haiti Right This Time: The U.S. and
the Coup,* ed. Noam Chomsky, Paul Farmer, and Amy Goodman, 165–69.
Monroe, ME: Common Courage Press.
Arnove, Anthony. 1995. "Criminal Habits: An Interview with Allan Nairn,
April 1995." *Z Magazine* (June): 22–29.
Asad, Talal. 1973. "Introduction." In *Anthropology and the Colonial Encoun-
ter,* ed. Talal Asad, 9–19. Atlantic Highlands, NJ: Humanities Press.
Ashforth, Adam. 2005. *Witchcraft, Violence, and Democracy in South Africa.*
Chicago: University of Chicago Press.
Avril, Prosper. 1999. *From Glory to Disgrace: The Haitian Army, 1804–1994.*
n.p.: Universal Publishers.
Balch, Emily Green. 1927. *Occupied Haiti.* New York: Writer's Publishing
Company.
Ball, Patrick, and Herbert F. Spirer. 2000. "The Haitian National Commission
for Truth and Justice: Collecting Information, Data Processing, Database
Representation, and Generating Analytical Reports." In *Making the Case:
Investigating Large Scale Human Rights Violations Using Information Sys-
tems and Data Analysis,* ed. Patrick Ball, Herbert F. Spirer, and Louise Spirer,
27–40. Washington, DC: American Association for the Advancement of
Science.
Barthélemy, Gérard. 1992. *Les Duvaliéristes après Duvalier.* Paris: Éditions
l'Harmattan.
Bataille, Georges. 1985. *Visions of Excess: Selected Writings, 1927–1939.* Trans.
A. Stoekl. Minneapolis: University of Minnesota Press.
———. 1988. *Oeuvres complètes XII.* Paris: Gallimard.
Becker, Anne. 1991. "Body Image in Fiji: The Self in the Body and in the Com-
munity." Ph.D. diss., Harvard University.
Bell, Beverly. 2001. *Walking on Fire: Haitian Women's Stories of Survival and
Resistance.* Ithaca, NY: Cornell University Press.
Bell, Madison Smartt. 2007. *Toussaint Louverture: A Biography.* New York:
Pantheon Books.
Bell, Vicki. 1991. "'Beyond the "Thorny Question"': Feminism, Foucault and
the Desexualisation of Rape." *International Journal of the Sociology of Law*
19: 83–100.

Bellegarde-Smith, Patrick. 1985. *In the Shadow of Powers: Dantès Belle-garde in Haitian Social Thought*. Atlantic Highlands, NJ: Humanities Press International.
———. 2004. *Haiti: The Breached Citadel*. Rev. and updated ed. Toronto: Canadian Scholars' Press.
Blackburn, Robin. 1988. *The Overthrow of Colonial Slavery, 1776–1848*. London: Verso.
Boddy, Janice. 1988. "Spirits and Selves in Northern Sudan: The Cultural Therapeutics of Possession and Trance." *American Ethnologist* 15 (1): 4–27.
Boltanski, Luc. 1999 [1993]. *Distant Suffering: Morality, Media and Politics*. Trans. Graham Burchell. Cambridge: Cambridge University Press.
Bornstein, Erica. 2005. *The Spirit of Development: Protestant NGOs, Morality, and Economics in Zimbabwe*. Stanford, CA: Stanford University Press.
Bouchereau, Madeleine Sylvain. 1957. *Haïti et ses Femmes: Une Étude d'Évolution Culturelle*. Port-au-Prince: Imp. Les Presses Libres.
Boulding, Kenneth E. 1981. *A Preface to Grant Economics: The Economy of Love and Fear*. New York: Praeger.
Bourgois, Philippe. 1990. "Confronting Anthropological Ethics: Ethnographic Lessons from Central America." *Journal of Peace Research* 27 (1): 43–54.
———. 1995. *In Search of Respect: Selling Crack in El Barrio*. Cambridge: Cambridge University Press.
———. 2004. "US Inner-City Apartheid: The Contours of Structural and Interpersonal Violence." In *Violence in War and Peace: An Anthology*, ed. Nancy Scheper-Hughes and Philippe Bourgois, 301–7. Malden, MA: Blackwell.
Bourguignon, Erika. 1984. "Belief and Behavior in Haitian Folk Healing." In *Mental Health Services: The Cross-Cultural Context*, ed. Paul B. Pedersen, Norman Sartorius, and Anthony J. Marsella, 243–66. Beverly Hills, CA: Sage.
Bracken, Patrick J., and Celia Petty, eds. 1998. *Rethinking the Trauma of War*. London: Free Association Books.
Brodwin, Paul. 1996. *Medicine and Morality in Haiti: The Contest for Healing Power*. Cambridge: Cambridge University Press.
Brown, Karen McCarthy. 1979. "The Center and the Edges: God and Person in Haitian Society." *Journal of the Interdenominational Theological Center* 7 (1): 22–39.
———. 1987. "The Power to Heal: Reflections on Women, Religion, and Medicine." In *Shaping New Vision: Gender and Values in American Culture*, ed. Clarissa W. Atkinson, Constance H. Buchanan, and Margaret R. Miles, 123–41. Ann Arbor: UMI Research Press.
———. 1989. "Afro-Caribbean Spirituality: A Haitian Case Study." In *Healing and Restoring: Health and Medicine in the World's Religious Traditions*, ed. Lawrence E. Sullivan, 255–85. New York: Macmillan.
———. 1991. *Mama Lola: A Vodou Priestess in Brooklyn*. Berkeley: University of California Press.
Brown, Wendy. 1995. *States of Injury: Power and Freedom in Late Modernity*. Princeton: Princeton University Press.

Brownmiller, Susan. 1975. *Against Our Will: Men, Women and Rape*. New York: Simon and Schuster.

Bustos, Enrique. 1992. "Psychodynamic Approaches in the Treatment of Torture Survivors." In *Torture and Its Consequences: Current Treatment Approaches*, ed. Metin Basoglu, 333–47. Cambridge: Cambridge University Press.

Cadet, Jean-Robert. 1998. *Restavec: From Haitian Slave Child to Middle-Class American*. Austin: University of Texas Press.

Callaghy, Thomas M., Ronald Kassimir, and Robert Latham. 2001. "Preface." In *Intervention and Transnationalism in Africa: Global-Local Networks of Power*, ed. Thomas M. Callaghy, Ronald Kassimir, and Robert Latham, ix–xi. Cambridge: Cambridge University Press.

Carothers, Thomas. 1991. *In the Name of Democracy: U.S. Policy toward Latin America in the Reagan Years*. Berkeley: University of California Press.

———. 1996. *Assessing Democracy Assistance: The Case of Romania*. Washington, DC: Carnegie Endowment for International Peace.

———. 1999. *Aiding Democracy Abroad: The Learning Curve*. Washington, DC: Carnegie Endowment for International Peace.

Charles, Carolle. 1995. "Gender and Politics in Contemporary Haiti: The Duvalierist State, Transnationalism, and the Emergence of a New Feminism (1980–1990)." *Feminist Studies* 21 (1): 135–64.

Charles, Jacqueline. 2003. "Aristide Pushes for Restitution from France." www.Miami Herald.com., Dec. 18.

Chomsky, Noam, Paul Farmer, and Amy Goodman. 2004. *Getting Haiti Right This Time: The U.S. and the Coup*. Monroe, ME: Common Courage Press.

CIA. 2008. *The World Factbook*. www.cia.gov/library/publications/the-world-factbook/.

CIFD. 1992. *La Situation des femmes haïtiennes*. Prepared by Francine Tardif. Port-au-Prince: Imprimerie Le Natal.

Clinton, William Jefferson. 1994. "Address to the Nation, September 15, 1994." *Weekly Compilation of Presidential Documents*, Sept. 19. http://frwebgate6.access.gpo.gov/cgi-bin/multidb.cgi.

CNVJ. 1997 [1995]. *Si M Pa Rele: 29 Septembre 1991–14 Octobre 1994*. Port-au-Prince: Ministère de la Justice.

Cohen, Lawrence. 1999. "Where It Hurts: Indian Material for and Ethics of Organ Transplantation." *Daedalus* 128 (4): 135–65.

Collectif de femmes Haïtiennes. 1980. *Femmes Haïtiennes*. Montreal: Maison d'Haïti and Carrefour International.

Comaroff, Jean, and John L. Comaroff. 1999. "Occult Economies and the Violence of Abstraction: Notes from the South African Postcolony." *American Ethnologist* 26 (2): 279–303.

———. 2003. "Ethnography on an Awkward Scale: Postcolonial Anthropology and the Violence of Abstraction." *Ethnography* 4 (2): 147–79.

Comaroff, John L., and Jean Comaroff. 1992. *Ethnography and the Historical Imagination*. Boulder, CO: Westview Press.

Conférence des Religieux Haïtiens. 1990. "Communiqué." Dec. 4 press release.

Copelon, Rhonda. 1994. "Surfacing Gender: Reconceptualizing Crimes against Women in Time of War." In *Mass Rape: The War against Women in Bosnia-*

Herzegovina, ed. Alexandra Stiglmayer, trans. Marion Faber, 197–218. Lincoln: University of Nebraska Press.

Crelinsten, Ronald D. 1995. "In Their Own Words: The World of the Torturer." In *The Politics of Pain: Torturers and Their Masters,* ed. Ronald D. Crelinsten and Alex P. Schmid, 35–64. Boulder, CO: Westview Press.

Csordas, Thomas J. 1993. "Somatic Modes of Attention." *Cultural Anthropology* 8 (2): 135–56.

———. 1994. *The Sacred Self: A Cultural Phenomenology of Charismatic Healing.* Berkeley: University of California Press.

Danieli, Yael. 1984. "Psychotherapist's Participation in the Conspiracy of Silence about the Holocaust." *Psychoanalytic Psychology* 1 (1): 23–42.

Daniels, Ronald J., Donald F. Kettl, and Howard Kunreuther, eds. 2006. *On Risk and Disaster: Lessons from Hurricane Katrina.* Philadelphia: University of Pennsylvania Press.

Danner, Mark. 1987. "The Struggle for a Democratic Haiti." *New York Times,* June 21.

Danroc, Gilles and Daniel Roussière. 1995. *La Répression au quotidien en Haïti (1991–1994).* Prepared for the Commission Justice et Paix du Diocèse des Gonaïves. Paris and Port-au-Prince: Éditions Karthala and Haïti Solidarité Internationale.

Das, Veena. 1995. *Critical Events: An Anthropological Perspective on Contemporary India.* Oxford: Oxford University Press.

———. 1997. "Language and Body: Transactions in the Construction of Pain." In *Social Suffering,* ed. Arthur Kleinman, Veena Das, and Margaret Lock, 67–91. Berkeley: University of California Press.

Das, Veena, Arthur Kleinman, Margaret Lock, Mamphela Ramphele, and Pamela Reynolds, eds. 2001. *Remaking a World: Violence, Social Suffering, and Recovery.* Berkeley: University of California Press.

Das, Veena, and Ashis Nandy. 1985. "Violence, Victimhood, and the Language of Silence." *Contribution to Indian Sociology,* n.s., 19 (1): 177–95.

Dash, J. Michael. 1997. *Haiti and the United States: National Stereotypes and the Literary Imagination.* 2nd ed. New York: St. Martin's Press.

Davis, Angela Y. 1981. *Women, Race and Class.* New York: Vintage Books.

Davis, David Brion. 2006. *Inhuman Bondage: The Rise and Fall of Slavery in the New World.* Oxford: Oxford University Press.

Davis, Wade. 1988. *Passage of Darkness: The Ethnobiology of the Haitian Zombie.* Chapel Hill: University of North Carolina Press.

Dayan, Joan. 1991. "Vodoun, or the Voice of the Gods." *Raritan* 10 (3): 32–57.

Deleuze, Gilles. 1988. *Foucault.* Trans. Seán Hand. Minneapolis: University of Minnesota Press. Originally published in French by Les Éditions de Minuit, 1986.

Deleuze, Gilles, and Félix Guattari. 1987. *A Thousand Plateaus: Capitalism and Schizophrenia.* Trans. Brian Massumi. Minneapolis: University of Minnesota Press.

Deren, Maya. 1970 [1953]. *Divine Horsemen: The Voodoo Gods of Haiti.* New York: Documentext.

Desjarlais, Robert R. 2003. *Sensory Biographies: Lives and Deaths among Nepal's Yolmo Buddhists.* Berkeley: University of California Press.

Desmangles, Leslie G. 1992. *The Faces of the Gods: Vodou and Roman Catholicism in Haiti*. Chapel Hill: University of North Carolina Press.

De Vaissière, Pierre. 1909. *Saint-Domingue: La Société et la vie créoles sous l'ancien régime (1629–1789)*. Paris: Perrin.

Diederich, Bernard, and Al Burt. 1986. *Papa Doc and the Tonton Macoutes*. Port-au-Prince: Éditions Henri Deschamps.

Dolan, Catherine S. 2002. "Gender and Witchcraft in Agrarian Transition: The Case of Kenyan Horticulture." *Development and Change* 33 (4): 659–81.

Donnelly, Jack. 1989. *Universal Human Rights in Theory and Practice*. Ithaca, NY: Cornell University Press.

Douglas, Mary. 1966. *Purity and Danger: An Analysis of the Concepts of Pollution and Taboo*. London: Ark Paperbacks.

Drake, Paul W. 1991. "From Good Men to Good Neighbors: 1912–1932." In *Exporting Democracy: The United States and Latin America, Themes and Issues*, ed. Abraham F. Lowenthal, 3–40. Baltimore: Johns Hopkins University Press.

Drummond, Tammerlin. 1997. "A Constabulary of Thugs: Haiti's U.S.-Trained Police Force Has Turned into a Gang of Rogue Cops Who Torture and Murder." *Time* (Feb. 17): 62–63.

Dubois, Laurent. 2004. *Avengers of the New World: The Story of the Haitian Revolution*. Cambridge, MA: Belknap Press.

Duffield, Mark. 2001. *Global Governance and the New Wars: The Merging of Development and Security*. London: Zed Books.

Dunne, Tim, and Nicholas J. Wheeler, eds. 1999. *Human Rights in Global Politics*. Cambridge: Cambridge University Press.

Dupuy, Alex. 1989. *Haiti in the World Economy: Class, Race, and Underdevelopment since 1700*. Boulder, CO: Westview Press.

———. 1997. *Haiti in the New World Order: The Limits of the Democratic Revolution*. Boulder, CO: Westview Press.

Dworken, Jonathan, Jonathan Moore, and Adam Siegel. 1997. "Haiti Demobilization and Reintegration Program: An Evaluation Prepared for U.S. Agency for International Development." CNA Corporation/Institute for Public Research, Alexandria, VA.

Enloe, Cynthia. 1993. *The Morning After: Sexual Politics at the End of the Cold War*. Berkeley: University of California Press.

Escobar, Arturo. 1995. *Encountering Development: The Making and Unmaking of the Third World*. Princeton: Princeton University Press.

Étienne, Sauveur Pierre. 1997. *Haïti: l'invasion des ONG*. Port-au-Prince: Éditions du CIDIHCA.

Evans-Pritchard, E.E. 1976. *Witchcraft, Oracles, and Magic among the Azande*. Oxford: Oxford University Press.

Fabian, Johannes. 2000. *Out of Our Minds: Reason and Madness in the Exploration of Central Africa*. Berkeley: University of California Press.

Farmer, Paul. 1988a. "Bad Blood, Spoiled Milk: Bodily Fluids as Moral Barometers in Rural Haiti." *American Ethnologist* 15 (1): 62–83.

———. 1988b. "Blood, Sweat, and Baseballs: Haiti in the West Atlantic System." *Dialectical Anthropology* 13: 83–99.

———. 1990. "Sending Sickness: Sorcery, Politics, and Changing Concepts of AIDS in Rural Haiti." *Medical Anthropology Quarterly* 4 (1): 6–27.

———. 1992. *AIDS and Accusation: Haiti and the Geography of Blame.* Berkeley: University of California Press.

———. 1994. *The Uses of Haiti.* Monroe, ME: Common Courage Press.

———. 1996. "On Suffering and Structural Violence: A View from Below." *Daedalus* 125 (1): 261–83.

———. 2003. *Pathologies of Power: Health, Human Rights, and the New War on the Poor.* Berkeley: University of California Press.

———. 2004. "An Anthropology of Structural Violence." *Current Anthropology* 45 (3): 305–25.

Farmer, Paul, Margaret Connors, and Janie Simmons, eds. 1996. *Women, Poverty, and AIDS: Sex, Drugs, and Structural Violence.* Monroe, ME: Common Courage Press.

Fass, Simon M. 1988. *Political Economy in Haiti: The Drama of Survival.* New Brunswick, NJ: Transaction Books.

Fassin, Didier. 2005. "Compassion and Repression: The Moral Economy of Immigration Policies in France." *Cultural Anthropology* 20 (3): 362–87.

———. 2007. "Humanitarianism as a Politics of Life." *Public Culture* 19 (3): 499–520.

Fatton, Robert, Jr. 2002. *Haiti's Predatory Republic: The Unending Transition to Democracy.* Boulder, CO: Lynne Rienner.

Favret-Saada, Jeanne. 1980 [1977]. *Deadly Words: Witchcraft in the Bocage.* Trans. Catherine Cullen. Cambridge: Cambridge University Press.

Ferguson, James. 1994. *The Anti-Politics Machine: "Development," Depoliticization, and Bureaucratic Power in Lesotho.* Minneapolis: University of Minnesota Press.

Fick, Carolyn E. 1990. *The Making of Haiti: The Saint Domingue Revolution from Below.* Knoxville: University of Tennessee Press.

Figley, Charles R., and Rolf J. Kleber. 1995. "Beyond the 'Victim': Secondary Traumatic Stress." In *Beyond Trauma: Cultural and Societal Dynamics,* ed. Rolf J. Kleber, Charles R. Figley, and Berthold P.R. Gersons, 75–98. New York: Plenum Press.

Fischer, Michael M. J. 1991. "Anthropology as Cultural Critique: Inserts for the 1990s Cultural Studies of Science, Visual-Virtual Realities, and Post-Trauma Polities." *Cultural Anthropology* 6 (4): 525–37.

———. 2008. "To Live with What Would Otherwise Be Unendurable, II: Caught in the Borderlands of Palestine/Israel." In *Postcolonial Disorders,* ed. Mary-Jo DelVecchio Good, Sandra Teresa Hyde, Sarah Pinto, and Byron J. Good, 260–75. Berkeley: University of California Press.

Fisher, William F. 1997. "DOING GOOD? The Politics and Antipolitics of NGO Practices." *Annual Review of Anthropology* 26: 439–64.

———, ed. 1995. *Toward Sustainable Development: Struggling over India's Narmada River.* Armonk, NY: M.E. Sharpe.

Fortun, Kim. 2001. *Advocacy after Bhopal: Environmentalism, Disaster, New Global Orders.* Chicago: University of Chicago Press.

Foucault, Michel. 1988 [1965]. *Madness and Civilization: A History of Insanity in the Age of Reason.* Vintage Books ed. New York: Random House. Originally published as *Histoire de la Folie.* Paris: Librairie Plon, 1961.

———. 1990 [1978]. *The History of Sexuality. Vol. 1: An Introduction.* Trans. Robert Hurley. Vintage Books ed. New York: Random House. Originally published as *La Volonté de savoir.* Paris: Éditions Gallimard, 1976.

———. 1979. *Discipline and Punish: The Birth of the Prison.* Vintage Books ed. New York: Random House. Originally published as *Surveiller et Punir; Naissance de la prison.* Paris: Éditions Gallimard, 1975.

———. 1980. *Power/Knowledge: Selected Interviews and Other Writings, 1972–1977.* Ed. Colin Gordon, trans. Leo Marshall, John Mepham, and Kate Soper. New York: Pantheon Books.

———. 1991. "Governmentality." In *The Foucault Effect: Studies in Governmentality,* ed. Graham Burchell, Colin Gordon, and Peter Miller, 87–104. Chicago: University of Chicago Press.

Frank, Jerome D., and Julia B. Frank. 1991. *Persuasion and Healing: A Comparative Study.* 3rd ed. Baltimore: Johns Hopkins University Press.

Fraser, Nancy. 1995. "From Redistribution to Recognition? Dilemmas of Justice in a 'Post-Socialist' Age." *New Left Review* 212 (July–Aug.): 68–93.

Fuller, Anne, and Amy Wilentz. 1991. *Return to the Darkest Days: Human Rights in Haiti since the Coup.* New York: Americas Watch, National Coalition for Haitian Refugees, and Physicians for Human Rights, Dec. 30.

Gaines, Atwood D. 1992. "Ethnopsychiatry: The Cultural Construction of Psychiatries." In *Ethnopsychiatry: The Cultural Construction of Professional and Folk Psychiatries,* ed. Atwood Gaines, 3–49. Albany: State University of New York Press.

Gaines, Atwood D., and Paul E. Farmer. 1986. "Visible Saints: Social Cynosures and Dysphoria in the Mediterranean Tradition." *Culture, Medicine and Psychiatry* 10: 295–330.

Galtung, Johan. 1969. "Violence, Peace, and Peace Research." *Journal of Peace Research* 6 (3): 167–91.

———. 1990. "Cultural Violence." *Journal of Peace Research* 27 (3): 291–305.

Gardner, Katy, and David Lewis. 1996. *Anthropology, Development and the Post-modern Challenge.* London: Pluto Press.

Garrity, Monique Paul. 1981. "The Assembly Industries in Haiti: Cause and Effects." *Journal of Caribbean Studies* 2: 25–37.

Geggus, David Patrick. 2002. *Haitian Revolutionary Studies.* Bloomington: Indiana University Press.

Geschiere, Peter. 1997. *The Modernity of Witchcraft: Politics and the Occult in Postcolonial Africa.* Charlottesville: University of Virginia Press.

———. 2003. "On Witch Doctors and Spin Doctors: The Role of 'Experts' in African and American Politics." In *Magic and Modernity: Interfaces of Revelation and Concealment,* ed. Birgit Meyer and Peter Pels, 159–82. Stanford, CA: Stanford University Press.

Ghachem, Malick W. Forthcoming. *The Old Regime and the Haitian Revolution.* Cambridge: Cambridge University Press.

Gibbons, Elizabeth D. 1999. *Sanctions in Haiti: Human Rights and Democracy under Assault.* Washington Papers/177. Westport, CT: Praeger in association with the Center for Strategic and International Studies, Washington, DC.

Giddens, Anthony. 1979. *Central Problems in Social Theory: Action, Structure, and Contradiction in Social Analysis.* Berkeley: University of California Press.

————. 1984. *The Constitution of Society: Outline of a Theory of Structuration.* Berkeley: University of California Press.

Girard, René. 1977 [1972]. *Violence and the Sacred.* Trans. Patrick Gregory. Baltimore: Johns Hopkins University Press.

Gobodo-Madikizela, Pumla. 2004. *A Human Being Died That Night: A South African Woman Confronts the Legacy of Apartheid.* Boston, MA: Mariner Books.

Godelier, Maurice. 1999 [1996]. *The Enigma of the Gift.* Trans. Nora Scott. Chicago: University of Chicago Press.

Goffman, Erving. 1959. *The Presentation of Self in Everyday Life.* New York: Anchor Books, Doubleday.

Good, Byron J. 1977. "The Heart of What's the Matter." *Culture, Medicine, and Psychiatry* 1: 25–58.

————. 1994. *Medicine, Rationality and Experience: An Anthropological Perspective.* Cambridge: Cambridge University Press.

Good, Byron J., Mary-Jo DelVecchio Good, Jesse Grayman, and Mathew Lakoma. 2006. *Psychosocial Needs Assessment of Communities Affected by the Conflict in the Districts of Pidie, Bireuen, and Aceh Utara.* Jakarta: International Organization for Migration.

Good, Mary-Jo DelVecchio. 1995. *American Medicine: The Quest for Competence.* Berkeley: University of California Press.

————. 2001. "The Biotechnical Embrace." *Culture, Medicine, and Psychiatry* 25 (4): 395–410.

Good, Mary-Jo DelVecchio, and Byron J. Good. 2008. "Indonesia Sakit: Indonesian Disorders and the Subjective Experience and Interpretive Politics of Contemporary Indonesian Artists." In *Postcolonial Disorders,* ed. Mary-Jo DelVecchio Good, Sandra Teresa Hyde, Sarah Pinto, and Byron J. Good, 132–56. Berkeley: University of California Press.

Good, Mary-Jo DelVecchio, Byron Good, Jesse Grayman, and Mathew Lakoma. 2007. *A Psychosocial Needs Assessment of Communities in 14 Conflict-Affected Districts in Aceh.* Jakarta: International Organization for Migration.

Goodale, Mark. 2006. "Ethical Theory as Social Practice." *American Anthropologist* 108 (1): 25–37.

Gordon, Avery F. 1997. *Ghostly Matters: Haunting and the Sociological Imagination.* Minneapolis: University of Minnesota Press.

Grunwald, Joseph, Leslie Delatour, and Karl Voltaire. 1984. "Offshore Assembly in Haiti." In *Haiti—Today and Tomorrow: An Interdisciplinary Study,* ed. Charles R. Foster and Albert Valdman, 231–52. Lanham, MD: University Press of America.

————. 1985. "Foreign Assembly in Haiti." In *The Global Factory: Foreign Assembly in International Trade,* ed. Joseph Grunwald and Kenneth Flamm, 180–205. Washington, DC: Brookings Institution.

Hallward, Peter. 2007. *Damming the Flood: Haiti, Aristide, and the Politics of Containment.* London: Verso.

Haraway, Donna. 1991. "A Manifesto for Cyborgs: Science, Technology, and Socialist Feminism in the 1980s." In *Feminism/Postmodernism*, ed. Linda J. Nicholson, 190–233. New York: Routledge.

Hartman, Saidiya V. 1997. *Scenes of Subjection: Terror, Slavery, and Self-Making in Nineteenth-Century America.* New York: Oxford University Press.

Hartsock, Nancy. 1990. "Foucault on Power: A Theory for Women?" In *Feminism/Postmodernism*, ed. Linda J. Nicholson, 157–75. New York: Routledge.

Hayner, Priscilla B. 2001. *Unspeakable Truths: Confronting State Terror and Atrocity.* London: Routledge.

Herskovits, Melville J. 1975 [1937]. *Life in a Haitian Valley.* New York: Octagon Books.

Herzfeld, Michael. 1985. *The Poetics of Manhood: Contest and Identity in a Cretan Mountain Village.* Princeton: Princeton University Press.

———. 1992. *The Social Production of Indifference: Exploring the Symbolic Roots of Western Bureaucracy.* Chicago: University of Chicago Press.

Holland, Douglas W., and Jane C. Wellenkamp. 1994. *Contentment and Suffering: Culture and Experience in Toraja.* New York: Columbia University Press.

Hopgood, Stephen. 2006. *Keepers of the Flame: Understanding Amnesty International.* Ithaca, NY: Cornell University Press.

HRFII. 1997. *Results Framework: October 1, 1997 to June 30, 1998.* Port-au-Prince.

HRW. 1993. *Human Rights Watch World Report 1994: Events of 1993.* New York: Human Rights Watch.

HRW and NCHR. 1994. "Rape in Haiti: A Weapon of Terror." Vol. 6, no. 8 (July).

HRW/A, JRS/USA, and NCHR. 1994. "Fugitives from Injustice: The Crisis of Internal Displacement in Haiti." Vol. 6, no. 10 (Aug.).

HRW/A and NCHR. 1994. "Terror Prevails in Haiti: Human Rights Violations and Failed Diplomacy." Vol. 6, no. 5 (Apr.).

HRW/A, NCHR, and JRS/USA. 1993. "No Port in a Storm: The Misguided Use of In-Country Processing in Haiti." Vol. 5, no. 8 (Sept.).

HRW/A, NCHR, and WOLA. 1997. "Haiti: The Human Rights Record of the Haitian National Police." Vol. 9, no. 1B (Jan.).

IACHR. 1995. *Report on the Situation of Human Rights in Haiti.*

"Insécurité et banditisme: Quelle solution?" 1998. *Haïti Observateur* 29, no. 49 (Dec. 2–9): 1, 11, 24.

Ives, Kim. 1994. "The Coup and U.S. Foreign Policy: The Unmaking of a President." In *The Haiti Files: Decoding the Crisis,* ed. James Ridgeway, 87–103. Washington, DC: Essential Books.

———. 1995. "The Lavalas Alliance Propels Aristide to Power." In *Haiti: Dangerous Crossroads,* ed. Deidre McFadyen and Pierre LaRamée (with Mark Fried and Fred Rosen from the North American Congress on Latin America [NACLA]). Boston: South End Press.

Jackson, Jean E. 2000. *Camp Pain: Talking with Chronic Pain Patients.* Philadelphia: University of Pennsylvania Press.

James, C. L. R. 1989 [1963]. *The Black Jacobins: Toussaint L'Ouverture and the San Domingo Revolution.* 2nd ed., rev. New York: Vintage Books.

James, Erica Caple. 2003. "The Violence of Misery: 'Insecurity' in Haiti in the 'Democratic' Era." Ph.D. diss., Harvard University.

———. 2004. "The Political Economy of 'Trauma' in Haiti in the Democratic Era of Insecurity." *Culture, Medicine and Psychiatry* 28: 127–49.

———. 2008. "Haunting Ghosts: Madness, Gender, and *Ensekirite* in Haiti in the Democratic Era." In *Postcolonial Disorders,* ed. Mary-Jo DelVecchio Good, Sandra Teresa Hyde, Sarah Pinto, and Byron J. Good, 132–56. Berkeley: University of California Press.

———. 2009. "Neo-Modern Insecurity in Haiti and the Politics of Asylum." *Culture, Medicine and Psychiatry* 33: 153–59.

Juhan, Deane. 1998. *Job's Body: A Handbook for Bodywork.* Expanded ed. Barrytown, NY: Barrytown Ltd. under Station Hill Openings.

Kapur, Ratna. 2005. *Erotic Justice: Law and the New Politics of Postcolonialism.* London: Glasshouse Press.

Katzenstein, Peter J., ed. 1996. *The Culture of National Security: Norms and Identity in World Politics.* New York: Columbia University Press.

Keck, Margaret E., and Kathryn Sikkink. 1998. *Activists beyond Borders: Advocacy Networks in International Politics.* Ithaca, NY: Cornell University Press.

Kleinman, Arthur. 1988. *The Illness Narratives: Suffering, Healing, and the Human Condition.* New York: Basic Books.

———. 1995. "Violence, Culture, and the Politics of Trauma." Originally written with Robert Desjarlais. In *Writing at the Margin: Discourse between Anthropology and Medicine,* 173–89. Berkeley: University of California Press.

———. 2006. *What Really Matters: Living a Moral Life amidst Uncertainty and Danger.* Oxford: Oxford University Press.

Kleinman, Arthur, and Joan Kleinman. 1991. "Suffering and Its Professional Transformation: Toward an Ethnography of Interpersonal Experience." *Culture, Medicine and Psychiatry* 15 (3): 275–301.

Konfidan, Deniz. 1997. "San Jistis pa gen lapè, san lapè pa gen lavi." *Libète* 5, no. 271 (Dec. 17–22): 5.

Kovats-Bernat, J. Christopher. 2006. *Sleeping Rough in Port-au-Prince: An Ethnography of Street Children and Violence in Haiti.* Gainesville: University Press of Florida.

Kristeva, Julie. 1982. *Powers of Horror: An Essay on Abjection.* Trans. Leon S. Roudiez. New York: Columbia University Press.

Laguerre, Michel Saturnin. 1976. "The Black Ghetto as an Internal Colony: Socio-Economic Adaptation of a Haitian Urban Community." Ph.D. diss., University of Illinois at Urbana-Champaign.

———. 1980. "Bizango: A Voodoo Secret Society in Haiti." In *Secrecy: A Cross-Cultural Perspective,* ed. Stanton K. Tefft, 147–60. New York: Human Sciences Press.

———. 1984. *American Odyssey: Haitians in New York City*. Ithaca, NY: Cornell University Press.

———. 1987a. *Afro-Caribbean Folk Medicine*. South Hadley, MA: Bergin and Garvey.

———. 1987b. "Migration and Urbanization in Haiti." *Sociologus* 37 (2): 118–39.

———. 1989. *Voodoo and Politics in Haiti*. New York: St. Martin's Press.

———. 1993. *The Military and Society in Haiti*. London: Macmillan.

Lambek, Michael. 1996. "The Past Imperfect: Remembering as Moral Practice." In *Tense Past: Cultural Essays in Trauma and Memory*, ed. Paul Antze and Michael Lambek, 235–54. London: Routledge.

Larose, Serge. 1977. "The Meaning of Africa in Haitian Vodu." In *Symbols and Sentiments: Cross-Cultural Studies in Symbolism*, ed. Ioan Lewis, 85–116. London: Academic Press.

Latour, Bruno. 2005. *Reassembling the Social: An Introduction to Actor-Network Theory*. Oxford: Oxford University Press.

Lawless, Robert. 1992. *Haiti's Bad Press*. Rochester, VT: Schenkman Books.

LCHR. 1990. *Paper Laws, Steel Bayonets: Breakdown of the Rule of Law in Haiti*. New York: Lawyers Committee for Human Rights.

Le Bon, Gustave. 1974 [1894]. *The Psychology of Peoples*. New York: Arno Press.

———. 1999 [1895]. *The Crowd*. New Brunswick, NJ: Transaction Publishers.

Lemoine, Patrick. 1997. *Fort-Dimanche: Dungeon of Death*. Freeport, NY: Fordi9.

Lévi-Strauss, Claude. 1969 [1949]. *The Elementary Structures of Kinship*. Rev. ed. Boston: Beacon Press.

Levi, Primo. 1989 [1986]. *The Drowned and the Saved*. New York: Vintage Books.

Lewis, Oscar. 1959. *Five Families: Mexican Case Studies in the Culture of Poverty*. New York: Basic Books.

LFAS. 1946. *La Femme Haïtienne répond aux attaques formulées contre elle à l'Assemblée Constituante*. Port-au-Prince: Société d'Éditions et de Librairie.

Little, Cheryl, and Charu Newhouse al-Sahli. 2004. *Haitian Refugees: A People in Search of Hope*. Miami: Florida Immigrant Advocacy Center. May 1.

Locher, Huldrych Caspar. 1978. "The Fate of Migrants in Urban Haiti—A Survey of Three Port-au-Prince Neighborhoods." Ph.D. diss., Yale University.

Lock, Margaret, and Nancy Scheper-Hughes. 1996. "A Critical-Interpretive Approach in Medical Anthropology: Rituals and Routines of Discipline and Dissent." In *Medical Anthropology: Contemporary Theory and Method*, rev. ed., ed. Carolyn F. Sargent and Thomas M. Johnson, 41–70. Westport, CT: Praeger.

Logan, Rayford W. 1941. *The Diplomatic Relations of the United States with Haiti, 1776–1891*. Chapel Hill: University of North Carolina Press.

Low, Setha. 2003. *Behind the Gates: Life, Security, and the Pursuit of Happiness in Fortress America*. London: Routledge.

Lowenthal, Ira P. 1984. "Labor, Sexuality and the Conjugal Contract in Rural Haiti." In *Haiti—Today and Tomorrow—An Interdisciplinary Study*, ed.

Charles R. Foster and Albert Valdman, 15–33. Lanham, MD: University Press of America.

———. 1987. "Marriage Is 20, Children Are 21: The Cultural Construction of Conjugality and the Family in Rural Haiti." Ph.D. diss., Johns Hopkins University.

Lundahl, Mats. 1979. *Peasants and Poverty: A Study of Haiti.* New York: St. Martin's Press.

———. 1983. *The Haitian Economy: Man, Land, and Markets.* New York: St. Martin's Press.

———. 1992. *Politics or Markets? Essays on Haitian Underdevelopment.* London: Routledge.

MacKinnon, Catherine A. 1989. *Toward a Feminist Theory of the State.* Cambridge, MA: Harvard University Press.

Malkki, Liisa. 1995. *Purity and Exile: Violence, Memory, and National Cosmology among Hutu Refugees in Tanzania.* Chicago: University of Chicago Press.

———. 1996. "Speechless Emissaries: Refugees, Humanitarianism, and Dehistoricization." *Cultural Anthropology* 11 (3): 377–404.

Manigat, Sabine. 1997. "Haiti: The Popular Sectors and the Crisis in Port-au-Prince." In *The Urban Caribbean: Transition to the New Global Economy,* ed. Alejandro Portes, Carlos Dore-Cabral, and Patricia Landolt, 87–123. Baltimore, MD: Johns Hopkins University Press.

Marcus, George E. 1998. *Ethnography through Thick and Thin.* Princeton, NJ: Princeton University Press.

Mars, Louis. 1977 [1946]. *The Crisis of Possession in Voodoo.* Trans. Kathleen Collins. New York: Reed, Cannon and Johnson.

Martinez, Samuel. 1995. *Peripheral Migrants: Haitians and Dominican Republican Sugar Plantations.* Knoxville: University of Tennessee Press.

Marx, Karl. 1990 [1867]. *Capital: A Critique of Political Economy.* Vol. 1. Trans. Ben Fowkes. New York: Penguin Books.

Maternowska, M. Catherine. 2006. *Reproducing Inequities: Poverty and the Politics of Population in Haiti.* New Brunswick, NJ: Rutgers University Press.

Mattingly, Cheryl. 1998. *Healing Dramas and Clinical Plots: The Narrative Structure of Experience.* Cambridge: Cambridge University Press.

Maurer, Bill. 2005. *Mutual Life, Limited: Islamic Banking, Alternative Currencies, Lateral Reason.* Princeton, NJ: Princeton University Press.

Mauss, Marcel. 1950. *The Gift: The Form and Reason for Exchange in Archaic Societies.* Trans. W.D. Halls. New York: Norton.

Mbembe, Achille. 2001. *On the Postcolony.* Berkeley: University of California Press.

———. 2003. "Necropolitics." Trans. Libby Meintjes. *Public Culture* 15 (1): 11–40.

McAlister, Elizabeth. 2002. *Rara! Vodou, Power, and Performance in Haiti and Its Diaspora.* Berkeley: University of California Press.

McCoy, Jennifer L. 1997. "Introduction: Dismantling the Predatory State—The Conference Report." In *Haiti Renewed: Political and Economic Prospects,* ed. Robert I. Rotberg, 1–26. Cambridge, MA: World Peace Foundation.

Méndez, Juan E., Guillermo O'Donnell, and Paulo Sérgio Pinheiro, eds. 1999. *(Un)Rule of Law and the Underprivileged in Latin America*. Notre Dame, IN: University of Notre Dame Press.

Merry, Sally Engle. 2006. *Human Rights and Gender Violence: Translating International Law into Local Justice*. Chicago: University of Chicago Press.

———. 2007. "Introduction: States of Violence." In *The Practice of Human Rights: Tracking Law between the Global and the Local*, ed. Mark Goodale and Sally Engle Merry, 41–48. Cambridge: Cambridge University Press.

Métraux, Alfred. 1972 [1959]. *Voodoo in Haiti*. Trans. Hugo Charteris. New York: Schocken Books.

Miller, Jake C. 1984. *The Plight of Haitian Refugees*. New York: Praeger.

Ministère de la Justice et de la Sécurité Publique. 1999. "Le Bureau Poursuites et Suivi et les victimes du coup d'état de 1991–94." Port-au-Prince, Jan. 29.

"Ministè Edikasyon, Konsèy Inivèsite, Jwèt Pou Nou." 1997. *Libète* 5, no. 257 (Sept. 10–16): 1.

Ministry of Welfare, Health, and Cultural Affairs, Rijswijk. 1987. *Health Hazards of Organized Violence: Proceedings of a WHO Working Group on Health Hazards of Organized Violence,Veldhoven, April 22–25, 1986*. Geneva: WHO.

Mitchell, Timothy. 2002. *Rule of Experts: Egypt, Techno-Politics, Modernity*. Berkeley: University of California Press.

Moore, Henrietta L. 1994. "The Problem of Explaining Violence in the Social Sciences." In *Sex and Violence: Issues in Representations and Experience*, ed. Penelope Harvey and Peter Gow, 138–55. London: Routledge.

Moore, Henrietta L., and Todd Sanders, eds. 2001. *Magical Interpretations, Material Realities: Modernity, Witchcraft and the Occult in Postcolonial Africa*. London: Routledge.

Moore, Sally Falk. 1987. "Explaining the Present: Theoretical Dilemmas in Processual Ethnography." *American Ethnologist* 14 (4): 727–36.

Moser, Caroline O.N. 2001. "The Gendered Continuum of Violence and Conflict: An Operational Framework." In *Victims, Perpetrators or Actors? Gender, Armed Conflict and Political Violence*, ed. Caroline O.N. Moser and Fiona Clark, 30–51. London: Zed Books.

Mutua, Makau. 2001. "Savages, Victims, and Saviors: The Metaphor of Human Rights." *Harvard International Law Journal* 42: 201–45.

Myers, Dee Dee. 1994a. Press Briefing. White House Office of the Press Secretary, Washington, DC, Apr. 26.

———. 1994b. Press Briefing. White House Office of the Press Secretary, Washington, DC, Apr. 29.

Nachman, Steven R. 1993. "Wasted Lives: Tuberculosis and Other Health Risks of Being Haitian in a U.S. Detention Camp." *Medical Anthropological Quarterly* 7 (3): 227–59.

Nader, Laura. 1999 [1969]. "Up the Anthropologist—Perspectives Gained from Studying Up." In *Reinventing Anthropology*, ed. Dell Hymes, 284–311. Ann Arbor: University of Michigan Press.

National Labor Committee. 1994. "Sweatshop Development." In *The Haiti Files: Decoding the Crisis*, ed. James Ridgeway, 134–54. Washington, DC: Essential Books.

NCHR. 1995. *No Greater Priority: Judicial Reform in Haiti*. New York: NCHR.

NCHR and Americas Watch. 1986. *Haiti: Duvalierism since Duvalier*. New York: National Coalition for Haitian Refugees and the Americas Watch Committee.

———. 1990. *In the Army's Hands: Human Rights in Haiti on the Eve of the Elections*. New York: Human Rights Watch. Dec.

Nelson, Diane M. 2001. "Indian Giver or Nobel Savage: Duping, Assumptions of Identity, and Other Double Entendres in Rigoberta Menchú Tum's Stoll/en Past." *American Ethnologist* 28 (2): 303–31.

Nguyen, Vinh-kim. 2005. "Antiretroviral Globalism, Biopolitics, and Therapeutic Citizenship." In *Global Assemblages: Technology, Politics, and Ethics as Anthropological Problems*, ed. Aihwa Ong and Stephen J. Collier, 124–44. Malden, MA: Blackwell.

Nicholls, David. 1985. *Haiti in Caribbean Context: Ethnicity, Economy and Revolt*. New York: St. Martin's Press.

———. 1996. *From Dessalines to Duvalier: Race, Colour and National Independence in Haiti*. Rev. ed. New Brunswick, NJ: Rutgers University Press.

"Nightmare in Haiti." 1994. *60 Minutes*, CBS, New York. Apr. 17.

Le Nouvelliste. 1997. "Le Ministre de la Justice donne de nouvelles assurances aux victimes du coup d'état de 91." Port-au-Prince, Sept. 30.

Nordstrom, Carolyn. 1997. *A Different Kind of War Story*. Philadelphia: University of Pennsylvania Press.

———. 2004. *Shadows of War: Violence, Power, and International Profiteering in the Twenty-first Century*. Berkeley: University of California Press.

Nussbaum, Martha C. 2003. "Compassion and Terror." *Daedalus* 132 (1): 10–26.

Ong, Aihwa, and Stephen J. Collier, eds. 2005. *Global Assemblages: Technology, Politics, and Ethics as Anthropological Problems*. Oxford: Blackwell.

Pandolfi, Mariella. 2003. "Contract of Mutual (In)Difference: Governance and Humanitarian Apparatus in Contemporary Albania and Kosovo." *Indiana Journal of Global Legal Studies* 10 (1): 369–81.

———. 2008. "Laboratory of Intervention: The Humanitarian Governance of the Postcommunist Balkan Territories." In *Postcolonial Disorders*, ed. Mary-Jo DelVecchio Good, Sandra Teresa Hyde, Sarah Pinto, and Byron J. Good, 157–86. Berkeley: University of California Press.

Pateman, Carole. 1988. *The Sexual Contract*. Stanford, CA: Stanford University Press.

Patterson, Orlando. 1982. *Slavery and Social Death: A Comparative Study*. Cambridge, MA: Harvard University Press.

Pearlman, L.A., and K.W. Saakvitne. 1995. "Treating Therapists with Vicarious Traumatization and Secondary Traumatic Stress Disorders." In *Compassion Fatigue: Coping with Secondary Traumatic Stress Disorder in Those Who Treat the Traumatized*, ed. Charles R. Figley, 150–77. New York: Brunner/Mazel.

Petryna, Adriana. 2002. *Life Exposed: Biological Citizens after Chernobyl*. Princeton, NJ: Princeton University Press.

Pietz, William. 1985. "The Problem of the Fetish. Part 1." *Res* 9 (spring): 5–17.

———. 1987. "The Problem of the Fetish. Part 2." *Res* 13 (spring): 23–45.

———. 1988. "The Problem of the Fetish. Part 3a." *Res* 16 (autumn): 105–23.

———. 1993. "Fetishism and Materialism: The Limits of Theory in Marx." In *Fetishism as Cultural Discourse*, ed. Emily Apter and William Pietz, 119–51. Ithaca, NY: Cornell University Press.

Pigg, Stacey Leigh. 1992. "Inventing Social Categories through Place: Social Representations and Development in Nepal." *Comparative Studies in Society and History* 34 (3): 491–513.

Platform (Plate-Forme des Organizations Haïtiennes des Droits de l'Homme). 1994. Memorandum to U.S. Ambassador William Lacy Swing. Port-au-Prince, July 29.

———. 1999. "Reyaksyon Platfòm Dwa Moun kont zak entimidasyon ki kontinye ap fèt kont Enstitisyon manm li yo ak moun kap travay nan sekretarya a" (Reaction of the Human Rights Platform against the acts of intimidation that continue to be made against the Institution's members and persons working in the secretariat). Port-au-Prince, March 2.

Plesset, Sonja. 2006. *Sheltering Women: Negotiating Gender and Violence in Northern Italy.* Stanford, CA: Stanford University Press.

Pluchon, Pierre. 1984. *Nègres et juifs au XVIIIe siècle: Le racisme au siècle des Lumières.* Paris: Tallandier.

Plummer, Brenda Gayle. 1992. *Haiti and the United States: The Psychological Moment.* Athens: University of Georgia Press.

Price-Mars, Jean. 1983. *So Spoke the Uncle.* Trans. Magdaline W. Shannon. Washington, DC: Three Continents Press.

Povinelli, Elizabeth A. 2002. *The Cunning of Recognition: Indigenous Alterity and the Making of Australian Multiculturalism.* Durham, NC: Duke University Press.

Rabinow, Paul. 1999. *French DNA: Trouble in Purgatory.* Chicago: University of Chicago Press.

Racine, Marie M.B. 1995. "The Long Journey toward Freedom." *Roots* 1 (3): 7–12.

Redfield, Peter. 2005. "Doctors, Borders, and Life in Crisis." *Cultural Anthropology* 20 (3): 328–61.

———. 2008. "Sacrifice, Triage, and Global Humanitarianism." In *Humanitarianism in Question: Power, Politics, Ethics,* ed. Michael Barnett and Thomas G. Weiss, 196–214. Ithaca, NY: Cornell University Press.

Reich, Wilhelm. 1991 [1945]. *Character Analysis.* 3rd enl. ed. Trans. Vincent R. Carfagno. New York: Farrar, Straus and Giroux.

Renda, Mary A. 2001. *Taking Haiti: Military Occupation and the Culture of U.S. Imperialism, 1915–1940.* Chapel Hill: University of North Carolina Press.

Rey, Terry. 1999. "Junta, Rape, and Religion in Haiti, 1993–1994." *Journal of Feminist Studies in Religion* 15 (2): 73–100.

Rey, Terry and Alex Stepick. 2009. "Refugee Catholicism in Little Haiti: Miami's Notre Dame d'Haiti Catholic Church." In *Churches and Charity in the Immigrant City: Religion, Immigration, and Civic Engagement in Miami,* ed. Alex Stepick, Terry Rey, and Sarah J. Mahler, 72–91. New Brunswick, NJ: Rutgers University Press.

Riles, Annelise. 2000. *The Network Inside Out*. Ann Arbor: University of Michigan Press.

Robben, Antonius C.G.M. 1995. "The Politics of Truth and Emotion among Victims and Perpetrators of Violence." In *Fieldwork under Fire: Contemporary Studies of Violence and Survival*, ed. Carolyn Nordstrom and Antonius C.G.M. Robben, 81–103. Berkeley: University of California Press.

Robinson, Randall. 2007. *An Unbroken Agony: Haiti, from Revolution to the Kidnapping of a President*. New York: Basic Books.

Rosaldo, Michelle Zimbalist, and Louise Lamphere, eds. 1974. *Women, Culture, and Society*. Stanford, CA: Stanford University Press.

Rose, Nikolas, and Carlos Novas. 2005. "Biological Citizenship." In *Global Assemblages: Technology, Politics, and Ethics as Anthropological Problems*, ed. Aihwa Ong and Stephen J. Collier, 439–63. Malden, MA: Blackwell.

Ross, Fiona C. 2003. *Bearing Witness: Women and the Truth and Reconciliation Commission in South Africa*. London: Pluto Press.

Rotberg, Robert I. 1971. *Haiti: The Politics of Squalor*. Boston: Houghton Mifflin.

Rothschild, Emma. 1995. "What Is Security?" *Daedalus* 124 (3): 53–98.

Roussière, Daniel, and Gilles Danroc. 1998. "Soif de justice en Haïti." *Le Monde Diplomatique* (May): 22–23.

Sabatier, Renée. 1988. *Blaming Others: Prejudice, Race and Worldwide AIDS*. Philadelphia: New Society Publishers.

St. John, Sir Spenser. 1884. *Hayti or the Black Republic*. London: Smith, Elder, & Co.

Sanday, Peggy Reeves. 1981. "The Socio-Cultural Context of Rape: A Cross-Cultural Study." *Journal of Social Issues* 37 (4): 5–27.

Savic, Obrad, ed. 1999. *The Politics of Human Rights*. London: Verso.

Scarry, Elaine. 1985. *The Body in Pain: The Making and Unmaking of the World*. Oxford: Oxford University Press.

Scheper-Hughes, Nancy. 1995. "The Primacy of the Ethical: Propositions for a Militant Anthropology." *Current Anthropology* 36 (3): 409–40.

Scheper-Hughes, Nancy, and Philippe Bourgois, eds. 2004. *Violence in War and Peace: An Anthology*. Malden, MA: Blackwell.

Scheper-Hughes, Nancy, and Loïc Wacquant, eds. 2002. *Commodifying Bodies*. London: Sage.

Schmidt, Hans. 1995. *The United States Occupation of Haiti, 1915–1934*. New Brunswick, NJ: Rutgers University Press.

Scott, Joan Wallace. 1999. *Gender and the Politics of History*. Rev. ed. New York: Columbia University Press.

Seifert, Ruth. 1994. "War and Rape: A Preliminary Analysis." In *Mass Rape: The War against Women in Bosnia-Herzegovina*, ed. Alexandra Stiglmayer, trans. Marion Faber, 54–72. Lincoln: University of Nebraska Press.

Shannon, Magdaline W. 1996. *Jean Price-Mars, the Haitian Elite, and the American Occupation, 1915–1935*. New York: St. Martin's Press.

Shore, Chris, and Susan Wright, eds. 1997. *Anthropology of Policy: Critical Perspectives on Governance and Power*. London: Routledge.

Shute, Stephen, and Susan Hurley, eds. 1993. *On Human Rights. The Oxford Amnesty Lectures*. New York: Basic Books.

Sikkink, Kathryn. 1993. "Human Rights, Principled Issue-Networks, and Sovereignty in Latin America." *International Organization* 47 (3): 411–41.

"Sispann bay lanmò ochan." 1997. *Libète* 5, no. 271 (Dec. 17–22): 1.

Slyomovics, Susan. 2005. *The Performance of Human Rights in Morocco.* Philadelphia: University of Pennsylvania Press.

Smith, Jennie M. 2001. *When the Hands Are Many: Community Organization and Social Change in Rural Haiti.* Ithaca, NY: Cornell University Press.

Speed, Shannon. 2006. "At the Crossroads of Human Rights and Anthropology: Toward a Critically Engaged Activist Research." *American Anthropologist* 108 (1): 66–76.

Stamm, B. Hudnall, ed. 1995. *Secondary Traumatic Stress: Self-Care Issues for Clinicians, Researchers, and Educators.* Baltimore: Sidran Press.

Steiner, Henry J., and Philip Alston, eds. 2000. *International Human Rights in Context: Law, Politics, Morals.* 2nd ed. Oxford: Oxford University Press.

Stewart, Pamela J., and Andrew Strathern. 2004. *Witchcraft, Sorcery, Rumors, and Gossip.* Cambridge: Cambridge University Press.

Stiglmayer, Alexandra, ed. 1994. *Mass Rape: The War against Women in Bosnia-Herzegovina.* Trans. Marion Faber. Lincoln: University of Nebraska Press.

Stoler, Ann Laura. 1995. *Race and the Education of Desire: Foucault's History of Sexuality and the Colonial Order of Things.* Durham, NC: Duke University Press.

Stoll, David. 1999. *Rigoberta Menchú and the Story of All Poor Guatemalans.* Boulder, CO: Westview Press.

Stotzky, Irwin P. 1997. *Silencing the Guns in Haiti: The Promise of Deliberative Democracy.* Chicago: University of Chicago Press.

Strathern, Marilyn, ed. 2000. *Audit Cultures: Anthropological Studies in Accountability, Ethics, and the Academy.* London: Routledge.

Tambiah, Stanley J. 1996. *Leveling Crowds: Ethnonationalist Conflicts and Collective Violence in South Asia.* Berkeley: University of California Press.

Taussig, Michael T. 1980. *The Devil and Commodity Fetishism in South America.* Chapel Hill: University of North Carolina Press.

———. 1992. *The Nervous System.* New York: Routledge, Chapman and Hall.

Taylor, Charles. 1994. "The Politics of Recognition." In *Multiculturalism: Examining the Politics of Recognition,* ed. Amy Gutmann, 25–73. Princeton, NJ: Princeton University Press.

Terry, Fiona. 2002. *Condemned to Repeat: The Paradox of Humanitarian Action.* Ithaca, NY: Cornell University Press.

Thornhill, Randy, and Craig T. Palmer. 2000. *A Natural History of Rape: Biological Bases of Sexual Coercion.* Cambridge, MA: MIT Press.

Tickner, J. Ann. 1992. *Gender in International Relations: Feminist Perspectives on Achieving Global Security.* New York: Columbia University Press.

Ticktin, Miriam. 2006. "Where Ethics and Politics Meet: The Violence of Humanitarianism in France." *American Ethnologist* 33 (1): 33–49.

Trouillot, Ertha Pascal. 1983. *Analyse de la Législation Révisant le Statut de la Femme Mariée: Le Décret du 8 Octobre 1982 et le Code Civil.* Port-au-Prince: Imprimerie Henri Deschamps.

Trouillot, Michel-Rolph. 1990. *Haiti—State against Nation: Origins and Legacy of Duvalierism*. New York: Monthly Review Press.

————. 1995. *Silencing the Past: Power and the Production of History*. Boston: Beacon Press.

Turner, Victor. 1957. *Schism and Continuity in an African Society: A Study of Ndembu Village Life*. Manchester: University of Manchester Press.

UNDP. 2000. *Human Development Report 2000*. New York: Oxford University Press.

"Une cargaison d'armes serait ensevelie dans le ventre de 'Fierté Gonâvienne.'" 1997. *Haïti-Observateur* 28, no. 42 (Oct. 15–22): 18.

UNHCR. 1979. *Handbook on Procedures and Criteria for Determining Refugee Status: Under the 1951 Convention and the 1967 Protocol Relating to the Status of Refugees*. Geneva: UNHCR.

UN/OAS International Civilian Mission (Mission Civile Internationale en Haïti OEA/ONU). 1995. "Medical Skills at the Service of Human Rights." *MICIVIH News* 1, no. 1 (Aug.).

————. 1997. *Haïti: Droits de l'homme et réhabilitation des victimes*. Préparé par le Département pour la Promotion et la Protection des Droits de l'homme. Port-au-Prince: Imprimerie Henri Deschamps.

USAID. 1998. *Results-Oriented Assistance: A USAID Sourcebook*. Draft for Discussion. Washington, DC, March 10.

USAID/Haiti. 1994. "Human Rights Fund." Port-au-Prince, May 20.

————. 1995. "Human Rights Fund." Port-au-Prince, Oct.

————. 1996. "Status Report." Port-au-Prince, Feb. 7.

————. 1997. "FY1999 Results Review and Resource Request." Port-au-Prince, June.

————. 1998. "Administration of Justice Programs Evaluation Team Guidelines." Port-au-Prince, Jan.

U.S. Congress. 1995. *An Assessment of the Current Situation in Haiti*. Hearing before the Subcommittee on the Western Hemisphere of the Committee on International Relations, House of Representatives. 104th Cong., 1st sess., Oct. 12.

————. 1996. *Haiti: Human Rights and Police Issues*. Hearing before the Committee on International Relations, House of Representatives. 104th Cong., 2nd sess., Jan. 4.

————. 1999a. *United States Policy towards Victims of Torture*. Hearing before the Subcommittee on International Operations and Human Rights of the Committee on International Relations, House of Representatives. 106th Cong., 1st sess., June 29.

————. 1999b. *U.S. Policy Toward Victims of Torture*. Hearing before the Subcommittee on International Operations of the Committee on Foreign Relations, United States Senate. 106th Cong., lst sess., July 30.

Vesti, Peter, and Marianne Kastrup. 1992. "Psychotherapy for Torture Survivors." In *Torture and Its Consequences: Current Treatment Approaches,* ed. Metin Basoglu, 348–62. Cambridge: Cambridge University Press.

Vieux, Serge-Henri. 1989. *Le Plaçage: Droit coutumier et famille en Haïti*. Paris: Éditions Publisud.

Warren, Kay B. 1993. "Introduction: Revealing Conflicts across Cultures and Disciplines." In *The Violence Within: Cultural and Political Opposition in Divided Nations*, ed. Kay B. Warren, 1–23. Boulder, CO: Westview Press.

Weber, Max. 1946. "Politics as a Vocation." In *From Max Weber: Essays in Sociology*, ed. H.H. Gerth and C. Wright Mills, 77–128. New York: Oxford University Press.

———. 1968 [1956]. *Economy and Society: An Outline of Interpretive Sociology*, vol. 2. Ed. Guenther Roth and Clause Wittich. Berkeley: University of California Press.

Weinstein, Brian, and Aaron Segal. 1992. *Haiti: The Failure of Politics*. New York: Praeger.

Weldes, Jutta, Mark Laffey, Hugh Gusterson, and Raymond Duvall. 1999. "Introduction." In *Cultures of Insecurity: States, Communities, and the Production of Danger*, ed. Jutta Weldes, Mark Laffey, Hugh Gusterson, and Raymond Duvall, 1–33. Minneapolis: University of Minnesota Press.

West, Harry G. 2005. *Kupilikula: Governance and the Invisible Realm in Mozambique*. Chicago: University of Chicago Press.

West, Harry G., and Todd Sanders, eds. 2003. *Transparency and Conspiracy: Ethnographies of Suspicion in the New World Order*. Durham, NC: Duke University Press.

Wilentz, Amy. 1989. *The Rainy Season: Haiti since Duvalier*. New York: Simon and Schuster.

Williams, Dessima. 1994. "Courage Washing Misery: Haitians Told Us Their Stories." Report of the New England Observers' Delegation to Haiti, Boston, July 21.

Wilson, Richard A. 2001. *The Politics of Truth and Reconciliation in South Africa: Legitimizing the Post-Apartheid State*. Cambridge: Cambridge University Press.

WOH. 1994. *Fundwatch Report on the USAID Human Rights Fund in Haiti*. Washington, DC: Washington Office on Haiti. Sept..

World Bank. 2001. *World Development Report 2000/2001: Attacking Poverty*. New York: Oxford University Press.

Wrangham, Richard, and Dale Peterson. 1996. *Demonic Males: Apes and the Origins of Human Violence*. New York: Houghton Mifflin.

Young, Allan. 1995. *The Harmony of Illusions: Inventing Post-Traumatic Stress Disorder*. Princeton, NJ: Princeton University Press.

Index

aid apparatus (*continued*)
and conflicts in, 2, 7–8, 37–38, 82,
113–16, 246, 293–94; "doing good"
intentions and, 34, 127, 238, 288,
289; *ensekirite* of *viktim*, and role
of, 7–8, 86; ethical dilemmas for,
16–17, 36–37, 47–48, 89–92, 94,
112, 130, 238, 291, 299n17; France,
and workers in, 102, 227, 249,
250, 256; gift economy and, 36, 84;
GOH, and contests between *viktim*
and, 104–5; graft and, 180, 183,
232, 245, 248, 256, 292, 310n15;
human rights, and goals of, 7,
14–15, 39, 82; inequalities of power
between *viktim* and, 178, 195, 221,
292; intervention by, 2, 8, 12–15,
26, 90, 271, 287, 289, 291; locations
in Port-au-Prince for, 20–21; media
discourses and, 46, 107, 111; medical community activities and, 95–96;
militarization in, 239–42; military
personnel rehabilitation program
and, 123–29; as mobile sovereigns
in global political economy, 25–26,
35, 44, 45, 175, 292, 300n7; occult
economies and, 30–32, 87–88, 288,
292; political economy of trauma,
and intersection with, 26, 85–86,
104, 288; politics of truth and, 30,
32, 48–49, 82–83, 303n2; pro-
democracy groups and, 86, 140;
scandal publicity and, 82–83, 91,
94, 127–28, 130, 278, 291, 303n2;
security, and transformation of
predatory political practices by, 2–3,
291; sovereignty, democracy, and
intersection with, 2, 82, 113; summary, 23, 37–38, 81–87, 130–31,
303n4; tension and controversial
dynamics within and between
actors in, 7, 48, 85, 92, 236; terror
apparatus, and role of, 44, 300n6;
truth, and conflicts in, 2, 48–51,
82, 113, 246, 301n12; "unforeseen
circumstances" and management
by, 185, 205, 245, 288; verification
processes, and assistance for *viktim*
from, 32–33, 84–85, 91; *viktim*, and
attitudes towards, 23; *viktim*, and
challenges of working with, 92, 252,
253, 291–92, 310n16; Vodou, and
ambivalence in, 9; witchcraft accusations and, 31–32, 92, 180, 206,
210–11, 224, 280–81, 287, 293;
women's tribunal, and representatives from, 173. *See also* bureaucraft;

grant economy; social life of aid;
U.S.-funded aid apparatus; *specific
aid agency or program*
AIDS, 12, 80, 137–38, 172, 247,
301n12
Albright, Madeleine, 115–16
alliance relationships: aid apparatus and,
230–31, 237, 241, 243–46, 288; aid
apparatus patron-client relationships
and, 246, 250, 252, 254–60, 264–65,
310n18
Ambroise, Maxine, 233–34, 245, 246,
277–82
American Association for the Advancement of Science (AAAS), 199–200
America's Development Foundation
(ADF). *See* ADF (America's Development Foundation); *specific aid
agency or program*
Améry, Jean, *At the Mind's Limits,* 1
amnesty, for political crimes, 125,
305n33
Amnesty International, 24, 98, 99, 103
angajman (agreement), 243, 266
angels, guardian, 150
angry *(cho),* 170
animasyon (political theatrical group),
166
ankadreman (support): aid apparatus,
180, 268; anxiety, frustration, and
anger, and decline in, 224; described,
24; *viktim* and, 24, 164, 169, 177,
179
an mawonaj (hiding inside Haiti), 67,
165, 255, 302n24
anteroom or veranda *(galeri),* 145
anthropology and anthropologists. *See*
ethnographic research
*Anthropology and the Colonial Encoun-
ter* (Asad), 17
Antoine, Caroline, 156–61, 283
Antoine, Pierre Max, 200, 221, 263, 271,
276, 309n19
AOJ (Administration of Justice Program),
119, 122, 229, 274, 309–10n10,
310n11
Appadurai, Arjun, 35–36, 288, 300n7
AQOCI (Quebecois Association for International Assistance), 303n13
Aristide, Jean-Bertrand: amnesty for
political crimes granted by, 305n33;
exile of, 12–13; Governors Island
Accord and, 73, 108, 196, 305n33;
military coup d'état against, 2, 11,
66, 83; *Neptune* ferry capsize tragedy, and actions by, 219; political
charismatic activism and, 2, 65;

extraction: economies of, 10–11, 52–54, 64–65, 77–78, 209, 293–94; of truth during coup period, 32, 41–42, 68–69

Fabien, Dany, 235, 236, 278
Faculty of Law, 135
FAD'H (Forces Armées d'Haïti; Armed Forces of Haiti): as agents of terror apparatus, 67, 251, 300n6; amnesty for, 125; disarmament during MNF intervention, 300n6; documents seized from headquarters of, 84, 300n6, 303n3; Duvalierist regime and, 1–2; HNP training, for former members of, 126; IPSF, and former members of, 125; military personnel rehabilitation program and, 123–24
families: coup period, and violence against, 79–80; Denise Jules story, and brigad vijilans actions against, 260–67; rape as form of torture against, 39. See also victims' advocacy groups
fanm deyò ("wife" or partner living outside the primary household), 61
fanm kadejak (wife of the rapist), 160
fanm saj (lay midwives), 134
Fanm Viktim Leve Kanpe (FAVILEK; Women Victims Mobilize), 233, 234, 277
Farmer, Paul E., 137–38, 301n12, 307n16
Fass, Simon M., 306n3
[to] fast (fè jèn), 28
Father Paul, 208, 211, 212, 214
Fatton, Robert, 262
FAVILEK (Fanm Viktim Leve Kanpe; Women Victims Mobilize), 233, 234, 277
FDM (Fon Dwa Moun; Le Fonds des Droits Humains), 21, 243. See also the Fund (Human Rights Fund; HRF)
fear, or peace, of the cemetery (lapè simityè), 57, 67, 139, 301n16
fè jèn (to fast), 28
feminist organizations, 173–75
La Fierté Gonâvienne ferry incident: alliance, obligation and exchange relationship invoked for assistance after, 243–46; bereavement and appropriation of suffering in, 213–21; community reactions to, 210–13; death statistics, 207, 209, 214, 308n15; described, 207, 208–9;

the Fund inquiry and advisory position on, 207–13, 217, 222, 228; GOH accountability and failures in, 209–10, 216–18, 219; international resources to assist victims of, 216, 217; Montrouis memorial, 215, 216; "phantom" weapons cache accusations, 219; political economy of trauma, and burial rites for victims of, 214–15; psychosocial experience and, 213; summary, 205–7, 221–22; victim verification process for, 215; Vodou epistemology, and experience of emotions, body, and spirit after, 212; witchcraft accusations and, 207, 210–11
Fischer, Michael M.J., 294
flight (mawonaj), 154, 165, 255
FNCD (Front National pour le Changement et la Démocratie; National Front for Change and Democracy), 167, 307n18
FOCAL (Fondation Connaissance et Liberté; Open Society Institute of Haiti), 198
focalization and transvaluation concepts, 206, 215, 218, 274
Fondasyon 30 Sektanm (September 30th Foundation), 104–6, 107, 192, 198, 236, 277, 278
Le Fonds des Droits Humains (Fon Dwa Moun; FDM). See also the Fund (Human Rights Fund; HRF)
Fon Dwa Moun (FDM; Le Fonds des Droits Humains), 21, 243. See also the Fund (Human Rights Fund; HRF)
food scarcity: ADF goals and, 114; during embargo, 5, 187; HWA assistance and, 94; MOVI-30 protests against, 278, 280; Rehab Program and, 278, 289; riots, 65; SOs, and recognition of, 187; women's role in traditional Haitian culture, and effects of, 71
Forbes, Phyllis, 187, 207, 274, 281, 286
forced incest, 39, 45, 72, 73
Forces Armées d'Haïti. See FAD'H (Forces Armées d'Haïti; Armed Forces of Haiti)
Fortun, Kim, 89–90
Foucault, Michel, 23, 41–44, 45, 88, 300n5, 308n8; The History of Sexuality, 41
foufòl (crazy), 252

CALIFORNIA SERIES IN PUBLIC ANTHROPOLOGY

The California Series in Public Anthropology emphasizes the anthropologist's role as an engaged intellectual. It continues anthropology's commitment to being an ethnographic witness, to describing, in human terms, how life is lived beyond the borders of many readers' experiences. But it also adds a commitment, through ethnography, to reframing the terms of public debate—transforming received, accepted understandings of social issues with new insights, new framings.

Series Editor: Robert Borofsky (Hawaii Pacific University)

Contributing Editors: Philippe Bourgois (University of Pennsylvania), Paul Farmer (Partners in Health), Alex Hinton (Rutgers University), Carolyn Nordstrom (University of Notre Dame), and Nancy Scheper-Hughes (UC Berkeley)

University of California Press Editor: Naomi Schneider

Compositor:	BookComp, Inc.
Text:	10/13 Sabon
Display:	Sabon
Indexer:	J. Naomi Linzer Indexing Services
Printer and Binder:	Maple-Vail